W9-AOL-552

A Poor Man Reads The Bhāgavatam

A Poor Man Reads The Bhāgavatam

Volume One

First Canto

Chapters 1–3

Satsvarūpa dāsa Goswami

GN Press

Persons interested in the subject matter of this book are invited to correspond with our secretary:

GN Press, Inc.
R.D. 1, Box 832
Port Royal, PA 17082

Printed in India
ISBN 0-911233-68-7

GN Press Inc. gratefully acknowledges the BBT for the use of verses and purports from Śrīla Prabhupāda's books.

Library of Congress Catalog Card Number: 96–079135

Printed in India at Rekha Printers Pvt. Ltd.,
New Delhi-110 020

CONTENTS

Dedicated to
His Divine Grace
A. C. Bhaktivedanta Swami Prabhupāda
my spiritual master
on the 100th annual celebration of
his appearance day.

Thank you, Śrīla Prabhupāda,
for rendering Śrīla Vyāsadeva's *Śrīmad-Bhāgavatam*
so expertly into English. Your Bhaktivedanta Purports are
sublime for the pure devotees who seriously want to contact
the Supreme Lord, easy for the neophytes, and accessible even
to the spiritually poor man.

He lives forever by his divine instructions
and the follower lives with him.

You ask one question about the nature of books I want you to write as my disciples; on this point Krsna consciousness is not limited. Persons like all of the Gosvamis wrote so many books. Visvanatha Cakravarti and all the acaryas wrote books and still I am writing books. Similarly, also my disciples will write. So any self-realized soul can write unlimited books without deviating from the original ideas.

—Letter by Śrīla Prabhupāda to Satsvarūpa dāsa

Foreword

The Bhāgavata Purāṇa is one of the most revered scriptures of Vaiṣṇavism, occupying a central place in their devotion as well as in their thought. It was the great ambition of Swami Bhaktivedānta, the founder-*ācārya* of the International Society for Krishna Consciousness, to make this great work available to the English speaking world, by providing its translation and his own commentary in a sixty-volume set. Satsvarūpa dāsa Goswami takes up that tradition and presents in his *A Poor Man Reads The Bhāgavatam*, of which the first volume is now appearing, a beautiful re-rendering of this scripture, together with a lively and contemporary commentary of his own. Dedicated to Śrīla Prabhupāda, the founder-*ācārya* of ISKCON at the occasion of his 100th birthday, it is a testimony of love and devotion. It documents a Western devotee's growth in *bhakti* as well as the problems and doubts that accompany this process. Satsvarūpa dāsa Goswami writes beautifully, poetically, spiritually. I am certain that this work will succeed in conveying to many the genuine spirit of Vaiṣṇavism in a garb that is woven of Eastern as well as Western strands, and that reveals the beauty as well as the depth of that tradition. I hope that *A Poor Man Reads The Bhāgavatam* will find many readers. Nothing could have been dearer to Swami Bhaktivedānta than such a 100th birthday gift from his Western devotees.

Professor Klaus K. Klostermaier
Chairman, Department of Religious Studies
University of Manitoba, Canada

Prologue

Room 42, Guesthouse, Krishna-Balaram Mandir, Vṛndāvana, India, 4:50 A.M.*, January 11, 1996*

We have been trying to make a master plan for an opus, praying and waiting. We may have to begin before it comes. When there was only bare land in ISKCON Māyāpur, Śrīla Prabhupāda ordered his GBC man to start construction. Tamāl Krishna then sent Prabhupāda a photo of the recently-arrived bricks and other building materials. Prabhupāda wrote back, "I see a pile of materials, but no building. What is this? Build something at once!" With no plan in mind, but impelled by the guru's order, the devotees and workmen began to lay bricks.

A few hours after writing the above paragraph, while brainstorming and praying with Baladeva Vidyābhūṣaṇa dāsa, the master plan came to me. It's called *A Poor Man Reads The Bhāgavatam.* I'll start with the first verse of *Śrīmad-Bhāgavatam*, begin reading Śrīla Prabhupāda's translation and purport, and then stop and free-write. Then back to reading, then back to writing. No other structure. Everything is allowed.

This plan satisfies many of my needs. The writer in me can stay anchored to Śrīla Prabhupāda's and Lord Kṛṣṇa's book. The free-writer can express his mind and heart. And the hankering for a long-term project is satisfied because the *Bhāgavatam* has 18,000 verses.

I don't know if readers will be satisfied by such an unorthodox *modus operandi*, but I am reminded of the haiku master, Basho's, words: "I always feel when sitting in company with Kikaku at the same party that he is anxious to compose a verse that will please the whole company. I have no such intention."

My purpose is to be fully engaged in a personal and Kṛṣṇa conscious writing project, and through my imperfect senses, mind, and intelligence to tell the glories of Kṛṣṇa, His devotees, and the purifying process of *bhakti*. I hope to work through my karma in this way and to keep writing to reach the goal of unalloyed surrender at Kṛṣṇa's lotus feet.

I offer my full obeisances here and throughout the book at the feet of my beloved spiritual master, His Divine Grace A. C. Bhaktivedanta Swami Prabhupāda, and through him, the whole disciplic succession of Gauḍīya Vaiṣṇavas, followers of Lord Caitanya. Through these masters, especially the Six Gosvāmīs of Vṛndāvana, one can offer obeisances and loving service to Rādhā-Kṛṣṇa and all Vrajavāsīs. That is my goal, strange as my method may sometimes seem.

Read the *Bhāgavatam* with me. The *Bhāgavatam* is complete and perfect; it cuts the knot of material desires and gradually grants love of Kṛṣṇa to sincere and submissive hearers.

I like the sound of *A Poor Man Reads The Bhāgavatam* because everything can go into it—poems, diary, drawings, me, you, the universe, the way, and the goal: loving transcendental service to Kṛṣṇa.

Invitation to the Reader

I aspire to write on topics in the *Śrīmad-Bhāgavatam*. I would like to be pure and potent. Does it require that I study Sanskrit first, that I become deeply learned, that I have communion with Jīva Gosvāmī's *Ṣaṭ Sandarbha* and Viśvanātha Cakravartī's comments as well as India's *ṣaṭ-darśana* philosophies? I am not on that standard. In some future life, perhaps, my words, dreams, drawings, thoughts, and feelings may all be completely immersed in the spiritual world, but for now I can only mold my life to become a reader of my spiritual master's translation of the *Bhāgavatam*. This is what I do. It is a wonderful path. *A Poor Man Reads The Bhāgavatam* includes whatever happens along the way of such a life lived for reading *Bhāgavatam*. Will you join me?

Śrīmad-Bhāgavatam is wonderful—usually. If it seems dry to me, I try various methods to make it more fun or to get through the reading blocks. Sometimes it seems impossible to penetrate the hard rock wall of my skepticism, so I go around it. There are many strategies one can use to overcome inattentive or shallow reading. Sometimes I turn to my diary and let off steam. When I do that, I am trying to find out why I think *Śrīmad-Bhāgavatam* is dry. Sometimes I make lists of things that concern me, and from time to time, I turn to those lists to see if the *Bhāgavatam* verse I am reading can help me to deal with anything mentioned on those lists. *Śrīmad-Bhāgavatam* also inspires me to draw. Drawing is another way to meditate on the *Bhāgavatam* subjects or whatever is going on at the time.

I'm a writer; that's my service to Śrīla Prabhupāda and Lord Kṛṣṇa. I'm always trying to improve. Therefore, dear reader, if you like, we can read *Bhāgavatam* together and sometimes talk.

I call this *A Poor Man Reads The Bhāgavatam* because I am spiritually impoverished. I am bereft and in need of Lord

Caitanya's abundant mercy. The *ācāryas* are magnanimous and the holy name's blessings are always available, I know. I seek them every day. Śrīla Prabhupāda has also given us vast and easily available mercy in his Bhaktivedanta Purports and his many instructions for spiritual life.

My *A Poor Man Reads The Bhāgavatam* is like my spiritual life—poor, humble, and not at the usual standard of *Bhāgavatam* writers. It is, in fact, outrageous that I am attempting such a thing at all. But as I will describe, the task was sent to me when I prayed and endeavored in Vṛndāvana as a way to keep a fellow like me safely anchored to my spiritual master's books while at the same time able to exercise my inevitable proclivity to write what I want out of my life's experience.

I feel I am responding to a genuine inner call by setting out on this adventure proposed as *A Poor Man Reads The Bhāgavatam*. I cannot help but think of my spiritual master's words in his Preface to *Śrīmad-Bhāgavatam* where he spoke of the great need to disseminate the message for peace in the world. Prabhupāda ended his purport with these words:

> I must admit my frailties in presenting *Śrīmad-Bhāgavatam*, but still I am hopeful of the good reception by the thinkers and leaders of society on the strength of the following statement of *Śrīmad-Bhāgavatam* (1.5.11):
>
> > "On the other hand, that literature which is full of descriptions of the transcendental glories of the name, fame, form and pastimes of the unlimited Supreme Lord is a transcendental creation *meant to bring about a revolution in the impious life of a misdirected civilization.* Such transcendental literatures, *even though irregularly composed, are heard, sung and accepted by purified men who are thoroughly honest.*" (emphasis added)

CHAPTER ONE

Questions by the Sages

Text 1

oṁ namo bhagavate vāsudevāya
janmādy asya yato 'nvayād itarataś cārtheṣv abhijñaḥ svarāṭ
tene brahma hṛdā ya ādi-kavaye muhyanti yat sūrayaḥ
tejo-vāri-mṛdāṁ yathā vinimayo yatra tri-sargo 'mṛṣā
dhāmnā svena sadā nirasta-kuhakaṁ satyaṁ paraṁ dhīmahi

O my Lord, Śrī Kṛṣṇa, son of Vasudeva, O all-pervading Personality of Godhead, I offer my respectful obeisances unto You. I meditate upon Lord Śrī Kṛṣṇa because He is the Absolute Truth and the primeval cause of all causes of the creation, sustenance and destruction of the manifested universes. He is directly and indirectly conscious of all manifestations, and He is independent because there is no other cause beyond Him. It is He only who first imparted the Vedic knowledge unto the heart of Brahmājī, the original living being. By Him even the great sages and demigods are placed into illusion, as one is bewildered by the illusory representations of water seen in fire, or land seen on water. Only because of Him do the material universes, temporarily manifested by the reactions of the three modes of nature, appear factual, although they are unreal. I therefore meditate upon Him, Lord Śrī Kṛṣṇa, who is eternally existent in the transcendental abode, which is forever free from the illusory representations of the material world. I meditate upon Him, for He is the Absolute Truth.

Comment

This first verse describes Śrī Kṛṣṇa as the Absolute Truth. He is *īśvara parama*, the Supreme Controller, the God of all. Śrīla Bhaktisiddhānta Sarasvatī Ṭhākura spoke on this verse for three months at Dacca. Our Prabhupāda wrote a ten-and-a-half-page purport on it. Viśvanātha Cakravartī Ṭhākura and other *ācāryas* have taken it to indicate *mādhurya-rasa*. Here I am, parrots chirping outside my window, crows cawing, reading it and feeling fortunate to be in Vṛndāvana. I am fortunate, despite my ill luck and tendency for headaches. I am fortunate to have been saved by His Divine Grace from Kali's worst.

I know well that reading the *Bhāgavatam* is often like chipping at stone. The author recites, *Oṁ namo bhagavate vāsudevāya*, "My Lord, I offer my obeisances unto You." I chip away with my lightweight hammer at the stone of my forgetfulness of Kṛṣṇa. The monkeys on the wall (ancient, ugly faces) beg my attention from me. I'm prone to give it to them. The monkeys of the mind too. Vṛndāvana prompts this metaphor.

Sick child
with warped ego,
in Vṛndāvana there are parrots
screeching.

Prabhupāda began the *Bhāgavatam* in Vṛndāvana soon after accepting *sannyāsa*. For years he wrote and published *Back to Godhead* whenever he had money. Then some acquaintances suggested he publish books because they were more permanent. He heard Kṛṣṇa speaking to him through those acquaintances and he launched his opus—a projected sixty volumes of no less than 350–400 pages each.

Prabhupāda believed the *Bhāgavatam* could save the world. He urgently wanted the world to receive it. Only the *Bhāgavatam* could provide the world with the missing ingredient,

God, and only God could pull humankind back from the brink of global war.

It does not matter that there are flaws in the English or in the printing ("I must admit my frailties in presenting the First Part"). The *Bhāgavatam* is meant to "bring about a revolution in the impious life of a misdirected civilization." Those who are thoroughly honest will accept it despite its "irregular" composition.

I beg the reader's pardon a thousand times on the same grounds. *I* cannot present *Śrīmad-Bhāgavatam*, so I won't even claim to be attempting that. Rather, I'm sheltering from the cold and giving myself something to do by staying close to the *Bhāgavatam's* texts and purports. Those who are thoroughly honest, and my friends, will accept it.

If ever there was a grand opener to a book, this first *śloka* is it. In it, we can behold everything at once. This verse immediately removes any doubt as to who the Absolute Truth is. Prabhupāda's purport is relentless: God is a person and the "stubborn atheists" are fools if they think anything can be moved in this universe without the will of the Supreme Being.

Vyāsadeva names for us the object of meditation: Kṛṣṇa, the cause of all causes. He then tells us that (1) we are in illusion and, (2) Kṛṣṇa is eternally existent. This is a beginner's knowledge of Kṛṣṇa. Therefore, this is one of several prelude verses, the beginning notes of a grand symphony. Only gradually do we learn more.

The *Bhagavad-gītā's* presentation of Kṛṣṇa is even more gradual. The first verse of the *Gītā* does not indicate at all, except indirectly, that the theme of the *Bhagavad-gītā* is surrender to Kṛṣṇa, the Supreme Lord. We get only a hint of it—a mention of *dharma-kṣetra* and Prabhupāda's comment about the power of such a holy place on the outcome of the battle. The *Bhāgavatam*, however, begins with a full presentation of Kṛṣṇa's position.

The first verse defines the essence of Kṛṣṇa: He is ever-existing, all-knowing, and completely independent. All *bhaktas* accept this version of Vāsudeva. *Bhaktas* may be divided into two main categories, *aiśvarya-bhaktas* and *mādhurya-bhaktas*. Within these categories, the *bhaktas* express a variety of moods. All, however, accept Kṛṣṇa as *parameśvara*.

I used to have to *slow down* to read the Swami, I tell people, describing myself as I read his First Canto at my desk in the welfare office. It was 1966. I was regularly smoking marijuana. I was also reading William Burroughs and other Beat generation authors. My mind raced to keep pace with their prose. I thought literature was supposed to do that to you, to speed the mind from word to word, phrase to phrase. Swamijī's book was different. There was something too deep and too valuable to miss by giving it too quick a reading.

Thirty years later I find that I still have to slow down. My mind no longer races ahead because I ingest drugs. Is it because I race through my temple duties? More likely it's because I'm not in direct touch with the Source of all.

"The world is too much with us; late and soon,/ Getting and spending, we lay waste our powers:/ Little we see in Nature that is ours;/ We have given our hearts away, a sordid boon!" ("The World Is Too Much With Us," William Wordsworth)

I want only to meditate upon Vāsudeva, the Supreme Truth, by whom even the demigods are put into illusion. Lord Śrī Kṛṣṇa is eternally existent in His transcendental abode, which is forever free from *māyā*.

But if the Absolute Truth is one, how can there be so much scope to view Him subjectively? We have to start with submission to this first verse of the *Bhāgavatam*, this absolute, dictionary meaning of Kṛṣṇa. Then as our personal relationship with Kṛṣṇa develops, our vision of Him becomes more subjective. Our personal, subjective relationship becomes fully developed at *svarūpa-siddhi*. We have a long way to go. The path to *svarūpa-siddhi* begins with acknowledging God's omnipotence and supremacy. Then we will surrender to the rules and regulations of *vaidhi-bhakti*. When *vaidhi-bhakti* becomes firmly established in our hearts, we will gradually come to understand our personal relationship with Kṛṣṇa. Therefore, first we accept the grand definition of Kṛṣṇa as God, and then we can take up our subjective relationship with that one inconceivable Person. Kṛṣṇa is omnipotent; therefore, He is able to simultaneously appear as the source of everything, the God of all, and to reciprocate individually with our loving feelings for Him.

In the first paragraph of his purport, Prabhupāda indicates that Śrī Kṛṣṇa, the divine son of Devakī and Vasudeva, is the Absolute Truth. I have no doubt about what Prabhupāda says and I am prepared to throw off all conceptions that relativize that statement. I don't have to convince myself, and right now, I'm not preaching to newcomers. I am trying to find direct nourishment in the *Bhāgavatam* and I don't want to filter that nourishment through my doubts. Allowing doubts while reading the *Bhāgavatam* is like trying to cook rice with the pot raised high above the flame. If I don't expose the pot to the heat, how will the rice cook? Similarly, if I don't expose myself to the heat of the *Bhāgavatam*, how will I hear, relish, and learn to pray?

Kṛṣṇa is the son of Vasudeva. Therefore, when we say *oṁ namo bhagavate vāsudevāya*, we refer to Śrī Kṛṣṇa, who was transferred by Vasudeva to Gokula where He took His natural place as the son of Nanda and Yaśodā, His eternal parents. Prabhupāda assures us that this subject matter will be described by Śrīla Jīva Gosvāmī in his *Kṛṣṇa Sandarbha* and that Lord Brahmā has also explained it in his *Brahma-saṁhitā*. I can read those books too and enter deeply into the science of Kṛṣṇa, but actually, everything is already here in the *Bhāgavatam*. I am here too, as I was in 1966, reading Prabhupāda's book—his *wondrous* book. I want to always open the *Bhāgavatam* and look for entrance.

Prabhupāda published this First Canto in 1962, '64 and '65. I like to think of him writing in his stone room at the Rādhā-Dāmodara temple and in the noisy room at Chippiwada in Old Delhi.

A project without end,
not something to whip up
for carrying and showing when he went abroad,
but a specific calling.
Whenever and wherever he might go,
this would be his life's work,
begun in Vṛndāvana
just after taking *sannyāsa.*
As Lord Kṛṣṇa had Vyāsa wait
until his mature stage
before compiling *Śrīmad-Bhāgavatam*,
so He perfectly prepared His Divine Grace
to begin the Bhaktivedanta Purports—on time,
at 64 years of age.
As Vyāsa worked from a vision,
so did Śrīla Prabhupāda.

The *Śrīmad-Bhāgavatam's* opening verse is a prayer by the author. He intones Kṛṣṇa's name Vāsudeva, the son of Vasudeva, the all-attractive Supreme Person, the source of everything. Meditate upon Him.

I write that down and study the text and purport to enter my own meditation. I am a student, after all, and am trying to become purified. Kṛṣṇa is God, the original Godhead. "Kṛṣṇa" is the principal name of God. Focus your distracted mind on His name and chant Hare Kṛṣṇa Hare Kṛṣṇa, Kṛṣṇa Kṛṣṇa Hare Hare/ Hare Rāma Hare Rāma, Rāma Rāma Hare Hare. Chanting Hare Kṛṣṇa drives out other thoughts and sounds. Or it should. It does so when we are blessed with offenseless chanting. Reading too has to go beyond the mechanical.

What about writing? Why do I advocate it for myself, even when my pen takes me to concerns that don't always seem strictly siddhāntic? Why? Because I'm not always in the *Bhāgavatam*. I'm often somewhere else. I need to write my truth as the distractions increase.

For example, someone just sent me a copy of *National Geographic* because it had a lead article on Ireland. He thought I might be interested. Then my secretary came into the room with yet another question: we have to schedule a meeting with a Godbrother who wants to talk with me. I can't refuse him on the plea of weak health. What to do?

Of course, that's how life is, but when I do get a chance to write, I want to cut through the distractions and leave them behind. When I am able to do that, I will write Kṛṣṇa, Kṛṣṇa, Vāsudeva, *oṁ namo bhagavate vāsudevāya*.

I am pleased at how this particular project began for me. I prayed and groped and considered different approaches, and then the Lord gave me this idea in Vṛndāvana: "Always write close to *Śrīmad-Bhāgavatam* and your spiritual master's purports."

Therefore, I want to follow the path Prabhupāda prescribed in his opening remarks to the first chapter of the *Ādi-līlā:*

> Since we belong to this chain of disciplic succession from Śrī Caitanya Mahāprabhu, this edition of *Śrī Caitanya-caritāmṛta* will contain nothing newly manufactured by our tiny brains, but only remnants of foodstuff originally eaten by the Lord Himself. . . . What will be described herein, therefore, has nothing to do with the experimental thoughts created by the speculative habits of inert minds. The subject matter of this book is not a mental concoction but a factual spiritual experience that one can realize only by accepting the line of disciplic succession . . .

My book will look different, but not because I am concocting or experimenting. Rather, I wander and even sometimes descend into the muck. I do it in order to pull at the golden thread William Blake said would unwind a ball that would lead us to Eternity. I am also trying to present Kṛṣṇa consciousness according to the Western mindset.

Śrīla Prabhupāda goes on in his introductory remark:

> This edition of *Śrī Caitanya-caritāmṛta* is presented for the study of sincere scholars who are really seeking the Absolute Truth. It is not the arrogant scholarship of a mental speculator but a sincere effort to serve the order of a superior authority whose service is the life and soul of this humble effort. It does not deviate even slightly from the revealed scriptures, and therefore anyone who follows in the disciplic line will be able to realize the essence of this book simply by the method of aural reception.

Prabhupāda is gold; I'm a chip of that gold still partly embedded in dirt. I don't say, "If anyone touches even a single page of this book, his life will become perfect." Yet Kṛṣṇa is here, His name, my calling to Him and desiring His service. Persons already wearing *dhotīs* and *sarīs*, householders, *saṅkīrtana* devotees, some lost souls if not too proud, can stumble onto this treatise, read of Kṛṣṇa consciousness, and benefit, I hope.

Paramahaṁsas always meditate on Śrī Kṛṣṇa (*dhīmahi*). I want to know Him too.

But it ain't easy.
I have a proclivity for cruising like
a seagull or screeching like a parrot
in the Vṛndāvana air—what's
on the parrot's mind?
Fix yours on the lotus feet of Kṛṣṇa.

I'll always come back to the *Bhāgavatam* like a cow tethered to a pole. In the meantime, this is a poor man's attempt to remember. "I am who I" am sort of thing.

A new standard of permissiveness? My actual being.

The spotless *Purāṇa* was compiled by Śrīla Vyāsa under Nārada's instructions. Vyāsa felt despondent even after compiling the *Vedas*. Then Nārada ordered him to write about Kṛṣṇa's transcendental activities. The pinnacle of those activities is featured in the Tenth Canto, "But, in order to reach to the very substance, one must proceed gradually by developing knowledge of the categories."

Prabhupāda's English is faulty, but his vision is perfect. English may be our mother tongue, although we may not be grammatically astute. We may be fluent talkers, quick notetakers, but we're slow to learn Kṛṣṇa consciousness.

May we be forgiven, even chastised if necessary, and corrected, but may we never quit reading the *Bhāgavatam*. Persistence despite obstacles is a symptom of faith and it leads us forward on the path of purification. Kṛṣṇa is the supreme cause, the Supreme Person behind the mirage of temporary reality. Let us meditate upon Him.

I love to read Prabhupāda's unedited English in his 1962 edition. "He sees at night in the sky and naturally thinks what are the stars, how they are situated, who lives there, and so on." Later, Prabhupāda told Hayagrīva, "Put it nicely." Then Jayādvaita dāsa began to edit because he told Prabhupāda he could bring it closer to the original. (I remember not wanting to change his *Teachings of Lord Caitanya*. After all, William Faulkner and James Joyce broke all the rules and created their own styles and people accepted their writings. Why couldn't Prabhupāda do that too?)

I've grown up since those days when Prabhupāda was on the West Coast, and we live on in his wake.

I am still trying to
come clean and be true and
surrendered, to work hard as
I did then.

I'm still waiting to become
Śrī Kṛṣṇa's unalloyed devotee,
but Śrī Jīva says time
has nothing to do with it.
You have to be pure and
love God and work for Him.
Read on.

When we did look up at the stars and wonder where they all came from, the *Bhāgavatam* was there to reply: the Lord is the origin of all creations. I still have that 1962 edition, although the pages are fading. I still exist, although Swamijī has disappeared. I think I'll go on existing while my cheeks grow thinner, but that is illusion, isn't it? "The world is the best place of all . . . but then right in the middle of it comes the smiling mortician."

They didn't discover Prabhupāda's *Bhāgavatam* in
San Francisco in the '60s, altho' they were so Beat
and hip.
Ginsberg told them confidentially
that the Swami was too conservative—
against most kinds of sex and
against all drugs (even tea!).
He was only into chanting
Hare Kṛṣṇa.
They missed it.
I didn't.
I'm still hanging on.

To live the life of a *Bhāgavatam* reader we have to practice the four regulative principles and chant Hare Kṛṣṇa. We have to understand Kṛṣṇa as Parameśvara, as Para-tattva. Otherwise, we'll miss the point. Reading—real, devotional reading—is deep, pure work. It's more important than constructing temples.

"Śrīla Vyāsadeva therefore gives the reader the chance to gradually develop spiritual realization before actually relishing the essence of the pastimes of the Lord." He distinguishes between the internal energy and the external potency, which is within our experience.

The material world is only a shadow of reality. The spiritual world is the real world. Still, the material world also comes from the Lord. In one sense, everything is Kṛṣṇa, but this world and that world are different. It is similar to the difference between freedom and imprisonment.

The *Śrīmad-Bhāgavatam* gradually takes us from the Lord as cosmic creator and director with His attendant demigods to His transcendental incarnations, to instructions on *bhakti* and its goal. Finally, the *Bhāgavatam* gives us Śrī Kṛṣṇa's eternal *svarūpa* in the Tenth Canto.

Once someone asked Prabhupāda about Joan of Arc and how she relates to the *Bhāgavatam*. The devotee couldn't understand why she wasn't mentioned in its pages. Prabhupāda said that she *was* present in the *Bhāgavatam*. Any God conscious effort is part of the *Bhāgavatam*.

Similarly, a devotee complained in a letter to Prabhupāda that he was trying to study the *Bhāgavatam* but that other devotees were making noise while constructing a new altar. Śrīla Prabhupāda said that the construction noise was also *Śrīmad-Bhāgavatam*. That's what I mean about my own life. A poor man begs and that's part of the *Bhāgavatam* too.

Since I'm on the subject, consider this (from Cc. *Antya* 1.211–212):

> Śrī Rūpa Gosvāmī said, "I do not know anything. The only transcendental words I can utter are those which Śrī Caitanya Mahāprabhu makes me speak.
>
> "Although I am the lowest of men and have no knowledge, the Lord has mercifully bestowed upon me the inspiration to write transcendental literature about devotional service. Therefore I offer my obeisances at the lotus feet of

> Śrī Caitanya Mahāprabhu, the Supreme Personality of Godhead, who has given me the chance to write these books."

This material world is *māyā*, unreal. Reality is bliss, the life of truth. There is no ultimate truth in this world or in its leaders and masses, although there is a yearning for it in the hearts of the pious. Even that yearning, however, is covered by layers of greed, anger, and illusion. We must remove those coverings. It takes a lot of work. It can also be done in a moment by Kṛṣṇa's grace if we are willing to submit to His process.

I don't advocate that devotees talk about the details of the material world just because that's where we're at. We don't want to stay at Brooklyn College or in the Manhattan subways forever. But what to do if we can't simply leap to Goloka? We're in Bhakti-devi's camp, preaching to each other in our *khādi dhotis*. We *know* the spiritual potency is real, but perhaps we haven't realized it yet. We're still repeating perfect knowledge while hoping to one day understand it.

Things appear real here only because Lord Kṛṣṇa, true reality, exists eternally in the spiritual world with all His transcendental paraphernalia. We have already purchased our tickets to go there. Therefore, we sing at the departure gate.

Reading *Śrīmad-Bhāgavatam* I think of many
things, alas not all connected
with the sports and
teachings of the Lord.
But I'll be okay, delivered
by virtue of holding the book,
the Indian brick-colored volume with
dust jacket art of Goloka emanating
brahmajyoti light and the Vaikuṇṭhas
and down under a cloud,
the material world.

God is omniscient. He knows what's going on in every corner of the universe. He's omnipotent, the Supreme Controller. This is classic, powerful, transcendental theism, fixed on Lord Kṛṣṇa as the One. This is Śrīla Prabhupāda's presentation. We are all tiny spirit souls, one in quality with Kṛṣṇa, but we never merge into Him; He doesn't disappear into a formless light. We are meant to live eternally in bliss and knowledge with Kṛṣṇa in His abode.

When I first read this as a young man, I awakened to my path. Now I continue to imbibe it. There is nothing else to do but read *Śrīmad-Bhāgavatam*. I hold onto the particular verses and purports for awhile, then read on. Do I retain anything? Some impression? Maybe. It seems to come unstuck from my mind and flow into forgetfulness, so I read it again, pointing with a pencil along the page, left to right and down, guiding myself, reading aloud. I am trying to stay with the *Bhāgavatam*, not abandon it for those other thoughts, those distractions. I keep it up for awhile, then take a break.

Why do I hesitate to say that I am
in Vṛndāvana,
hearing a *bhajana* loudspeakered
outside our ISKCON walls?

No one is *abhijñaḥ* or *svarāṭ* except the Supreme Lord. We all need to learn from someone, but God alone is independent. "Where does everything come from? Where does God come from?" We can't even contemplate it. No one can figure it out.

Many scientists and atheists dismiss it, but they can't explain how the universe came about without Kṛṣṇa. He has inconceivable potency and needs no origin other than Himself.

Prabhupāda argues that no one can approach God's intelligence and that the world's big brains should surrender to Him and become *mahātmās*. I close my eyes and hear it, register it, and think over what he has said, what it means. I don't want to miss anything, but I want to honor it and feel it in my heart.

In the *Padma Purāṇa*, Gautama advises Mahārāja Ambarīṣa to read *Śrīmad-Bhāgavatam* if he at all desires liberation from material bondage. It's complete in 18,000 *ślokas*. If we make a gift of the *Bhāgavatam* on a full moon day, we will go back to Godhead. There is no doubt about its authority. Many distinguished scholars since Lord Caitanya's time—Jīva Gosvāmī, Sanātana Gosvāmī, Viśvanātha Cakravartī Ṭhākura, and others—have written elaborate commentaries on the *Bhāgavatam*.

"Is this a commentary on the scripture?" I asked Swamijī, as I purchased the first three volumes from his hands.

"Yes," he said. I meant, is this your *subjective* commentary. I wanted to show off that I knew how to read books. But I was interested too.

The day I bought the books—
deliver me from *māyā*,
a Swami on the Lower East Side.

In this purport Lord Kṛṣṇa is described as all-knowing, all-pervading, and completely transcendental. Western theologians and philosophers, however, have been baffled about the nature of God throughout the centuries. They cannot understand how God can simultaneously be immanent and transcendent. Neither can they understand how He can simultaneously be all-powerful yet apparently inactive in the face of the world's miseries. How can God be all-good, and yet have a connection to this place of misery?

Christian theologians have particularly wrestled with these concepts. Therefore, in the early days of Christian thought, they debated about an appropriate understanding of Jesus Christ. Was he God? But then how could he experience the passions of a man and thereby feel compassion? Then was he a man? But how could he provide the direct and infallible link to God? Was he half-man and half-God? Eventually, the doctrine was formed: Jesus was both man and God, because in order for him to feel real compassion for man's suffering, he had to experience it himself, and in order for him to provide a tangible link to God, he could not be man.

We see it differently. Kṛṣṇa's compassion for all the living entities does not necessitate that Kṛṣṇa become flesh and blood. Kṛṣṇa loves His parts and parcels in a natural way because they are never separate from Him. God is inconceivable; He is beyond our comprehension. Therefore, it is wrong to measure God on our own scale. God has inconceivable potencies. Jīva Gosvāmī therefore sets this as the first criterion for acceptance and understanding of God—that we accept His *acintya-śakti*, His inconceivable power.

Inconceivable doesn't mean that God is beyond our love. Rather, one of His potencies is that He is *bhakta-vatsala*. He loves His devotee. Therefore, we should apply all intelligence, clarity, and humility in our approach to God.

We should become fixed in the basic definition of what God is. He is not a human being who is bound by time and space. He can simultaneously lose Himself in loving emotions with His pure devotees yet remain the all-knowing universal Supervisor. He simultaneously forgets Himself and yet remains in full remembrance of His power. Is this a contradiction? Yes. But all contradictions are resolved by His own inconceivable potencies.

Anyone who cannot accept this basic definition of God is an atheist or at best, an agnostic. A devotee thrills to hear of God's inconceivable powers. Therefore, the *Bhāgavatam* has something to give all religions. The *Bhāgavatam* teaches that

God is all-great and full of love. We should worship Him. It teaches that God does not want us to suffer but that the suffering is due to our own misbehavior. As soon as we regret our rebellion and turn again toward God, we are immediately lifted out of our suffering. This information is applicable to everyone in the world.

Don't make a mockery of
Śrīmad-Bhāgavatam scholarship
by adding your name to the list.
You don't dare.
I'll explain, "This is
not intended as a joke
or a serious attempt at
Bhāgavatam commentary.
It's not a take-off,
a burlesque
or minimization of what
the great commentators have done."
Then why have you dared?
Because He sent it to me in
my room in Vṛndāvana when
I prayed and I submitted to
Vṛndā-devi in Kāmyavan.
I asked Śrila Prabhupāda,
"Tell me what to do,
although you know I'm a madman,"
and I got this quick response.

Prabhupāda writes, surprisingly, about spiritual sex life (*ādi-rasa)* at the end of his first *Bhāgavatam* purport. He says that because sex is so prominent, it must be real. Its true feature, however, isn't found in this world, but in the spiritual world, free of material desire. "This *Śrīmad-Bhāgavatam* will gradually elevate the unbiased reader to the highest perfectional stage of transcendence."

I may say I've read the *Bhāgavatam* quite a few times in my life and therefore I'm ready to study spiritual *ādi-rasa*. Some devotees hanker for it, but I have decided to start again with the First Canto. That feels right to me. (That's perhaps another virtue of free-writing—it gives me release and also reveals the reality of my immature state.) I'm satisfied to read Prabhupāda's books provided I can be myself and work out the details of what his purports mean to me here and now. I guess you could call that a virtue too, if you know what I mean.

Text 2

dharmaḥ projjhita-kaitavo 'tra paramo nirmatsarāṇāṁ satāṁ
vedyaṁ vāstavam atra vastu śivadaṁ tāpa-trayonmūlanam
śrīmad-bhāgavate mahā-muni-kṛte kiṁ vā parair īśvaraḥ
sadyo hṛdy avarudhyate 'tra kṛtibhiḥ śuśrūṣubhis tat-kṣaṇāt

Completely rejecting all religious activities which are materially motivated, this Bhāgavata Purāṇa propounds the highest truth, which is understandable by those devotees who are fully pure in heart. The highest truth is reality distinguished from illusion for the welfare of all. Such truth uproots the threefold miseries. This beautiful Bhāgavatam, compiled by the great sage Vyāsadeva [in his maturity], is sufficient in itself for God realization. What is the need of any other scripture? As soon as one attentively and submissively hears the message of Bhāgavatam, by this culture of knowledge the Supreme Lord is established within his heart.

Comment

In the first chapter of the *Ādi-līlā*, Kṛṣṇadāsa Kavirāja Gosvāmī quotes this verse to explain how Gaura-Nitāi drive out the darkness of ignorance from the core of the heart. The first verse defines God in the classical way. The second verse focuses on the scriptures, specifically the *Bhāgavatam*, as the way to establish knowledge of God in the heart. Teach us, *Śrīmad-Bhāgavatam*, learned sages, and Lord Kṛṣṇa. You who can grant everything, grant us the *śruśrūṣubhiḥ*, the culture of hearing with faith and devotion. Let it be established in our hearts.

In this verse, reality is distinguished from illusion. The substantial reality is defined as the Supreme Personality of Godhead. Unless we realize this truth, we must suffer in the illusory concept of the self, which brings only misery.

For example, Śrīla Prabhupāda discusses competition in this purport. We all know the pain of competition because our materialistic upbringing constantly pitted us against others. Competition can attack our integrity, our sometimes delicate sense of worth, especially if we lose. But it is the law of material life. Getting ahead implies getting ahead of others. Everything we accomplish in this life is accomplished at another's expense. There are winners and losers. Ultimately, there is war. Only death ends the competition.

Prabhupāda writes that *paramahaṁsas* are above competition because they are detached from sense objects. If we become detached from material goals, there will be nothing left to fight over. That detachment starts with attraction to Kṛṣṇa.

This verse not only criticizes material competition, but it criticizes materially motivated religion as well. Religion is almost always practiced for material security. Therefore, religion is another source of competition. The goal may be gross material success or something more subtle—fame, adoration, and distinction—but such religious piety is always practiced at the expense of others. This verse and purport distinguish two categories of religion: material life means animal life—characterized by mating, eating, sleeping, and defending. When a human being steps a little beyond those propensities and recognizes a Supreme God, he becomes distinguished from the animal species. Then human beings willingly come under the control of the *Vedas* and their competition is civilized.

I remember the shock I felt when I first read in Prabhupāda's book that religion as I knew it at that time was sense gratification. I had to admit it was true. I had experienced it myself in my own religious upbringing. It seems contradictory that people use religion to satisfy lust. Doesn't religion traditionally teach restraint from the world? Not always, at least not always in practice. Rather, religion tries to govern lust by instilling fear of God, fear of damnation, or a tiny bit of piety. (I'll never forget the "baskets of joy," the big wicker baskets with a dozen bottles of liquor covered in cellophane being raffled off in the vestibule of Saint Clare's Church.) What the *Bhāgavatam* describes as "religion" is far above what passes for religion today. And beyond that is *bhakti*.

Pure devotion must be performed in pure consciousness of our spiritual identity. This implies that until we know who we are, we are not performing actual *sevā* but only going through the motions. Sometimes devotees find such statements depressing, but they shouldn't. *Bhakti* is far superior to materially motivated religion, even religion governed by Vedic injunction. It takes practice and sincerity to perform it. Going through the motions gives us that practice and provides us with an opportunity to express earnestness. We sweat and surrender and gradually learn that we are unworthy. Kṛṣṇa sees the dawning of our humility and helps us to approach Him. By "going through the motions," we gradually learn of our true identity and enter the stage of loving service to Kṛṣṇa as who we really are.

May the *Bhāgavatam* protect my
soul. I intend to write
without thinking or prevaricating.

May the *Bhāgavatam* protect
my wanderings: "Leave them alone
and they'll come home, wagging
their tails behind them."

Don't mind boring lectures.
When you listen to others—I
can't say, "Don't fidget," and
expect you to obey, but don't
condemn. See the good—as
in the fair, blue eyes and
slight smile of that Aussie
who gave class the other day,
who kept saying "the Lord" as
if he knew Him.

Cheating religion refers to praying for material goods, speculating on the impersonal, and so on. Sometimes readers say that these things are also mentioned in the *Bhāgavatam*, that it contains discussions on karma, *jñāna*, and yoga. Yes, but those discussions are there only to help us distinguish karma, *jñāna*, and yoga from pure *bhakti*. We'll gradually become elevated by the pure knowledge contained in the *Bhāgavatam* if we are not in a hurry and we hear with attention. As Issa wrote:

"Climb Mt. Fuji,
O snail,
but slowly, slowly!"

Prabhupāda writes that the *Vedas* regulate human activities so people won't unnecessarily compete with one another. Regulation is a lower function of religion. The *Bhāgavatam* goes beyond this. Therefore, it can only be understood by those who no longer wish to compete. The pure-hearted want only loving service to Kṛṣṇa and they want to help humankind establish a competitionless society with Kṛṣṇa in the center.

Śrīmad-Bhāgavatam is above all impurity because it stresses worship of the Supreme Personality of Godhead, Śrī Kṛṣṇa. Devotional service satisfies all other drives—to work, to have knowledge, to worship God—but in a way that brings no karma.

We are supposed to be setting an example of happy devotional life in our ISKCON temples and farm communities. Think of it: no competition, and devotion to God. Can it exist—a society where everyone recognizes that only God is the greatest and we can all only be His loving servants?

The jester can serve, the
Plymouth can serve, the
newborn, the marijuana
smoker can give up his habit
and serve in the kitchen
making *dāl* and cooking down
milk into *burfi* for those
who like that and
the man can serve with the
oxen and the temple manager
and the computer and the children
who talk out during *Bhāgavatam*
class disturbing the lecturer.
They can all serve,
but they need to
hear *Śrīmad-Bhāgavatam*.

Don't go out to the fields
to plant corn without
hearing, and don't think of
computer logic while Sūta is
speaking of absolute substance.

Advice to me too—
stay on track,
errant boy,
writer.

When we realize that we are Kṛṣṇa's servants, we become free of the threefold miseries. Prabhupāda meant that, and he lived in that experience when he wrote that statement. We simply have to look at him to become convinced.

Some contemporary *sādhakas* want to hear more about *mādhurya-līlā*. A *brahmacārī* who lived and worked for years with cows on an ISKCON farm now lives in Vṛndāvana outside ISKCON's shelter. He told an acquaintance that he chants sixty-four rounds a day and feels Prabhupāda's presence strongly. He said the *mañjarīs* love Rādhā more than they love Kṛṣṇa, and they know Her desire just by Her glance. Another devotee asked me to approve his reading of *Ujjvala-nīlamaṇi* and similar books.

I don't condemn them, but I want to enter what Prabhupāda says in his purport to 1.1.2. If we can realize servitorship, we'll be free of the threefold miseries. I am familiar with this statement—I have read it many times over the years—so I may tend to pass over it without letting it affect my heart. I know better; I know I can draw nourishment from such statements and that they have an infinite and fresh reverberation if only I can submit to hearing them with a clear mind. Vyāsa is an unquestionable authority. He recommends that we study *Śrīmad-Bhāgavatam* over all other Vedic literature.

I hope to overcome any challenging attitude left in me. The transcendental message has to be received submissively. Submission doesn't mean dull passivity. We must be anxious and interested to hear. We can become *paramahaṁsas* simply by hearing the *Bhāgavatam*.

I used to be a *paramahaṁsa*,
now I'm just a *parivrājakācārya*.
I was never an *uttama*.
Who cares about that
classification and the put-downs? They may
try to prove I'm a schmo,
an offender of their guru,
I don't know. I just want to
wear *khādī* and clean my bathroom,
and write it out.
Some go barefoot in winter,
stand on cold temple stone.
I wear two or three layers of socks. I say
I've got my own austerity. It's
to read and pray and to write all day.

All right, I summarized *Bhāg.* 1.1.1 and 2. 17,998 verses to go.

A poem is
a bell ringing.

I want to pray and pledge myself to the lifelong work of studying the *Bhāgavatam*. I want to continue it through thick and thin, through the days when I feel there are no easy answers and the days when I tremble and doubt. I am carefree and earnest, conservative and radical. I dare to write crazy things, "shack" notes, and then proceed with my sacred worship. I want to keep track of what Prabhupāda writes in his *Bhāgavatam* purports, but more than that.

Did you know that if you associate with a poor man, there are particular moments when his poverty will be exposed? According to your temperament, you may either be repulsed or you will accept his poverty and not hold it against him.

Imagine that you meet a poor man and he invites you to his home. Perhaps at first there is nothing so much to distinguish him as a poor man expect his simple or worn dress—nothing so bad. You walk along with him and accept an invitation to his house. Suddenly, his poverty is exposed. Perhaps he lives in one of those straw and mud shacks called *bastis* in India. As you step through the door of his shack, it could be a moment of truth for you, and although you might not say it aloud, you might think, "What? This is his house? I have to enter here?" There would be no way for him to hide his poverty from you.

Another way his standard of living would be exposed is in the meal he would be able to offer. When you sat down at this poor man's table, you might again think, "This is all there is? Just a few *capātis* and a small bowl of rice (or the American version of the same)?" Perhaps he even apologizes. It's all he's got.

Sometimes Lord Krsna accepted the invitations of poor people. Śrutadeva invited Kṛṣṇa and the sages to his house and could only offer them planks to sit on and a very simple meal, but because he was imbued with devotion, the Lord and His entourage were at ease and satisfied.

In the case of my *A Poor Man Reads The Bhāgavatam*, I think my poverty is painfully exposed when we come to the end of my comment. Perhaps while reading it, it was so relaxed and easygoing that you didn't notice that we had already reached the next verse. You might ask yourself, "You mean that's it? That's your entire comment on 1.1.2, a verse that has been commented on in depth by the *ācāryas*? You're already finished and that's all you have to say?!"

That's it and my spiritual poverty is exposed. Oh, I could say more about the verse, but I want to to cover the entire *Bhāgavatam*, so we have to move quickly. Therefore, please forgive me and just come with me to the next verse and purport. I count on your empathy and also on the principle that *sādhus* appreciate any sincere effort to glorify the Lord, even if it's filled with defects.

Text 3

nigama-kalpa-taror galitaṁ phalaṁ
śuka-mukhād amṛta-drava-saṁyutam
pibata bhāgavataṁ rasam ālayam
muhur aho rasikā bhuvi bhāvukāḥ

O expert and thoughtful men, relish Śrīmad-Bhāgavatam, the mature fruit of the desire tree of Vedic literatures. It emanated from the lips of Śrī Śukadeva Gosvāmī. Therefore this fruit has become even more tasteful, although its nectarean juice was already relishable for all, including liberated souls.

Comment

As the first verse defines God as Parameśvara and Paratattva, and the second verse defines reality, this third verse invites the reader to relish the *Bhāgavatam*. It's a more personal verse, a juicier verse, than the two preceding it. This verse is nectar, and it's the best advertisement I've read for any course of knowledge. I want to immediately throw myself at the feet of the person *bhāgavata* and beg to be included with his students. Please give me the eligibility to taste this nectar. "The *Bhāgavatam* is semi-solid, soft, and easily digestible nectar. Come on, expert and thoughtful men! Taste it!"

Just to hear the language of the old, brick-colored volume: "Oh the expert and thoughtful men! Please know it that *Śrīmad-Bhāgavatam* is the mature fruit of the desired tree . . . " It's not always easy reading, but there are real gems, such as this one: " . . . it is already readily swallowable nectarine juice which is relished . . . " I want that juice.

Prabhupāda is sitting at Chippiwada on a thin, straw mat placed on the hard floor, naked bulb overhead the only light, stones placed on manuscripts as paperweights, typing for hours. To reciprocate, I read for hours, for years, and now want to write on his points.

He gives a long explanation in his purport about the meaning of *rasa*. This is described in more detail in *The Nectar of Devotion*, where Rūpa Gosvāmī explains the five primary and the seven auxiliary *rasas*. Typical of Prabhupāda's manner, he gives us an overview of the subject in his purport to the third verse of the *Bhāgavatam*. Prabhupāda sometimes said that he wasn't sure he would live long enough to translate the entire *Bhāgavatam*. Therefore, he put everything into the First Canto, and much into the first few purports.

I remember reading it for the first time and mulling over this wondrous new information about a relationship with God in ghastliness, wonder, and conjugal love. No other religion teaches this. For me, the most wonderful thing in the purport comes at the end where Prabhupāda tells us about Śukadeva Gosvāmī. "The Vedic fruit which is mature and ripe in knowledge is spoken through the lips of Śrīla Śukadeva Gosvāmī, who is compared to the parrot not for his ability to recite the *Bhāgavatam* exactly as he heard it from his learned father, but for his ability to present the work in a manner that would appeal to all classes of men." Something in me responds to the idea that we should be more than parrots who mindlessly repeat the philosophy. We can instead faithfully repeat the philosophy, yet sweeten it with our own understanding.

The *Bhāgavatam* is something that is carefully handed down, a fruit that should not be bruised or handled roughly. Neither should it be kept under sterile wrapping without any sign of human touch. No, the devotees can add their reddened mark of sweetness as they hear from Śukadeva. Prabhupāda writes, "This process of disciplic succession of the *Bhāgavata* school suggests that in the future also *Śrīmad-Bhāgavatam* has to be understood from a person who is factually a representative of Śrīla Śukadeva Gosvāmī."

The sages ask us for patient and submissive hearing. To some degree, we have to offer our willingness to hear, our willingness to concentrate. We *could* choose to go to the cinema instead, but we don't. We try to center our lives around submissive hearing.

Although we submit our will, however, the quality of patient and submissive hearing is given as a blessing from guru and Kṛṣṇa. The pure devotees accept Kṛṣṇa as everything. When *they* hear the *Bhāgavatam*, they are maddened by it. They remain immersed in hearing, chanting, and remembering about Kṛṣṇa. Prabhupāda extends this invitation to us: taste the nectar. The nectar is for the highly advanced devotees, but we are not excluded. Just come forward and become eligible.

An example of the highest nectar made available to us is Prabhupāda's presentation in this purport about *rasa*. This scientific method of presenting love of God appeals both to the intellect and to the spiritual senses, and it clarifies the sometimes stark-sounding statement that there is no love in this world. All love is meant for Kṛṣṇa. By loving Kṛṣṇa, we can love all living beings in relation to Him.

The pure devotees understand these words in their ultimate perfection. We may understand them differently. Our material experience of perverted *rasa* spoils our conception of spiritual reality. We think we understand what is sex desire, but then we hear that what we know is only the lowest, perverted manifestation of that which is experienced as topmost in the spiritual world. Since we are so expert in trying to taste sexual consummation in this world, we become unlikely candidates to understand the higher pleasure of *ādi-rasa*.

Therefore, in the beginning, even when we still feel affection for so many material objects, and while our *rasa* for Kṛṣṇa is not developed, we can come to both acknowledge the truth and begin to approach its fulfillment in our own lives. ". . . as far as the spirit souls are concerned, they are one qualitatively with the Supreme Lord. Therefore, the *rasas* were originally exchanged between the spiritual living being and the spiritual whole, the Supreme Personality of Godhead."

Should we become frustrated? I remember in the beginning feeling envious of Kṛṣṇa. I thought I would be emasculated because I wouldn't be able to enjoy sex pleasure in the spiritual world. I took it as an insult to my masculinity. It took me a while to get over it, although now I laugh about it. It is difficult for those who so much ground their masculinity or feminity in their bodies to understand Kṛṣṇa. Conjugal *rasa* (or *any rasa*) is completely transcendental. Although the meeting of God and the *jīva* has some relationship with what we see in this world by reflection, because the reflected forms are so contaminated, they cannot give us direct experience of love of God. Therefore, we have to become free of contamination and material designation in order to go back to Godhead and to love Kṛṣṇa. We cannot impose the designations and relationships we know in this world upon spiritual love.

Having said that, we should note that we begin to approach the spiritual world by dovetailing whatever we have and are in this world. If we have loving sentiments for someone in this world, we can learn to transfer them to Kṛṣṇa. If we do not feel any affection, but live dry, emotionless lives, how will we awaken our spiritual emotion? Our love simply has to be purified and turned toward Kṛṣṇa, not rejected or abandoned.

Schizophrenic, a toad
became a prince. I mean Satsvarūpa.
I don't know how
the Swami picked my name or
who he really is and was,
but I didn't make this up, although
I was a mixed-up boy
in black sweater and pants.

I did get a name and "Steve"
became the young man who
gave money out of his socks
and typed for the Swami.

O expert and thoughtful *munis*, O fools and rascals, please relish *Śrīmad-Bhāgavatam*. It is the best fruit of the *Vedas* as spoken by Śukadeva Gosvāmī (whose name ushers in the third verse, as sweet to hear as Rādhā's, which he spoke later only once in a hidden form). Śuka has made the *Bhāgavatam* sweeter by first tasting the fruit himself.

When we are reading and all of a sudden we're not—when we lose attention—where do we go? The *where* I can tell, and the *why* I don't know except to say that I'm not a devotee or else my mind is *cañcala*. That's the way it is. I'm sure there are psychological and physiological explanations. Maybe we have a vitamin deficiency or our glucose level suddenly drops. I don't know. Maybe a lack of devotion for Kṛṣṇa.

Surrealists want automatic writing to catch the unconscious, but I want to pay attention and go deeper than even the intellect is capable. I like Prabhupāda's inspirational encouragement: "With great respect and attention, one should receive the message and lessons imparted by the *Śrīmad-Bhāgavatam*."

The highest spiritual realization is to know the Personality of Godhead as the reservoir of all mellows (*rasas*).

"You've given me enough to type all winter, Swamijī!"

"Enough," he replied, "to last you several lifetimes."

I remember thinking that I could always leave in a few months if I didn't like the Swami, just as I could leave a temporary job or the Boy Scouts or the Navy or even home.

I mean I could leave
any scene I didn't like—
I learned that from Beat life
and marijuana smoking.
"I don't need you, man!"

Walk out on a chick (girl)
or a cat (guy) I didn't like,
even a success scene if it
rubbed me the wrong way—
leave, split, go into the
street and run fast away, my
feet in winged sneakers.
That much I could do,
it was in my power—to *leave.*
But he said Kṛṣṇa will
capture you and you can't
get away. We laughed,
enjoyed sitting on the floor
eating hot rice and vegetables,
Howard in a plaid shirt, a big
beard, me and me and you and
it's true
I didn't make it up.

As proof that it wasn't a dream, I need only look at the book in my hands, printed in New Delhi in 1962. It's the same one I bought in New York City in 1966. I am sitting with it here in Vṛndāvana while the parrots screech. The Swami's gone and it's different, but

woe betide I ever
leave him and may die soon
in this dingy hall
stairway. I have to go despite
ISKCON's new building construction
and my private writing.
Go obediently down the
dark, narrow hall,
the forced mercy of Rādhā
on anyone in Vṛndāvana.

I too want
to die that way, but for
now, taste nectarean juice.

I know the dear reader doesn't have to be given a review (as in a student's "Cliff Notes") of the outline of the *Bhāgavatam* purports. I've made such reviews purport by purport as many devotees have in notebooks. This is meant to be different than that.

I heard Prabhupāda say last night, "Don't be lazy." He said it twice. He said we should study as Kṛṣṇadāsa Kavirāja Gosvāmī advocates. Learn the *siddhānta* even though it takes effort. The *siddhānta* will strengthen the mind. Prabhupāda added, "Don't concoct or express whimsical ideas." He himself was always true to *siddhānta* and he presented it for our benefit.

We repeated like chirping birds
or the way the *chaukīdār* at
Krishna-Balaram Mandir rings the bell
exactly on time even on a cold
night. He doesn't ring three times
when it's 4 o'clock and he
isn't early or late.

We might say the *chaukīdār* could be replaced by a machine and the *siddhānta* speaker too. That's what they do in Western churches where bell-ringing is automated. The human reader, however, has to assimilate the message and present it in his own way. If Vyāsa and Prabhupāda say there are five main *rasas* and seven auxiliary ones, we can't change that to six and two. We can't say that the conjugal *rasa* doesn't count as one on the list. The list is *siddhānta* and it is both literally true and transcendental.

What does it mean, then, to express *siddhānta* in our own words? It means we can express it according to time, place, and persons, but we must keep the spirit of the original. *Siddhānta* is not stereotyped or stagnant. Lord Caitanya's followers may make innovative presentations.

Rasa doesn't exist in the material world except in a perverted form. (That's quite a challenge to a humanist. Good!) It's true that a mother protects her child and that a lover is mad about his beloved, but all relationships in the material world end in tragedy or separation, and they always fall short. Material relationships are another part of the cosmos that gets swept away. Therefore, any coming together in this world is like the chance combination of straws on the waves of the sea. (Relationships among devotees may qualify as real, but they can't claim to be *rasa* until the devotees are liberated.)

Rasa means the relationship between the Lord and His *pariṣads*. Vyāsadeva gives a preliminary description of *rasa* in this verse, in the words *rasam* and *rasikā*. These words describe both the nectarean juice and the persons who are full of knowledge about the *Bhāgavatam's* mellows. We tend to use those terms less technically sometimes.

O learned and thoughtful men,
please let me read and
be one preacher among you.
Let me serve those whom you have sent
to the world.

Why do I want to dance and sing?
It's in me, it's
a way to spontaneously exult, and
I hope the *siddhānta*
appears in a suitable way.
(I was going to say, suitable for my ragtime notes,
but that's old jazz, although still
in the dictionary).

Remember those IQ tests we used to take? They often tested reading comprehension among other skills. Reading comprehension is only a beginning stage of reading the

Bhāgavatam. It's not the most important skill to have to be able to summarize a page after reading it.

One passage in the previous purport stated that the conditioned souls are always hampered by the threefold miseries, but if we become fixed as Kṛṣṇa's servants, we will be free of misery. If we read that page so poorly that we can't even give a comprehension report afterwards, then we have missed out. Therefore, we should pay attention.

Even more that that, however, we should enter a "mystical contemplation," as the Christians say. I can't express it exactly, but a mystical contemplation is when you get an inkling of Prabhupāda's special potency and his particular mood in bringing Kṛṣṇa to us in his writings. This kind of reading brings realization, *vijñāna*, to one who practices it carefully and submissively.

Reading *Śrīmad-Bhāgavatam* delivers *rasa* when it is heard and understood from the right source, from Nārada (who carried it from the spiritual world) to Vyāsa to Śukadeva to Mahārāja Parīkṣit. *Rasikās* such as Śukadeva are anxious to taste *Śrīmad-Bhāgavatam*, even though they are already *ātmārāmas*, liberated from matter.

Ordinary people acting under the modes of nature cannot taste the *Bhāgavatam* because they are still entangled in the perverted form of *rasa*. Therefore, it is important to be materially detached and to repose our loving feelings in the Supreme Lord and the narration of His pastimes.

Reading *Śrīmad-Bhāgavatam* is private, I say. We spend time alone with the *Bhāgavatam*. No one can pour it down to us. Oh, sure, Śukadeva delivered it to Mahārāja Parīkṣit, Sūta Gosvāmī delivered it to the sages at Naimiśāraṇya, and Lord Caitanya sent it to Śrīla Prabhupāda who gave it to us, but we each have to open our beaks like hungry birds and taste it. We have to do that alone. Only then may we speak realized *Bhāgavatam*.

I like that image of the fruit being handed down carefully. I want to draw a picture of it—the men up in the tree handing down the fruit from person to person and finally to me on the ground. We don't need to jostle each other; there's enough fruit for all. We simply have to reach up and take all we want, all we need.

"This process of disciplic succession of the Bhāgavata school suggests that in future also for all the time *Śrīmad-Bhāgavata* has to be understood from a person who is factually a representative of Śrīla Śukadeva Gosvāmī."

I'm a poor man and perhaps I can't reach up to accept the fruit from the man in the tree. Rather, I do like other poor men and gather the fruits that have fallen on the ground.

Śrīla Prabhupāda speaks of "stupid interpretation" of *Śrīmad-Bhāgavatam*. Did they change those words in later editions? No, they're still there, "stupid," "dogs and cats." Those who don't follow Śukadeva Gosvāmī are no better than hogs, dogs, camels, and asses. Their jeweled turbans will weigh them down at death.

Text 4

naimiṣe 'nimiṣa-kṣetre
ṛṣayaḥ śaunakādayaḥ
satraṁ svargāya lokāya
sahasra-samam āsata

Once, in a holy place in the forest of Naimiṣarāṇya, great sages headed by the sage Śaunaka assembled to perform a great thousand-year sacrifice for the satisfaction of the Lord and His devotees.

Comment

The *Bhāgavatam* was spoken for a second time in Naimiṣāraṇya. The sages performed a *yajña* intended to please Lord Viṣṇu and His devotees and to bring peace to the world. Sometimes devotees wonder how it is possible for sages to bring peace to the world when they are off in the forest, living apart from humankind. What tangible good could come from simply hearing from Sūta Gosvāmī?

The sages were not activists in the usual sense, but by engaging in spiritual life for the good of others rather than working for newspapers or attending political rallies, they were able to bestow blessings on the world. Hearing produces preachers. Prayer can also be preaching if we pray sincerely and with the right intent. And after hearing, as Prabhupāda suggested to his forty mostly Western disciples during his 1972 *Nectar of Devotion* talks at Rādhā-Dāmodara temple in Vṛndāvana, "the sages could then go out . . ."

Another form of preaching by sages is when they write books. The Six Gosvāmīs lived apart from materialistic society in the sanctified and protected atmosphere of Vṛndāvana-dhāma, but their books were meant to benefit all humanity. Prabhupāda too wrote books, which contain the essence of the Gosvāmīs' books. Such powerful sages can also benefit others by praying for them or wishing them well.

We sometimes hear of *tapasvis* giving their religious merit to others, devotees offering candles at Kārttika on others' behalf, watering *tulasī* for others, and other forms of devotional service. In *Mādhurya-kādambinī*, Viśvanātha Cakravartī Ṭhākura explains that Kṛṣṇa gives the power of attorney to the devotees; it is the devotees who determine who will receive *bhakti*. The devotees avail themselves of direct mercy, but others in the world may not even know that they are being blessed. Whether the people know it or not, the sages should continue to serve the world in this way.

I once spoke on this verse and purport to a group of Christian social activists at Boston University during the rise of the peace movement in the 1960s. It wasn't an auditorium lecture, but a regular club meeting, and I was there not to lecture but to ask them to sponsor Prabhupāda as a lecturer. It was a winter evening, and I remember how nervous I was in that informal setting. It was a typical college scene—a bulletin board covered with notices for political rallies, upcoming concerts, rooms to rent, and a girl was sitting in the corner playing the piano while young men were laughing and fooling around. Although I was dressed like them, my short hair and Vaiṣṇava *śikhā* set me apart as a stranger.

When the meeting began, the chairman read the agenda, which included planning an anti-Vietnam march in Washington, D.C. Then he said, "Before we start, we have some minor business to get through first. This man has come to tell us about a swami."

I sat up and spoke to the dozen or so lounging students. "I am a follower of A. C. Bhaktivedanta Swami. He is coming to Boston this May, and since he is a significant spiritual leader, I thought it would be beneficial for the students at Boston University to get a chance to hear him speak."

I then read this verse and purport because I felt it would explain Prabhupāda's relevancy to the peace movement. Prabhupāda's purport explained it clearly:

> [The sages] are sincere friends to all living entities, and at the risk of great personal inconvenience they are always engaged in the service of the Lord for the good of all people. Lord Viṣṇu is just like a great tree, and all others . . . are like branches, twigs and leaves of that tree. By pouring water on the root of the tree, all the parts of the tree are automatically nourished. Only those branches and leaves which are detached cannot be so satisfied. Detached branches and leaves dry up gradually despite all watering attempts. Similarly, human society, when it is detached from

the Personality of Godhead like detached branches and leaves, is not capable of being watered, and one attempting to do so is simply wasting his energy and resources.

I knew this Christian group was oriented toward activism. Therefore, I emphasized that Prabhupāda's message was also active and that Prabhupāda wanted to overcome evil in the world. This purport also delivers the ultimate activism: chanting Hare Kṛṣṇa is the means by which the living entity can wake up from false identification with matter.

I don't know how seriously the students took my presentation. After they agreed to sponsor Prabhupāda and I was out in the coatroom preparing to leave, I heard a burst of laughter come from the room. Prabhupāda did speak there, however, and deliver his message of peace and goodwill.

Prabhupāda makes it clear in this purport that both he and the *Śrīmad-Bhāgavatam* think in absolute terms. There is Kṛṣṇa and there is *māyā*. If we are not in Kṛṣṇa consciousness, we are in *māyā*. The two conditions are side by side, like shadow and light. If we lean a little to one side, we will be in darkness; a little to the other side and we will be in light. If we choose darkness, our lives are useless.

When I first came to Prabhupāda, this absolute presentation attracted me. He was not overbearing about it, yet he left no room for compromise. It's difficult to explain what Prabhupāda was like in those days. He was soft, elderly, wise, humble, and inviting. He was surrounded by an aura of kindness, gentility, and mendicant poverty. Even we could see that he depended on Kṛṣṇa. When he spoke, however, he was absolute. It's inconceivable how we who were so relative and eclectic were able to accept what Prabhupāda said.

I remember thinking at the beginning that Prabhupāda would teach a different spiritual book every week. After I attended my first *Bhagavad-gītā* class, I asked one of the other students what book he would speak on the next week. I suggested he might like to speak on *The Tibetan Book of the Dead*. "No, Swamijī says everything's in the *Bhagavad-gītā*." I accepted that quickly. How could we accept Prabhupāda's absoluteness? It is inconceivable; it is only his mercy.

I was and am thankful to Prabhupāda for describing the sages' purpose and all the other things he has explained. His noncompromising statement that everything must be done for the pleasure of Viṣṇu is not oppressive, but welcome. Sometimes we hold festivals and propaganda drives on ISKCON's behalf, but many of us participating miss the point. Many are dissatisfied with the leaders' direction. Regardless, somehow we have to perform *yajña* to please Lord Kṛṣṇa, and only that will bring peace to the world and to ourselves. When we are finally peaceful, we will know we have succeeded.

"In this age, the congregational chanting of the holy names of the Lord is the prescribed method for waking up. The ways and means are most scientifically presented by Lord Śrī Caitanya Mahāprabhu, and intelligent persons may take advantage of His teachings in order to bring about real peace and prosperity."

I'm gathering my wits, subpersons, wherewithal, good intentions, concentration as my master's *śiṣya* around the Naimiṣāraṇya in the center of my heart. I hope. I can't stay in one place for long with the great sages in India's peaceful forests. I'm moving about and sometimes feel plagued and pressed by duties that don't feel connected to my inner calling. Therefore, I've begun my own *yajña*, which is my "one-thousand-year" poor man's sacrifice of *prāṇa, artha, dayā,* and *vāca*. May Lord Viṣṇu and His devotees grant me protection so that there will be no hindrance to this *yajña*. Or, if there are hindrances, please let me overcome them. May I be aware that I too am working for world peace.

O *Śrīmad-Bhāgavatam*, if I stay within your aura, I can do good to others, sprinkling on them the nectar of your teachings. *Oṁ śānti, śānti, śānti oṁ*. Hare Kṛṣṇa.

Text 5

ta ekadā tu munayaḥ
prātar huta-hutāgnayaḥ
sat-kṛtaṁ sūtam āsīnaṁ
papracchur idam ādarāt

One day, after finishing their morning duties by burning a sacrificial fire and offering a seat of esteem to Śrīla Sūta Gosvāmī, the great sages made inquiries, with great respect, about the following matters.

Comment

The author of the *Bhāgavatam* now begins to give concise descriptions of the *Bhāgavatam* recital at Naimiṣāraṇya. It is a holy place, in the forest, and although many sages are present, the atmosphere is calm and quiet. This is not a loud or restless crowd. It is morning, the best time for spiritual practices. We can imagine them, those quiet, controlled sages listening intently, and we can feel the drama as each sage awakens to his own aspiration to see Kṛṣṇa in the heart. When Kṛṣṇa actually appears in the heart of an avid listener, that person is transformed by ecstasy. Expectation of ecstasy adds an intensity to the scene.

The sages offer the *vyāsāsana* to Sūta Gosvāmī and inquire from him with great respect. All Vyāsadeva's representatives are *gosvāmīs* who control their senses and who do not change the message they have heard from the previous *ācāryas*: "The *gosvāmīs* do not deliver lectures on the *Bhāgavatam* capriciously. Rather, they execute their services most carefully, following their predecessors who delivered the spiritual message unbroken to them."

What about that? I turn to a later purport where Prabhupāda states that Lord Caitanya's followers are dexterous and innovative in presenting the *Bhāgavatam* and who can therefore find a variety of ways to inject it into the dull brains of modern people. Kṛṣṇa consciousness is not stereotyped; we can present it in many different ways as long as we preserve the original spirit.

The sages ask their questions with great respect. I imagine Śaunaka Ṛṣi standing while the others sit at Sūta's feet. Śaunaka wants Sūta Gosvāmī to hear him as he speaks on behalf of the assembled sages. Sūta, clear-eyed and transcendental, alert and respectful of Śaunaka's own high qualifications, listens carefully.

One must question the *Bhāgavatam* speaker with respect to elicit the clear meaning. There is a difference between listening alertly just to find the speaker's faults and listening alertly to understand the Absolute Truth from a speaker whom we trust. Both listeners may ask questions, but the first listener will challenge and the second will ask with respect. It is recommended that we adopt the second mood.

It is inevitable that at the beginning of our spiritual lives, our true inquiries may be mixed with challenge. The speaker may consider our challenging doubtfulness as a sign of intelligence. If we are sincere about hearing, however, we soon learn to follow a certain etiquette of politeness and respect in asking our questions, and the challenge is overcome by trust. Lord Caitanya said, "Etiquette is the ornament of a devotee." We learn to inquire gently, to admit our doubts without false ego. Prabhupāda invited us to ask our questions with logic and argument. If we present our question within the bounds of etiquette, the spiritual master may feel more obliged to respond.

If the questioner accompanies his inquiry with acts of service, he will come more quickly to accept the spiritual master. He may then continue to present himself as foolish or ignorant, but one with a spiritual master knows everything because by his loving relationship with the guru, his doubts can easily be cleared. We see this in the relationship between Kṛṣṇa and Arjuna on the battlefield. Prabhupāda says that as friends, their talks were not helping Arjuna to overcome doubt. As friends, their opinions had equal weight. When Arjuna saw that his opinions did not relieve his grief, however, and when he understood that Kṛṣṇa had superior intelligence, he surrendered: *śiṣyas te 'haṁ śadhi māṁ tvāṁ prapānnam*, "Please instruct me."

We cannot expect to ask questions from a vacant heart. We can report on the sounds we hear in the hallway of the Krishna-Balaram Guesthouse—a young child's chatter echoing, and outside, a distant *bhajana*. Sūta was offered the guru's seat, but we were not there. I was present, however, when Prabhupāda was first offered a *vyāsāsana* (a big upholstered chair). Therefore, we direct our praises toward him. That's not unnatural. One *sādhu* here in Vṛndāvana warned me that ISKCON devotees overdo their praise of Prabhupāda. He said that we keep ourselves separate from the *sampradāya* because we praise Prabhupāda so much. He also said that Prabhupāda's true glory was that he was a humble servant of the *paramparā*—one of many such humble servants. I don't agree. Śrīla Prabhupāda's contribution was extraordinary. He did what no one else could do. I feel he allows me to write in his wake.

Ekadasi parikramers, Jan 17

Madhu has a cold and his voice is hoarse. He looks so skinny walking around in his long underwear. At breakfast he brings in Prabhupāda's plate, but forgets mine. Five minutes later I call him. "This isn't nice." I want him to feel bad for the oversight, but the guy is sick. What do I expect? I sit down to my belated fruit plate (it's Ekādaśī).

Put it *all* in.
Put the whole diary in,
the frankincense and myrrh. It's
all *Bhāgavatam*. Hazret Mohammed
and Akbar and the Hindu-hater
Aurangzeb who tore down Govinda's
upper stories in jealousy.
Blood all over Vṛndāvana in
those years and here
we are rich, not venturing out
"in case I get a headache."

Put it all in.
Devayāṇī grows old,
slack skin under her chin,
Stevie dies of heart failure like
his Dad. What else?

Text 6

ṛṣaya ūcuḥ
tvayā khalu purāṇāni
setihāsāni cānagha
ākhyātāny apy adhītāni
dharma-śāstrāṇi yāny uta

The sages said: Respected Sūta Gosvāmī, you are completely free from all vice. You are well versed in all the scriptures famous for religious life, and in the Purāṇas and the histories as well, for you have gone through them under proper guidance and have also explained them.

Comment

The sages told Sūta he was free from all vice, that he knew the scriptures, especially the *Purāṇas*. Therefore, he was entitled to sit on the *vyāsāsana*. No one should assume to give *Bhāgavatam* lectures from the *vyāsāsana* unless he is following the four rules. No one should bluff on that point. Besides that, he should know the scriptures. Of course, for us, knowing the scriptures means knowing Prabhupāda's four basic books: *Bhagavad-gītā As It Is*, *Śrīmad-Bhāgavatam*, *The Nectar of Devotion*, and *Caitanya-caritāmṛta*. These four books contain the essence of all the *Vedas*. Even if we know only *Bhagavad-gītā*, we can understand that essence. Śrī Kṛṣṇa states, "I am the subject of *Vedānta* and its goal and its knower as well."

Śrīla Prabhupāda writes in his purport to verse five, "The Gosvāmīs do not deliver lectures on the *Bhāgavatam* capriciously . . . " Here we see the high standard set for the speaker of the *Bhāgavatam*. It was a rare privilege to speak, and only one sage among thousands was awarded that privilege. Then what about ISKCON? Speaking the *Bhāgavatam* is open to almost anyone because Prabhupāda deputized his followers to speak. So those who speak should understand the responsibility, and they should meet at least minimum requirements: they should control their senses by following the four rules, chant sixteen rounds a day, and never concoct, become frivolous, or go against Vaiṣṇava *paramparā*. They shouldn't speak capriciously.

As we gain experience as speakers and as we study the scriptures, we will become more knowledgeable, both about what the *Bhāgavatam* is and how to present it effectively. If we remain faithful to guru, we will also learn to speak openly from the heart.

Prabhupāda states more qualifications for the *gosvāmī* who is eligible to speak the *Bhāgavatam*. He doesn't exclude people, but trains as many as possible as representatives of Vyāsadeva and Sūta Gosvāmī. He does not expect us to be able to speak as *mahā-bhagavatas*, but he establishes the minimum requirements in this purport: we must be free from the four major vices of Kali-yuga and be well-versed in all the revealed scriptures. He mentions the *Purāṇas*, *Mahābhārata*, and *Rāmāyaṇa*, and adds, "The *ācārya* or the *gosvāmī* must be well acquainted with all these literatures."

Prabhupāda did not translate the *Mahābhārata* or the *Rāmāyaṇa*, nor did he necessarily encourage us to study them thoroughly. Simply by reading Prabhupāda's books, we can assimilate the essence of the histories and important *Vedas*. For us, we may define "well versed in all revealed scriptures" as meaning well versed in the verses of the books he gave us and his Bhaktivedanta Purports.

There are qualifications for the audience too. The audience should be controlled enough to only hear from the right source. If someone is speaking with questionable connection to the *paramparā*, we should not hear from him. In reference to reading scriptures, Prabhupāda states, "To hear and explain them is more important than reading them." This means that we have to understand scripture by having it explained to us by an *ācārya*. Unless I hear the *Bhāgavatam* or other books explained by Prabhupāda, I don't feel I can invest the same simple sincerity and trust.

The principle of faithfulness to hearing from the spiritual master is not an introductory instruction but something that becomes more and more important as we enter deeper into Kṛṣṇa consciousness. Ultimately, we have to become fixed in hearing from someone who can guide us in a particular mood with a particular emphasis. We are not looking to have only a superficial grasp on scriptural knowledge, but to please Kṛṣṇa with our śāstric conviction. We want to realize the fruit of Kṛṣṇa consciousness.

It is a great blessing that Prabhupāda has given us both the opportunity to speak and the opportunity to hear the *Bhāgavatam*. We can hold in our minds the image of the pure devotee sage who speaks the *Bhāgavatam* filled with remembrance of Kṛṣṇa. Such sages want to stimulate love of God in themselves and awaken it in others by hearing and speaking. We can aspire for that awakening and learn to hear with rapt attention as Kṛṣṇa supplies the intelligence from within.

To recite the *Bhāgavatam*, we need to know Lord Kṛṣṇa; He is the goal of Vedic study. Who knows Him? We all know Him. If we chant Hare Kṛṣṇa, regularly read the scriptures, avoid sinful life, and repeat whatever we have heard in *paramparā* without adding to it or subtracting from it, we can carry the same torch Sūta Gosvāmī passed down to the sages: the torch of Kṛṣṇa consciousness in the dark age of Kali.

I doubt my own proficiency from head to foot. I ought to overcome it, but you see, I'm always afraid I may misbehave and lose Prabhupāda's grace. I heard the Swami say I have to please Kṛṣṇa. It doesn't matter if I am a *pūjārī* or a floor sweeper because one form of service is not more exalted than another. It doesn't matter whether I am a *brāhmaṇa* or low-born. All that matters is whether Kṛṣṇa is satisfied by my efforts. If I am a *brāhmaṇa* (learned, clean, able to meditate, highborn), but I don't please Kṛṣṇa, then my work is *śrama eva hi kevalam*. Prabhupāda told us this again and again. Then he said, "Thank you very much," ending his lecture.

"He sure is clear."

"Yeah," Madhu said.

Therefore, I doubt. How do I know whether I am pleasing Him by eating the delicious grapes and papayas someone prepared for our Ekādaśī breakfast? Did I eat too voraciously and thus spoil the Lord's pleasure? Why was I so irritable this morning? I'd like to overcome that doubt and speak with the confidence of Sūta's follower, yet I want to speak everything that's on my mind and then some, to confess and break loose into dancing and singing.

All I can say is the more, the better, as long as it all rings true. I hope the cut of truth is pleasing to Kṛṣṇa. Otherwise, it's not worth being said.

Sūta upheld the *Bhāgavatam's* honor. We who come after must uphold it too. Four rules and no addition or subtraction. No politically motivated speeches or long, rambling stories with no connection to Kṛṣṇa. This is the responsibility of one who speaks the *Bhāgavatam*. We should feel the weight of it.

I may be a poor man, which signifies that I am spiritually humble and bereft of *ruci* (Prabhupāda used to call us "poor students"), but poor doesn't mean deliberately sinful or somehow not honorable in our speech.

You see, that's where my problem lies. Sometimes I have something on my mind and I need to speak out about it or unburden it. Can I talk it out with friends? I mean, do I always have to be a perfect speaker?

You know what I mean. I am an ordinary fellow. I need to speak in a friendly way among my friends, even though my speech isn't always perfect. We all assume that we want to be perfect. Therefore, I want to expand the field of what we may write in a book offered to devotees. This is daring and the source of my fear and trembling. I dare to extend the boundaries and include what hasn't been included by the perfect *ācāryas* in their books, their perfect *śāstras*. That's what's on my mind and the main point behind the "extra" in this poor man's writing.

The judges can decide.
Sit on your case. Meantime,
write it out.

Don't add insult to injury but be
aware at all times
I want to be
Kṛṣṇa conscious and am coming around
to that—
at His lotus feet with loud *japa*.
Felt bad about my shortcoming and
my admitting it purified the ether.
Did not stay angry but gave it up.
Didn't practice *mauna* but
corrected my guff.
To hear and explain that is more important than reading.
I wept and tried.

Do you remember your thirty years in ISKCON?
Sure, you must have a lot of memories.
What gets churned up nowadays as
you read a purport? Is anybody
listening?

I can say that Sūta followed
the four rules and repeat over and over again, "We
should do this and we should do that"
until my audience is bored sick even
though what I said was
technically perfect.
I think you can
be private and say, "I actually feel
okay and grateful, but these
things I recall . . . "

Then maybe you even tell
of times you were shaky on the
4 rules if it's edifying to hear—
how you overcame it.
Or you could tell a dream
where you were running away
from your Godbrothers, the big ones,
who were going, "Tsk, tsk,
why do you go apart?"
You didn't want love?
You hid in order to write.

It was a kind of neurotic
dream, naked as so many of them
are, and a puzzle, not clear
paramparā conclusion—but
somehow important, some-
how full of implicit
release from *māyā*.

A lot of official stuff in
an institution may be bunk.
More and more devotees
admit it. They are sick of
pretensions of perfection.
I don't want to rant and rail
against any group or anyone.
Just to speak and be allowed.
Actually I only wish to preach,
I guess. But it comes
this way.

Sūta obeyed the four rules. I
do too. And you, I hope.
If you don't you may tell me.
I won't hold it against you.
I'll help as I can.
It won't help you to sin.
But . . .
I know an *ācārya*
should be grave.

This isn't a "should" book. It's an actual declaration. I fear it's run-on. I fear to go on, but fear to stop.

Ask Kṛṣṇa what He likes. With each line I write, I pray for forgiveness and pray to improve.

Sūta obeyed the rules and knew all the relevant scriptures. They honored him, the son of Romaharṣaṇa (who was not so gentle, but that's another story). I'm talking of Sūta and myself in limited time.

Sūta was obedient. He was standard. He stood up straight and didn't make a mockery of his position. The captains look me up and down for inspection as I stand in the ranks. Are my shoes polished? Right creases in the *dhotī*? *Tilaka* on straight? I know I'm not the best. But do I pass? Squeak by?

They look me up and down and I feel that even if they say, "Mr. Sats, you look a little seedy, as if you slept in that shirt," I know I won't be punished or rejected by the *ācāryas*, although I may be held back.

Oh, but time is up.
I can't write more today.

It was long ago when Śaunaka and the sages thanked Sūta Gosvāmī and invited him to speak on the *Bhāgavatam*. First Vyāsadeva wrote his three prelude verses which clarified the topic: Śrī Kṛṣṇa, the Absolute Truth, the Personality of

Godhead. Viśvanātha Cakravartī Ṭhākura stated that *janmadyasya*, the source of all, includes the source of *ādi-rasa*, conjugal love. And Prabhupāda hammered at once on the atheists in his purport. We get ready to go with them into *Bhāgavatam-kathā*. Now the stage is set where we can include ourselves and feel welcome among the sages at Naimiṣāraṇya, where everyone hears the speaker submissively. Of course, for us, submissive hearing means accepting Prabhupāda and his purports as our guide in the life of *sādhana-bhakti* he gave us.

Here we are in the morning in the perpetual cycle of days, for as much time as we have left in our life. We don't have "*sahasra*" (1,000) years left at our disposal. Mahārāja Parīkṣit had only seven days. Please speak, Sūta Gosvāmī. We are eager to hear.

I read again the qualifications one must have before he can dare sit on the *vyāsāsana*, but my mind flits off to a letter I have to write, a piece of luggage I have to pack, and the *chaukīdār* knocking his stick against the gate outside. I hear a *bhajana* in the distance, and the sound floats this way as unclear as fog. Shall I try again to think about a *gosvāmī's* qualifications, or should I try to pick up another thread?

"He not only should be freed from all such vices, but must also be well versed in all revealed scriptures or in the *Vedas.*" Śrīla Prabhupāda is concerned not only with the historical Sūta Gosvāmī of five thousand years ago, but with the continuation of *Bhāgavatam* recital today. He wants us to qualify ourselves to speak it. It's not impossible. We simply have to follow the four rules, give up sinful life, and know the conclusion of Prabhupāda's books. (The essential Vaiṣṇava *smṛti* gathered from all *śrutis*, *smṛtis*, and previous commentaries are poured out sweetly from his experience.) Be with Prabhupāda and enter the topics of the spotless *Purāṇa.*

Sūta was qualified. We must not remain unqualified. Study the books, hear them explained, and then write. As

Śrīla Prabhupāda said of himself, "Because I was good at hearing (*śravaṇam*), now I am good at *kīrtana* (glorifying Lord Kṛṣṇa and the *saṅkīrtana* movement of Śrī Caitanya Mahāprabhu)."

Text 7

yāni veda-vidāṁ śreṣṭho
bhagavān bādarāyaṇaḥ
anye ca munayaḥ sūta
parāvara-vido viduḥ

Being the eldest learned Vedāntist, O Sūta Gosvāmī, you are acquainted with the knowledge of Vyāsadeva, who is the incarnation of Godhead, and you also know other sages who are fully versed in all kinds of physical and metaphysical knowledge.

Comment

Sūta Gosvāmī is praised as the seniormost learned Vedāntist. He is acquainted with Vyāsadeva and other sages, the leaders of ancient India's *ṣaṭ-darśana*, six philosophies. Most of them are materialistic or atheistic. They give little importance to the cause of all causes.

The *Śrīmad-Bhāgavatam* speaker, however, is expected to know these six philosophies before he can sit on the *vyāsāsana* and "present fully the theistic views of the *Bhāgavatam* in defiance of all other systems." We learn about them from Prabhupāda.

I remember from my BBT Library Party days when Professor Troy Organ of Ohio State University read this line in a book we had given him for review. He objected to what he considered Prabhupāda's sectarianism. He didn't like it that Prabhupāda defied all teachers other than those who taught the pure *Bhāgavatam*. The professor believed in neutrality in the name of scholarship. But we are not interested in neutrality. We want to go back to Godhead. We want peace and accord among all people. Since five out of six of the Indian philosophies defy God, how can we not defy them? *Śrīmad-Bhāgavatam* is God's book *par excellence*, and we must know how to defend it.

But what about the professor's challenge? Sūta Gosvāmī is described as learned in Vyāsadeva's knowledge and in the teachings of other sages, which include "all kinds of physical and metaphysical knowledge."

Does this surprise us? Why should a representative of Kṛṣṇa consciousness be expected to know more than a few Vaiṣṇava scriptures? Someone may criticize our more exclusive approach and say, "You ISKCON devotees are disdainful of all knowledge outside of what you consider transcendence. You're almost anti-intellect, anti-culture, and anti-metaphysics, and because of that, you don't develop an overall perspective of either the strength of the *Bhāgavatam's* philosophy or the shortcomings of other systems. Not only that, you close off the universe until it contains only one small corner of what you consider absolute philosophy, and you deny the value of everything else. That may leave you feeling safe, but it also makes you dogmatic. How can you become wise if you are dogmatists? How can you have the power to discern what is true and right?"

By knowing Kṛṣṇa, one knows everything. *Yasmin vijñāte sarvam, evam vijñātaṁ bhavati*, "If one can understand the Supreme Personality of Godhead, the controller of all controllers, one can understand everything else." Kṛṣṇa also assures Arjuna in the *Bhagavad-gītā* that if he simply hears from the Lord, he will learn everything noumenal and phenomenal.

Śrīla Prabhupāda took this approach. He rarely refused to answer a question on any topic, although he freely admitted that he did not know the teachings of every philosopher or that he was not a trained scientist. However, if Prabhupāda heard the name of a Western philosopher unfamiliar to him, he would say, "What is his philosophy?" As soon as he got a handle on the philosophy, he would respond to it from his context of the Absolute Truth as presented in the Vaiṣṇava *paramparā*.

The *Śrīmad-Bhāgavatam* itself tells us that all knowledge originated in the *Vedas*. It later branched out and spread throughout the world, sometimes in perverted or defiant forms, and became known as various departments of knowledge. Of course, we can be dogmatic and fail to appreciate the worth of reflected spiritual truth found in so many philosophies, political causes, altruistic pursuits, and world religions *because* they are not strictly Vedic. Better, however, is to be properly grounded in Vedic knowledge, especially in Kṛṣṇa conscious practices, and to have a broad outlook on how Vedic knowledge has expanded, has jurisdiction, and either finds sympathetic expression or contradicts all other branches of knowledge throughout the world.

To reach that stage of broad-mindedness takes maturity. In the beginning stages of Kṛṣṇa consciousness, we tend to become negative toward other knowledge because we are afraid for our new and delicate faith. The more we understand Kṛṣṇa consciousness and feel at ease in our practice of it, however, our outlook will broaden, although we will remain satisfied to hear about Kṛṣṇa only from the purest and best sources.

Śrīla Bhaktisiddhānta Sarasvatī Ṭhākura was an advocate of *yukta-vairāgya*, of using whatever we have in Kṛṣṇa's service. He was not opposed to university knowledge, for example, but said that it should be used in the Lord's service. If a person who is already trained in academic knowledge meets a pure devotee and takes to Kṛṣṇa consciousness, then he may use his academic knowledge to explain Kṛṣṇa consciousness to attract other academicians. Prabhupāda also encouraged this spirit of *yukta-vairāgya* when he asked his scientist disciples to form the Bhaktivedanta Institute.

While Śrīla Bhaktisiddhānta Sarasvatī said that one should immediately turn over all that he has to Kṛṣṇa's service, if we don't already have academic knowledge, then it's not necessary to get it once we become devotees. We do not need to waste our time developing mundane knowledge. We should be satisfied that we have all the knowledge required to go back to Godhead and to preach to people in almost all circumstances.

Birds chirping outside. Only two more days in Vṛndāvana. Then we will drive through a dangerous morning fog for sixteen hours. We need to take a health break. I plan to spend my time reading the *Bhāgavatam*.

Dog whining outside. It's remarkable that I rarely leave this room. When I look out my window, I see an extended monkey family—males and females, children and grandchildren—loping along the wall. I want to live the life of a *Bhāgavatam* reader. A young man wrote me that he used to love to read the *Bhāgavatam*. Now he has lost his taste. "No, I just have to do it regularly," he tells himself. "The taste will return." Yes.

In defiance of all other systems.
We won't swallow what they say.
Be the right type of teacher—hear
from the literary incarnation,
Vyāsa in his book.

Text 8

vettha tvaṁ saumya tat sarvaṁ
tattvatas tad-anugrahāt
brūyuḥ snigdhasya śiṣyasya
guravo guhyam apy uta

And because you are submissive, your spiritual masters have endowed you with all the favors bestowed upon a gentle disciple. Therefore you can tell us all that you have scientifically learned from them.

Comment

In the previous verse, the sages describe Sūta as a great scholar of religious scriptures and of related knowledge. In this verse, they reveal the secret of his success: "You have been given all the favors bestowed upon a gentle disciple."

Sūta was blessed because he was submissive. The sages at Naimiṣāraṇya, therefore, assume that his gurus have given him confidential knowledge, and so they ask him to impart it to them.

Materialists are usually not fond of submitting to others. In spiritual life, however, we are attracted to those who are submissive, who have humbled themselves in obedience and yielded to the power and authority of the Vaiṣṇava guru. Coming under the guru's influence can transform anyone into a first-class devotee. Prabhupāda compares the relationship between guru and disciple with the relationship between a "critical student" and an expert master. The student, by submitting to the master, in turn becomes a master himself.

Submission offered out of respect and affection makes us gentle. The guru does not bribe the disciple; there is no need for the disciple to submit out of fear or coercion. Rather, because the guru is himself completely dependent on Kṛṣṇa, the disciple becomes attracted to hear from him and to offer service. When a guru sees that the disciple is eager and willing to pay any price to learn—to himself become gentle and submissive to Kṛṣṇa—he feels impelled to help him in any way he can. We don't become dead or worthless by submitting to the spiritual master, because spiritual submission is active and creative. We have to surrender our intelligence and actively employ it, creatively and constantly, to serve the guru's order. When we approach the guru in this way, the spiritual master is won over by our sincerity and attempts at devotion.

Therefore, *The Nectar of Devotion* lists submission as a devotional principle. Prabhupāda writes that devotees may offer their submission to Kṛṣṇa (and guru) by "very feelingly offering prayers" composed from their own hearts. The disciple does not remain proud of any education or any other qualification but faces his insignificance and prays for the perfectional stage of spiritual life. Submission leads to *laulyam*, which is sometimes expressed in tears of eagerness: ". . . one should learn how to cry for the Lord. One should learn this small technique, and he should be very eager and actually cry to become engaged in some particular type of service. . . . such tears are the price for the highest perfection." (NOD, p. 83)

In the *Bhagavad-gītā* (4.34), Kṛṣṇa states, and Prabhupāda concludes in his purport, that submissive inquiry accompanied by service is the key constituent to spiritual advancement. "In this verse, both blind following and absurd inquiries are condemned. Not only should one hear submissively from the spiritual master, but one must also get a clear understanding from him, in submission and service and inquiries. A bona fide spiritual master is by nature very kind toward the disciple. Therefore when the student is submissive and is always ready to render service, the reciprocation of knowledge and inquiries becomes perfect."

I don't know how I measure up in terms of submissiveness. Some say it doesn't matter as long as we speak the truth, but we would have to be dead stones or mindless hypocrites not to question our level of submission to the spiritual master. "By pleasing the spiritual master, one pleases Kṛṣṇa; if one displeases the spiritual master, his destination is unknown." How do we know whether we are pleasing the spiritual master or not? Sometimes we can't know and we just have to continue without knowing. Other times, it may be more obvious.

We can, however, always analyze our position and try to understand how to improve.

A disciple should want to milk his guru; he should want to learn as much as possible from him. *Tasmād guruṁ prapadyeta, jijñāsuḥ śreya uttamam.* Only when one wants absolute knowledge is he a candidate for approaching a spiritual master.

The sages in the *Bhāgavatam* want to hear; they are prepared to listen for a thousand years! What will they do out there in the forest besides hear the *Bhāgavatam*? Not much. Live simply, without sense gratification. A little eating and sleeping, no mating, no intoxication. That's how they can go on hearing. They must have been powerful and controlled, not fidgety sitters who suddenly have to run off to make a phone call or send a fax.

They say Sūta is *saumya*, "one who is pure and simple." We can become *saumya* too, but first we have to remove ourselves from all the controversies. It's good that some people deal with controversy, attend meetings, and develop their communication skills, but it's also good that some people don't. Those who don't can learn to sit like sages, silent and *saumya*, prepared to hear long discourses from Sūta's representatives. They can remain undiverted. The success of either type of person is his ability to please his spiritual master.

Someone is talking in the hall: "*Accha*. Thank you, Prabhu." I hear a chair scraping against a floor somewhere in this building. Sounds rise up—birds' notes and *bhajanas*, monkeys and children. If we follow each sound, we can become lost to ourselves. One man told me that he has been spaced-out for months, ever since he got married. Now he's in Vṛndāvana, but he still feels spaced-out. His older, serious friend preached to him and told him to use his opportunity of being in Vṛndāvana. Therefore, he said, he's going to try again to hear and chant.

I have an older friend in my mind who preaches to me. Seek clarity, he tells me. I imagine the future outside Vṛndāvana and wonder whether I will remember the unfathomable, sweet mystery of Vṛndāvana, which I have felt even though I have stayed in my room.

I want to be a gentle disciple. Husbands and wives quarrel, but in Kali-yuga, a person divides himself and then quarrels with himself. These sages gathered to bring peace to the heart of the world. They are like the older sons of a family who wish it well.

They start by congratulating Sūta as ideal. If we please the spiritual master, he will give us knowledge. If we receive that knowledge, we will have received his blessings. We don't have to be extremely intelligent, because his giving and our receiving is based on mercy, not intelligence. However, it is also based on inquiring and reason. "The disciple can receive such teachings not exactly intellectually, but by submissive inquiries and a service attitude." (*Bhāg.* 2.1.10, purport)

We say that everything depends on *śāstra* and that evidence must be given, but people twist and torture it to prove their own points. "That's another thing," Śrīla Prabhupāda said. He admonished those who would misuse *śāstra*. If we use *śāstra* to support our material motivation, then it becomes dangerous. An institution can go awry when leaders disobey the spiritual master.

Therefore, Prabhupāda's books in the association of Vaiṣṇavas are our ultimate shelter. We too can join in the discussion with the sages at Naimiṣāraṇya. It doesn't matter what else goes on; we will always be sustained by *kṛṣṇa-kathā*. The sages' discussion is full of knowledge, goodness, and sincerity, and it has been extant for thousands of years. It cannot be destroyed. Remember Prabhupāda's words from the 1962 edition? "The foreign invaders of India could break down some of the monumental architectural work in India, but they were unable to break up the perfect ideas of human civilization so far kept hidden within the Sanskrit language of Vedic wisdom."

Kṛṣṇa consciousness as it is expressed in the *Bhāgavatam* cannot be destroyed. Śrīla Prabhupāda went on to say that he had just begun to render the *Bhāgavatam* into English with a broader outlook. He wanted Kṛṣṇa consciousness not merely preserved in the Sanskrit, but available outside India. He said it was the duty of all Indians "to spread this culture all over the world at this momentous hour of need."

It's time for Kṛṣṇa consciousness to enter our culture too. Even a poor man can help spread it. I'm appealing here to anyone who will hear, including myself: don't be cruel. Don't abuse others in the name of religion. Uphold only the truth.

The sages want to hear from a bona fide guru. A bona fide guru becomes obliged to his disciples because he has agreed to take charge of them. When they offer him service, he doesn't accept it for his sense gratification. He is like a king's viceroy who accepts tribute on behalf of the king and then delivers it to the king. In service to *his* guru, our guru becomes obliged to us. He teaches us and accepts the burden of our neophyte problems. It's a chore and sometimes it exhausts him. He sometimes privately expresses that he's tired of dealing with neophyte quarrels and mixed motives: "I don't have to put up with this! I'll go back to Vṛndāvana!" But he doesn't. He stays and tolerates and goes on teaching and managing.

The *Kṛṣṇa* book describes how sages sometimes speak and are sometimes silent, like streams and waterfalls that flow during the rainy season and don't flow in the dry season. This means that the sage (or guru) "is not obliged." He reserves the right to be grave. He doesn't have to respond to his disciples' constant demands. He can go apart. Jesus used to go apart and pray to get strength for his mission. Maybe the sage will read more on his own, do more what he needs to do and not what they want him to do all the time.

Drawings don't always have to make sense because sometimes they are born of the moment. That's the spirit of this whole endeavor. The heart has things to say and they're not always coherent. We have to trust each other as devotees.

It starts out this way,
the 10,000 mile journey.

And poem words too—

The *sannyāsi's* copper beard—
in search of surreal.
What comes of it he
doesn't know at first. He
follows blindly, the guru-
voice within. *Be true to*
me, it says.

The copper path is winsome.
Brown, harsh hills of India
await us, and terrible roads,
tolls, police (they are always
pious underneath their
smiles). A rich *sādhu*
in the back seat in many layers
of clothes.

A copper-heated hell awaits
the sinner, the killer of cows,
the one lusty for illicit sex.
I'm free of that, but searching
new lands.
Beg mercy, hard little heart.

One student wrote to me in response to a writing assignment. He said, "I don't like to talk to the GBC. I prefer to read 'Archie' comics because they are humorous and make me laugh." He was responding to my question, "Tell of some aspect of the Kṛṣṇa conscious philosophy that you find dry and how you overcome it." A wife wrote that marriage is dry because her husband always insists he's the boss. Another student wrote, "I find every aspect of Kṛṣṇa consciousness dry at one time or another, so I vary my activities. If I get bored with reading, I get up and chant, or I walk to the temple or talk with devotees. Variety is the spice of life."

I wanted them to write about how parts of the *Bhāgavatam* seem dry, but they expanded on that topic. Some said that when a *Bhāgavatam* chapter talks of Sāṅkhya or the universal structure or defends Vaiṣṇavism from the Māyāvādīs, they find it dry. Then they tried to correct their feelings by giving examples of how what caused the dryness might be made relevant and interesting.

Most of us will agree, however, that we are now reading a nectarean section of the *Bhāgavatam*—these opening praises. The actual *Bhāgavatam* topics haven't really begun. It's early morning and we are entering the first chapter fresh.

Text 9

tatra tatrāñjasāyuṣman
bhavatā yad viniścitam
puṁsāṁ ekāntataḥ śreyas
tan naḥ śaṁsitum arhasi

Please, therefore, being blessed with many years, explain to us, in an easily understandable way, what you have ascertained to be the absolute and ultimate good for the people in general.

Comment

The sages describe Sūta as blessed with many years. They ask him the first of their questions: "What is the absolute and ultimate good for everyone?" This question indicates the sages' concern not only for themselves as fortunate elite, but for the entire population. The answer has to come from the *Vedas* because material well-being can come only from spiritual well-being.

Neither the sages nor Sūta Gosvāmī are interested in introducing political or material welfare programs. There are already so many people working for political upliftment, cessation of poverty, and conservation of the planet's dwindling resources. All of these people can argue that their cause is the most urgent, or even that it is a spiritual program. But those causes aren't the most urgent. Only those practicing Kṛṣṇa consciousness can be confident that their work is purely spiritual and that it is for the absolute and ultimate good of all people.

Unless people come to understand that they are spirit souls, servants of the Supreme Soul, and that they must perform sacrifice to please God, then no relative cause can save them. Therefore, to educate and enlighten people about their constitutional nature is the most urgent work; education can save them from ruin at death.

Spiritual knowledge is difficult to attain, however. The *Vedas* contain volumes of detailed information. How can an average person go through the *Vedas* and arrive at the right conclusion? These are the thoughts that prompted Śaunaka's question: "Blessed Sūta, give us a summary, the essence—the *ekāntataḥ śreyaḥ*, the singlemost best practice which people can actually hope to follow."

Ekānta means "absolutely." This word has also been translated as "single-minded." We are reminded of Kṛṣṇa's language in the *Bhagavad-gītā* when He says *mām ekaṁ śaraṇaṁ vraja*, "surrender unto Me alone." Arjuna also asked Kṛṣṇa, *ekaṁ vada*, "Which one would You prefer?" when he asked Kṛṣṇa whether it is better to work or to cultivate *jñāna*. Therefore, we should seek out the one, very best absolute. We should try to understand the one source, the one activity, the one purpose which will benefit everyone, including ourselves. Is there actually such a panacea? Is there one act that will accomplish all good for everyone? This is what the sages are asking and this is what we should want to understand.

It is impressive that the sages have formulated such a question and that Sūta is prepared to answer it with confidence. This indicates the great power and learning on the part of speaker and hearer. People often claim cheaply to know the best thing or to have the most important information, although they actually don't know anything at all. Recently, I saw an ad for a New Age book which claimed to teach the knowledge "most worth learning," and that this knowledge was derived from the author's family. The sages of

Naimiṣāraṇya would never accept such an audacious claim—a claim based on whimsy and bluff. Their question is all-encompassing, but they can be confident that Sūta Gosvāmī, who is not only mature in age but blessed by his spiritual masters, can give authorized knowledge.

No, but it will take time to sort things out. There's no point being impatient. Sūta gives everything immediately, but at the same time, he gives it gradually. It unfolds with our lives. We hear and then live and then hear again and then apply what we have heard. The answer to all their questions is, of course, *bhakti*. That is the theme of the

Bhāgavatam, how to understand *bhakti-yoga*. Sūta will now explain how to engage in *bhakti-yoga* by engaging in hearing, chanting, remembering the lotus feet of the Lord, etc. All of these practices are contained in the Hare Kṛṣṇa mantra—Hare Kṛṣṇa Hare Kṛṣṇa, Kṛṣṇa Kṛṣṇa Hare Hare/ Hare Rāma Hare Rāma, Rāma Rāma Hare Hare—because chanting God's names is the *yuga-dharma*.

Now that I have said all that, we will have to assimilate it. We don't just say, "Class is over" and go home. We have to hear repeatedly and at length to occupy our minds with Sūta's teachings. We have to then assimilate those teachings according to our backgrounds, culture, and knowledge. If I tell everyone to chant Hare Kṛṣṇa, how will they take it seriously? Perhaps they'll have questions.

It's also true, however, that Prabhupāda wanted everyone to begin chanting despite their questions. In 1966, Swamijī started us off at once with his drum rhythms and powerful *kīrtanas*. Soon he was handing out *karatālas* and teaching us how to keep the beat. We clashed and sang along happily. Then immediately he gave philosophy to sustain us. The philosophy flowed through the hard rocks of our hearts, the dirty chunks of coal, the long habits of unclear and abusive thinking. "This is going on." Both instantly and gradually, he revealed the Absolute Truth.

Śrīla Prabhupāda described Sūta Gosvāmī in 1962: "Out of your considered and made easy opinion." These words were edited out of later editions, but they are sweet. Prabhupāda made it easy for us to understand the grave and multivolumed *Vedas*. We can't know the Absolute Truth by logic, by mechanical following, by becoming great philosophers, or by directly reading the scripture. The secret is hidden in the sages' hearts. Therefore, *mahājano yena gataḥ sa pantāḥ*. When the sage speaks, the truth is revealed. Why can't we find the truth by reading the *śāstras* ourselves? Because the *śāstras* need to be *explained* by the sages' "considered and made easy opinions."

"The *ācāryas* and *gosvāmīs* are always compact in thought for the well being of the people in general, especially for their spiritual well being." They're compact, concentrated, *ekānta*, always meditating on how to serve the world. Kṛṣṇa inspires them to achieve universal well-being. Lord Caitanya devised the trick of taking *sannyāsa*. Prabhupāda allowed women to join his movement. He allowed spiritually poor men to become devotees, to chant Hare Kṛṣṇa, to become initiated as *brāhmaṇas*, to take *sannyāsa*. He showed them kindness and engaged them as preachers. That was his preaching dexterity.

There are so many ways to preach. Prabhupāda told the scientists and musicians, "Will you suffer if you dovetail your individual consciousness with the Supreme Consciousness? No, not a pinch! It is not at all difficult!" To gourmets he gave the principle of *prasādam*, and he did not turn away even the slow people with the Kali-yuga brains.

André Breton, a surrealist poet, wrote, "Put yourself in as passive, or receptive, a state of mind as you can. Forget about your genius, your talents, and the talents of everyone else. Keep reminding yourself that literature is one of the saddest roads that leads to everything. Write quickly, without any preconceived subject, fast enough so that you will not remember what you've written and be tempted to re-read what you have written. The first sentence will come spontaneously, so compelling is the truth that with every passing second there is a sentence unknown to our consciousness which is only crying out to be heard. It is somewhat of a problem to form an opinion about the next sentence; it doubtlessly partakes both of our conscious activity and the other . . . Go on as long as you like. Put your trust in the inexhaustible nature of the murmur."

I like the idea of writing like that. I have a desire, which I hope is Kṛṣṇa conscious, to write not just from the mind—the flickering or academic student's brain—but directly from the arm-body, "the unconscious," and then to dovetail it with the Supreme consciousness, with Kṛṣṇa's purpose. Can I connect with Kṛṣṇa and not with the demon babbler within?

If you paint over the surface as fast as you can, you eventually get bored. Better to go deeper, or rather, more toward the unconscious.

A peripheral memory wants to insert itself. I dreamt I was with a group of honored devotees at Harvard. I was the first one tested in public (on TV too) by Harvey Cox, who asked a question from higher mathematics. How could he expect a bloke like me to know? I was humiliated. Fortunately, Hṛdayānanda Mahārāja was next and he tackled the same problem with unique and clever logic and got the right answer. I removed myself from the honor group and sat with an old school friend from the '50s.

I woke and realized that my Godbrother had been kind in his letter by suggesting I write a book of simple prayers and then illustrate it like Leunig. I'm more diffuse and inclusive, however.

What does he say, the poet?
Something about loneliness and that people all
have masks. His impressions of how
a fluorescent bulb flickers before it
goes on. He ought to go to India
where the tubes wait a long
time before clicking on.
Hey, he ought to get a haircut and
a job. That silly saffron skirt.

I just realized my brother
wrote *me*.
He said, "Why don't you
write a book with
little prayers?" No, I
won't tell him. It's a secret.
I want a big book with long
prayers and many asides and
straight *śāstra*.

What about confession? Where does that urge to tell all come from? From the peripheral? From the actual emotions I hold back? I bowed down to the students at the end of the seminar. A lady moved forward; she didn't want to be left out.

Fake teeth, we know,
but false hearts are worse.
False hats. "Thank you." False
words. I'm going now, make a quick
exit out side gate. I couldn't
see or attain Vṛndāvana, but I'm
bringing the dirt from my room
where I claim Kṛṣṇa and His angels
of mercy told me to write
A Poor Man Reads The Bhāgavatam.

I prayed and tried and this is what came. Why deny it? Take it. It's Vṛndāvana's dust. I craved the authorization for my imagination to be used in Kṛṣṇa's service. I want to say, "This is the form given to me to preach to people at this time and I'm only an instrument."

It's my whole self. As WCW wrote in *Kora
in Hell:* "The imagination . . .
delights in its own season,
reversing the usual order at will."

He then describes the dedication
of artists and says, " . . . But the sad truth is that since
the imagination is nothing, nothing will
come of it."

You see, that's the difference. We work under Prabhupāda, so if he allows the use of imagination, then it's Kṛṣṇa conscious compassion, like that of the sages at Naimiṣāraṇya. You can give it out like a feast at a festival, the miracle of the loaves.

I want to go to a list I made of words and expressions of things I care about. I want to hold them up to the scripture and say, "How does this look in the light of the *Bhāgavatam*?"

Making a list is a writing technique, but it's also useful for clearing one's thoughts. I listed names: Hayagrīva, Rūpānuga, Brahmānanda. Who knows, I might develop enough courage to say something from that list.

Right now, though, I want to bid adieu to the ancient churches dredged up from the unconscious memory. Let me say good-bye to Vṛndāvana before it's too late. I'm in Vṛndāvana only a few hours more. Unfortunately, I can't stay. There are just too many people here who want to see me.

I'm on my way, but I want to remember Vṛndāvana. I am bringing photos of Kṛṣṇa-Balarāma, Rādhā-Śyāmasundara, and Gaura-Nitāi.

Unseen spirits of Vṛndāvana known only to pure devotees, please bless me and Madhu and Śamīka Ṛṣi and our taxi driver as we make our way to the next place.

I won't say good-bye,
but please be with me as I
travel. I won't say, "I failed
to be in Vṛndāvana," but I will
continue to try.

The next verse describes people's condemned affairs in this age. You see these "affairs" every time you travel West. Do you want to save them? Do you have such nobility? We used to go out on the streets to beat drums and chant Hare Kṛṣṇa. We thought that would save them. We still think that, although the city councils rarely agree.

Angels of Mercy
Came to our
Room, #42
and gave us
Idea & Blessing
For this Book
Jan 1996
I leave today
promising
to always
continue it.
What can I do
to help people
of this Age?
I say A Book like this
PM's
Bhag
VRNDABAN ke JAYA

Went for *darśana* of the Deities. Touched Prabhupāda's foot and took a rose. Felt, "I want to hear your lecture tapes, love you, and be dedicated to you." Went before Gaura-Nitāi and felt good, the best for this visit to Vṛndāvana. Thought of Them in Māyāpur and felt a desire to return there. Went to Kṛṣṇa-Balarāma and saw Their beauty. Thought of Śrīla Prabhupāda on tape saying that everyone knows They are made of stone from Jaipur, yet They are Kṛṣṇa and Balarāma. Prayed for spiritual strength *(bala)* to write *A Poor Man Reads The Bhāgavatam*. Went to Rādhā-Śyāma and prayed, "I know You are the pinnacle of Vṛndāvana and I will reach You as Prabhupāda desires." Then Their *pūjārī* gave me a garland and some *tulasī* leaves. We bowed before Tulasī and took *caraṇāmṛta* from the old, saintly *brahmacārī* who always serves it and who is always so sweet to us.

Text 10

prāyeṇālpāyuṣaḥ sabhya
kalāv asmin yuge janāḥ
mandāḥ sumanda-matayo
manda-bhāgyā hy upadrutāḥ

O learned one, in this iron age of Kali men have but short lives. They are quarrelsome, lazy, misguided, unlucky and, above all, always disturbed.

Comment

When we read this verse, we become amazed at the *Bhāgavatam's* relevance. Although spoken thousands of years ago, the *Bhāgavatam* draws a picture of the worsening condition of human life. We are living through it now. Hearing this verse should make us more alert to understand that the *Bhāgavatam* is speaking to our times and that the remedy the sages propose is actually meant to be taken up by people in the world today.

This verse summarizes the disadvantages people experience in Kali-yuga over past ages. Reading this overview of the effects of Kali-yuga on people's lives and intelligence, we may feel hopeless. How can we hope to preach to such a stunted population? School systems for hundreds of years have taught children only mundane knowledge or presented them with ignorance and untruth. One generation after another grows up and educates their children in the same way. How can we change the tide? If they are so lazy and misguided, if they're so unable to understand their own self-interest, what can the *Bhāgavatam* or the sages do for them?

It was with this in mind that Lord Caitanya decided to give the most direct means of spiritual upliftment, the Hare Kṛṣṇa *mahā-mantra*. Chanting Hare Kṛṣṇa is itself so simple and pure that we can attain love of God just by chanting it. Unfortunately, the people of Kali-yuga tend to reject that too. Chanting Hare Kṛṣṇa can overcome their disadvantages, but because of their general unluckiness, and because they have been misguided for generations, they refuse to take it.

Somehow or other we have taken the Hare Kṛṣṇa mantra. Therefore, instead of feeling hopeless in preaching, we can consider that if someone as unlucky as ourselves can chant, anyone can chant. This is not a sectarian treatise. Kṛṣṇa says He will be pleased by the performance of the *yuga-dharma*, and He will be especially pleased if we attempt to spread it to others. As the *Vedas* state, "In the age of Kali there is no other way, no other way, no other way to the ultimate good, except chanting of the holy names of God."

Śrīla Prabhupāda says that people are *victims* of "many different types of sense-gratificatory diversions . . . " His list includes enterprises and activities which almost everyone admires or considers worthwhile, including cinemas, mundane libraries, smoking, drinking, bickering and so on. He even includes religious faiths which are not based on revealed scriptures but which allow sense gratification and which attract followers on that basis. "Consequently, in the name of religion so many sinful acts are being carried on that the people in general have neither peace of mind nor health of body."

How unlucky and disturbed are the people of Kali-yuga. They live such short lives. Eventually, a man who lives to the age of thirty-five will be considered old. It's getting worse, not better, as the optimists think. People are lazy, misguided, and always quarreling, "Life's a bitch."

"Concentration camps, gas chambers, the Nuremberg Trials, atomic bombs, and radioactive fallout ended the age of American isolation and innocence. . . . Suddenly the old reality was filled with devils and death."

It's just getting warmed up, this hell called Kali. "This is *my* age!" cries out Kali, "And this is my consort, Sin!"

People lie lazily in the fire, although they are burning. They live for the illusions: "We have our shopping malls." "The politicians and the people's good sense will stop the governments from dropping nuclear bombs." "We have to pay off our national debts and let gays and women have their rights." Or, "We have to bring prayer back into the schools." "We can set things right." "America will lead in morality and economy and the world will follow."

Bosh.

Back to Naimiṣāraṇya. We should always return to Naimiṣāraṇya with the help of Prabhupāda's purports.

There's a reference in Prabhupāda's purport to people's vitality being sapped by too much dependence on others, by overeating, by laziness, bad habits, and so on. In order to be fit for the struggle for existence, we have to be healthy and sound in body and mind. We can remain healthy by a simple and regulated life, as given to us by the *Śrīmad-Bhāgavatam* and the spiritual master. Kali-yuga presents difficulties even for those who seek an alternative path. We are surrounded by an atmosphere of pollution on so many levels and it's hard to be pure. How can we be pure when our neighbors are emanating impure sound vibrations all around us? At least we should not be dependent on the materialists' infrastructure. Self-sufficiency is essential to vitality.

Śrīla Prabhupāda thought that along with book distribution we should create a society where people can live apart from the normal dependence on material society. In the society of devotees, vitality can be maintained by simple living and high thinking. The society of devotees is meant to protect us from Kali-yuga's vices. Therefore, we should maintain a pure standard of living and clean out any artificiality in our lives.

In Kali-yuga, people are less intelligent and always harassed. Famine comes from the mismanagement of natural resources. Taxes are imposed by heartless rules. Drought, disease—people are forced to leave the "shelter" of civilization and live as primitives in the hills.

There are still *sādhus* in India and crowds of people who go to hear from them. They speak *rāma-kathā* and *kṛṣṇa-kathā* even while India introduces Ferris wheels and night fairs. The ancient life of going to bathe in the Ganges or the Yamunā side by side with material culture.

The anomalies of the age are more fully described in the Twelfth Canto. This verse gives a quick summary. All bad news. Therefore, people in Kali-yuga need special dispensation.

Some people think we're on the verge of a worldwide spiritual breakthrough. *Śrīmad-Bhāgavatam* says we're not. As a matter of fact, the way to tell that we're not on the way to a worldwide spiritual breakthrough is to count the self-proclaimed gurus who cheat their followers. That's another symptom of our misfortune in Kali-yuga. When people show interest in yoga, prayer, and meditation, cheating gurus take advantage of their innocence.

The *Bhāgavatam* sages, however, are not cheaters. They are more like our elder brothers. Their compassion is broad. In Sanskrit, two terms are usually used to denote compassion, *kṛpa* and *dayā*. *Kṛpa* refers to compassion for people we know—our family and friends—and *dayā* refers to compassion for all living entities regardless of who or what they are. Here the sages are expressing *dayā*, universal compassion. Their magnanimity is free from envy and malice. No ordinary, compassionate soul can feel such love toward all.

We are therefore fortunate to receive their program for freedom. If it is not obvious that they have made a practical impact on the world, then that is a sign of further misfortune in this age. However, their knowledge is never lost. It is up to persons who are well meaning to take up the *Śrīmad-Bhāgavatam's* cause. Śrīla Prabhupāda was the greatest champion of this cause and he was well aware of all the benefits of Kṛṣṇa consciousness.

We pray that more and more devotees, including ourselves, may become convinced of the need and efficacy of Kṛṣṇa consciousness, aware of its *dayā* (mercy for all) and its dynamism, and practice Kṛṣṇa consciousness with all our hearts. We may also be confident that our chanting and prayers do not fall on deaf ears, and they actually have an effect against the tide of ill luck in Kali-yuga.

Bad age, sad age
selfish me and little you,
our body's bondage.
What about all the people
dying and dead in the newspapers'
reportage? (Don't name
them now; we want the *Bhāgavatam*.)
But what about them?

What I probably want above all in my reading is to relish it. Prabhupāda said that people challenged him to show them God. He replied that we should first become mad after God. Then when we don't see Him, we will feel the whole world vacant in His absence. Seeing also means understanding, hearing.

In Kali-yuga, our lives are shorter because of our irregular habits—overeating (over-sense gratification) and overdependence on others' mercy. We *want* to live. We need time to progress in Kṛṣṇa consciousness.

The sages wanted to serve the people by introducing them to the process of devotional service, but people are lazy. They are also slow and bad. They miss the purpose of life. "Human life is a means by which the living entity can end all the miseries of the hard struggle for life in material existence and by which he can return to Godhead, his eternal home." Because they are misled, they understand only illusion, and material education confirms their understanding in the name of theories and isms. " . . . men are victims . . . of many types of sense-gratificatory diversions, such as cinemas, sports, gambling, clubs, mundane libraries . . . " etc.

Yes, libraries, those seemingly innocent places where you sit at a table to read after taking books off the shelf, discussing your selections with a friendly librarian. Because what's in all those books, in Proust and the latest novels and the classics and the self-help books?

Man-made religions—religions not based on revealed scripture—appeal to people addicted to sense gratification because they allow sinful activities. Students don't have to follow *brahmacarya* and householders don't have to observe the rules of the *gṛhastha-āśrama*.

It's a bad age. A hard rain's
going to fall.
What did *you* see of it?
Want to broadcast your vision, poet?
No, I am only scratching here.
The truth is another thing.
Odes are for Kṛṣṇa worship.

It's late in Kali. Jagadīśa
Mahārāja is spending the year
at Śaraṇāgati to show us
how to live on whatever food
they produce in the mountain
valley, although the men
are new to farming.

I set an example of a writer
wandering. Plan to travel in
a Kali-yuga Ford to cities and
campgrounds and hide in the back
of the van, cursing disco music
when I hear it,
hiding in someone's home
and spying on America.

Kali needs *harināma*, needs to
see Prabhupāda's books distributed
(and a few of mine).
Kali needs to die to sin,
needs the mask of education
removed and the real thing established—
songs to Kṛṣṇa,
English and Sanskrit in
learned God consciousness.

Is ISKCON up to the task?
Give us a few moon-like
devotees, not hordes of
insignificant, faraway stars.
Lord Caitanya's moon is rising.
If only they don't drop the bombs.
Even then . . .
It's predicted.
Devotees like the sages
come to cities with *Bhāgavatams*
but seem overrun.
Bhaktisiddhānta Sarasvatī said just one *pūjārī*
ringing the bell at noon *ārati*
when no one attends the *darśana*
of Rādhā and Kṛṣṇa
has more value than all the
hospitals and welfare workers in the world.
Pray for Kali's redemption.

There is no faith in Kali-yuga. It's worse now than even fifty years ago. Young kids take drugs. You can't speak against homosexuality without seeming old-fashioned. You can't curb the flow of semen without being thought of as repressed. No one knows or cares for the art of raising semen to the brain except a few old men in India.

No faith in God. Yes, faith is required to understand higher topics. We have to transfer our faith to God and away from Freud, Marx, Darwin, and company. Prabhupāda predicted his audience's reaction to his preaching: "Oh, Swamijī is talking of God? What old-fashioned things." People hear of Kṛṣṇa in Dvārakā and disbelieve. God can't be a person or why does He allow wars? God is a light at best, a feeble, yellow drizzle diminished by pollution. This is a bad age.

"The sages of Naimiṣāraṇya are anxious to disentangle all fallen souls, and here they are seeking the remedy from Śrīla Sūta Gosvāmī."

Dear readers, I have summarized the verse and purport. Now I want to say more, something unique and personal. I don't want to fall short. Therefore, I want to try to get beneath the surface and peek at what flows below. God knows, you and I are victims of Kali, but we also know of Lord Caitanya and Kṛṣṇa consciousness. Maybe we can say something that will help. I mean, by allowing words to just come.

Start with images to loosen up. Water murmuring. My senses report a flowing river and a dam project nearby. It's night. I can't understand what people are suffering from in this country. I have no preconceived subject, but I have holes in my right-hand glove where I have worn it away by vigorous chanting.

O holy name, holy night, do I have a right to sing the blues? I don't belong to America and certainly not to India. Where's a man to go in this world, or should he stay put?

Burnt ashes of smithy
burnt what it read,
with a poker, sift through
clever Shredded Wheat
junk food. My companion
and I happy for another day.
We ought to be able to tell you something.
When we chant and when
we walk outdoors,
it's blissful to be simple in *brahmacārī khādī*
and avoiding sin as far as possible.
I want to leave a record against the
swollen tide of madness.
Our bodies aren't happy
but our hearts sing in the simple
joy of accomplishment
under our master's plan.

We'd like to study at least.
I can't let loose.
What's the sense
of indulging in the madness of
incoherent speech? As for
evil and torture of Kali,
you know it or heard it
and don't want to hear more.
You turn your face away.
Give us peace, you say.
Give us frosted Applejacks
and our *TV Guide*.
Give us a moment of awareness,
a life absolved
of bad karma, and a chance
to go back to Godhead.

"Where will your disciples
be?" the mad poet asked,
when hearing of Kali's worsening
from A. C. Bhaktivedanta Swami.
He replied, "They will
be with Kṛṣṇa."
We sure hope so.

Michaelmass ale, billboards showing naked women, bad offal in the streets of Milan. We are free of it. It's sad, then, when we can't inspire the devotees, and they go to mundane shrinks who say our original Swami and even the *Vedas* are not enough. I speak against that in these pages. Please let's read on what the *Bhāgavatam* says.

Text 11

bhūrīṇi bhūri-karmāṇi
śrotavyāni vibhāgaśaḥ
ataḥ sādho 'tra yat sāraṁ
samuddhṛtya manīṣayā
brūhi bhadrāya bhūtānām
yenātmā suprasīdati

There are many varieties of scriptures, and in all of them there are many prescribed duties, which can be learned only after many years of study in their various divisions. Therefore, O sage, please select the essence of all these scriptures and explain it for the good of all living beings, that by such instruction their hearts may be fully satisfied.

Comment

The sages ask Sūta to select the *sāram*, the essence, of all the scriptures in order to satsify everyone's heart. Without this selection by an experienced sage, how can ordinary people find the time or intelligence to go through the many varieties of scriptures? These studies and their application take years to complete, but a compassionate sage such as Sūta Gosvāmī can easily hand over the essence, the point, and save everyone so much time. This is what Śaunaka asks him to do.

Ātmā, the self, referred to here as "the heart," becomes satisfied only in spiritual subject matter. That's because the self is beyond matter. If you place the self in matter, it will feel awkward. When the *ātmā* is situated in the material body and world, it's at sea; the material world is not the natural habitat of the spirit spark. Spirit wants spirit. Give a hungry man something other than food—give him tickets to the cinema or a new car—and he'll remain dissatisfied. "Don't you know I want to eat?" Spirit wants spirit. The tiny individual spirit wants to take shelter of the Supreme Spirit. The self wants to join with the Self. The scriptures are therefore written for the self to guide him to the Supreme.

If the *ātmā* is one in quality in all beings, then why are there so many scriptures? Because people and cultures manifest in different lands and times. (Remember when we arrived at the Delhi airport? It was filled with Japanese people all wearing the same uniform of baggy, gray, cotton knickers, matching smocks, and both men and women had completely shaved heads. They appeared to belong to a Buddhist sect come to tour the holy places in India. Some of them were chubby-faced and beaming. All drank from water bottles. They were so different from the thinner, darker Indians and me.) Different scriptures for different folks. It's human nature, but it can get confusing. While building the tower of Babel, the people were suddenly cursed to speak in many different languages. As a result, they couldn't cooperate in their work. Besides, we just heard how unlucky they were due to the influence of this age. We can't expect people to go through the gradual process of *varṇa* and *āśrama*. It takes too long, and besides, who has that much time? We can't expect people to leave home and accept *sannyāsa*. "The whole atmosphere is surcharged with opposition."

This is an unlikely age for the *ātmā* to flourish. The *ātmā* needs a head start. Someone has to make it clear and quick. Is there such a person, such a way? Lord Caitanya accomplished this.

Here is a new section because I just skipped lines. I had better introduce this section as "Gnawing away." Is this poor man's *ātmā* satisfied? I summarize the *Śrīmad-Bhāgavatam* purport and then look around. What more is there to say? There is a cavity where there should be an *ātmā*, or at least a small, fleshy heart beating life. He criticizes the nondevotees and those who wrote in mockery of the Lord's Prayer, "Our Father who art in heaven/ Stay there and we'll stay here on earth." Where was *my* love of God?

"I got a triple bypass, but I'm all right now," the brother of a devotee said. Another man had a minor heart problem. They corrected it with a laser; cleared the artery with wind maybe.

These are *ātmā* clearings. I have always had a good heart. Still, it's not satisfied because it can't make sense out of too many scriptures (*prāyeṇālpāyuṣaḥ sabhya . . .*).

"Kṛṣṇa will make it clear."
Give us *sāram*.
Give marrow.
"I will, but you must have the
adhikāra (qualification).
Do you?"

You mean, am I interested,
brainy enough, or what?
"I mean, do you care to know
what your soul aches for?

Art is no substitute for the
soul's cry. Matter won't
suffice in any form although
it looks good at first."
I guess I do qualify—
I want to be happy and I sure agree
we need a direct dispensation.
So dish it out please,
smack it in my hand.
Gimme essence,
said a soiled, arrogant, covered over
soul.

Will Sūta disclose to such as he?

A List:

(1) Who am I and what do I want to do?

(2) Discuss Sinetar's *Ordinary People As Monks and Mystics* as springboard to #1.

(3) It's maddening to have to sit through a long lecture (even though you can do concealed *prāṇāyāma* to pass the time).

(4) Write on the phrase attributed to Cardinal Newman: "If I had to propose a drinking toast to the human conscience and to the Pope, I'd drink first to the conscience and second to the Pope."

(5) Why do I claim I have to wear earplugs even when others can get to sleep without them?

(6) Mouse phobia.

(7) "The fruit of Myrobaln kept in one's palm." *

Can these concerns be answered by the *Bhāgavatam* verse(s)?

Definitely. They are not the six questions asked by the sages at Naimiṣāraṇya, but they are much easier, inconsequential (I have many more). I can take them up one by one, but not just now.

I try to write even when someone comes into the room. Prabhupāda did this too wherever he traveled. I'll write a poem, and before lunch, I may go to the roof for a massage.

There's mouse stool on the rug. I'm okay, avoiding the crunch of writing here, but then suddenly feeling grateful, absorbed, quick to kneel.

He ain't no scholar like those men preparing the *Ṣaṭ Sandarbhas* in English or the painstaking overview of *The Nectar of Devotion*. Neither is he pounding wash by the river bank or singing in a nightclub. He's our man south of Indore dancin' "The Twist."

* This is a Sanskrit phrase typifying that which is clearly seen and easily understood.

Please select the essence of all the scriptures so that people don't have to go through all the departments of knowledge, but can immediately feel self-satisfaction. The selection of and emphasis on chanting Hare Kṛṣṇa is Lord Caitanya's gift. Drawing from scriptures such as the *Bṛhan-nāradīya Purāṇa*, Lord Caitanya's followers conclude that there is no other way for God consciousness in this age except to chant the holy names. Thus millions of verses and hundreds of books are studied or realized by one who simply chants Hare Kṛṣṇa.

That is certainly a stroke of genius by the Lord and the greatest boon for humanity. Still, we are inclined to read books. Therefore, we go to the library or bookshop or read them in school. We read junk, nonsense, and sophisticated, nonconclusive books. If we would just read the *Bhāgavatam* (or literature in pursuance of the *Bhāgavatam* version), we would become self-satisfied. Then we would make progress toward attraction for Śrī Kṛṣṇa and the reinstatement of a life of eternity, bliss, and knowledge.

If someone has received this confidential knowledge, then he should serve others who are searching for relief from *saṁsāra's* miseries. "Here it is, that which you have been looking for but couldn't find life after life. Here is the Lord you are seeking, the scripture, the hymn, the one work required."

When we speak of *ātmā*, the materialist doubts that it even exists. He recognizes only the body and the mind. We must affirm, therefore, the existence of our own self despite the detractors. Here's an expression of this affirmation by a contemporary spiritual author:

"But how do we search for our soul, our God,
our inner voice? How do we find this treasure
hidden in our life? How do we connect to this
transforming and healing power?

The search and the relationship is
a lifetime's work and there is help available,
but an important, perhaps essential part of this
process seems to involve ongoing, humble
acknowledgment of the soul's existence and
integrity. Not just an intellectual recognition but
also a ritualistic, perhaps poetic,
gesture of acknowledgment: a respectful tribute.

This do-it-yourself ceremony where the mind is on
its knees; the small ceremony of words which calls
on the soul to come forward. This ritual known
simply as prayer."

—*Common Prayer Collection*, by Michael Leunig

Personal prayer is one thing, but hearing has to come first. By hearing, we learn what is the self, what is God, and what is the loving relationship *(bhakta, bhagavān, bhakti)* between the two. We mold our lives in devotional service once we hear from the correct authorities. We cannot make full progress if we hear from an inadequate source or if we hear poorly.

Some Vedic scriptures teach the lower stages. By following these directions, we can achieve our material desires within religious bounds *(karma-kāṇḍiya)*. More advanced scriptures teach the futility of temporary pursuits, even that of worshiping the demigods to attain the heavenly planets. These advanced scriptures are the *Upaniṣads*, which center on knowledge of the eternal Brahman. Only that which is eternal is valuable. One should sacrifice everything to reach that supreme goal and become liberated.

Above the *Upaniṣads* is the personalism of the sattvic *Purāṇas* and ultimately knowledge of Lord Viṣṇu in His original form as Śrī Kṛṣṇa, the Lord of Vṛndāvana. This secret is revealed in *Śrīmad-Bhāgavatam*, where it will be declared, *kṛṣṇas tu bhagavān svayam*.

We have already read in the second verse of this chapter that the *Śrīmad-Bhāgavatam* kicks out all lesser, cheating religious principles, including the desire for liberation. The *Bhāgavatam* teaches love of God in the intimacy of spontaneous devotional service rather than in *aiśvarya,* where strict following of the rules cripples affection between the lover and the Beloved.

By mentioning this, I may be jumping ahead, but we want to know even at the start where an endeavor will lead. We should understand the basis of the *Bhāgavatam's* claim as topmost among all religious scriptures. Śrīla Prabhupāda explains this to us over and over again. He explains it to us in his own *Bhāgavatam*, even before the first verse of the first chapter. He tells us in the introductory essay identifying Lord Caitanya Mahāprabhu as the ideal preacher of *Śrīmad-Bhāgavatam*. By page five, Prabhupāda has given us a summary of Lord Caitanya's preaching work:

> . . . Lord Śrī Kṛṣṇa, who appeared at Vrajabhūmi (Vṛndāvana) as the son of the king of Vraja (Nanda Maharaja), is the Supreme Personality of Godhead and is therefore worshipable by all. Vṛndāvana-dhāma is nondifferent from the Lord because the name, fame, form, place where the Lord manifests Himself are all identical with the Lord as absolute knowledge. Therefore Vṛndāvana-dhāma is as worshipable as the Lord. The highest form of transcendental worship of the Lord was exhibited by the damsels of Vrajabhūmi in the form of pure affection for the Lord and Lord Śrī Caitanya Mahāprabhu recommends this process as the most excellent mode of worship. He accepts the *Śrimad Bhāgavata Purāṇa* as the spotless Literature for understanding the Lord and He preaches that the ultimate goal of life, for all human beings, is to attain the stage of *prema* or love of god.

This is a glimpse of what we will attain if we are faithful and persistent, but we have to take it step by step. "The only qualification one needs to study this great book of transcendental knowledge is to proceed step by step cautiously and not jump forward haphazardly like with an ordinary book. It should be gone through chapter by chapter, one after another. The reading matter is so arranged . . . that one is sure to become a God-realized soul at the end of finishing the first nine cantos." *(Bhāg.* Preface, p. *xxii)*

It all begins by choosing the right speaker, in this case, Sūta Gosvāmī, and inquiring respectfully from him. In this case, Śaunaka is inquiring brilliantly and we are fortunate to be able to hear the exchange of the two sages. Mahārāja Sūta, please save us precious time. You already know all the scriptures. We are unable to study them in detail. We are poor and slow, bad and cheated; we won't live much longer. Please be merciful and give us the *sāram*.

I am following a similar process in 1996. It's the way of sages. We don't want to waste time, yet we know that the whole self has to surrender. I am not capable of too much concentration and I can't take much stress. I also crave to express my experiences. I inquire from Prabhupāda and then I express my experience. In this way, I am a true member of Prabhupāda's *sampradāya*.

"Sir, you have just stated the necessity of getting to the point. So is this personal side of A Poor Man necessary?"

He says yes, it's necessary for him. It's his personal surrender. He wants to come out of *māyā* with his hands in the air.

Sometimes it's necessary to sing and dance. I acknowledge that this may not be necessary for all who read the *Bhāgavatam*. Therefore, this is not a required text for everyone. But it seems necessary for me. Either I do this or I play the jukebox or read Proust.

Come, you don't mean that.

I mean, my *ātmā* is satisfied to stay with the *Bhāgavatam* when I give vent to my whole self. I like to hear what Prabhupāda says in his Introduction to the *Bhagavad-gītā*: "At the time of death either we can remain in the inferior energy of this material world, or we can transfer to the energy of the spiritual world. . . . Now, how can we transfer our thoughts from the material energy to the spiritual energy? There are so many literatures which fill our thoughts with the material energy—newspapers, magazines, novels, etc. Our thinking, which is now absorbed in these literatures, must be transferred to the Vedic literatures. . . . in that way it will possible for us to remember the Supreme Lord at the time of death." (Bg., Introduction, pp. 26–7)

True, Prabhupāda says "Vedic literature." I claim I'm within that. Anyway, this is not a matter of debate. This is how I'm transferring my thoughts and emotions to Kṛṣṇa. That's the whole point, isn't it? Prabhupāda directly told his disciples not to be dull. He said we should write our realizations daily. "You are hearing, but you must also write. Be active always."

"Satisfaction of the mind can be obtained only by taking the mind away from thoughts of sense enjoyment. . . . The best course is to divert the mind to the Vedic literature, which is full of satisfying stories, as in the *Purāṇas* and the *Mahābhārata*. One can take advantage of this knowledge and thus become purified." (Bg. 17.16, purport)

(1) I don't know where I am in India. Go out and walk until an idea comes.

(2) So many flies on the windowpanes. Reminds me of how in *Crime and Punishment*, Raskolnikov fastened his attention on a fly on the windowpane when the police were questioning him.

(3) Explain, defend, explain, defend. We are near a dam. The owners of this house are kind to us, but I don't know why people pass this house all day since it's so out of the way. Do they come to stare? Did they stare at Naimiṣāraṇya? I bet no white man was there. Prabhupāda was kind to include us.

(4) Fly in my ear. Who is he or she? What *jīva* got itself caught in a fly body and now dives again and again into my ear and nose while I try to swat it away?

I said we can't always stay with the *Bhāgavatam* text, but we can stay in close proximity to it. We are like cows on long ropes. Don't worry. We don't have to explain, defend, apologize: "Now I'm grazing in the south field, now I'm in the east pasture, now I'm on that ridge, now near the stream. I'm eating grass, now alfalfa, now chewing my cud. Don't beat me." We can roam.

Here comes Madhu back from market
with the house servant.
I look out from the *Bhāgavatam*.
Can't understand
Hindi. Shadow on page.
Rest, rest. You'll make it, Prabhu.
Your questions will get answered and
some not. Keep going until it stops.
You don't stop blood beat pulse
until interrupted and you look up,
"What?" You are a civil boy
caught in the act of
private prose
with a gnat on your hand.
You were about to say
when he entered
I . . . I . . . and *Śrīmad-Bhāgavatam*, we
form a good team, huh?
I was about to call myself
a cow when he opened the
door.

In writing this book, I seek my true self and try to express it. I summarize each verse and purport because I need to. It's the rock, the anchor. Then I need to go beyond that act. I don't claim my knowledge goes beyond *Śrīmad-Bhāgavatam*, but I trust you will understand my meaning. I have to express myself *more*, and more personally, after I have done the summary. The review of the purport doesn't exhaust me. It barely gets me started.

I realize I am not in *love* with the Absolute or the *Śrīmad-Bhāgavatam*, although I have a strong affinity for them and feel safe in their company. Therefore, I need to explore without shame who I am—this person who is not yet in love with Kṛṣṇa. Why am I this way? I won't swat at myself superficially with words while remaining untouched at heart. I need to keep speaking it out. That's why the automatic writing and poems, the lists, and so on are worth employing. This is my personal book of discovery and I hope it can be shared with others. Each of us is a person, in God. If I can help others in their search, this is how I will help them —by giving my whole self to the search and the continual act of expression. That's why I'm grateful to Kṛṣṇa for giving me such a long-term project to carry out where I can be myself as much as possible, yet not in a whimsical way. Rather, I'll be speaking *Bhāgavatam*, as a *sannyāsī* should. Through self-expression, I also avoid cutting myself off from others.

Text 12

sūta jānāsi bhadraṁ te
bhagavān sātvatāṁ patiḥ
devakyāṁ vasudevasya
jāto yasya cikīrṣayā

All blessings upon you, O Sūta Gosvāmī. You know for what purpose the Personality of Godhead appeared in the womb of Devakī as the son of Vasudeva.

Comment

Lord Kṛṣṇa is directly alluded to here and described by the words *patiḥ* and *bhagavān*, defined as the protector and all-opulent one. God protects all living beings, but He especially protects His devotees who seek His shelter. This is described in the verse, *samāṣritā ye pada pallava-plavaṁ*. The world is an ocean of peril with danger at every step, but for one who takes shelter of Murāri (Kṛṣṇa, the killer of Mura), the ocean shrinks to the size of a puddle he can easily cross.

How often Prabhupāda impressed upon us that material life is miserable. He never wanted us to forget that point.

"Why are we turning the fan?" he said in one August lecture in Vṛndāvana. In summer, heat is misery, and in winter, cold is misery. All our activities are usually centered around coping with natural misery.

When we are in illusion, we call this happiness—the beautiful wife (who later becomes ugly and dies), the sweet children (who later suffer the same fate), the big bank balance, the powerful nation, the good health that allows us to enjoy our senses. Even if we think we are enjoying, we have to pay the karmic debt for all our sins.

Why did Bhagavān appear? The *Bhāgavatam* will tell us. We already know something about that from *Bhagavad-gītā*. Kṛṣṇa comes to rescue His devotees. We need to be rescued: "For them I am the swift deliverer from the ocean of birth and death." All this will be explained. Without delay, the sages indicate that they have chosen Sūta as their guide because he knows Bhagavān's purpose. Therefore, his speech will not be impersonal, but focused on the Personality of Godhead.

Bhagavān sātvatāṁ patiḥ. Lord Kṛṣṇa is the protector of the *sātvatas*, the servitors of the Absolute Truth. Vasudeva is the name of Kṛṣṇa's "father," but it also indicates "pure goodness": "the symbol of the transcendental position wherein the appearance of the Supreme Lord takes place." Each and every Sanskrit word has great meaning and may be expanded upon. Still, Prabhupāda has given a purport of only eleven lines.

Bhagavān, *bhadraṁ te*, *sātvatām*, the Lord, Vasudeva and Devakī, *patiḥ*, the protector—let all these words ring through us and soothe us. We should embrace them if we can, feel their warmth and assurance, their authority. Live in these sounds as we pronounce them in our rooms. Eyes and electric power at midnight are for this purpose; otherwise, we remain asleep in the dark.

Bhadraṁ te, blessings to Sūta. Blessings to our brain and mind. May Kṛṣṇa protect us in our devotional service. May the knowledgeable spiritual masters speak to us and may we have the sense to be anxious to hear the Absolute Truth from them.

Who am I and who are you and what
are our concerns?
O *Sātvata*, my name is Sats
derived from Stevie and I can
sing and play harmonium in the
storefront. But only one note. I
pump it again and again, or a chord.
I know the purpose for which
the Lord, the protector of the
sātvatas, appeared as the son
of Devakī and Vasudeva.
I know more—my
chill in breast, the mouse stool
on my sole, the striving to please
and to play like a jazz man
after playing the main melody.
I don't want to displease
the pure devotee or leave his
shelter in the name of "I
got a right to sing."
But it's inevitable I turn to my list and pursue my
occupation, in light of the *Bhāgavatam*.

Here is another list of concerns and some responses:
Concern: What does Kṛṣṇa want from me?
Response: He wants me to surrender to Him.

I reply, "That I'm doing," and in the course of it, I'm alert and inquiring about what He wants. He knows I'm in process. I think He wants me to write all day in whatever way I can to suit His purpose of, "Think of Me always, become My

devotee, bow down and worship Me; surely you will come to Me." He wants me to be happy and fully engaged in devotional service and to help others. He wants me to get rid of my shackles and return back to Godhead after fully executing the preaching duties given to me by my spiritual master. He wants me to chant Hare Kṛṣṇa.

He wants me to get to know Him however I can. He wants me not to waste time. He wants me to preach in an appealing way and not to be harsh or overbearing. " . . . one should not talk nonsense. The process of speaking in spiritual circles is to say something upheld by the scriptures. . . . At the same time, such talk should be very pleasurable to the ear. . . . There is a limitless stock of Vedic literature, and one should study this. This is called penance of speech." (Bg. 17.15, purport)

Bhadraṁ te, he wants to play. He wants permission to look at his list. He wants the sages and folks to say, "Yes, do it."

Other list items:

(1) Reading Śrīla Prabhupāda's books, chanting the holy names—I can write on these without end, and especially on how to remain chaste in reading and how to improve. I can also praise the process, tell of good times by candlelight, *japa* in my room. I can also write about calling out Kṛṣṇa's names, the perfection of *bhajana* and breath.

(2) Breaking into prayer while writing.

(3) Prabhupāda *mūrti*, his new scarves and my desire to always be with him. My fear that his body may break. My attempt to take close personal care of him; he is not a statue.

(4) Honesty.

(5) Can I become more compassionate?

(6) My father is dead and my mother rejects me—good, I'm free of that and can serve full-time.

(7) Jesus Christ.

(8) Interest in Kṛṣṇa's pastimes in Vṛndāvana.

(9) ISKCON's controversy over *ṛtvik*.

(10) What would I do if I had to stop traveling?

Bhadraṁ te. We have to die. That we know whether we keep it in the back or the forefront of our minds. A poet, Paul Celan, wrote that death is always on our minds, even if we write all day of other things, such as, "Your golden hair, Margareta." Death is a "gang-boss" who commands us to dig a grave and to play music and dance.

Death is a gang-boss *aus Deutsche* and his eye is blue
he hits you with leaden bullets his aim is true
there's a man in this house your golden hair Margareta
he sets his dogs on our trail he gives us a grave in the sky . . .

He sings this fugue over and over. I smear the ink by mistake with my left hand. Our "death fugue" is different because we know the purpose for which Bhagavān appeared as the son of His devotees.

I don't get so deeply bothered by mice or flies or death, I claim, because the Lord is protecting me. Maybe I have not been so tested—tortured by Yamarāja's associates—or I can't recall it right now. I want to be a writer, but when the day's work is done, I don't live a death fugue, but Kṛṣṇa consciousness through and through. We have the desire to come through death even as we cope and drive off mosquitoes and flies and other forms of torment Prabhupāda assures us pervade life in this world. We sing a better song because we mold our lives according to Kṛṣṇa's fugue. We believe in the ultimate destination.

We go out to shovel snow or tend to the barn, and while out there we get cold and hungry. Or we don't have such manual duties, but we go out to walk a poet's walk and we become just as cold and hungry. We want to return to the fireplace of *kṛṣṇa-kathā*, the meal of Kṛṣṇa *upadeśa*, and the friendly companionship of Kṛṣṇa's devotees. We must have this, so we try our best to arrange for it. We are never far away from the Lord in book form, mantra form, even while we struggle to "create." By His grace, ours is a thanksgiving fugue, not a call to death. But yes, that too—Kṛṣṇa waits for us as Death.

One poet (Heissenbüttel) wrote a list of all the things he would be homesick for:

for the clouds above the garden in Papenburg
for the small boy that I was
for the black flakes of peat in the bog

for the smell of the highways when I turned 17
for the smell of footlockers when I served as a soldier
for the trip with my mother through the desolate city
for the spring afternoons on small-town train platforms
for the walks I took with Lilo Ahlendorf in Dresden
for the sky one snowy day in November
for the face of Jeanne d'Arc in the movie by Dreyer
for the cancelled dates on old calendars
for the cries of the gulls
for the nights without sleep . . .

Sounds musical and poignant, we agree, and we probably all remember similar moments in our lives that allowed us to empathize, to enter a moment of emotion. A poet's job is to evoke empathy and emotion. Let's become poets of our own lives and fill our lines with the particulars of moments in ISKCON, acceptance of what we have been through, even the superficiality we have felt in our hearts.

Don't cut those moments down. Don't reject them. O Lord, we are petty children who demand Your love and who know that because we are unqualified and lacking in desire (*laulyam*), You don't appear fully when we chant Your name. You see our restless spirits, our pettiness, our desires for power and fame. We know better; these are all material pursuits and they end only in the grave. Useless profits. But we lack the courage and confidence and humility.

Still, You are kind. We let go and touch the moments we have experienced, taste the small emotions we have felt, and aspire for more. We follow the schedule. Time can only be lived in small measurements, a bit at a time, as You allow.

Text 13

tan naḥ śuśrūṣamāṇānām
arhasy aṅgānuvarṇitum
yasyāvatāro bhūtānāṁ
kṣemāya ca bhavāya ca

O Sūta Gosvāmī, we are eager to learn about the Personality of Godhead and His incarnations. Please explain to us those teachings imparted by previous masters [ācāryas], for one is uplifted both by speaking them and by hearing them.

Comment

This verse describes the conditions or requirements for a successful *Bhāgavatam* exchange. Both speaker and hearer must be qualified. The audience needs to be eager and sincere. They must listen submissively, not with a challenging attitude. The speaker, to be potent, has to come in *paramparā*. He repeats what his guru taught him and that is in line with the previous, bona fide spiritual masters, *śāstras*, and *sādhus*. When these conditions are met, then all the transcendental topics about Lord Kṛṣṇa can be easily understood.

We understand the theory, but are we qualified to hear or speak *Bhāgavatam*? We have to possess eagerness. That's not artificial. We can't just drum it up. Rūpa Gosvāmī says that if we hear that *kṛṣṇa-prema* is for sale in the market, then we should go at once to purchase it. But can we pay the price? The price is our *laulyam* to possess it. However, *laulyam* is rarely attained, even after many births of seeking it.

Eager hearing is a gift. Later in the *Bhāgavatam*, Prabhupāda writes of "rapt attention." He says for that we need a pure mind to hear. For a pure mind we need pure habits of eating, mating, sleeping, and defending. We can practice *sādhana*, sattvic reading, and that will increase our eagerness. We may procrastinate due to our lack of eagerness, but if we are regulated, we will submit to a schedule, open the *Bhāgavatam*, and read. That is how to cultivate interest. If we live lives according to vows and in the mood of *guru-sevā*, if we regularly chant Hare Kṛṣṇa, and if we aren't grouchy bastards but are kind and tolerant toward others (*tṛṇād api*), then there's hope that we can become lively students and speakers of *Bhāgavatam*.

Prabhupāda says that we can also increase our eagerness by praising Kṛṣṇa and His devotees. Praise Sūta. It's not flattery. We are truly grateful to a qualified speaker such as Sūta and a qualified commentator such as Prabhupāda. It is the best moment of the day when we can peacefully, openly hear from them. They may be describing *varṇāśrama-dharma* "as I have told you many times," telling a pastime of Kṛṣṇa and His pure devotees, or telling us that the *gopīs* are the topmost devotees, but whatever they say is relevant and uplifting. I want to be eager. I want to get myself in shape for attentive hearing and then stay in shape. That is faithfulness.

Laḍḍu Kṛṣṇa holds His hand out. The night we arrived here, they had a pot with many *tulasīs* growing in it, and in front of them, cotton wicks for us to worship *tulasī*. Pious people.

Voice within head: I'm all right. I am following my inner way. Kṛṣṇa speaks in His book and I believe His words. Therefore, I want to mold my life to surrender. But *I* have to do it, not this or that person telling me how and what. I had to surrender to the Swami in 1966 and in 1976 and in every year in between and since. Me, not his servant telling me, "Prabhupāda is like this. You should surrender as I deem fit." I need to find my own way, my own heart.

"You'll be sorry!" other voices say.

But no, I accept the calling of my inner self. Just because I try to surrender according to someone else's direction, even if he can quote Prabhupāda, even if he's technically right, doesn't mean I'll succeed.

O Swami, O boss, O ruler of me, you know my tendency. I am weak, a wiseguy, a monkey jumping, and I cannot manage men and money, but I love you.

I refuse to criticize or reject my love for you as sentimental. I pray to be stronger, but this is what I am now, this delicate self who wants his own way. Is it lesser?

I don't know—maybe it's good. *If* I go all the way in writing life, it can count as work for you. You said in 1976 in Vṛndāvana that your Guru Mahārāja didn't give disciples the opportunity to be idle and neither did you. Don't claim, "I can't go out, I'm chanting all day." No, you said, "Go out and work hard and sell books!" Well, I work hard at this wooden desk—as many hours as possible.

Re-enter—in his last ten minutes he dove underwater and felt the water's pressure pressing on his lungs. One day he has to die. Until then, he has to write and preach (at the Lion's Club?), quoting Sanskrit and telling people how the Swami rescued him and he studied *Bhagavad-gītā* and taught how the *Gītā* has been misinterpreted.

But one day . . .

Nicanor, give us a line

hip poet slant against door, heavy vibes,

No, I am at peace. "Shine! Shine!" Dago black clothes, shoeshine men on Staten Island Ferry, and me with magazines inside a brown paper bag inside my Brooklyn College gym bag along with books on French and Spanish and Shakespeare and English Romantic poets and Geology I and II. I wanted good grades. I hated my father and his ignorance. I didn't know anything yet.

You dope, you hadn't even begun to smoke pot. You were still drinking beer at the Swiss Chalet. I remember you now. I got you by the throat, your full-length black overcoat your parents bought you, them both looking at it and you in the mirror. Then you got that three-quarter-length, stylish Greenwich Village black coat to replace it. Didn't wear that old one anymore.

Banish these thoughts! Clear a new path to peace. Put it in your book. It doesn't belong in a nice man's house or that of a qualified *Bhāgavatam* hearer or reciter.

Or does it?

Ease yourself and take your Nature Cure massage. Think over how to again become a nice *sādhu*, deep and peaceful. Bring yourself to approach the *Bhāgavatam* and read and write as you have been trained all these years.

May we live to pen many volumes and in the process surrender and become pure devotees who only speak the truth.

The automatic
writer recites the words
+ writes 'em down
w'out a frown,
hopes his love for
Swami will own out.
Beer

Prabhupāda compared the coming together of a potent *Bhāgavatam* speaker and an eager audience with the combination of a man and women in healthy sexual intercourse. Conception is the result of sex and the injection of *bhakti* into the heart is the result of hearing *Bhāgavatam* from the right speaker. Up sprouts one's dormant love of God in the form of the *bhakti-latā*, the creeper of devotional service. This plant must be fenced in against *aparādhas* and regularly watered with chanting and hearing. It's capable of penetrating the material coverings, then the *brahmajyoti*, and finally entering Kṛṣṇa's eternal planet.

I believe this, but do I care? Do I tremble with excitement when I hear it? Or if that's too intense (don't want to give you a headache, old man), does it make me pleased to hear it? Does it seem right? Or do I write it down because I know it's a relevant reference, "Oh yes, put that thing in there about the *bhakti-latā*"? What is my honest response?

Well, I can honestly pick up the rope on Jagannātha's cart (forty feet high, wooden wheels, huge Deity eyed suspiciously by the police) and pull along with the others to move the Lord of the Universe, *if* He wants to be moved. I can honestly say that the spiritual art of submissive hearing has to be learned in many ways under the spiritual master's order—whether by scrubbing pots, milking cows, or begging donations. As we serve, we learn to please him and receive his blessings to hear better and with faith. I can honestly pray, "Please let me hear, O Lord." And I can honestly quote, "*Ataḥ śrī kṛṣṇa nāmādi.*" We can't know Kṛṣṇa's names, pastimes, forms, or qualities with our blunt, material senses. Gradually the mind and senses have to be purified, starting with the tongue.

I honestly conceive of, imagine a place
where sages speak the truth
and no ordinary mortal poet is allowed
to go like a rat newspaper reporter
to later write down rancid lines.

Naimiṣāraṇya is an actual place,
near Nimsar railroad station
where today . . . I need to go there in my imagination—
any quiet time. I'm there—in suit and tie?
No, I'll wear *khādī* always now that
I've re-discovered it, the perfect cloth
for the saffron Hare Kṛṣṇa *brahmacārī* monk.

I'll wear Indian-dyed *khādī*
and sit in a half-lotus *no more than*
forty minutes at a time
and hear the angels speak—a
figure of speech meaning that the divine
speaks through Sūta's latest
representative.

He says, "Kṛṣṇa," he says, "*ātmā*,"
and I listen to whatever he says.
Then in this vision I have, I
become transformed into a
better person. I love others,
I'm not afraid. I even
cure my indigestion and
headaches for awhile
(although flesh is mortal and pained).
I hear with faith and
devotion for Kṛṣṇa and His
parts and plenary parts.
I like it very much and I
don't forget it, some of it.
Kṛṣṇa blesses me with
the desire to preach
whatever I've heard.

My friend comes in and says, "It's time," and I say, "You've interrupted me again, but I'm glad for the relief."

Yes, we have summed it up in brief. A bored Angora stretches its fat limbs in the sunlight. A retired dentist tells a friend he'd like to take a vacation to read *Bhāgavatam*. Those who are fortunate are either *Bhāgavatam* audience or speaker as described herein. Let's hear what happens to them.

I don't mean to be sarcastic or make cynical asides, but I must be honest. My brain leaks. I have to go to the bathroom. There's a hole in my shoe. There's something rotten in the state of Denmark. True words are spoken and they can bust all doubters. This isn't a propaganda war, however. Only the pure and qualified are admitted.

In other words, you have to be qualified, but if you are *even a little bit qualified*, Kṛṣṇa's mercy will come through. Therefore, we recommend repeated hearing of these topics at choice times in your day.

Dance of animals, spirits & plants when Srimad Bhagwatam meeting gets rolling.

Text 14

āpannaḥ saṁsṛtiṁ ghorāṁ
yan-nāma vivaśo gṛṇan
tataḥ sadyo vimucyeta
yad bibheti svayaṁ bhayam

Living beings who are entangled in the complicated meshes of birth and death can be freed immediately by even unconsciously chanting the holy name of Kṛṣṇa, which is feared by fear personified.

Comment

Kṛṣṇa's name is feared by fear personified. That is, the most ferocious demons, Rāvaṇa or Hiraṇyakaśipu, are openly afraid of the Almighty's rage. Yamarāja is also fear personified as the king of death, but he is God's servant and operates out of fear of the Supreme Lord's displeasure. We can call for the shelter of the all-powerful Godhead just by calling His name. This is because Kṛṣṇa's name is non-different than Kṛṣṇa. Lord Kṛṣṇa's power, which subdues all fear, is available to protect the devotee-chanter.

It's not that we become Kṛṣṇa when we chant, but we come under His shelter. As we read later in the *Bhāgavatam*, many great devotees in the past (as well as in the present) recommend chanting Kṛṣṇa's name as protection against danger and fear. Śukadeva Gosvāmī tells Mahārāja Parīkṣit, "My dear King, wherever people in any position perform their occupational duties of devotional service by chanting and hearing [*śravaṇaṁ kīrtanaṁ viṣṇoḥ*], there cannot be any danger from bad elements." (*Bhāg.* 10.6.3) In his purport to that verse, Prabhupāda states:

> Śrīla Bhaktivinoda Ṭhākura has sung: *nāmāśraya kari' yatane tumi, thākaha āpana kāje.* Everyone is thus advised to seek shelter in the chanting of the Hare Kṛṣṇa *mahā-mantra* and remain engaged in his own occupational duty. There is no loss in this, and the gain is tremendous. Even from a material point of view, everyone should take to chanting the Hare Kṛṣṇa mantra to be saved from all kinds of danger. This world is full of danger (*padaṁ padaṁ yad vipadām*). Therefore we should be encouraged to chant the Hare Kṛṣṇa *mahā-mantra* so that in our family, society, neighborhood and nation, everything will be smooth and free from danger.

Even Yaśodā-devī, Kṛṣṇa's eternal mother, resorted to chanting God's names in her attempts to protect Kṛṣṇa from demons. After Pūtanā was vanquished, the elderly *gopīs* told Yaśodā:

> The evil witches known as Ḍākinīs, Yātudhānīs and Kuṣmāṇḍas are the greatest enemies of children, and the evil spirits like Bhūtas, Pretas, Piśācas, Yakṣas, Rākṣasas and Vināyakas, as well as witches like Koṭarā, Revatī, Jyeṣṭhā, Pūtanā and Mātṛkā, are always ready to give trouble to the body, the life air and the senses, causing loss of memory, madness and bad dreams. Like the most experienced evil stars, they all create great disturbances, especially for children, but one can vanquish them simply by uttering Lord Viṣṇu's name, for when Lord Viṣṇu's name resounds, all of them become afraid and go away.
>
> —*Bhāg*. 10.6.27–9

By stating that the chanting of the holy name will free us from *saṁsāra*, the sages at Naimiṣāraṇya indicate that chanting at the time of death will be effective. Certainly at death, if at any time, we will experience fear. Everyone is afraid of death. Prabhupāda heartily recommends chanting Hare Kṛṣṇa in our last hours. Death brings the most painful condition to the body and material mind, but calling out Kṛṣṇa's names is a relatively easy practice. Chanting brings remembrance of God by sound vibration which forces us to *hear Kṛṣṇa*. As Lord Kṛṣṇa states, "And whoever, at the end of his life, quits his body, remembering Me alone, at once attains My nature. Of this there is no doubt." (Bg. 8.5)

Prabhupāda reminds us, however, not to try to chant and remember Kṛṣṇa only as a last-hour resort. "Remembrance of Kṛṣṇa is not possible for the impure soul who has not practiced Kṛṣṇa consciousness in devotional service. Therefore one should practice Kṛṣṇa consciousness from the very beginning of life. If one wants to achieve success at the end of his life, the process of remembering Kṛṣṇa is essential. Therefore one should constantly, incessantly chant the *māha-mantra* . . ."

You know this, little soul.
You know that chanting is
the main practice to save you
from danger and
fear of death. And you chant every day,
starting as early as possible.
You chant especially fervently
when you're afraid.

As I write, a guard outside the house—he sleeps outdoors—coughs again and again. He sleeps on or near the front porch, like a personal protector. The owner has provided him for us. We approved of his coming because this is a remote house near a river and a dam. Thugs may have seen that two Westerners are living here and I'm sure there have been rumors about how our rooms are crammed with Western amenities. The *chaukīdār*, however, carries only a bamboo stick as a weapon, and he bundles up in his quilt and coughs.

Yes, mine is a little life. I want silence as I read. I get distracted. The flow of the river sounds peaceful. Otherwise, it is silent here (except when he's coughing). Or so I say. Actually, it's not silent here, not as silent as I would like. But I can't have things my way. My own mind coughs and starts and veers from concentration on the *Bhāgavatam*. Holy name, please bring me back to You. I neglect You and forget Your power in my life. I fail to remain devoted to You, as Dakṣa failed to appreciate Lord Śiva's supremacy.

Please don't let my asking for forgiveness be even partly a literary exercise. That's what I seek to escape—the academic, literary, social, institutional gesture. The outward act of what one is expected to do in a given situation. It's just not enough. Better an unconscious cry to God in fear, or better still, an act of personal, sincere devotion to the Lord.

This is one reason why I keep trying for honesty—even when it takes me some steps back from the *Bhāgavatam* topics. The topics are best, but after some initial participation in them, I may lose attention. Then I ask myself, "What's up? Where are you going?" I may slap myself, force myself, beat that old horse of myself back to workmanlike concentration.

I know it doesn't always work. Who wants to be beaten constantly? Therefore, I try tenderness with myself: "Dear heart, what's on your mind? Why don't you stay with the speaker at Naimiṣāraṇya or with your own spiritual master in his books?" Maybe all it takes is a little caring attention. My conditioned, injured self may just want a thorn removed from his foot so he can go back to Naimiṣāraṇya. It may not be that serious.

Hare Kṛṣṇa Hare Kṛṣṇa, Kṛṣṇa Kṛṣṇa Hare Hare/ Hare Rāma Hare Rāma, Rāma Rāma Hare Hare. Chant, chant—this is the time for it. The sages talk about it. It's recommended for all. Tell parents and children and students and disciples. Ask teachers to discourse on it. Engage tongues and voices in chanting Hare Kṛṣṇa. This is the time for it. While fear and danger stalk, while the pitiful, cold guard coughs as he tries to sleep too near me as I try to read the holy name's glories, chant Hare Kṛṣṇa.

My hand is growing tired and cramped. I push him on. I have no typewriter. I can write. I am willing. Breathe in and out and keep going. Willy, how is your *Bhāgavatam* study going? Oh, okay, I guess.

If I look out over that ridge, I see smoke from a cabin chimney. We see those sights and think of all the practical work it takes to maintain them—like Turīya dāsa cutting wood, driving to the hospital. I told him to practice Nature Cure, but he said, "That's your way, not mine." He's into doctors and running tests. Maybe he needs that. Who am I?

I think we just caught a mouse in this trap. It's one of those traps that doesn't kill the mice, but I'll have to pick it up with gloves on and remove it from my room. I usually leave it outside so someone can come by and let it out far away from this house (so it doesn't just trot right back in).

It's what I said earlier. We want silence—no coughing, no mice intruding on our page—just be with God without thinking about what these others are doing, why they're coughing or how it applies to teethy, whiskered, long-legged, claw-pawed rodents feeling fear as they find themselves caught in a steel cage.

Turn to chanting.

When you're afraid, chant Hare Kṛṣṇa. You *are* afraid, so chant. When you're not afraid, chant anyway. You can get over the hurdle of birth and death because Kṛṣṇa is His name.

Now the questions come: does a casual or unconscious utterance of the holy name, or even a most fervent calling, actually banish all those Piśācas and goblins? Say you got mugged by several young men. Do you think if you chanted, "Kṛṣṇa!" or "Nṛsiṁha!" they would go away? Probably not. They'd laugh and say, "Where's Lord Nṛsiṁha now when you need Him?" We can't expect God to come to us like that, like the Amazing Spiderman or Shazaam!, as if Hare Kṛṣṇa is the call that brings Captain Marvel.

I don't know what it means, how it works, or *when* it works. I leave that up to Kṛṣṇa. I don't have to know all that. Besides, when Kṛṣṇa says His devotees never perish, it doesn't mean His devotees have to win all the World Series games, the tennis cup champions, the political elections, or even the battles, and that if they don't, Kṛṣṇa is disproved. It means His unflinching devotees remember Him at death and go back to Him. It means even imperfect devotees like me may not go back to Godhead at once, but we don't perish, don't get pushed down to the lower species.

"When chanting the *mahā-mantra*, we are completely safe, even in this most dangerous position. We should always be aware that in this material world, we are always in a dangerous position. *Śrīmad-Bhāgavatam* confirms: *padaṁ padaṁ yad vipadāṁ na teṣām*. In this world, there is danger at every step. The devotees of the Lord, however, are not meant to remain in this miserable, dangerous place. Therefore we should take care to advance in Kṛṣṇa consciousness while in this human form. Then our happiness is assured." (*The Path of Perfection*, p. 152)

Kīrtana-rasa and *japa-rasa* are the safest places in the world to be. Whatever provokes us to chant, whether it be fear or joy or duty or impulsiveness, we can suddenly find ourselves safe. Prabhupāda writes, "When chanting the *mahā-mantra*, we are completely safe, even in this most dangerous position." He doesn't say that the dangerous position goes away, even for the devotee. Rather, a devotee should realize from the tribulations that the material world is a dangerous place. We should get out.

How? *Bhagavad-gītā* states, "Having come to this temporary, miserable world, you should engage in My devotional service." We have to be careful, however, not to seek safety in the material world itself, in its apparent comforts and facilities, in the name of peaceful execution of service. We want self-confidence, self-esteem, and a nice lunch. Don't worry, we'll offer the lunch to Kṛṣṇa. We want and we demand. We count our years and consider ourselves senior devotees; we want honor. We look at the color of our cloth and think, "I'm wearing saffron and I walk back and forth before sunrise chanting Hare Kṛṣṇa. I ought to be given a round-trip plane ticket to anywhere I want to go."

"May the glorification of the transcendental name, form, qualities and paraphernalia of the Supreme Personality of Godhead protect us from the influence of bad planets, meteors, envious human beings, serpents, scorpions, and animals like tigers and wolves. May it protect us from ghosts and the material elements like earth, water, fire and air, and may it also protect from lightning and our past sins. We are always afraid of these hindrances to our auspicious life. Therefore, may they all be completely destroyed by the chanting of the Hare Kṛṣṇa *māha-mantra*." (*Bhāg*. 6.8.27–8)

The holy name is merciful. We don't have to be expert or learned to chant it, and according to *Bhāg*. 1.1.14, we don't even have to chant deliberately or consciously. We can chant unconsciously (*yan-nāma vivaśo gṛṇan*) and still be freed from *saṁsāra*.

Fear personified—demons, terrorists, bullies—may not become afraid when we chant in their faces, but when Kṛṣṇa impresses upon them that He is supreme, then they will fear even His name. Arjuna says the demons flee upon hearing Kṛṣṇa's names, although the devotees rejoice. Even the demigods: "Some of them, very much afraid, are offering prayers with folded hands. Hosts of great sages and perfected beings, crying, 'All peace!' are praying to You by singing the Vedic hymns." (Bg. 11.21)

The Universal Form of Kṛṣṇa can frighten *anyone*. " . . . demigods are disturbed at seeing Your great form . . . Your many terrible teeth; and as they are disturbed, so am I. I see all people rushing full speed into Your mouths, as moths dash to destruction in a blazing fire. O Viṣṇu, I see You devouring all people from all sides with Your flaming mouths.

Covering all the universe with Your effulgence, You are manifest with terrible, scorching rays." (Bg. 11.23, 29–30)

God can cause fear, yet He brings peace to His simple devotees when they chant continually. No matter what happens, the devotees cling to *kṛṣṇa-nāma* and are ultimately saved. They are unshakable in their faith and practice of chanting, even until death and beyond.

Text 15

yat-pāda-saṁśrayāḥ sūta
munayaḥ praśamāyanāḥ
sadyaḥ punanty upaspṛṣṭāḥ
svardhuny-āpo 'nusevayā

O Sūta, those great sages who have completely taken shelter of the lotus feet of the Lord can at once sanctify those who come in touch with them, whereas the waters of the Ganges can sanctify only after prolonged use.

Comment

Lord Kṛṣṇa declares in *Bhagavad-gītā* 9.32 that He will give shelter to anyone regardless of birth and thus they can become elevated, pure souls. The best way to seek shelter at Kṛṣṇa's lotus feet is to surrender to His pure devotee and accept him as spiritual master. The qualified spiritual masters are known by names such as Prabhupāda and Viṣṇupāda, which indicate that they have taken shelter of Lord Viṣṇu, Kṛṣṇa. If a fallen soul follows a pure devotee and becomes his disciple, he'll become free of sin and trained up in *bhakti-yoga*. He becomes a *sādhaka*, a practicing devotee.

In the seventh verse of the "*Gurvaṣṭakam*," it is stated that the spiritual master is the direct representative of Lord Hari because he is the confidential servant of the Lord. In the purport to *Bhāg.* 1.1.15, Prabhupāda states that the spiritual master's confidential service is to preach and to train disciples. "Such devotees of the Lord are honored equally with the Lord because they are engaged in the most confidential service of the Lord, for they deliver out of the material world the fallen souls whom the Lord wants to return home, back to Godhead." Thus the fortunate disciple (unlike the unfortunate Kali-yuga victim who is cheated by false, so-called gurus) becomes a humble servant of the servant of the Lord.

The sages praise Sūta and all pure devotees and point out the effect the spiritual master's benediction can have upon those to whom they preach. What is the nature of their potency? It is that they purely represent the previous *ācāryas* in all that they speak and write.

There are qualifications to becoming a spiritual master. The first qualification is that they control their senses. "*Gosvāmī*" means one who controls his senses. Rūpa Gosvāmī writes in *Upadeśāmṛta* that a *gosvāmī* (by controlling the tongue, mind, anger, words, belly, and genitals) is fit to make disciples all over the world.

Even this first qualification we have yet to attain. Do we know anyone among our contemporaries who has achieved actual sense control? Maybe not, but at least we are all aspiring for it, even if we have not yet reached it.

We will attain it when we are looking at the ground, at the dust particles at the spiritual master's feet. "The sincere disciple of the pure devotee considers the spiritual master equal to the Lord, but always considers himself to be a humble servant of the servant of the Lord. This is the pure devotional path."

What's on my list and how does it look in the light of the *Bhāgavata*?

Dreams. I wake nowadays and grasp only fragments. Remembering dreams is not a practice I give time to, but dream life can be compelling. When I do remember a dream, I ask, "What does this say about my Kṛṣṇa consciousness?" I think the dream may signify the fear of transmigration and the threefold (or fourfold) miseries.

Other list items: Things overhead, epiphanies.

I can't work a list.
I don't have the gumption.
It's too long, too short, too heavy,
each one could be a whole
report but too personal and what
connection does it have with
Prabhupāda and Viṣṇupāda and
prolonged use of the Ganges?

I first saw the Ganges from an airplane
when I was 33 years old.
Before that I had always lived in New York City.
My mother's mother and father came from Ireland.
My father's mother and father came from Italy.
My list then was Elvis, devil's food cakes,
sugar, and unmentionables.
I learned what a scum bag was
when some kids and I were playing
hooky sitting in a tree and we saw
the bags floating in the pond below.
I learned all sorts of things from
the kids during recess in the
dirt lot outside the wooden school.

So my list—*New York Daily News*,
the top song hits from Allen Freed's show—
is not so good for seeing by the
light of the *Bhāgavata*.
The *Bhāgavatam* would kick it out.

Tear down and shred and burn your
list and start a new one
from *śraddhā* to *sādhu-*
saṅga to *bhajana-kriyā*.

Is it right to destroy things?
Was it right to toss a thousand pages
of writing into the incinerator in the hallway of
the 26 Second Avenue apartment building,
my agony poems "Li'l Chaos"
and the short novels I wrote?
Yes, it was right.
Started a new life,
new lists, maybe,
but they still include at
least something of the past.
I admit I'm tainted.
How else will I demonstrate that
Bhāgavatam can uplift the fallen?
I can't prove *Bhāgavatam* is my
constant life and soul ever since I
was born. I was not given an infant's
choice between *Bhāgavatam* and coins.
Can't sing a *Bhāgavatam* verse in 5 tunes
as Raghunātha Bhaṭṭa did, so that even the
animals cry when they hear it.
But I can testify—
a hell-bound, eclectic reader now
enters *Bhāgavatam* daily.
My list? Later.

Instead of attempting to explain anything, I could just list it for now and let it go. This morning when I went outdoors to chant in the first slanting rays of sunlight, I saw five fifty-pound sacks of something lying just inside our front gate. One sack was torn open and taken from. Were they sandbags for the dam? Wheat for our meals? How did they get here? I don't know. Why is the sun . . . List it, that's all.

(1) Preparing for the time of death.

(2) Losing passport.

(3) How far away the reality of going back to Godhead seems.

(4) Devotees in Rome temple sitting down after 10 P.M. for extra pasta snack.

(5) Picking blackberries in stainless steel pot in Great Kills, late 1940s.

(6) Whole concept of writing about childhood or adolescence and how it seems off limits because it's "*māyā.*" And yet it's part of my life.

(7) Influence of Zen Buddhism, the ultimate turn-off to it.

(8) The loneliness of the writing life.

(9) "Don't tread on me."

(10) The question of money: how much do you need and what do you do to get it?

(11) The human illusion that life will go on more or less like it's going on now. Not living as Prabhupāda said to live, "With death at your front."

(12) Members of ISKCON sub-culture talking about the earth changes that will take place with entire new geography and survivor populations in America, and the people from outer space who told them this and who are "okay."

(13) Assuming attitudes which are not my actual attitude at heart just to make a literary pose of apparent spirituality, broad-mindedness, or just to have a niche in the world.

(14) Avoiding Vaiṣṇava *aparādha*—a serious business, not just a theory or philosophy.

(15) Faith in *śāstra* and my own simple faith. Arguments against agnosticism and atheism.

(16) Letter from a Godbrother in Barcelona, vituperative attack—said anyone who considers you humble is in ignorance.

(17) Morning walks in the country or the seashore. How blissful. Walk with a cane.

(18) Slave to the clock, to the schedule.

(19) Swamijī, Swamijī.

(20) My sister.

(21) How *karma-yoga*, as described in the *Bhagavad-gītā* verse *yat karoṣi*, is not pure devotional service, but I sometimes tried to say it was.

(22) The Australian artist about whom Baladeva sent me an article, who spent his last years living in a shack on the beach and painting. Madman.

(23) Episodic technique in *Mahābhārata*, Victory at Sea, *Don Quixote*.

Śrīla Prabhupāda asked his audience in Vṛndāvana, "You are coming from different parts of the world, so is there any school where they are teaching this science?" No, not as a

science, not in all details, not with the full *bhakti* conclusions as taught in *Vedānta*, *Bhagavad-gītā*, *Bhāgavatam*, *Caitanya-caritāmṛta*. You have to learn it here, individually, not waiting for your governments to send it to you or for your parents to put you in the right school where you can learn it properly. Understand and *practice it* under the direction of a qualified spiritual master. He gives Kṛṣṇa's mercy faster than the Ganges does.

The devotees represent the Supreme Lord's feet because that's where they are situated in loving service. We'll find them there and we'll best please Kṛṣṇa by serving those pure Vaiṣṇavas. Therefore, they may be called Kṛṣṇa's vice-lords; honor given to them goes directly to Kṛṣṇa. Any questions?

What is the cost of discipleship?

You must give your life. Viśvanātha Cakravartī Ṭhākura describes this complete surrender in his commentary to *Bhagavad-gītā* 2.41, *ekeha kuru-nandana*. He writes in his *ṭīkā* that as the life air (*prāṇa*) gives vital sustenance to a living being, so single-minded service to the spiritual master is the life of the disciple. He cannot live without it. It's not just one of many interests in life.

That question woke me out of my stupor. It piqued my interest. I also see a tendency for glassy-eyed boredom in my role of giving out Kṛṣṇa conscious teachings. It's as if I only become interested if I can play with one of my lists or go into free-writing. What is this?

Guru's mercy. He gives it out. We have to take it. My guru has gone back to Godhead. I suppose this mental stupor I find myself in may be attributed to that—a sign of suffering in separation. Remember what Uddhava found when he visited Vṛndāvana? Kṛṣṇa's mother and father were distracted from their daily routine because they were suffering so much separation. The *gopīs* and *gopas* were drying up like people who had been fasting until death or like lotuses withering in the dry season.

I no longer receive his letters telling me what to do. I can no longer inquire about my doubts. He's not there to drag me back in the door. That may be the cause of the deficiency you see in me.

Of course, a good disciple never feels that his spiritual master is absent. "He's always by my side," Prabhupāda wrote of his own Guru Mahārāja. Therefore, he writes his books and preaches Kṛṣṇa consciousness knowing that his Guru Mahārāja approves. He becomes empowered with the guru's good wishes.

If I want to press this point of my own deficiency, I could say my low level is due to not pleasing him. I'm sure I could find Godbrothers who will give that diagnosis. And their treatment will be to preach in the ISKCON department which they prescribe to me, perhaps under them in one of their temples. "Be accountable," "Distribute his book," "Get off your butt," "Stop the madness of being alone."

But I don't want to dwell on this.

He worries what's wrong, his brain's in a spiel, saw irrational fear and didn't like it—a violent jump and a shout unseating the Moby Dick concealed in the shadowed mouse hole. *Ayi nanda*!

The hand presses down, seeking a fresh flow of ink to be satisfied. First comes the past, the lint on the old-fashioned phonograph needle. I remember it, scratch-scratching across the surface of old favorites. The hand presses down further, conscientious, looking for Kṛṣṇa consciousness.

Knots in wood. When I look closely at small things like that, I can't believe others' analogies that eternity is contained in the concentric circles of a wood knot. They also say that the personal worship of God is meant to help us understand impersonal Brahman. *Śāstra* doesn't agree.

Strain, yoga, dizzy, the body stretches and I ask myself what Prabhupāda would say about me today. My hand works for him. I am a survivor, like most.

We'll be okay, don't worry. They make kids so afraid that Śamīka Ṛṣi's fine-bred son is afraid to wear a hat in winter and must have white bread for his sandwiches.

Ah, to be born again. The sages say gurus are found at the Lord's feet and that we ought to go there rather than lingering in a mudpack on the bank of the Ganges or chanting silent *gāyatrī*. Go to guru and type for him, ask relevant questions, recognize him as God's viceroy. Have we neglected guru? Have we neglected offering reverence and affection and showing a willingness to do whatever he asks or go wherever he wants us to go?

My conscious self just suggested that this was the cause of *ennui*. I miss him. I love him. I know he is at Kṛṣṇa's lotus feet, so I have to go there. I write this book to be close to him even if I suffer from *malaise* as a disciple. I know I have faults, but I want to go to him anyway. Sometimes he seems harsh in his condemnation of the rascals, but never mind. His institution is sometimes too top-heavy or judgmental, never mind. I may be *way off* the mark, but I want to go to him anyway, meet with him in mind and deed and serve him however I can.

My hand presses down to touch these points.

Poem bounce— it took us
16 hours to get here and to settle
in took days. Takes months
to adjust to the new body we
got from Nature Cure diet and
takes years to be a devotee,
lifetimes to get *laulyam* and
we may never—like Nārada
or Lakṣmī—be allowed to
enter the *rāsa* dance.
Then?

Then go at a pace, e-mail or
snail mail it doesn't matter.
Not time,
but guru's grace is required.
Do you find *Ṣaṭ Sandarbhas* dry?
Is your brain too small?
You find *Ujjvala-nīlamaṇī*
too "wet"?
What's your speed? *Bhagavad-gītā*? Yeah, I love it
when the Lord speaks.
Then why do we waste our
time with poets
who know only
"With your eyes
with your eyes
with your Death full of Flowers"?
They speak of Death as the only
God they'll know.

Why consort with them?
For rhythm and blues?
Sometimes they see people
in naked detail,
a kind of tenderness.

Here goes—to Kṛṣṇa, my Father,
to unstainable Sanskrit names
like Nirañjana, to memories
of ISKCON dualities—
Suhotra playing the twisted
saṅkīrtana horn in Boston temple,
the Murphys' sueing and sueing and
never relenting even until they
die.

Someone asks, "You are
reluctant and cautious to criticize
your ISKCON while
other brothers speak out. Is it
because you are not troubled
much by its wrongs?"

At the feet of the Lord—
whose feet are spiritual,
who is not a dead stone,
from whose feet the Ganges emanates,
who is a transcendental source of
all that be, *janmādy asya yataḥ*—
stay with His pure devotees.
I serve His one, Swami
Prabhupāda. His followers
are many different characters
and quarrel and this is all a symptom
of our missing his
generalship,

loving fatherly direction,
sure hand. But he had
to leave, giving us
the Comforter (Supersoul and
himself in our hearts).
Tell it straight—the Lord's devotees are at His feet and
that's where you'll get His
mercy. Sūta says so.

Text 16

ko vā bhagavatas tasya
puṇya-ślokeḍya-karmaṇaḥ
śuddhi-kāmo na śṛṇuyād
yaśaḥ kali-malāpaham

Who is there, desiring deliverance from the vices of the age of quarrel, who is not willing to hear the virtuous glories of the Lord?

Comment

Śrīla Prabhupāda speaks against the world's foolish leaders whom we take to be presidents, prime ministers and their cabinets, the men and women who carry out their orders, and other leaders who wield insolence. They cannot save people from the bad habits of the age. They cannot even stop quarreling.

In Kali-yuga, "there is a great fight at the slightest misunderstanding." Prabhupāda boldly asserts that the only help is to follow the path of the pure devotees: accept and surrender to the Supreme Lord. The leaders, however, don't know about *kīrtana*. Rather, they deny God's existence and oppose the propagation of God's glories because they run a secular state. As such, the leaders and their people in this age fail to establish peace and friendship, although they can't seem to understand why.

"But here is the hint to get over the hurdle. If we want actual peace, we must open the road to understanding of the Supreme Lord Kṛṣṇa and glorify Him for His virtuous activities as they are depicted in the pages of *Śrīmad-Bhāgavatam.*" Again I glimpse Śrīla Prabhupāda in his bare Chippiwada room, typing and writing and correcting printer proofs, placing the stones on the piles of pages to keep them from blowing away. His round eyeglasses, long hours sitting upright on the floor, him burning with the desire to carry the relevant *Bhāgavatam* message into the world's affairs. He knew that what he was doing could help everyone. This is exactly what the sages at Naimiṣāraṇya thought about what they were doing. If a lesser swami were to think of world betterment, he would himself become entangled in worldly politics, but not Prabhupāda. He insisted that we need to hear about Kṛṣṇa from the *Bhāgavatam* if we don't want to remain shackled by the vicious habits which are "natural" for this age.

Srila Prabhupada's Bhagavatam Labors at Chippiwada

It's hard to keep up that vision. Well, not hard to keep it up for one's self, but for the world. Or at least to know how to apply it to the world. I can see the need to keep myself as Kṛṣṇa conscious as possible, and to do that it seems I have to keep apart from Kali-yuga and the world's leaders and followers. When we practice Kṛṣṇa consciousness, we do it as religious people. To see our efforts as changing the current of the age, however, is harder. We know that the world sees us as Hare Kṛṣṇa people, a cult. Eyed suspiciously, tolerated, miniscule. In one sense, we are facing what Prabhupāda faced in India in the 1950s—a voice crying in the wilderness. Prabhupāda was so powerful. He cried in the wilderness, but at the same time, he went on contacting the prime minister to urge him to at least read the headlines of his *Back To Godhead* essays and to trust that Prabhupāda was not a madman when he said that he could bring his fellow men back to Godhead. It is not madness to say that Kṛṣṇa consciousness can transform the world's pandemonium into peace and prosperity.

We also have to work in this field. The preachers feel compassion and a deep sense of purpose and inner satisfaction in their preaching. We cannot know right now what the ultimate effect will be. We may not have the satisfaction to see a revolution from atheism and materialism to Kṛṣṇa conscious theism in our own lifetimes. Theism—politicians avoid the very word; speaking of love of God doesn't get votes. Politicians fear theocracies and fundamentalists and give evidence that these "types" breed fanatical cruelty, communal riots, and wide-scale wars. "You want God praised? But the God of which religion? You want more countries like Khomeini's Iran? You want a world ruled from the viewpoint of North Ireland's Ian Paisley? Christian? Muslim? Oh—Hare Kṛṣṇa! Sure, sure, just what we all need, to shave our heads, dress in orange skirts, and chant all day. No meat and liquor, right? Sure. Anyway, you people are cheaters. Get lost."

People read Prabhupāda's purports and feel their hearts changed. I saw a young man in front of me in the Krishna-Balaram Mandir. On the back of his T-shirt was the logo, "World revolution through book distribution." The small band of young devotees traveling in vans distributing Prabhupāda's books, fueled with a vision by their ISKCON leader, think that book distribution will save the world. This is what Prabhupāda also says in this purport. It seems highly unlikely, but many things seemed highly unlikely when they were first introduced to the world. Communism was once just an obscure German scholar's idea. Freud and his theories were once unknown. These things can grow and sweep into power. Everything is under the control of Providence .

Without calculating the possibility of winning elections or popularity polls, the Lord's devotees first believe in Kṛṣṇa, second, speak *kṛṣṇa-kathā*, and third, if they share the preaching vision, work to inject Kṛṣṇa consciousness into Kali-yuga's mainstream against all odds.

At least we should not feel foolish because we are Hare Kṛṣṇas. We shouldn't think we are incapable of improving the world situation, and that therefore we should consign ourselves to living in a little room in a temple with no sphere of influence except over a few pious congregational members who happen to be mostly Indians. In the world of influence, we are not anathemas.

As I write, my companion is chanting on his beads in the next room. Why is he up at 1 A.M. chanting?

Silence is a form of strength; in it, we find our conviction without distraction. We have to know ourselves, see ourselves at our most Kṛṣṇa conscious. We must strive every day to recover our relationship with our integrity, our previously sacrificed and discarded uniqueness, our sacred interior self which is complete and lacks nothing. Lord Kṛṣṇa also advocates this in the *Bhagavad-gītā*. He doesn't want us to get caught up in a life of sense gratification, even though that is the path chosen by most. ("What is night for most people is the time of awakening for the sage.")

Silence and solitude are part of our lives as revolutionaries, at least at a certain stage. Some never give it up. Śrīla Prabhupāda internalized his Kṛṣṇa consciousness so thoroughly that he didn't need to hide out from the world, although he lived alone for years at Rādhā-Dāmodara temple in Vṛndāvana. He thrived there, felt the peace and inner meditation on Rādhā-Kṛṣṇa's eternal pastimes—which have nothing to do with this world and its movements and māyic suffering. He knew, however, that Kṛṣṇa, his spiritual master, and the previous *ācāryas* wanted the basic teachings of Kṛṣṇa consciousness to go into the world. "It is the duty of leading Indians to spread this culture all over the world at this momentous hour of need."

I've got that broader outlook too, rendering this cultural variety of *Śrīmad-Bhāgavatam*, the offshoot weed known as *A Poor Man*. I pray, but hardly dare to expose it even to myself, that I'd love my work to become influential. Yet we fear it too because we know popularity creates the greatest strain on integrity. Therefore, we leave the fulfillment of that dream up to Kṛṣṇa, whether we will see our work spread. We should plant the seeds and grow a hardy devotional plant. That will appeal to the hearts of honest people. Make it true. We can't—I can't—do both things at once—make it true and popularize it by active propaganda. Others may come and together we may do it—the League of Devotees, the International Society for Krishna Consciousness.

I tap into what gives me the most energy and the best results. That seems realistic. Why work at that which turns me off and leaves me a dissatisfied member? Rather, I write a book, now a long book, and pray my work and I will be accepted. Even within a religious movement, one might be disregarded, seen as a fringe character. Or his preaching may spread in a quiet way. So be it. I've got to write and produce in the quiet of flowing time.

I made another list this morning. What should I do with it? I could ask the same about anything I write, my *Śrīmad-Bhāgavatam* summary, my little comments and insights. Should I fold them into small pieces of paper, place them inside bottles, float them on the river? Polish them? Print them? Put them into more acceptable written forms?

A list looks incomplete, like something to remind us of what we have to do later. "Buy figs and raisins." I could share the list in a more calculated way, but poems are often lists. In other words, our perceptions can be *listed* and that is also a literary form. *Śrīmad-Bhāgavatam* verses contain lists of kings and genealogies. Even Kṛṣṇa's sixty-four qualities can be listed, or the devotee's twenty-six qualities. We can expand on them later. Here's a list. Let it fly if it will.

(1) How to become popular. Why I don't care for this.

(2) Dream scenario that you became popular and tried to escape it. Write on, write on, and fuel the revolution in your own way.

(3) Preserving integrity at all costs.

(4) Wooden desks I've known. Joy of writing at a desk.

(5) Keen hunger.

(6) Fears, phobias.

(7) Body not in control.

(8) Peaceful hours. Sound of surf as heard from a solitary house.

(9) Reality of *guṇḍas* attacking remote temples and *sādhus* at Govardhana and other places.

(10) Too many people around—a hassle.

(11) Privacy.

(12) Claiming people's time and attention through the books I write.

(13) Following the path of the *One*.

(14) Avid student of *Bhāgavatam* texts and learned devotees' commentaries.

(15) Fading light of old age.

(16) Being useful.

(17) The body, the soul.

(18) Birds. Fading eyesight.

(19) Alone, shut in room.

(20) *Brahma-muhūrta* worship and the sun's first slanting rays. Sun ball on the horizon.

(21) Poems as lists, peony and paeon.

(22) One God above all—awareness it can't be accepted by all people in the form of Lord Kṛṣṇa.

(23) Propagate, share it with like-minded.

(24) A poem on the run.

(25) Squatting toilets as superior to sitting ones.

(26) Picking up ideas from books and schools of thoughts.

(27) Plagiarize. Fill your book.

(28) Finding your own unique view even if it is in little personal things. Be true to self—actual experience.

(29) Sheaffer pens.

(30) Your comforts.

(31) Precious days are given to you by God. *You* worship first, never mind if others do not. Introduce it to yourself—for example, chant Hare Kṛṣṇa mantra heart and soul.

We can't get out of the estrangement of this age unless we're pure devotees. The Māyāvādīs can't get out even after declaring that the whole universe is false. Certainly the *karmīs* can't get out. The devotees serve the Lord completely with body, mind, and words. They have nothing left by which they can become ensnared by *māyā*. Even if *māyā* comes to them, they go on chanting Hare Kṛṣṇa. If *māyā* says—in the form of the police or torturers—"Stop chanting!" the devotee chants or prays to God within. He asks God to forgive him for not being able to chant aloud.

As long as he's not so oppressed, he chants loudly. He helps others try to understand how not to become ensnared by *māyā*. He remains aloof even in the midst of bombings, famines, or temptations for sense enjoyment. Try to become him, the devotee who is a lotus on water. As rivers enter the ocean and yet the ocean remains undisturbed, so the sage of steady mind is not disturbed by the incessant flow of desires entering the mind.

Śrīla Prabhupāda was always calm and confident that chanting Kṛṣṇa's glories was the way to save the world and ourselves. Chanting is simple, but world leaders don't recognize it as valid. The next President of America wouldn't be caught dead chanting Hare Kṛṣṇa. "On the contrary, such leaders of the people are against the process of ventilating the glories of the Lord."

They don't know it's the deliberate intervention by the Lord's *māyā* that frustrates all their plans for progress. No eyes to see.

Oh, give me eyes to see
that Kṛṣṇa's beauty is form
and the peace and joy of His names
is our way.
Not so easy I know—
got to desire it.

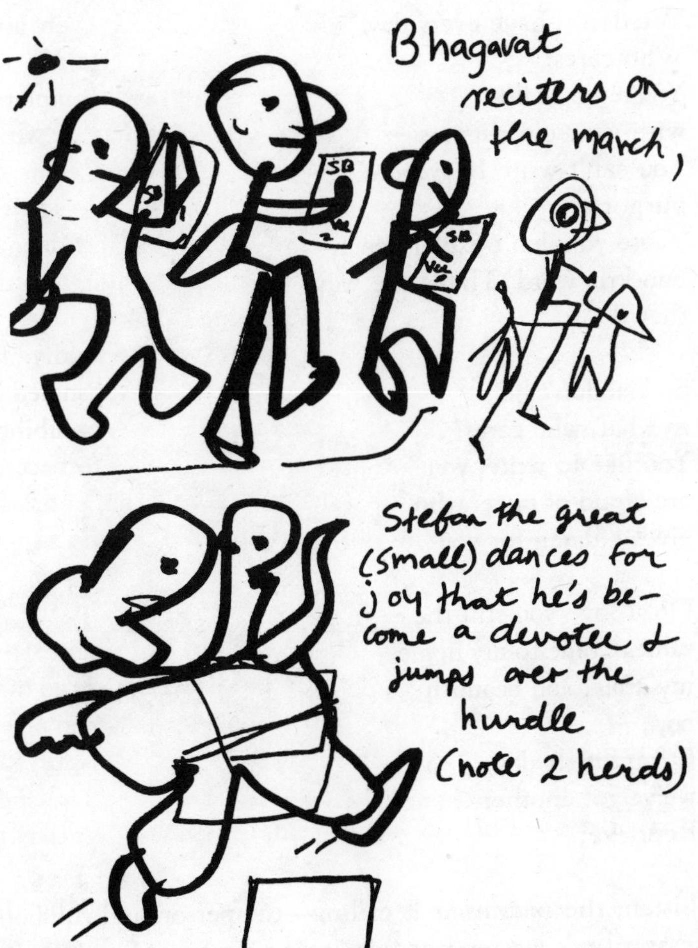

If we become
potent and influential, where
would we lead the world?
Kṛṣṇa may think we would
not bring it to His feet.
Get over the hurdle, open the road.

You don't shave every day.
Who cares?
You're no *sādhu*
with your old slippers.
You can't write *Bhāgavata*
purports
'cause you don't explain each
Sanskrit word. That's the way
they do it.

So you don't lie,
so what, who cares?
You like to write, you
are afraid of mice, who
gives a damn for you?

Oh, I love you still the
same. Come to my home,
my *arms*, you beamish
boy.
O rapturish day,
we've got another chance.
Reprieve.

Listen, the *Bhāgavata* is calling—the person and the book. Our spiritual master wants us to be happy. My volume of *Bhāgavatam* is mine to read. I can even write in the margin if

I care to. What does it say? That fools and asses deride Kṛṣṇa. Those who praise Him can bring peace to the world and they work hard for it.

Guru-like
figure
protects
a
little
one

Text 17

tasya karmāṇy udārāṇi
parigītāni sūribhiḥ
brūhi naḥ śraddadhānānāṁ
līlayā dadhataḥ kalāḥ

His transcendental acts are magnificent and gracious, and great learned sages like Nārada sing of them. Please, therefore, speak to us, who are eager to hear about the adventures He performs in His various incarnations.

Comment

Prabhupāda describes that the Personality of Godhead is the creator of both material and spiritual worlds. Both worlds contain wonders and opulence, but the material energy is like a cinema compared to the spiritual reality. Foolish people think the false show is all there is (as in Plato's analogy of the cave-dwellers). Sages such as Vyāsa and Nārada are interested in the spiritual world. Those who are unaware of this Truth are sometimes favored by the Supreme Lord when He descends to this material world and enacts His transcendental pastimes here. At that time the earth is as good as Vaikuṇṭha because Kṛṣṇa and His direct associates are manifest with all their eternal paraphernalia of *dhāma*, pastimes, and teachings.

There are many incarnations. Some are partial, empowered incarnations and others are full-fledged Viṣṇu *avatāras*, but "Lord Śrī Kṛṣṇa is the fountainhead of all incarnations, and He is therefore the cause of all causes."

Here I am, not only writing a summary of a *Bhāgavatam* verse, but taking time to discover myself. The other day while sitting in the backyard writing this book, I discovered that I like the mixture of self-reflections and *Bhāgavatam* topics. I also felt confident that my self-searching was part of *Bhāgavatam* appreciation and could be valuable to others. One cannot always sustain such confidence, but at that time when I saw it, it felt as if I had just mined a gem. Yesterday when asking myself why I felt bored to repeat the philosophy, I decided it might be a symptom of feeling separation from my spiritual master. This was another good discovery for me and helped me to see positive value even in the seeming negative attitude toward writing straight *paramparā*.

I must go on mining. I'm taking my time and the time of friendly readers to do this. Of course, I already told the readers that they may jump off this train if they're not interested in the asides. I'll say it again, for my sake and yours: this train is stopping at local junctions, where most scriptural commentators never stop. At other times, we're speeding through places where people usually stop. Does that make this trip erratic? Singular? Each one of us is his own engineer and can take folks along his own journey—if they're willing to go. Yet I do it all as service to guru.

Lord Kṛṣṇa comes to this planet as an *avatāra* and walks the earth. The earth planet is then transformed. He's still here and rare souls can see His *līlās* enacted, especially in His "country estates" of Vṛndāvana, Māyāpur, and other sacred places. You can feel it, if you're lucky, even if you can't see the spiritual *dhāma* in full manifestation. You can feel Kṛṣṇa's presence anywhere and everywhere. "Indeed the self-realized soul sees Me in all beings and sees all beings in Me."

God the person. As long as we read *śāstra*, Kṛṣṇa will not fade from our intelligence. That's why the participants at Naimiṣāraṇya were grateful; they had a perfect opportunity to be with *kṛṣṇa-līlā* by hearing from an authorized speaker. By their behavior the sages suggest that everyone should leave the world of vicious habits and fights. Trust in the reality of the spiritual domain, by hearing.

I'm hoping to change by writing this book, not just accumulate pages as I "go through" the *Bhāgavatam*. I'm hoping to benefit by drawing myself close, several times a day, to yet another verse and purport by my spiritual master. I'm hoping to have fun and overcome fear.

Some admissions:

(1) After I do a short summary, I don't feel inclined to say more.

(2) If I had to lecture on this verse, I might get interested and find references.

(3) I admit I catnapped in the chair during writing time. My head slumped forward, I dreamt something, but can't remember what.

(4) I like to range out, write what's on my mind. But even that . . .

(5) I admit I doubt sometimes whether my reflections are worth reading. Maybe they are like the soup the British served the Irish during the famine, a watery, unnourishing liquid. Of course, if I raise such doubts, readers máy agree.

(6) I talk about myself when I write as I please.

(7) So far I find reading the *Ṣaṭ Sandarbhas* dry.

(8) Don't know what to "do" with this list of admissions except select from it and present it. This is all I can do right now.

(9) I don't like the tenor of so much psychological jargon and frame of reference in Sinetar's *Ordinary People As Monks And Mystics*. I do like other things, though, such as the basic pattern or process she finds in people who withdraw from the worldly norm and who have the guts to become socially transcendent, heed their inner calling, become fulfilled and enlightened to some degree, then take the responsibility to care for others. She writes: "The person who fears his own thoughts, who needs others too much, who is overly self-critical or severely attached to his own cultural belief systems and values may not be able to do this work."

Most devotees went through these changes in order to join ISKCON. Some of us, years later, feel a further inner calling. In some cases, devotees leave ISKCON in answer to this. What I liked about the participants in the Sinetar study is that they obeyed their inner calling but stayed in contact with the world. In order to be true to ourselves and our full inner development, we may have to withdraw from some aspects of ISKCON, especially sociopolitical interaction or whatever. But it's not necessary to break ties with society, and certainly not to give up one's relationship with the spiritual master, essential vows, association with devotees, and full acceptance of Kṛṣṇa conscious *siddhānta*.

Sages, ISKCON's illustrations of bearded men
with topknots—probably looked
only a little like that.
Did they get up and "go to the bathroom"
sometimes? Of course they did.
But their needs were simple and mostly
they sat.
When they did walk away and meet
each other, they exchanged soft words.
The life of a monk.

I can't imagine it. I believe they
were highly advanced, their semen
never lost,
their thoughts
and brains enriched by pure cow's milk and
moderate eating. Never mixed with
rot or sold themselves.
They could comprehend. Maybe some
of them were lacking in
pure devotion to Kṛṣṇa, but
that could be taken care of
as they heard submissively
what Sūta heard from Śukadeva.

Text 18

athākhyāhi harer dhīmann
avatāra-kathāḥ śubhāḥ
līlā vidadhataḥ svairam
īśvarasyātma-māyayā

O wise Sūta, please narrate to us the transcendental pastimes of the Supreme Godhead's multi-incarnations. Such auspicious adventures and pastimes of the Lord, the supreme controller, are performed by His internal powers.

Comment

Lord Kṛṣṇa's activities are called *līlās* because they are voluntary acts done with no pressure or taint of karma. We must always remember that we come to this world forced by our past activities of good or bad karma. We are suffering or enjoying our reactions. To take birth in the material world, even into what is considered a materially advantageous or pious birth, is still bad. All material life must go through the miseries common to every *jīva:* birth, death, disease, and old age. These are always miserable and life is temporary—*duḥkhālayam aśāśvatam*. Therefore the *Vedas* teach that the human being's chief purpose is to seek liberation from further birth and death.

Since the Supreme Lord's appearance and incarnations are transcendental and part of the internal energy, they are called *līlās*. Lord Kṛṣṇa states in *Bhagavad-gītā*, "Although I am unborn and My transcendental body never deteriorates, and although I am the Lord of all living entities, I still appear in every millennium in My original transcendental form." (Bg. 4.6)

So auspicious are His *līlās* on earth that those who understand them achieve the highest goal of life. "One who knows the transcendental nature of My appearance and activities does not, upon leaving the body, take his birth again in this material world, but attains My eternal abode, O Arjuna." (Bg. 4.9)

This is true for those who personally witness the *avatāra*'s movements during His appearance on earth as well as for those who hear about Him later.

Someone may ask, "If the *avatāra* is not actually born, then why do we hear of His mother and father? Does He die? Even if He 'disappears' without dying, where does He go?" These and many more questions will be answered in due course by the *Bhāgavatam* speakers. Suffice to say that despite all inquiries about His nature, the Supreme Lord knows His own purpose and is always beyond the view of ordinary people. Lord Kṛṣṇa says He puts a curtain of *yogamāyā* between Himself and the world's fools. Sometimes He deliberately deludes them about Himself. In *Śrīmad-Bhāgavatam*, however, we will learn whatever we need to know to develop a correct understanding and real attraction for Kṛṣṇa and His incarnations. We cannot know everything about God because He is infinite and we are infinitesimal, but correct hearing will invoke our dormant love of Kṛṣṇa, and that is the point.

Kṛṣṇa is our best friend, parent, lover, and master. He is the original guru and protector. The material world ravages all beings in the form of time and devastation. We are tiny pieces of straw on a vast, stormy sea. Only Kṛṣṇa can save us. We seek love, we strive for knowledge, and these come only in our eternal and natural relationships with Lord Kṛṣṇa.

All paths are misleading and fall tragically short of the goal except the path of devotional service unto the Supreme Lord. Most forms of spirituality remain vague, partial. It is unclear in their practice who is God and how one can love Him fully. The ultimate destination is especially vague except in a broad and elementary word, "heaven." *Śrīmad-*

Bhāgavatam, however, will satisfy us on all accounts. It is not Hinduism or "religion." It is science.

Śaunaka seems to be repeating himself some in these verses, but that shows his eagerness and gratitude. He wants to begin. He has already expressed his receptivity and respect toward the guru in *paramparā*. By hearing him, we also become better prepared to be present—no one seems to object—as listeners at this auspicious gathering.

Someone may smile and say, "A few years ago you knew nothing of Kṛṣṇa and the *Vedas*, and now you assert them as irrevocable facts. How did you become such an advanced Vedāntist?" They think we are raw converts repeating the party line.

It's true that we didn't know anything and that now we have adopted and espoused a Vedic life. Someone may have known us before when we were feckless and spouted doubts. They may even spot discrepancies in our present behavior. But we acknowledge them. Prabhupāda praised what might appear as the naive conversion of his disciples. He didn't call it naive, but he appreciated that within a few short years, people who had never even heard about Kṛṣṇa had now made Him the goal of their lives.

The other half of Prabhupāda's comment on that subject: "They were not envious." Therefore, we could hear from him. That nonenviousness was (and is) our qualification.

More admissions and some assertions:

(1) I run on.

(2) I want to convince myself. I feel good when I get worked up by the rhetoric of *kṛṣṇa-kathā*.

(3) When I sit on the *vyāsāsana*, I can't go for more than an hour or an hour and a half. I can answer most questions. Even if the questions are too technical, I've learned to scale them down to basic and important points. I can see people's

motives in their questions. I assert and defend the *Bhāgavatam* conclusion. It's a performance, but a sincere one.

(4) I admit I was a jerk and that I am still foolish, but I've also improved. I used to be even more self-centered than I am now, believe it or not.

(5) I curb my tongue, anger, genitals, and belly, and even my mind and words. I dare to initiate disciples on behalf of my spiritual master.

(6) I realize that it's not proper or standard to talk about one's self so much while speaking Kṛṣṇa consciousness to an audience. Therefore, this writing is more like talking to myself.

(7) Maybe I shouldn't be writing a spiritual diary here, tracking my progress and noting my faults. Such a diary is valuable, but why put it side by side with *Bhāgavatam* purports? I've told you (and me) why I do it, but I know it's odd. What else can I do? "Repairs are under way to make a better airport for you. Please excuse the temporary inconvenience."

(8) He's sorry.

(9) He's voluble (flowing speech).

a confused person somehow starts listening to Krsna katha

(10) Brr. Grunt. Hunkers and hunch.

(11) Learned this run-on not at school. Where? Some New Age writing teachers?

(12) Turn the guy off. Turn down the volume of self. Let's hear the wind in the trees and bushes and under that, waterfalls over a dam.

(13) He writes because a headache twinge is not far away, so he wants to get a quota done before that. The sun is setting quickly. Forgive us. We mean to glorify Kṛṣṇa and His incarnations.

(14) We are each part and parcel of Kṛṣṇa. We are each tiny *īśvaras*. We have a little power of speech. Better use it in His service. God is nigh.

I'm out of touch with the world. I remember my first poems written in imitation of e.e. cummings: "That moment billowing brave and white/ when I loved it/ Is it gone forever?"

I grew up in ISKCON. I feel restless in the institution. There are so many opinions as to what's wrong with ISKCON or what's wrong with those who say what's wrong.

I will die. If I can go to Vṛndāvana to die, if I get such warning, won't it be similar to my last visit—that I won't want to meet people, and so on? Maybe stay at Baladeva's house and die there.

These random thoughts come, but how are they connected to the *Bhāgavatam*? In this way: these thoughts occur while I live and read the *Bhāgavatam*. I read about Naimiṣāraṇya five thousand years ago and think of Prabhupāda in 1960 writing the first volume of his *Bhāgavatam* translation. I am here now in India doing this while these things come to mind. That's the connection. Now whether others think it's a worthy or publishable connection, that's a different topic, but the connection is a natural one. I can't pretend I'm always living in the *Bhāgavatam* texts, but at least I always return to them.

Text 19

vayaṁ tu na vitṛpyāma
uttama-śloka-vikrame
yac-chṛṇvatāṁ rasa-jñānāṁ
svādu svādu pade pade

We never tire of hearing the transcendental pastimes of the Personality of Godhead, who is glorified by hymns and prayers. Those who have developed a taste for transcendental relationships with Him relish hearing of His pastimes at every moment.

Comment

Prabhupāda states that devotees go through their whole lives reading *Bhagavad-gītā* and *Śrīmad-Bhāgavatam* and they keep finding "in them new light of information." Mundane stories and news are static because matter is static. Spirit is dynamic. ("Yes," I say, "yes, I want that dynamism. I want to read and write with new lights and always with relish. Please awaken it in me, dear Lord. I know regular practice will make me eligible for it. I won't be eligible merely by wishing it without opening the books.")

This whole purport swings with positive recommendation for continuous reading and hearing. "Transcendental literature is above the mode of darkness, and its light becomes more luminous with progressive reading and realization of the transcendental subject matter." That's an important point—you don't merely go on reading, but you gain realization and attraction for hearing about Kṛṣṇa. Prabhupāda used to say that attraction was the main criteria: "We don't finally know all about Kṛṣṇa, but we increase our pleasure in hearing about Him."

When we say, "Kṛṣṇa is not a myth," is that dogma? If He's *not* a myth, then what is He? He's the Supreme Personality of Godhead, the Supreme Controller. *Mattaḥ parataram nanyat.*

Yes, but what is He in *your life*? Do you always want to hear more news and instruction about Him? As Prabhupāda writes in a *Bhagavad-gītā* purport, ". . . those who are devotees heartily welcome the statements of Kṛṣṇa when they are spoken by Kṛṣṇa Himself. The devotees will always worship such authoritative statements of Kṛṣṇa because they are always eager to know more and more about Him." (Bg. 4.4, purport)

"Śrī Kṛṣṇa, the Personality of Godhead, who is the Paramātmā [Supersoul] in everyone's heart and the benefactor of the truthful devotee, cleanses desire for material enjoyment from the heart of the devotee who has developed the urge to hear His messages, which are in themselves virtuous when properly heard and chanted." (*Bhāg.* 1.2.17)

Since my service is to write, I certainly want to be in the spiritual camp, not living among the hackneyed modes of ignorance and passion. How can I ensure this? By faithfully reciting scripture. By using my pen, words, life, intelligence, descriptive powers, joys, and struggles in Kṛṣṇa consciousness.

When I taught a seminar on "Prabhupāda Appreciation," I asked the devotees to imagine themselves living in 1966 and meeting Swamijī. One young man, Paramānanda dāsa, wrote that instead of writing poetry as he usually does, he wrote about his struggle to come to Kṛṣṇa consciousness. "And you know what? I felt better when I did." That's transcendental writing too, the aspiring devotee's earnest attempts, his jotting down how he's trying to be a devotee. It's "literature in pursuance of the Vedic version," even though the pursuance is at a great distance and the *Vedas* are being pursued by a beginner.

Prabhupāda said (while on the Bowery), "I am glad to say that this Mr. Paul sometimes says to me, 'Swamijī, I want to attain spiritual life immediately!' Yes, I say to him, be patient, be patient. Surely with such determination, Kṛṣṇa will help you."

Patient but active in spiritual life. Tell us what you know about Kṛṣṇa. Pray. Beg to become a Vaiṣṇava. Beg the senses to stop driving you. Describe the world as hellish without Kṛṣṇa. Track your progress. Admit your wrongs. Express yourself, but be careful that you don't indulge in feeling yourself the creator. You're not the creator who is to be exulted, or the main actor who is to be described, by your "*uttamaśloka*." Turn to Kṛṣṇa, that Other Person in your life. He is maintaining all beings. You are one of them. Your acts are insignificant compared to His. Your worth is only in your turning to Him in *sambandha*, *abhidheya*, and hopes for *prayojana*. Don't be envious of Kṛṣṇa enjoying with the *gopīs* and speaking so expertly.

Hear patiently. Stay in the fire with all your iron rods. And please write.

I'm just coming from the potency and enthusiasm of that purport. Keep reading *Bhagavad-gītā* and *Śrīmad-Bhāgavatam* your whole life; don't read or write mundane news.

"Mundane news" does not include what we do in connection to our Kṛṣṇa consciousness. If that includes sometimes talking of birds, we forgive each other. Even Prabhupāda sometimes spoke of the old days in Calcutta and didn't always say, "Kṛṣṇa said this, Kṛṣṇa said that." Of course, those moments were small ones amid his preaching, but we relished *anything* he said. It helped us relax with him and see him as a person who also grew up, who played with friends and rode bikes through Dalhousie Square to the Maidan, who flew kites with his sister, both praying to Bhagavān to please let it fly. Yes, he was always thinking of Kṛṣṇa. He wanted Kṛṣṇa Deities as his worshipable couple, went to see Rādhā-

Govinda and liked to gaze at Them, satisfied, for hours. He was no ordinary child.

I want to recite the *Bhāgavatam* naturally. Do I mean that it will eventually be pure and all dross will be excluded? Prabhupāda even near the end sometimes remembered how his Scottish teachers pronounced "duty" as "jyuty." We relished it!

But I'm not Prabhupāda. When I speak a "mundane" reference, it's not so relishable because matter—stale cigarette smoke, the jangling of the cash register at the bar while the jazz band plays on—is static and spirit is dynamic.

Tell us of *uttama-śloka* even
while the mice make noise and
run in and out under the
door. Let them do their thing—
do you think Mahārāja Parīkṣit or the
sages at Naimiṣāraṇya were disturbed if
a mouse ran by?
"What if it were a lion?"

Uttama-śloka lifted the earth
on His snout, Govardhana
on His left pinkie. He spoke
as befits in *Bhagavad-gītā*. A
friend of Prabhupāda's said to him,
"I like Kṛṣṇa of the battlefield
of Kurukṣetra, but not Kṛṣṇa
of Vṛndāvana." Śrīla Prabhupāda replied,
"That's all right. If you are not so fortunate
as to like Kṛṣṇa in Vṛndāvana, then
go to Arjuna-Kṛṣṇa. That's
also Kṛṣṇa." But hear from
Him. *Tat śṛṇu.*
Kṛṣṇa says He's the taste in water.

He grants fearlessness to *nārāyaṇa-para.*
I . . . I don't know Sanskrit
but my Guru Mahārāja
has told me about Kṛṣṇa.

The sages are fired up, not hyped. It is their natural state to feel deep appreciation. They make it clear what they want to hear. No Māyāvādī talk, no nonsense, nothing mundane. "We never tire, we shall never be at rest or satiated by hearing the transcendental pastimes of the Personality of Godhead. We enjoy associating with Him and relish hearing of His pastimes at every moment."

From the back of the head, hand, the smooth pen leaves behind the text only to find it later at sea.

"Nonsense!" Prabhupāda said it was nonsense to tell Americans to give up Christianity for Hinduism. "If I said that," Prabhupāda said, "they would have kicked in my face. I never said such nonsense that you become Hindu. I said *here is God*, Kṛṣṇa." Many friends told him that he should name his movement the International Society for God Consciousness, but he said it was better to be plain and straight: Kṛṣṇa is God. Kṛṣṇa is not a Hindu God; Kṛṣṇa consciousness is a science.

Switch pens and let it rip. Pinto panting breaths and my hand doesn't judge what comes out, which memories, I mean. My hand can't write fast enough. I remember suicides and other men and women now dead and gone. Me too, me too. That will be the real laugh. I am not an exception.

Murray gave up Lucky
Strike cigarettes after 20 years he wrote
and sent me a card by Chagall of Moses
giving 10 Commandments, cultural item
no doubt. Good-bye forever. If I
see any old pals, I'll tell them, "Hare Kṛṣṇa Hare Kṛṣṇa,
Kṛṣṇa Kṛṣṇa Hare Hare.
Hare Rāma Hare Rāma, Rāma Rāma Hare Hare."
Reichean Ph.D is Harry Lewis. I got some smart
Jewish friends, you bet.
Hare Kṛṣṇa Smith. Guarino joined that
cult. Heard his Irish mom rejected
him. Good for her. Cabbage
and potatoes.
God and the strength of my good right arm.
Mom, I bless you.

Steer to the sages at Naimiṣarāṇya. They were eager to hear. Mundane stories are static. We get tired and can't read *Ulysses* or *The Brothers Karamazov* endlessly. *Bhāgavatam* and *Bhagavad-gītā*, yes. They discuss Uttama-śloka.

The 1962 edition of *Bhāgavatam*, which Prabhupāda himself printed in New Delhi and later brought to America, has a special flavor. Sometimes I like to read this unedited version to get a more precise focus on the actual meaning. To describe this flavor, I was going to use the word "quaint," but that won't do. All that means is old-fashioned, unusual, strange. His Indian-printed book is pleasing but can't be savored by nondevotees or grammarians or people who don't love Prabhupāda. Here's his translation to *Bhāgavatam* 1.1.19:

> We shall never be in rest even though continuously hearing the transcendental pastimes of the Personality of Godhead who is glorified by good prayers. Those who have developed the particular humour of transcendental mellow, do relish in every step such description of pastimes of the Lord.

It's potent. It rescued many of us. It gave us God. What more could we ask?

Text 20

kṛtavān kila karmāṇi
saha rāmeṇa keśavaḥ
atimartyāni bhagavān
gūḍhaḥ kapaṭa-mānuṣaḥ

Lord Śrī Kṛṣṇa, the Personality of Godhead, along with Balarāma, played like a human being, and so masked He performed many superhuman acts.

Comment

Since the original Godhead and His first expansion are mentioned here, Prabhupāda takes the occasion to deride false incarnations. He comes close to naming names when he says self-made incarnations are especially popular in Bengal, and that God cannot "be manufactured or declared" by popular vote.

Śrī Kṛṣṇa was always God, even in the lap of His mother. He killed Pūtana when He was three months old and lifted Govardhana Hill when He was seven years old. These are extraordinary feats, almost unbelievable, if we consider Kṛṣṇa to be an ordinary child.

The *Bhāgavatam* verse states that He masks Himself as a human being but He is actually the Supreme Being. As the Supreme Lord, He kills everyone through the time factor and holds up all the earth's mountain ranges, all the planets in outer space, and all the seas and skies. We shouldn't be so astounded that we cannot believe that Kṛṣṇa performed superhuman acts in His human-like incarnation.

Kṛṣṇa's birth and activities are all transcendental. If we understand them properly, that knowledge alone can grant us entrance into the spiritual world. The sages would not be interested in hearing about an ordinary, or even an extraordinary, mortal. They are only interested in hearing about Kṛṣṇa and Baladeva, who, although resembling human brothers, were actually the Supreme Lord and His first expansion.

When Śrī Kṛṣṇa appeared in Vṛndāvana, His mother and father mistook Him to be their child. This misunderstanding was dictated by their intense desire to protect Kṛṣṇa in parental love. Kṛṣṇa's internal energy, Yogamāyā, allowed Kṛṣṇa and His parents to enjoy the sweet exchanges of parents and child without being bothered by the awe and majesty usually felt in a relationship between God and His devotee.

It's not that Yaśodā and Nanda saw Kṛṣṇa as human due to a lack of devotion, as is the case with philosophers and fools who deride Kṛṣṇa when they hear of His activities in Vraja. Of those nonbelievers, Kṛṣṇa says, "In that deluded condition, their hopes for liberation, their fruitive activities, and their culture of knowledge are all defeated." (Bg. 9.12) In his purport to that verse, Prabhupāda states, "There are many devotees who assume themselves to be in Kṛṣṇa consciousness and devotional service but at heart do not accept the Supreme Personality of Godhead, Kṛṣṇa, as the Absolute

Truth. For them, the fruit of devotional service—going back to Godhead—will never be tasted."

This statement is startling in that Śrīla Prabhupāda detects a lack of conviction even in those who want to be seen as devotees. Our conviction about Kṛṣṇa must therefore become deep and real. We should clear our doubts by inquiring from the spiritual master, just as Arjuna expressed doubts about Kṛṣṇa ("How could You have spoken to the sun-god so long ago?") to his guru, the Supreme Lord.

Arjuna's conversation with Kṛṣṇa took place a long time ago, but the record of it still exists in this world in authorized books. The *mūḍhas* deny Kṛṣṇa and receive their just punishment. I'm not among them, but neither can I claim to be a devotee who accepts Kṛṣṇa "at heart." If I did love Kṛṣṇa, how could I live so complacently? Yesterday, the high point of my day was the delicious taste and satisfaction I felt while eating lunch. My low point was when I met a headache at 4 P.M. A pure devotee's lows and highs are all intimately connected with Kṛṣṇa ("I could not attain the Lord of Mathurā!" Or, "I am so grateful to be able to chant, despite my fallen nature, that tears are flowing from my eyes."). All his ups and downs are transcendental.

Kṛṣṇa and Balarāma, masked as human beings, running through the forest with Their cowherd boyfriends, blowing horns and trading lunches, tending cows and calves, wrestling in the grass, imitating animals and encountering demons easily subdued by Keśava—why doesn't that picture rise in my heart throughout the day? At least I'm always engaged in His service and anxious to not waste time.

We do much wrong and don't dive deep into *bhakti*. Last night Madhu said that his low point was a moment when he saw his *japa* was inattentive and couldn't get it under control. When I heard that, I thought, "Why don't I have such profound low points? That's where it's at, chanting and hearing and lamenting our lack of devotion to *sādhana*."

Personally, I like it when an author tells us what he's doing while he writes his book. Most authors don't do that, but I always look for it when I read. I recall an essay on Thoreau by E. B. White where White tells us he is writing in a shack and a chipmunk or some similar animal is nearby. He says that his setting for the writing seems appropriate for the subject, the naturalist-philosopher Thoreau. Why don't authors do this more?

What about me? If a writer is defined as someone ordered by his spiritual master to write in *paramparā*, fine; it's a traditional service and the guru is proud of a disciple who prosecutes it nicely. It may be that the disciple inherited his writing proclivity from past karma and that it was once a misused talent. Now, however, he uses it to purify himself.

If he is climbing out of past karma, he may still be impressed with mundane authors. Names pop up from the psyche—the backlog of authors whose books he's read. The list seems endless.

There were many authors I once loved, or pretended to love, so I could carve the image of myself as a literary man. I didn't want to be a carpenter, a naval officer, a baseball hero, a chemist, or a businessman. I read and assimilated novels, poems, and essays. I discovered at seventeen that I could write passable English compositions—not just for school grades, but for my own use as a growing person (secret diary) and as—dare I hope?—material for a literary career. Now I want to make literature and simultaneously write to purify and discover myself and my way. But be careful about that creative drive; use it all in *bhakti*.

The birds are chirping. This place has a funny name, Khargone. English, they say, is pitifully irregular and corrupt compared to Sanskrit. It's filled with allusions to beefeaters, bullies, Christians, and a doctrinaire's life, whereas Sanskrit is Kṛṣṇa-ized, or at least closer to that. Still, we speak English and Prabhupāda said it was the best language for preaching because people all over the world speak it and it can also be easily translated.

Text 21

kalim āgatam ājñāya
kṣetre 'smin vaiṣṇave vayam
āsīnā dīrgha-satreṇa
kathāyāṁ sakṣaṇā hareḥ

Knowing well that the age of Kali has already begun, we are assembled here in this holy place to hear at great length the transcendental message of Godhead and in this way perform sacrifice.

Comment

In former ages, people lived for thousands of years under more favorable circumstances. In Kali-yuga no one lives more than a hundred years. Violent death often occurs in car accidents, murders, wars, etc. People are slow and bad, especially when it comes to self-realization. With all this in mind, we have been given only chanting and hearing about Kṛṣṇa as He is presented in *Bhagavad-gītā* and *Śrīmad-Bhāgavatam* to perform. If someone tries to advance spiritually by any other method, even if that method was valid in a previous age—yoga, meditation, sacrifice, *jñāna-yoga*, and so on—he will be wasting his time. Lord Caitanya taught Rāmānanda Rāya that even the gradual development through *varṇa* and *āśrama* isn't possible in Kali-yuga because the eternal *varṇāśrama-dharma* is jeopardized by Kali-yuga's inauspicious features.

Therefore, chant and hear, chant and hear. That's what Lord Caitanya recommends and it's what the sages at Naimiṣāraṇya encourage.

"Only this process will work." It sounds like a desperate statement, but it's true. It's an injunction that must be followed. Therefore, it is declared in the *Bṛhan-nāradīya Purāṇa* that there is "No other way, no other way, no other way except chanting the holy names of God."

Hearing and chanting is presented as an easy dispensation which makes for pleasant progress despite the age of Kali. Kali is an ocean of vice, but the process of chanting and hearing has such power that it alone makes up for all the disadvantages. Thus the worst age becomes the best age for making quick spiritual progress.

Śrīla Prabhupāda alludes to *bhāgavata-dharma*, a system of preaching *Bhagavad-gītā* and *Śrīmad-Bhāgavatam*, repeatedly. He urged his disciples to hold *bhāgavata-dharma* discourses, as he himself did for a week at New Vrindaban in 1972. Kṛṣṇa's message should be broadcast widely by capable speakers, especially *sannyāsīs*. Indian citizens should be aware of their duty to participate in such discussions, and they should help broadcast the message in whatever way they can.

This is the rhetoric devotees use, but we mean it. Participation in such preaching also lies on our shoulders. *Yāre dekha, tāre kaha 'kṛṣṇa'-upadeśa*, tell whomever you meet about Kṛṣṇa. Become guru. Be evangelistic. Go out and preach. Don't live only for your own comfort. Be a preacher. Support preachers.

People who are initiated into *hari-nāma-dīkṣā* and who have taken second initiation may slow down after years of forced or forceful preaching and take care of themselves and their families. They also sometimes get soured running errands for the big, recognized preachers and *sannyāsīs*. And the institution sometimes turns preaching into mostly fund-raising. Or the call to "Preach!" becomes strident and appeals mostly to young recruits. There are not as many young recruits, however, as there were in the past.

There are problems, but the call still comes down through the ages, and persons still receive the divine preaching spark, the desire to give Kṛṣṇa consciousness to others. We eagerly await the time when *bhāgavata-dharma* days will usher in Kṛṣṇa consciousness for the masses. We hope to be part of that even now.

> " . . . you should always be humble: 'Kṛṣṇa, I am quite unfit. So whatever I could collect with my capacity, kindly accept.' This is our only plea. Otherwise, don't be proud that 'I am doing so much for Kṛṣṇa. Kṛṣṇa will be obliged to accept it.' It is not like that. *Tṛṇād api sunīcena taror api suhiṣṇunā*. This is wanted."
>
> —Śrīla Prabhupāda lecture, August 15, 1974, Vṛndāvana

That is my mood in writing this book. Please accept it, dear Lord Kṛṣṇa, dear Śrīla Prabhupāda. I am a poor man. I was born in the darkness of ignorance. *Nīca jāti nīca-saṅgī, patita adhama:* my birth, upbringing, association, and habits are all bad. Even my inclinations are not perfect. I chant, but poorly. Never mind. I offer you the best I can; I offer you my love.

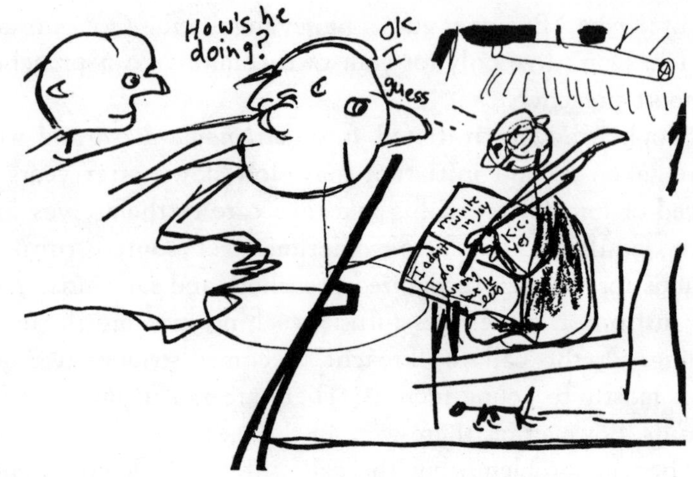

Some admissions and complaints:

(1) I'm grouchy.

(2) Sometimes Madhu and I sound like two tired old men as we complain how others let us down and don't bring things on time or the way we like them. At times like that, I don't like to be with such a tired old monk and I don't like to be one either.

(3) I don't like it when someone argues with me when I say, "I think I'm too thin and would like to put on weight."

(4) Don't be too self-critical, the psychologists say. Okay. Shall I say that my chanting of *japa* and *gāyatrī* is the best I can do?

(5) This is an unusual, diffuse, "poor" book. Nevertheless, I assert it.

(6) Be humble, Śrīla Prabhupāda says. I am proud and weak. I stumble. I talk anyway.

I don't know how the sages expected to live a thousand years to do the *yajña* if in Kali no one lives that long, but the numbers don't trouble my brain. They could do it—Kṛṣṇa could let them live that long for such a noble purpose. I hope He lets me live twenty more years or whatever. I hope He lets me keep at this *yajña* for a great length, the *saṅkīrtana* of *A Poor Man Reads The Bhāgavatam*. "A prolonged programme," Śrīla Prabhupāda calls it in his 1962 edition of *Śrīmad-Bhāgavatam*.

"The sages of Naimiṣāraṇya began this process in that specific land for the devotees of the Lord. They became ready for hearing for a prolonged time even for one thousand of years as the programme was so made."

Juice is coming just now
a glass of it watered
from a well—in India!
Juice is coming in a stainless steel cup,
a small gold-plated one to place
on Śrīla Prabhupāda's altar
and a bigger one for me.
Will it be grape?
It will be disappointment if I
live to drink, to eat, to be
merry, and then die.

Sages returning to the Naimisaranya yajna after passing stool and bathing.

A blackbird sings one sweet note as the sun goes down. Servant Lakshman's duties with Madhu mostly done. He walks to the bridge above the dam and looks down at the water. What is real? I could muse.

Real tired. Sweater frayed. Sound of water through dam. Late sounds. Labor is easy but constant.

A long work projected for Sūta and the sages. How could they last a thousand years just on the *Śrīmad-Bhāgavatam's* 18,000 verses?

Can I last? I once calculated for Prabhupāda on a morning walk in Allston, "Swamijī, you've completed the Third Canto. At this rate, if every X number of months you do another canto, how many years would it take?" Prabhupāda stopped to calculate for a few moments—it caught his interest—but then he let it go. Wearing a coat and a swami hat, walking those dreadful, dirty streets near Boston University, he said something like, "I'm trying my best. *It is up to Kṛṣṇa.*"

Text 22

tvaṁ naḥ sandarśito dhātrā
dustaraṁ nistitīrṣatām
kaliṁ sattva-haraṁ puṁsāṁ
karṇa-dhāra ivārṇavam

We think that we have met Your Goodness by the will of providence, just so that we may accept you as captain of the ship for those who desire to cross the difficult ocean of Kali, which deteriorates all the good qualities of a human being.

Comment

Human life is meant for self-realization, but people nowadays are blind to this purpose. They live only for sense gratification. There are, of course, some people who speak of self-actualization, finding one's self, becoming healed, whole, spiritual, and so on. They are even willing to give up one sense satisfaction for another. But who understands plainly that one life leads to another? Prabhupāda states in his '62 edition, " . . . they do not know that this spot-life is but a fragment of our journey towards self-realization."

I keep finding that Kṛṣṇa consciousness is of a singular standard. It occupies the spiritual ground by itself. It is way above the rest. This is why I am justified in reading only Kṛṣṇa conscious books. (By the way, I'm anxious to rectify my earlier statement that the *Ṣaṭ Sandarbhas* are dry. I'm back reading them in the little spare time that I have, and I'm finding them profitable. Śrīla Jīva Gosvāmī is our worshipable master, another captain for all Gauḍīya Vaiṣṇavas. It's true that his conclusions are already gathered in Prabhupāda's purports, but reading him verse by verse, as well as reading the comments by my learned Godbrothers, is edifying. Jīva Gosvāmī's *Sandarbhas* are that type of literature—singular, distinguished, above everything outside the Gauḍīya Vaiṣṇava tradition. Nothing else matches their standard.)

Transmigration—living this life with awareness that I have many lives to go and that I must make progress for going back to Godhead. This is the beginning of education for a human being, although it's largely denied or thought of in a dreamy, speculative way in the West. Buddhism's concept of it also seems unstated. The plain facts are in Kṛṣṇa consciousness. Who else provides this ship for crossing Kali? "The ship is the message of Lord Śrī Kṛṣṇa in the shape of *Bhagavad-gītā* or the *Śrīmad-Bhāgavatam*."

We may sometimes feel uneasy about our exclusive studies. If as a writer I wish to reach out and be accepted by readers in addition to my Kṛṣṇa conscious friends, then following *siddhānta* may seem confining. But this is my home. How can I abandon clear and definite knowledge in favor of compromises with the vague? I may try to present Kṛṣṇa consciousness in a way others will appreciate, but not that I should feel that Kṛṣṇa consciousness is sectarian. It stands apart by its superiority. People outside it regard it as insular, but that's their mistake. They will always reject Kṛṣṇa because He is so much a person. Kṛṣṇa will not be compromised. He's not just one of many gods or a symbol of what we can all become—a well-actualized man, a theistic concept introduced by early mankind, an Indianism, and so on. Śrī Kṛṣṇa cannot be trifled with. Take Him as the Supreme Person or not.

I take Him. I accept. I bow down, I chant His names, I want the International Society for Krishna Consciousness to thrive and improve and accept many souls in its shelter. If we appear cut off from the masses and even from New Age and other religious faiths, we can try to overcome that by better communication, but we cannot deny the clear facts of transmigration and all the other essential and beautiful gems of Kṛṣṇa conscious *siddhānta* as presented in *Bhagavad-gītā* and *Śrīmad-Bhāgavatam*, our ship for crossing Kali.

Even though I jump off to personal talk, I feel faithful. I need room, I claim, to talk about how I feel, to divest myself of a straitjacket feeling that I'm only allowed to say what's perfect. But it's not that I am inclined to spout doctrines other than Kṛṣṇa conscious ones, or to switch ships or captains.

" . . . this brief life is but a moment on our great journey towards self-realization." Don't live for the pleasure of the tongue or body, or for fame or security of flesh and blood. We'll have to give it up anyway and then it will be burned on the funeral pyre or put in a coffin to rot. Think of the soul's interest, which goes on to a next life according to our activities in this life. Our deeds start with prayer and thought *and with whatever we hear*.

One might ask, "Why do the sages praise Śrīla Sūta Gosvāmī as a captain? Why make him sound more important or better than the rest? All he's doing is *speaking*." Speaking and hearing are important. If we hear from someone, he becomes our captain and can guide us or misguide us. In this case, a person who can steadily, unfailingly speak Kṛṣṇa's message in *paramparā* is certainly worth being called the captain and is worth following with obedience.

Apollinaire never
was a devotee in Kṛṣṇa consciousness and part of
the GBC meetings where one leader
jumped over the table to contest the
challenge from another who wanted to take
over the Canary Islands.

Apollinaire never
joined ISKCON. He did not accept Sūta
as the captain of the ship. He did however
write strange poems of the modern
(19th century) saying the Eiffel Tower
was great and women are wonderful,
soft arms and wet eyes and
all that.

I better be a straight *sannyāsī*
and not talk of what Apollinaire
didn't do. Or maybe I should
persist
for the cause of humankind—
men and women happy together in ISKCON.
Make best use of my brief time
in the ship as we cross
together. It's a fact we make
progress as a crew.

I praise the individual.
I learned that from Śrī Kṛṣṇa and
Śrīla Prabhupāda—we each go alone and
a good son improves the whole
family just as one flower improves
the fragrance of the forest.

Apollinaire never changed his socks
the way I do. He didn't live for
awhile in South India or south of
Paris with the bliss to be given
a task of *staying close to*
the *Bhāgavatam*. That's what my master said
(as I envisioned in
room 42 of Krishna-Balaram Guesthouse):
"Whatever you do, stay close to
Śrīmad-Bhāgavatam, faithful to its words, and
don't go away. As for your
own nonsense, what can I say?
If you don't take it so seriously,
I won't either."

Or to put it another way—
I do declare a little life is
truth, but it's within Kṛṣṇa consciousness.
We are all *jīva* servants.
Only our *tapasya* will reveal these truths.
I too am pulling at the rope
in the Ratha-yātrā of the spirit.
My soul is young but
I sometimes feel sad and tired, an old monk,
at different times of the day.
I just want to be myself.

We accept Sūta Gosvāmī as the captain of the ship and we accept Prabhupāda as the captain of the latest ship in the Kṛṣṇa conscious armada going back to the spiritual world. If you don't become perfect on this cruise, then you'll be born as a crew member in another fleet ship with another competent captain. Or, it is said, you will find your eternal spiritual master life after life.

Please accept me, Gurudeva. Let me come onboard not with a heavy heart but with my duffel bag manfully on my shoulder and eager to meet adventure. May I serve and sit at the dinner table satisfied with whatever *prasādam* is offered to the crew and take up work under the petty officer assigned to us. Even though he may be imperfect, he is part of the hierarchy where the captain is beloved and the ship guided unerringly.

The mice, it seems, are stirring under the bed. Maybe that other sound is the branches scratching against the window. Tiny gnats under the desk light. Remember? One day Prabhupāda was leaving Krishna-Balaram Mandir (1976) to go on his morning walk. Viśala dāsa stood before him and recited this *śloka* out loud: "We think that we have met Your Goodness . . . " Prabhupāda interrupted him and said, "Do something useful. Here is a puddle of dirty water. Clean it up." Viśala was shocked, but he gave up his loud recitation in favor of practical service.

We think your goodness—
do something useful!

Words don't make sense. They can't convey what's in Turīya dāsa's heart as he goes to the hospital, or me,
a pea
a lunch plate for all.
God . . .

Words don't always have to be logical. They have a sense of their own. This, therefore, is a different kind of literature. It will arrive at Kṛṣṇa consciousness in its own way and I'll be satisfied.

Poor man! Poor man!

Beggar! He's got bugs in his hair, smells bad, old clothes. Not like us clean Americans with our cheap, store-bought clothes and fads and rings. He ain't got a TV and he lives in an old refrigerator carton house. Ha! Poor man, your *Bhāgavatam* notes are a joke. It's a patched quilt with a hole in it.

He smiles at them like Charlie Chaplin's man, little fella.

What do you want?
Big happy book, Cheerios for b'fast
want highway rip-roar at pre-dawn
Snyder poems, mine even better—
better, best, superlative Kṛṣṇa battleship
Potemkin, Russian soul ballet
snows and springs and wheat and cows munching and Paramānanda back. Oh, you can't have heaven on earth your way.

I mean, what do you want in your *book*? Where do you want to go with it?

I want categories and growth, memories, exercises. The inner voice of wisdom (doesn't have to be logical), Kṛṣṇa consciousness. Allow many people to teach the VIHE. Yamarāja dāsa is designing BTG. I've got my own world.

Sometimes I repeat like a lecturer instead of a rumba man. (They met us as our plane landed in Santo Domingo, five guys playing merengue and offering passengers Cola drinks on a tray. No thanks, we feel harassed enough just filling out the tourist forms before we're allowed to enter the world of simple devotees.)

"I think we have met Your Goodness by the will of providence." Yes, Prabhupāda's coming was providential.

Give us some drawings of the sages accepting Sūta as the captain of their ship.

We caught a frog in a rat basket.

But why write memories?

Because they're another source leading to Kṛṣṇa.

Sūta answered the questions one by one. But this is the age of Kali. No quarter is given. They shot the Civil War soldiers. "Run!" they yelled. "Run for your lives." When they tried to run away, they shot them dead.

I shouldn't tell that? What should I tell instead? About lemonade on a creaky, old, wooden porch? About lynched black men? Pinched apricots? Kali-yuga is a stink pile of life's garbage.

Text 23

brūhi yogeśvare kṛṣṇe
brahmaṇye dharma-varmaṇi
svāṁ kāṣṭhām adhunopete
dharmaḥ kaṁ śaraṇaṁ gataḥ

Since Śrī Kṛṣṇa, the Absolute Truth, the master of all mystic powers, has departed for His own abode, please tell us to whom the religious principles have now gone for shelter.

Comment

Dharmaṁ tu sākṣāt bhagavat-praṇītaṁ—the Supreme Lord Himself enacts religious principles. Religion refers to God's laws. The Supreme Person not only gives the religious codes, but He appears to establish their prestige and to support them whenever they are neglected.

"Whenever and wherever there is a decline in religious practice, O descendent of Bharata, and a predominate rise of irreligion—at that time I descend Myself. To deliver the pious and to annihilate the miscreants, as well as to reestablish the principles of religion, I Myself appear, millennium after millennium." (Bg. 4.7–8)

The sages are aware of Lord Kṛṣṇa's recent *līlās*, His birth in Mathurā, His childhood in Gokula and Vṛndāvana, His killing Kaṁsa in Mathurā, His adventures in and out of Dvārakā, and His disappearance from the earth. They have already expressed their eagerness to hear of Kṛṣṇa's activities. They know that the Supreme Lord upheld religious principles by His personal prowess and that He killed the demons. They also know that He killed many demons during His other incarnations and that He taught ultimate *dharma* in the *Bhagavad-gītā*. Therefore, it may be that they are feeling apprehensive as they ask this last question in Chapter One: now that Kṛṣṇa has disappeared from our sight, who will protect humankind from evil elements?

Prabhupāda assures us that the answer will be given later. It is one of the most important questions the sages ask and Sūta will directly reply to it in the third chapter. However, Prabhupāda ends his last purport of Chapter One with this statement: "The *Śrīmad-Bhāgavatam* is the transcendental sound representation of the Personality of Godhead, and thus it is the full representation of transcendental knowledge and religious principles."

That's the answer. Whenever Kṛṣṇa is absent—as He travels from universe to universe—the *Śrīmad-Bhāgavatam* acts on His behalf. Everything Kṛṣṇa is is also in the *Śrīmad-Bhāgavatam*; hearing, studying, and practicing the *Bhāgavatam's* teachings are as good as being in Kṛṣṇa's personal presence.

Therefore, Kṛṣṇa's devotees cleave to the *Bhāgavatam* and teach it to others. Śrīla Jīva Gosvāmī's *Ṣaṭ Sandarbhas* were written to establish the *Bhāgavatam* as the supreme *pramāṇa*, the standard of knowledge. Prabhupāda chose to translate and write purports on the *Bhāgavatam* as his vocation and literary opus. We can feel safe playing and studying in the backyard and lecture hall of the *mahā Purāṇa*.

We might say in an analagous way that as Kṛṣṇa protects religion through the *Śrīmad-Bhāgavatam*, so ISKCON and Prabhupāda's followers protect his translation of the *Bhāgavatam* after his disappearance. Prabhupāda's books will become the law books for thousands of years. Beyond that, by studying Prabhupāda's *Bhāgavatam*, we can be with him.

At breakfast, Madhu and I heard Prabhupāda say that we can't stick only to *vaidhi-bhakti*. We have to go further. He said that *rāgānugā-bhakti* was above following the rules and regulations, although follow we must. How to get there? We can't just jump up and become *gopīs*. He said that we should become serious and sincere.

That's a lifetime's worth of work—become serious and sincere. Therefore, best we don't give up. After declaring that they would stay for a prolonged sacrifice, do you think the sages at Naimiṣāraṇya took a week off and went home to their wives, beds, and jobs? Neither did Śrīla Vyāsadeva sigh and quit after twenty-three verses and say, "I've run out of things to say." And of course, Prabhupāda didn't quit writing when he lived in Vṛndāvana and had to travel to Delhi to get it printed. The sages had a vision; Vyāsadeva had a vision; Prabhupāda had a vision, a dream of going to America with several printed volumes of his *Bhāgavatam* and giving them to the world. No one quit. Neither will I.

I mentioned earlier that memories can lead to Kṛṣṇa consciousness. How do they do that? Memories are a reservoir of expression. Something happened, got buried, and still lives. Without them, what are we? Only the present—narrow and instant. For example, without memories, where is my relationship with Śrīla Prabhupāda? I wouldn't know him as my friend and guru and I wouldn't be able to continue reading his book unless I had memories.

Does that mean we should open the floodgates to our memories? How will we discriminate between those memories that will lead us to Kṛṣṇa consciousness and those that won't? Maybe we can't make the discrimination. At least not all at once. Sometimes we have to just allow them to come and receive them with respect. They'll pass through us. What's valuable will stick and the dross will float away. It's like *yukta-vairāgya*. You can use an old scarf and you can use an old memory.

I remember many things, but right now I can't choose one to share. My memories are like fish looking at the opening I made in their tank and deciding who will come through first. I can't take much time with any one of you fellows, so come on, one of you come through. Don't be scared. I'm not going to eat you.

Roberta Kaplan walked up to the bench where I was sitting on the Brooklyn College campus. She was a few years younger than me. We were mildly attracted to each other. She wanted a man to attack her like a leopard, she said. I was too Catholic for that. I was a sad lad in a drab olive raincoat.

I remember, but I don't want to—those Brooklyn College days.

Then how about ISKCON memories? In Dodge vans driving with the library party *brahmacārīs* all over America, mapping out the country, each university, me their caretaker reading *Caitanya-caritāmṛta* manuscripts before they were published by the BBT and talking about the Swami.

Nothing vivid in my head. My memory of Mahābuddhi dāsa is vivid though—an ex-football player from San Diego State University. Everything I touch seems sad now. Mahābuddhi, the last I heard, was an unhappy administrator at a Florida hospital. Am I equally estranged? I dreamt I was crying in loneliness. I was on a big civilian ship. I went to the area where I usually slept, but different people now occupied that space. I knew that it shouldn't matter where you lie down, so I took a place there saying, "This looks like a new neighborhood." Then I began to shed profuse, lonely tears.

Remember shopping bags, *Śrīmad-Bhāgavatam* books, shopping carts—metal A&P carts on wheels, remember this morning chanting the first nine rounds loud and clear but with no devotion? An hour ago outside, I looked at the sun ball and walked in the grass yard, feeling empty, counting beads, and chanting Hare Kṛṣṇa Hare Kṛṣṇa, Kṛṣṇa Kṛṣṇa Hare Hare/ Hare Rāma Hare Rāma, Rāma Rāma Hare Hare.

Where are religious principles now
that Lord Kṛṣṇa has departed?
Why did He depart and
when is He coming back?
O Sūta, select from the
scriptures that which will interest
and sustain us.
What are the six questions of the
sages? Who knows? Who cares?
How many angels dance on
the pin of the Āyur-Dhanur-
Viveka *śāstra*? How
many declensions to the verb "to be"?
Oh, open your mouth wide.
You appear to have
no teeth.

I remember losing them all, my friends, in a past life. I went out to sea in high tide. Drowned in a storm. A sailor I was with had hives all over his skin from eating too many strawberries and a sore throat from sucking too many ice pops. Doctor Workman diagnosed him under the Eltingville train station overpass. Yeah, he knew.

Can't remember,
can't care
right now
Oh Krsna,
You know
my plight-
I dont

CHAPTER TWO

Divinity and Divine Service

Texts 1–2

vyāsa uvāca
iti sampraśna-saṁhṛṣṭo
viprāṇāṁ raumaharṣaṇiḥ
pratipūjya vacas teṣāṁ
pravaktum upacakrame

sūta uvāca
yaṁ pravrajantam anupetam apeta-kṛtyaṁ
dvaipāyano viraha-kātara ājuhāva
putreti tan-mayatayā taravo 'bhinedus
taṁ sarva-bhūta-hṛdayaṁ munim ānato 'smi

Ugraśravā [Sūta Gosvāmī], the son of Romaharṣaṇa, being fully satisfied by the perfect questions of the brāhmaṇas, thanked them and thus attempted to reply.

Śrīla Sūta Gosvāmī said: Let me offer my respectful obeisances unto that great sage [Śukadeva Gosvāmī] who can enter the hearts of all. When he went away to take up the renounced order of life [sannyāsa], leaving home without undergoing reformation by the sacred thread or the ceremonies observed by the higher castes, his father, Vyāsadeva, fearing separation from him, cried out, "O my son!" Indeed, only the trees, which were absorbed in the same feelings of separation, echoed in response to the begrieved father.

Comment

Śukadeva Gosvāmī was liberated from birth and that is why he didn't undergo the purificatory ceremony of brahminical initiation. For most people, these various ceremonies are necessary. We are born from our material mother and father. Then when we are somewhat grown, we approach the spiritual master to receive instructions in the *Vedas*. When the guru accepts us and gives us initiation, we become twice-born, *dvija*. Only then can we study Vedic knowledge and become further qualified as *brāhmaṇas* and then Vaiṣṇavas.

Śukadeva Gosvāmī was a Vaiṣṇava from birth. In Indian socio-religious life, caste conscious people say that one can become a *brāhmaṇa* only by birth. Lord Caitanya Mahāprabhu, however, accepted persons from lower birth, such as Haridāsa Ṭhākura, and recognized them according to their actual spiritual status. Thus Śrī Caitanya Mahāprabhu assigned Haridāsa Thākura as the *ācārya* of the holy name and considered him a first-class Vaiṣṇava, far beyond the status of the ordinary *brāhmaṇas*.

Lord Caitanya's action is supported by the scriptures. If one acts as a *brāhmaṇa*, he should be accepted as a *brāhmaṇa*, even if born as less than a *śūdra*. If by one's occupation and lack of proper behavior one acts as a lower-class person, then even if he is born in a *brāhmaṇa* family, he should be considered a fourth-class man. By the spiritual master's mercy and the chanting of the Lord's holy names, any person can be raised to the highest stage.

Long before ISKCON was formed, Śrīla Bhaktisiddhānta Sarasvatī Ṭhākura accepted lower-class persons and gave them first and second initiation (*hari-nāma* and *brāhmaṇa* initiations). Our Prabhupāda did the same. Thus Kṛṣṇa consciousness has spread to cultures outside India.

I like to think of Śukadeva Gosvāmī abruptly leaving home with his father in pursuit. It touches my heart to think of Vyāsadeva calling out, "O my son!" Śukadeva didn't turn back. "Only the trees . . . echoed in response to the be-grieved father."

Śukadeva's story is so unusual. The Ninth Canto states that Śukadeva stayed in his mother's womb for sixteen years before he agreed to take birth. He didn't want to become entangled in material life and apparently didn't trust that his father, a family man, could teach him how to become liberated. Vyāsadeva went and asked Kṛṣṇa to come and preach to Śukadeva in the womb, assuring him that he would be able to follow the path of spiritual perfection even if he took birth. Only then did Śukadeva agree to appear in the world. As soon as he was born, he left home at once. Before going, he received instructions from Vyāsadeva, who inspired him with attraction for Kṛṣṇa. In other words, although Śukadeva was liberated from birth, he was not yet a personalist. This will be explained in later verses of the *Bhāgavatam*.

Vyāsadeva was attached to his illlustrous son and wanted his company. It's natural that he should desire this, both for his son's welfare and to satisfy his own yearning. Śukadeva, however, had a higher mission. He set out naked, wandering until it was time to meet up with Mahārāja Parīkṣit. Kṛṣṇa as Providence arranged that Śukadeva should be the one to instruct the world in *Śrīmad-Bhāgavatam* through Mahārāja Parīkṣit's inquiries and Śukadeva's responses. Vyāsadeva was Śukadeva's teacher as well as the compiler of his words. That in itself is intriguing. Therefore, not only is Śukadeva's birth and renunciation interesting, but the whole transcendental arrangement of the Lord.

Even more interesting is that we are all connected to this, as long as we are hearing in disciplic succession.

I feel connected too. I know my daily or hourly feelings are not a matter of great concern to others, and even I don't take my ups and downs so seriously. I'd like to be sober toward the disturbances in the world, not affected; and toward Kṛṣṇa and devotional service, I'd like to be softhearted and eager to please. Unfortunately, I have to contend with my physical, emotional, and mental ups and downs. I can't claim I'm something that I'm not.

Still, I relish what's being said in this section and I am trying to pass it on to you in whatever way I can manage.

I like to present my *Bhāgavatam* summaries in installments and then take a break in between. In ISKCON, we don't sit for seven-day marathons to hear the *Bhāgavatam*. We hear "always" (*nityam bhāgavata sevāya*), regularly, every day. For those who go to the morning program, we hear a one-hour class in the morning. Then the devotees usually eat breakfast and then go about their duties. Twenty-four hours later, they attend another *Bhāgavatam* class. In between those classes, Śrīla Prabhupāda advised us to read, especially *Bhagavad-gītā* and *Śrīmad-Bhāgavatam*, for two or three hours a day. He also wanted us to work and maintain and broadcast the Kṛṣṇa consciousness movement. All that creates a rhythm in our lives.

I remember hydrants opened in summer and the tremendous force of water pouring out. I used to be afraid that too much water would flow out because I was a fireman's son and I knew that we depended on fire hydrants to put out fires in people's houses.

This has nothing to do with the *Śrīmad-Bhāgavatam*. I remember sitting in the temple room in Los Angeles and feeling the pageant mood of that place. Three hundred devotees were hearing from Prabhupāda, who sat on a red-upholstered, gold-trimmed *vyāsāsana*. He read with his spectacles on, scholarly and pure. I still like to hear the tapes of those talks.

I remember keeping Prabhupāda's first Indian edition of the *Śrīmad-Bhāgavatam* in my drawer at the welfare office and reading a page every now and then to keep me going. I also remember feeling Swamijī's presence while I was at work—he was only a few blocks away.

I used to like to recall being struck or enlightened by something particular I read in the *Bhāgavatam*. Or maybe it wasn't like that. I did, however, and do, like to read in a steady, peaceful way. Sometimes I can enter it and feel, "This is it. Now I am entering Kṛṣṇa consciousness." This usually happens when I read more than one verse and purport. It happens more if I read for at least half an hour to an hour, especially in the early morning. There's a limit to my ecstasies, but I'm satisfied.

This is an authorial aside: I told you that I like it when an author tells us what's going on with him as he's writing his book, so here goes. I hit on something important today.

First came a feeling of resistance. Then I pushed that out of the way and began writing. I found myself saying how nice it is to read the *Bhāgavatam* in an unmotivated way. Then I realized that reading a verse and purport in order to write *A Poor Man Reads The Bhāgavatam* as I'm doing now doesn't produce the best reading experience. I may also be projecting this lack of reading satisfaction into what I'm writing. I noticed it—I write a short, perfunctory summary of the

Kṛṣṇa conscious topics and then I write "what I want." In this way, I may be setting myself up for something that's not really in my best interests, or in the interests of the reader.

I've been writing full-time now for six days. I give myself no time for leisurely reading. All day long I read one verse and purport, then write the review in a preacher's straight prose, then break out into free expression. It's writing work and I've been driven to it due to my vocation. It's been joyful too, with the emphasis on *accomplishment*. I'm writing a book. It's projected as the first of many, my opus, given to me by Kṛṣṇa.

Yet everything has to find a natural level, especially if I expect this to last for years. I'll have to change the pace sometimes. I see at least two reasons to change the pace immediately: (1) so that writing on the verse and purport doesn't become a chore while I prefer to write something else, and (2) so that I don't deny myself more extended, unmotivated reading, which in turn will promote a deeper experience and appreciation of the *Bhāgavatam*.

Do I really want to read *Bhāgavatam*? Yes. Then the next question is, "What is the best way for me to do that?"

After these thoughts I decided to let myself read in an unmotivated way in Prabhupāda's *Caitanya-caritāmṛta*. This will cut down on my daily production of *A Poor Man Reads The Bhāgavatam*, but it will be worth it if I can get Kṛṣṇa's *darśana*. Then my straight, *paramparā* writing will also improve. Who knows? Even the wild stuff may improve.

Text 3

yaḥ svānubhāvam akhila-śruti-sāram ekam
adhyātma-dīpam atititīrṣatāṁ tamo 'ndham
saṁsāriṇāṁ karuṇayāha purāṇa-guhyaṁ
taṁ vyāsa-sūnum upayāmi guruṁ munīnām

Let me offer my respectful obeisances unto him [Śuka], the spiritual master of all sages, the son of Vyāsadeva, who, out of his great compassion for those gross materialists who struggle to cross over the darkest regions of material existence, spoke this most confidential supplement to the cream of Vedic knowledge, after having personally assimilated it by experience.

Comment

Śrīla Prabhupāda declares that this prayer of obeisance summarizes the introduction to *Śrīmad-Bhāgavatam*. It describes the *mahā Purāṇa* as the commentary on *Vedānta-sūtra*, which is the cream of the *Vedas*. The prayer also praises Śukadeva for being a master of *Bhāgavata* knowledge and for bringing relief to unhappy persons who are struggling with birth and death.

If a conditioned soul actually feels pain and wants to rid himself of material entanglement, he can do so. The problem is that most *karmīs* don't think of their endeavors as innately unhappy. They calculate that if they can just improve their situations in a few critical areas, they will attain happiness. They never stop trying. Those who are more advanced seek knowledge and the way out of material misery. They are known as *jñānīs*. The *Vedānta-sūtra* was directed toward the *jñānīs*.

Even better than *Vedānta-sūtra* is Vyāsadeva's own commentary on it. "By the mercy of Śrīla Śukadeva, the *Bhāgavata-vedānta-sūtra* is available for all those sincere souls . . ." The Māyāvādīs may deride *Bhāgavatam* out of ignorance, but the *paramahaṁsas* (those without malice toward God or His creatures) will appreciate the *Bhāgavatam*. Even a beginner on the spiritual path can come to appreciate the *Bhāgavatam* and receive the topmost benefit if he receives it from the right source.

I like to hear Sūta praise his guru in a learned way. He immediately presents himself as a humble disciple, informing us of his spiritual master's awe-inspiring position. Through Sūta, we also accept Śukadeva Gosvāmī as *śikṣā-guru* and worship him with submissive hearing. (This was hinted at in the previous *śloka* when we were informed that Śukadeva Gosvāmī "can enter everyone's heart.")

It is also good to be reminded of the *Bhāgavata Purāṇa's* unique place among scriptures. We are not going to hear concocted "wisdom" from a self-appointed teacher. We are about to receive the knowledge usually reserved for the most advanced and confidential transcendentalists.

Thought-asana
I wonder what Gurudeva
thinks of me now. I
so desire to please him.
An idea for my
book?....

More admittances:

(1) I'm low in energy.

(2) The clouds cover the sun this morning. It may not be so nice receiving a massage from Lakshman on the roof, not if it's chilly.

(3) The sun is blessed and blesses us. The rays come from the bodies of persons on the sun planet.

(4) I admit myself into the chapel at Saint Clare's in Great Kills, but I discover I don't belong there. My place is with the sages, the Viṣṇu *avatāras*, and Kṛṣṇa's pure devotees, the Six Gosvāmīs of Vṛndāvana—all of whom bless me through my spiritual master, Śrīla Prabhupāda.

(5) I admit I made mistakes in ISKCON. I was part of it.

(6) I admit I want to storm ahead into the school of plain truth, but my sneakers are untied and I'm afraid if I try too hard, I'll get a headache, which I dread.

(7) Śukadeva and Sūta seem far away—long ago—in a book. Yes, I also admit that it's *the* book and that they are the greatest, but I'm like a frog in the mud who can't appreciate a human poet's sonorous recital. He prefers his own, "Brr-rivet! Brr-rivet!"

(8) I admit I love the breakfast fruits.

(9) I admit that time is running and that I want to get something out, some pages, just as any worker pushes out units of work—sewing clothes, tapping rubber heels onto shoes while listening to Italian radio stations, laying steaming hot macadam on highways and walking around in thick, heat-resistant shoes, shoveling, leveling, bricklaying with a crew of cursing men. Or faking it as a civil service clerk, yawning and blinking back tears while looking at his watch.

(10) *Śrīmad-Bhāgavatam* is for those who pray. They're called swan-like men because they can extract pure milk from a mixture of milk and water.

(11) I admit that my low energy may be purely physical. Can I pick myself up?

I think I'm too skinny. Madhu says,
"No. We just need energy,
wiry we can be." Anyone else
would look at us and say we
look like we were both in a
concentration camp. I thought maybe
I could write head and spirit
and big body's not necessary, just
enough to move a smooth pen.

Some deficiency's in me.
Can't expect to crank out odes
on my own. It's a lesson that
mercy descends. At least I
repeat it straight:
Sūta praises Śuka and
Śrīmad-Bhāgavatam is the cream of
Vedas and those fools who work
hard in *māyā* never inquire how
to get out of it. But for those
who want relief,
Śuka's speaking.

Text 4

nārāyaṇaṁ namaskṛtya
naraṁ caiva narottamam
devīṁ sarasvatīṁ vyāsaṁ
tato jayam udīrayet

Before reciting this Śrīmad-Bhāgavatam, which is the very means of conquest, one should offer respectful obeisances unto the Personality of Godhead, Nārāyaṇa, unto Nara-nārāyaṇa Ṛṣi, the supermost human being, unto mother Sarasvatī, the goddess of learning, and unto Śrīla Vyāsadeva, the author.

Comment

In his purport, Prabhupāda focuses on the word "*jayam*" from the verse, which he translates as "all that is meant for conquering." We use this definition when we say, "*Jaya* Prabhupāda!" It's a call for victory. We want to be victorious and conquer material life. We seek to free ourselves from the cycle of birth and death wherein a soul is sometimes pushed into the animal species, is sometimes born as a demigod, and then is again forced to descend to hell.

Prabhupāda writes, "His struggle for existence in the material world is perpetual, and it is not possible for him to get out of it by making plans. If he at all wants to conquer this perpetual struggle for existence, he must reestablish his eternal relation with God."

To achieve this victory, we need to turn to the *Purāṇas*. They are supplementary Vedic literatures which are prepared to elevate persons in the various modes of nature so that they may eventually regain their pure, spiritual status, free from matter. *Śrīmad-Bhāgavatam* is the ultimate expression of this victory.

"Śrīla Sūta Gosvāmī shows the way of chanting the *Purāṇas*. This may be followed by persons who aspire to be preachers of the Vedic literatures and the *Purāṇas*." Some *Bhāgavatam* lecturers in ISKCON take this statement literally and recite verse 1.2.4, "*nārāyaṇaṁ namaskṛtya*," as if it were an absolute requirement. Śrīla Prabhupāda didn't chant it. Before beginning each *Śrīmad-Bhāgavatam* lecture, he sang Bhaktivinoda Ṭhākura's song, "*Jaya rādhā-mādhava, kuñja-bihārī*," which, as Prabhupāda said, gives "the real picture of God"—in Vṛndāvana, with Rādhārāṇī, the *gopīs* and *gopas*, Yaśodā-devī, the Yamunā, and all the Vrajajanas. Then Prabhupāda recited the *Bhāgavatam's* invocation, "*Oṁ namo bhāgavate vāsudevāya*," and commenced his recitation of the verse for the day. When he writes that we may follow Sūta Gosvāmī's way of chanting the *Purāṇas*, the essential meaning is that we should speak with full faith in guru, Kṛṣṇa, and *śāstra*, and call out for the victory of Kṛṣṇa consciousness over nescience. We should speak not as losers, but as conquerors, by the grace of *Śrīmad-Bhāgavatam*.

Before speaking, during speaking, and after speaking, we should always make humble obeisances to our Vaiṣṇava superiors, offer friendly wishes to our peers, and give mercy to our juniors. This is how we will conquer pride, forgetfulness of God, and all other kinds of ignorance. "*Śrīmad-Bhāgavatam* is the spotless *Purāṇa*, and it is especially meant for them who desire to get out of the material entanglement permanently."

Since what we are striving for is such a tremendous achievement for a *jīva*, we understand that the *Bhāgavatam* class is recommended not just for once a week attendance, or for seven-day *Bhāgavata-saptaha* recitations, but *nityam bhāgavata sevāya*, regularly and eternally. We have to hear every day, more than once a day, if we want to achieve the ultimate victory. Māyādevī tends the fortress of the material world with great power and stringency. She will not easily release us unless she is convinced of our sincere and persistent desire to hear and chant. Only then will she say, "Ah, he has conquered."

We've been in this house now for a week. We came here on the invitation of our host. He said that his brother-in-law had a nice solitary house we could borrow for awhile. Yesterday, however, we learned that the house doesn't belong to his brother-in-law at all, but to the Indian government. We also learned that a group of political ministers are about to visit this area to gather votes and that some of them want to stay in this house. We have to move out. When our host heard this he was angry and protested it. The house has apparently been abandoned for years. He had it cleaned and repaired, had the thorns in the yard cut down, and had filled in the roads leading to the house. Seeing these improvements, the government ministers are inclined to use it. It is certainly a peaceful spot on the bank of a quiet river with the soothing sound of the waterfall created by a dam nearby. It's rural and secluded, a rare treat in highly populated India.

Yesterday our host said he convinced the local assistant minister that we should be allowed to stay, but today he said we might have to leave after all, maybe—they don't know for sure yet—suddenly, during the night. Stand by for action.

Hearing this, Madhu and I are inclined to pack up and move without waiting for night alarms. They say after two days, the ministers will move on and we can return. If I move out once, though, I doubt I'll come back. We have been offered a place in town. It's not so quiet, but at least our host owns it.

This is a disturbance because my steady writing routine is threatened. I feel I have to mention it and that I am determined to minimize the interruption. I may miss a few scheduled writing sessions, and it will be a test whether I can hold on to the assignment. A substantial assignment won't collapse or disappear by changing houses. If need be, I'll pack my belongings all afternoon, put them in a car (myself too), Madhu will pack his kitchen and suitcases, and we'll relocate. If I'm very lucky, I'll rest early at night in a new place and rise at midnight, find a light, find a chair, a flat surface, have my *Bhāgavatam* and notepad with me, and write on *Śrīmad-Bhāgavatam* 1.2.5.

Be not wry or angry in purpose,
I tell myself. Accept your fate
to keep moving. Pack your notebooks
and empty your pens to refill in the
next place. Royal blue, blue-black,
before reciting this *Śrīmad-Bhāgavatam*
which is our very means of conquest.

I offer obeisances to Śrīla Prabhupāda,
to Lord Nārāyaṇa and Vyāsa and
Nara-nārāyaṇa and Sarasvatī and many
more,
Six Gosvāmīs, our
grand spiritual master, Bhaktisiddhānta Sarasvatī,
Gaurakiśora dāsa Bābājī, Bhaktivinoda Ṭhākura . . .
They are our exalted
spiritual family.

We get
pushed around but we conquer
if we are calm and go on
chanting Hare Kṛṣṇa and show ourselves
not petty but detached.
It's a great thing we hope to
achieve, so we have to work for it.

Prabhupāda tells us Daśaratha greeted
the sage, "How are you doing in
your attempt to conquer birth and death?"
Adhiṣṭaṁ yat tat punar-janma-jayāya.
Conquering over death
is the "business" of a sage and devotee.
It happens in little ways
when you control your tongue,
conquer momentary sex desire,
and let the ministers have their
way. It's their house, not
mine. I'm seeking to enter
the house of the spiritual
world. Give them this
bungalow and offer them the
real one, with you.

I deliberately wrote something easy so I could omit the hard-to-face crap of the world. Well, we don't have to move after all.

I'm glad because I preferred to stay here. Make sense. Ease your body, man. The mice were on the march all night.

A vivid fellow, a
scholar once looked over the
precipice of a white page. The
world is flat.

In P.S. #8 we learned to make sense out of chaos. Memories are a defective proof because they are based on our imperfect senses. Swami, if you had not come, I'd be lost. I mean it.

Nāndīmukhī dasī knows how rare and sweet
is 26 Second Avenue. We
were jerks saved and I don't have to tell you how low.
This poor man rides the rails.

Rail against the night. Sit and face yourself. I have little to say. A bird will sing, I'll close my eyes and dream, then stretch, go on until 3:30.

Before conquering this nescience, a motorbike starts up. I'm not against Sarasvatī *bhajana* and Nara-narāyaṇa, but I want to say that the Hare Kṛṣṇa mantra is good enough. I say what comes on the menu about conquering. Uncle Don used to say, "That's enough for the little bastards for today." That's how he felt—no goodwill. He was tired of playing the fool, Uncle Don, and I don't even know *how* I feel about *nārāyaṇa namaskṛta* except respectful (as usual) toward *any śloka*. I'm just trotting out what's on the surface and the tip of my tongue to fill the page. (There are no kids' initials on this desk, but someone wrote "Santosh" on the side of this house.)

Where's my depth and love? The socks, the tired feeling of afternoon when the chill is gone and the room warms and you don't need your long johns anymore—is this truth to me?

Lying in the sun and tolerating mistakes or checking ingratitude, preparing to move?

Am I confused? Then let me come back for more *Bhāgavatam*. Please be faithful and don't worry if it's not profound. The *Bhāgavatam* will take care of itself.

My dear Lord, You are taking good care of us. Please let me do this long-term work which I dedicate to You. Before reciting the *Bhāgavatam*, we had better really mean what we say, ask for blessings to conquer our lower natures, to conquer writing blocks, low self-esteem, the tendency to write at too low a standard, and all else that may hinder us.

I believe I will conquer. *Jaya*! *Jaya*! I say it all the time. I too want to conquer in a small way and help Lord Caitanya achieve His victory. "My devotees will never perish."

Text 5

munayaḥ sādhu pṛṣṭo 'haṁ
bhavadbhir loka-maṅgalam

yat kṛtaḥ kṛṣṇa-sampraśno
yenātmā suprasīdati

O sages, I have been justly questioned by you. Your questions are worthy because they relate to Lord Kṛṣṇa and so are of relevance to the world's welfare. Only questions of this sort are capable of completely satisfying the self.

Comment

Śrīmad-Bhāgavatam began (as *Vedānta-sūtra* begins) with the necessity to inquire into *janmady yasyataḥ*, the absolute source of everything. The Absolute Truth was immediately identified as Vāsudeva, Lord Kṛṣṇa, the son of Vasudeva. Here again the *Bhāgavatam* speaker affirms that inquiry into the Absolute Truth brings us to inquire about the Supreme Personality of Godhead, whose name is Kṛṣṇa. This immediate connection of Vedic knowledge to knowledge of Kṛṣṇa is affirmed in *Bhagavad-gītā* where Lord Kṛṣṇa states to Arjuna, "By all the *Vedas*, I am to be known. Indeed, I am the compiler of *Vedānta*, and I am the knower of the *Vedas*." (Bg. 15.15)

The Supreme Lord is so full that He writes the *Vedas* in His incarnation as Vyāsa, He teaches them as the teacher of *Bhagavad-gītā*, and He Himself is the ultimate Vedic subject matter. The Lord also provides the guru, both within the heart and externally as the *dīkṣā-* and *śikṣā-gurus*. Without guru, no one can understand Vedic literature.

Śrīla Prabhupāda analyzes that all interactions, not only among civilized humans, but among birds and beasts, can be boiled down to a series of questions and answers. In the lower forms of life, the questions are mostly, "Where is food? Where is sex? How can I defend myself?" Among humans, these questions are prominent along with many speculative inquires about religion, politics, money-making, sense gratification, and even liberation. "Although they go on making such questions and answers for their whole lives, they are not at all satisfied. Satisfaction of the soul can only be obtained by questions and answers on the subject of Kṛṣṇa."

It's unfortunate that people are consumed by questions and answers, but not by Kṛṣṇa. Therefore, their questions and answers provide only a diversion. One could call it an effective trick by *māyā* to keep the fools and rascals in bondage. Let them go on perpetually inquiring and supplying answers and thus maintain their own stupidity and illusion. If we want to become free from it, however, we have to feel dissatisfaction with mundane life and cry sincerely to know God—or at least to know how to become free from the suffering caused by nonsense questions and answers.

Persons ripe for devotional service sometimes ask themselves, "There must be something more to life than this, what I see everyone doing and inquiring into. What is it that's beyond this?" This line of reasoning is a crude version of the Vedānta's *athato brahma jijñāsa:* "Now that we have exhausted our inquiry into sense gratification and market prices, why are we still unhappy? Let's inquire into the Absolute Truth."

We're fortunate when we inquire and find answers within the context of the *Bhāgavatam*. As Sūta states, *Śrīmad-Bhāgavatam* is meant for inquiry about Kṛṣṇa, which alone brings satisfaction and welfare to the world and the self. Prabhupāda: "One should learn the *Śrīmad-Bhāgavatam* and make an all-around solution to all problems pertaining to social, political or religious matters. *Śrīmad-Bhāgavatam* and Kṛṣṇa are the sum total of all things."

People think they're being confined if we ask them to inquire only about Lord Kṛṣṇa and to take their answers only from the Vedic literature. They don't know that knowledge of Kṛṣṇa consciousness has jurisdiction over all matters, even over worldly affairs. The *Vedas* originally taught all material as well as spiritual knowledge.

I sometimes occupy myself with lesser inquires. Since I'm so much a part of my spiritual master's institution and the *saṅkīrtana* cause, my questions may be said to be connected to Kṛṣṇa. Sometimes, however, the link is tenuous.

Just last night I asked:

(1) Do we have to leave this house?

(2) Can I write books in peace?

(3) Will they come out "all right"?

(4) If not, how can I improve?

(5) Is my basic working method approved by guru and Kṛṣṇa?

(6) What are more subheadings and strategies I might use to release me into freer expression?

(7) Can I link this personal way with the Vedic way?

O Prabhupāda, where are you now? How can we serve you in this world? Everything is confused or superficial or political; so many are dissatisfied and the solutions are so multifarious it's like trying to build the tower of Babel after the curse.

Do we need to eat more? But how can we digest what we eat? What health regimen should we follow? What about my headaches? Lord, guru and Kṛṣṇa, what do you want me to do?

How many mice live in this house? What are their passageways into the rooms? (If I knew the answer to that, I might block them all up.)

What will happen? Will there be world catastrophes? Will seventy-five percent of the population be destroyed and the geography of the planet radically altered soon? If so, what will happen to my writings? (Why don't I first ask where Śrīla Prabhupāda's writings will go? But I already know that the Lord rescued the *Vedas* as Matsya-avatāra. I'm not sure if my books deserve to be saved.)

What about my friends? Will we continue to live? (As I pursue these questions, it occurs to me why people turn to astrologers. Astrologers seem to have all the answers. But are they the right answers? That's another question.)

Where are the snows of yesteryear? Is it all right to remember things that come to mind?

O Lord, I wish I knew the answers to questions such as, "When will my *japa* improve? When will I give up my selfishness and go out to preach the divine command as Bhaktivinoda Ṭhākura orders?"

Vaiṣṇava songs and prayers are sometimes presented in the form of personal, yearning questions. "When will my eyes be decorated with tears of love flowing constantly when I chant Your holy names?" "When will I be able to give up worldly attachment?"

These questions are often rhetorical questions to which no answer is expected. They are spoken in sincere and unpretentious language. When we say, "Oh, when will I attain love of Kṛṣṇa?" but at heart wonder whether there will be milk with breakfast today, we become ashamed.

Our core questions, the ones we really care about, are often the petty ones. Our curiosity is often masked faultfinding. We sit to hear a Godbrother answer questions from the *Bhāgavatam* and measure what we can see of his devotional service against the perfection of his responses. We also worry what he thinks of us.

How much money will we earn this year? And *details* on these questions. This is called "management." Did we get the best price on our tickets? How much commission is the travel agent making? In what form of currency is the money being carried by the man who is bringing it to Bombay? Did he get a bank draft? Is he going by train or plane? Are we okay? Will we get spinach? I'm fifty-six years old. How much longer do I have?

We also *beg* questions: "Kṛṣṇa, may I please serve You by being an author?" Begging the question means evading or dodging real surrender. The actual question should be, "Lord, how may I serve You?" but we dodge that and ask, "Will you please accept *this* service I want to do or will You let me off the hook? Please let me do what I want. Will You give me permission to marry this girl and enjoy in that way?"

Or there are petty questions, questions that are merely pious and therefore mundane. Mundane questions tend to be demanding: "When will You give me love of God?" "Why can't I see You?" "Where are the bananas?" "When can I expect relief from my suffering?"

Where is God? Can you show me God? Agnostic questions. Insincere time-fillers. Vapid, stupid, and irrelevant. Questions that reveal our mentality as mean, our motives impure. "Is your daughter young?" the guru asks the man. He means, "Is she attractive? Will I enjoy seeing her?"

We don't want to face our real questions because they're often so nasty. Neither do we want to face up to asking the questions that will bring us the most surrender, because to ask those questions would demand too much *tapasya.*

And we have to give answers. Are our replies verbose or superficial? Why bluff that we are capable answer-men? We can repeat what the books say, but the answers should live in our hearts. Don't give solutions if we can't follow them ourselves.

Don't just ask stupid, irrelevant questions. "How many years will I live, and out of those years, for how many will I enjoy good health?" Stupid questions. Ask only how you can serve. If you don't know how to ask, keep an inquiring mood by reading Prabhupāda's books. Ask Prabhupāda every day and answer the question with affirmative action. Then you'll stop feeling the need for so many sentences ending in question marks.

Drive to Canada,
the geese in spring,
we'll let you write if you promise to behave.

Kṛṣṇa in everyone's hearts. The drawings and words don't have to be logical. I'll escape that and write on.

Can I get residency in Ireland? Can we ship the van there? Will they believe us? If not, can we raise more money to pay the import tax? Will M.'s health hold up? Can I go on writing all year? Is this selfish or wrong?

What are you doing to celebrate the Centennial? Did you surrender? Why don't you push book distribution? Are you on COM, LINK, the Internet? Why not? No computer? Why? "Why is anything?"

Oh, shut up and chant Hare Kṛṣṇa. Try to be engaged in *that*.

Yessir.

Text 6

sa vai puṁsāṁ paro dharmo
yato bhaktir adhokṣaje
ahaituky apratihatā
yayātmā suprasīdati

The supreme occupation [dharma] for all humanity is that by which men can attain to loving devotional service unto the transcendent Lord. Such devotional service must be unmotivated and uninterrupted to completely satisfy the self.

Comment

Prabhupāda lectured often on this verse. He liked to present it as a nonsectarian definition of true *dharma* or religion. He said the dictionary defines religion as "a kind of faith," but true *dharma* is not a faith that can be changed as one converts from Hindu to Christian or Christian to Muslim. True *dharma* is the original, unchanging nature of the living being. That is, his tendency to render service to someone or something.

The innate serving nature is perfected when we render devotional service to the Supreme Personality of Godhead. That is our eternal occupation, just as it is the permanent "*dharma*" or nature of sugar to be sweet or of water to be liquid. The *sa vai puṁsām* verse, therefore, describes a first-class religionist without claiming that one world denomination is better than another. That religion which promotes unmotivated, uninterrupted, loving service to the Supreme Personality of Godhead is best.

By speaking this verse, Sūta answers the sages' first question. They requested him to go through all the Vedic literature and select the essence which could be given to the unfortunate people of Kali-yuga.

There are two paths prescribed by the *Vedas*, *pravṛtti-mārga*, the path of material enjoyment within the bounds of religion, and *nivṛtti-mārga*, the path of renunciation of material sense gratification. "The path of enjoyment is inferior, and the path of sacrifice for the supreme cause is superior."

Why is *nivṛtti-mārga* the best? Because it leads us out of false happiness into real happiness. The happiness one struggles for in family life, economic success, career, nationalism, etc., is short-lived. When we beat back the unending tide of misery for awhile, we consider that relief to be happiness. Then the miseries attack us again. In spiritual life, however, there is no misery; there is only eternity, bliss, and knowledge in transcendental service unto the Personality of Godhead.

To qualify for devotional service, it is best not to exaggerate or depend on material sense gratification for our well-being. *Bhakti* is described as *vairāgya vidyā nija bhakti-yoga*, renunciation from things not favorable for devotional service, and rich in *vidyā*, or Kṛṣṇa conscious knowledge. One should renounce the path of *pravṛtti* and situate oneself firmly in *nirvṛtti-mārga* or *bhakti-mārga*, taking direction from the bona fide spiritual master.

Pure devotional service is free of karma and *jñāna*. *Bhakti* is therefore an uncovering of or an awakening to who we actually are: the eternal, spiritual, blissful servants of the Supreme. "This relation of servant and the served is the most congenial form of intimacy."

I accept that. It's a clear, tight, scientific definition. I like to follow Prabhupāda's example and lecture on it too. It disarms the notion, "My religion is better than yours." But it is not vague sentiment. It reveals the pure current of *bhakti* as the essence and acknowledges that this current may be found in other world religions.

Prabhupāda was asked once his opinion about the Christian mystics. He said he hadn't studied their lives, but one could judge by the criteria of this *Bhāgavatam* verse. If you find someone anywhere in the world who is rendering devotional service without any motive other than to please God, and if he does it without interruption, then that is *bhakti*. It doesn't matter if such a person appears as a Christian, a Hindu, a Muslim, a Jew, or even a Buddhist. The *paro dharma* potentially exists in all cultures. It is always pure, just as gold is always pure no matter who possesses it. To actually find the symptoms of such a pure devotee is rare.

The criteria is sufficiently broad-minded, yet stringent. I am always happy to explain this verse point by point, elaborating on the words *para-dharma*, *bhakti*, *adhokṣaje*, *ahaituky*, *apratihatā*, and *ātmā-suprasīdati*.

May we be satisfied by discussing devotional service and not restless to move away from it. *Kṛṣṇa-kathā* should be so pleasing that we can engage in it all day, if not by speaking the philosophy and pastimes of Kṛṣṇa, then by chanting His holy names or rendering service with body and mind. When we get hungry, we may honor *prasādam* (but not too much), and when we are tired, we can rest. Be like Prabhupāda described himself during his Bowery days, "Always something reading and writing, something reading and writing. I tell you, I don't get fatigued."

I break my flow of devotional service if a fly buzzes too insistently around my face or if I suddenly see a rodent's tail peek out from under a picture on the wall. If Madhu comes in with news that's too worldly, I feel interrupted. When I sleep, I dream, but my dreams are often riddles with nothing in them impelling me to remember Kṛṣṇa—except when I wake and feel anxious that I have forgotten *bhakti*.

When my flow is challenged, I bite at a fingernail. I fear something unknown. Will I be dragged away from devotional service?

Where is taste? I'm afraid I'm just going through the motions. My allegiance to my schedule: read and write on *Śrīmad-Bhāgavatam* from 8–10 A.M., go to the roof for a twenty-five-minute massage and talk with our host (likely distractions there), come down and wash off the oil (was the enjoyment of sunbathing within *bhakti*?). At 11 A.M. I massage Prabhupāda, then bath, and dress him. Is this actually *ahaituky apratihatā*, unmotivated and uninterrupted?

I mean I believe and you try.
I get restless sometimes
in the confines of what I know
as *bhakti*. So I
peek around outside. But then
come back into the house where
it's safe.

Don't want no hideous danger.
Know that most men and women
I meet are *māyā* personified.
Don't want to be part of it.
Yet sometimes I feel unsatisfied or
bored and mostly lacking,
tired shortcoming.
Who could be happy
jawing his *japa* in such
a mechanical way?

Sa vai puṁsām's
theory to me, not realized fact.
It points to the supreme devotees.
I acknowledge them in any land
and I believe they have lived and
walked the earth (often barefoot).

I sing the song of the interrupted,
distracted. Please bless us as
we get back onto the track.
I must speak unrehearsed 'tho,
how I opened a bag and found
a running spider, how I looked
in *Pocket Poets* but found
only a *duskṛtina* spark . . .
and
here in India I met the red
orb on horizon at 7 A.M.,
to the desk on time,
silent, waiting, untouched,
reading *bhakti's* true form
and liking it; it's my own code
and I'll uphold it next week
in an advertised lecture.

Hurry up, hand, it's your turn. My brain drops the word "screwdriver." It's just a word. We're trying to discover a new place. I once saw a photo of Admiral Byrd in the dictionary. He wore a furry hood. I was looking for the word "beg," as in "beg the question."

I'm not a freak; I'm a normal, placid, freckled devotee. Rocket pen. Plastic gimmicks. Childhood toys. I haven't read Knut Hamsun. I want my own expression, not his.

This page is white. *Bhakti* is plain. Put aside the little concerns that draw you away from it.

The ISKCON bus is going to Indian towns. Nārāyaṇa-jvara is with them, showing videos and animated dolls to attract the village people. That's how he's spending the Centennial.

I'll see Jaya Gauracandra at Śaraṇāgati and tell him I want to stay alone to mine the depths. Maybe the editor will find some gold dust. I will work detached in a quiet house. Put in my time. This system of writing on *Bhāgavatam* verses is good. The *ślokas* reverberate in me. Although I appear to wander, I always return to them.

I don't hear voices in me but a crow cawing outdoors and someone speaking Hindi and the scrape on the roof. My blood flows quietly. I hope to eat again. Listen, listen, we want peace, no doors creaking. Don't startle me or I'll slam my fist on the desk in case you're a mouse. The mice bother me but the lizards don't—even the big, slithery ones. This proves it's something I got from my mother. Kṛṣṇa is bringing me close to mice this month so I'll remember that the world is not tailor-made for me. The cat I asked for never came, and neither did the typewriter.

Be happy, poet, that you are retired from the Navy. Lord Caitanya prayed (note it), *janmani janmani*. He didn't ask for liberation, something most transcendentalists want. He asked for pure devotional service life after life. The devotees want only to serve Kṛṣṇa. Kṛṣṇa sometimes grants liberation from birth and death, but Caitanya Māhāprabhu didn't even want that.

I heard it while eating today. I was thinking about how the bananas were small and he could have given me three. I may have to go on a nourishing diet to gain strength.

Sa vai puṁsām. It means that Saint Francis was a pure devotee, and Teresa of Lisieux, but I don't read them anymore. The Six Gosvāmīs certainly. I'm reading Jiva Gosvāmī's *Sandarbhas*. He wrote 400,000 lines or verses, as much as all the *Purāṇas* put together.

Don't forget to say "Kṛṣṇa, Kṛṣṇa," and pray He'll bless me with ability to write further into self-expression as woven into the *Bhāgavatam* text explication. *Jaya! Jaya*! to the spirit conquering over matter and the sages at Naimiṣāraṇya.

Text 7

vāsudeve bhagavati
bhakti-yogaḥ prayojitaḥ
janayaty āśu vairāgyaṁ
jñānaṁ ca yad ahaitukam

By rendering devotional service unto the Personality of Godhead, Śrī Kṛṣṇa, one immediately acquires causeless knowledge and detachment from the world.

Comment

Some uninformed persons consider *bhakti* to be an inferior, sentimental process suitable for the lower classes who are not able to meditate or study the *Vedas*. This idea is completely mistaken. *Bhakti* is actually the highest stage of spiritual development. When one takes directly to *bhakti*, the other good results of transcendental life—knowledge, detachment, sacrifice, and mystic powers—develop automatically as by-products. The beauty of *bhakti* is that it is easy to perform and can be practiced by neophytes and even children. At the same time, it is the path followed by the greatest scholars and devotees.

As we develop naturally, we acquire higher transcendental knowledge. Then we lose taste for hackneyed material pleasure. In other words, attachment for the spiritual equals detachment from the material. Prabhupāda sometimes compared this to a person who is given a superior meal and who as a result, rejects the offer of an inferior meal.

Detachment (*vairāgya*) doesn't imply the negation of all forms and activities. True *vairāgya* means to give up material values and to enthusiastically perform transcendental loving service to Lord Kṛṣṇa. Śrīla Prabhupāda: "That is the sign of a pure devotee. He is not a fool, nor is he engaged in the inferior energies . . . This is not possible by dry reasoning. It actually happens by the grace of the Almighty."

It's Lord Kṛṣṇa who awards pure devotional service through contact with His pure devotees. We may make a sincere effort, but *bhakti* is not attained by our karma, by cause and effect, or as result of hard work. Therefore, its attainment is called causeless. The devotee who is blessed with *bhakti* gradually manifests all the good qualities of a human being.

Impersonalists sometimes try to use the *Bhāgavatam* to support their conclusions, but as we read it from the beginning, we see *bhakti-yoga* as the basic foundation of *bhāgavata-dharma*. The very name "*Bhāgavatam*" pertains to the Supreme Personality of Godhead and His *bhāgavatas*, the devotees. Formless Brahman is not above Bhagavān. The entire work begins with the prayer *oṁ namo bhāgavate vāsudevāya* and an expression of sincere desire to meditate upon Him as the Absolute Truth. Forms of *dharma* other than pure devotional service are kicked out.

The sages want to hear from one who knows the purpose of Kṛṣṇa's advent and activities. Their questions about Lord Kṛṣṇa have been immediately appreciated by Sūta Gosvāmī, the authorized speaker. At every step, the *Bhāgavatam* recommends *bhakti* as the only valuable path. Other paths or items of knowledge are mentioned only to refute them or to give them their subordinate place at the feet of *para-dharma*. The *Bhāgavatam's* insistence on the predominance of *bhakti* is assuring.

We want *bhakti*. We want to hanker for it and be satisfied by it. We want to overcome dislike for any aspect of work done as *sādhana-bhakti*. We desire strength to persist through our daily sloughs. We want the stamina to climb hills and to see the view—a sense of accomplishment. Thus we pray for *bhakti* as both the means and the end.

May *bhakti* enter our thoughts and wishes. May we write, at least as aspiring *bhaktas*, as Prabhupāda describes, "just on the threshold of the house of *bhakti*." And may we enter that house and contact the Supreme Personality of Godhead, our Lord and Master, our Friend, the Beloved of the *gopīs*.

I want all that.

Silent and serious. The day is quiet, productive, offered to the spiritual master, lived with integrity and not distracted by the busy activities of fools. We are not confused by the riddles of the universe. We know the answer to the question, "Why is there anything?" Pleasure is the goal, *ānanda mayo 'bhyasat:* satisfaction of the self comes from rendering service for Kṛṣṇa's pleasure.

Kṛṣṇa is *bhava-grāhi-janārdana*: He accepts whatever little energy we are able to offer, and He accepts the best part of our desires and knows our inner heart. He extends Himself through His servants. It's they who inform us of the mercy available through His holy names. They also teach us by example and precept the right moods in which to practice.

Vāsudeve bhagavati. The more familiar verses sound musical. Sanskrit is rhythmic, but it is more than a language. These verses go beyond language and rhetoric; they make sense in a senseless world.

For example, I've been living in this government house for over a week. Over and over again I hear the chug-chug of a nearby engine. I still don't know whether it's a locomotive (passing so frequently?) or a factory engine. I don't know why they built this dam. I don't know why people come here and hang out. I can't understand Hindi. But if I murmur *vāsudeve bhagavati, bhakti-yogaḥ prayojitaḥ*, my worldview clears up. Everything I need to know falls into place. As Lord Kṛṣṇa says, "In this world, there is nothing so sublime and pure as transcendental knowledge. . . . And one who has become accomplished in the practice of devotional service enjoys this knowledge within himself in due course of time." (Bg. 4.38) A little later in *Bhagavad-gītā* Kṛṣṇa says, "When . . . one is enlightened . . . his knowledge reveals everything, as the sun lights up everything in the daytime." (Bg. 5.16)

I think I would like to write a letter to the sages at Naimiṣāraṇya. Not a cute, literary letter, but a real letter. Perhaps Kṛṣṇa can reveal to me what I should say, what mood I should write in. For now I'll add it to my list.

Dear locomotive or whatever you are, why don't you be quiet? What's the big chug-chug for? Are you forced to labor by the government ministers and their bosses? Just thought I'd ask.

The desire to eat *halavā* is starting to build in me. Is it wrong, sinful? Prabhupāda ate sweets and normal food, and he didn't follow Nature Cure. I dreamt last night I was licking up white cream. Śamīka Ṛṣi asked me how long I would follow this diet. I said, "Oh, forever. It's a way of life." But maybe I should modify it. Everything we eat each day fits into a little pot. I have to have keen hunger to appreciate it because half of it is raw. I am not mocking anything here, just confessing that I'm feeling discontent building up. It occurred to me to speak about it to someone, but to whom? Anyone I think of is already for or against it. No one is impartial. God may be amused.

I wrote a book at the health clinic asserting that Nature Cure is superior to other diets and the best method to control the tongue. Sense control is a virtue. It's a mistake, as they say, to keep loading the belly even after we belch and we're not hungry any more. We cram it all in anyway. It becomes morbid, toxic, and the poisons circulate undigested in the blood. That's where sickness comes from. It *makes* sense, doesn't it? But how come I'm so skinny now and feel so weak? At least I'm not burping and belching all day long, and I have a clearer head.

I was trying to keep up my meditation on *Bhāgavatam* 1.2.7 without drifting. Those little asides just came. They are part of the life of a *Bhāgavatam* reader. He reads a text, then takes off his shoes. If he's a father, his son may read comic books. The father may pick one up at an odd moment and look at something. Of course, I'm not a father and there are no comic books here. I just mean I drifted off on a raft in order to come back to you, dear *Śrīmad-Bhāgavatam;* you are the riverbank and the holy river. I'm just an imitative fool drifting in literary currents who wants the ecstasy of *vairāgya-vidyā*, knowledge and detachment.

Text 8

dharmaḥ svanuṣṭhitaḥ puṁsāṁ
viṣvaksena-kathāsu yaḥ
notpādayed yadi ratiṁ
śrama eva hi kevalam

The occupational activities a man performs according to his own position are only so much useless labor if they do not provoke attraction for the message of the Personality of Godhead.

Comment

Śrīla Prabhupāda's expressions are unique. He first describes the crippled attitude of materialists who know only the life of the senses. They work for a "concentrated and extended selfishness" in connection with their own bodies or the bodies of others. In either case, the goal is gross, bodily comfort.

Above the hard-core materialists are the *jñānīs*, the dry, mental speculators who indulge in "making poetry and philosophy or propagating some *ism* with the same aim of selfishness limited to the body and the mind."

It's interesting how Śrīla Prabhupāda calls sense gratification selfish. By contrast, devotional service is truly for the broad-minded, broad-hearted *mahātmās*. Once we connect with Lord Kṛṣṇa, we're able to actually care for all *jīvas*. Therefore, we cannot claim to be devotees and yet still be selfish. That would be hypocrisy. Becoming a devotee completely transforms us into a higher order of consciousness. Being a devotee is much more than religious sentiment expressed by a poor-hearted person.

The needs of the spirit soul—that vital self which activates all life, in the absence of which there is death—is the prime consideration. The materialists know nothing about those needs. Out of ignorance of the soul, no *dharmī* or *karmī* can find satisfaction in his work. "Simply by cleansing the cage of the bird, one does not satisfy the bird. One must actually know the needs of the bird himself."

Prabhupāda waxes poetic in this wonderful purport about the spirit soul's need to get out of material bondage and to fulfill his desire for complete freedom. "He wants to get out of the covered walls of the greater universe. He wants to see the free light and the spirit." Ultimately, this means meeting the Personality of Godhead, for whom all souls have either dormant or active affection.

Prabhupāda's advice is grounded. We each have an occupational duty by which we make a living. That work should not, however, separate us from Kṛṣṇa consciousness or cover the soul's needs. Many of today's occupations are soul-killing. We have to stay fixed in our spiritual consciousness even when we are engaged in our practical, daily work. We should not become proud of our incomes or struggle at a job with no relief. We are not asses. Whether we are wealthy or poverty-stricken, a person needs to link up with Kṛṣṇa through his work. Otherwise, work is useless. Prabhupāda says specifically, " . . . any occupational activity which does not help one to achieve attachment for hearing and chanting the transcendental message of Godhead is said herein to be simply a waste of time."

Work without *bhakti* dooms us to the bondage of *saṁsāra*. Therefore, how to work in connection with Kṛṣṇa is a great science. Sūta Gosvāmī has introduced the subject while glorifying the process of *bhakti*. He thus anticipates a possible disparity between *bhakti* and karma. We cannot excuse ourselves from the path of *bhakti* by saying, "*Bhakti* may be all right for monks, but I have to work; I have no time for *bhajana*." Don't be a fool.

Of course, all this is easier said than done. Each of us has to figure out how to apply it in our own lives. We should be convinced that we live and eat at Kṛṣṇa's expense, not as a result of our work in this world. If we have to work in someone's office or shop, we have to learn how to do it so that it provokes, or at least doesn't diminish our attraction to, hearing and chanting in Kṛṣṇa consciousness. We have to save the soul.

Some revolutionaries have realized that factory work is soul-killing, but they don't know what actual freedom is for. Or they think freedom means not having to perform any work. We should work, but in Kṛṣṇa consciousness. Then it is not karma, bondage.

As I said, this is easier said than done in Kali-yuga because the age itself seems to limit even a sincere devotee's options. Somehow we can save ourselves anyway. We can build our own society and infrastructure, we can turn more to the land and the cow. I don't have all the answers, but I can read what is written plainly in this verse: *śrama eva hi kevalam*. It's clear. Don't get caught up in work and lose your soul. If you find yourself becoming trapped in your work, get out. Make the sacrifice and break away. Don't become a *karmī*. Become a *bhakta*.

I remember Śrīla Prabhupāda saying, "Rich men's sons don't work," as we walked through the Denver park together one early, sunny morning. He thrilled me right down to my soul when I heard him preaching on the Lower East Side. He taught something so different than what I had learned from my parents, who worshiped the Almighty Buck. My parents had penetrated my psyche with the conviction that I had to have a job, hire myself out, that this was virtue, manliness. This would take care of almost all the problems of existence—a steady, decent-paying job. They wanted me to work like an ass for forty hours a week (with weekends off). They would have liked it if I could have become a fireman like my father, or something better by higher education. "Get it together, Stevie. Don't waste time, but start your career. Get a good job like your brother-in-law, Tommy, the stock market analyst. Don't be a ne'er-do-well."

When I hinted to my father that I might like to become a college professor, he snuffed that out. "That's the end of the line." Then what? Join an insurance company and work my way up? Make money as a writer? No, too chancey. Keep your head out of the clouds. Maybe on Madison Avenue writing ad copies. It was up to me exactly what I did, but I was expected to choose something sensible and presentable and to surrender my life to making money, raising a family, paying a mortgage, buying a new car every three years, etc.

Śrīla Prabhupāda threw that away. He laughed at it, scorned it, exposed it as illusion. Don't become a slave, he said, an ass who works all day carrying cloth for a morsel of grass. I learned. At first I missed the point and resigned from the welfare office. No, he said, keep that job because you can donate to ISKCON. I got it: work for Kṛṣṇa. I wrote two essays for *Back to Godhead* called, "*Karma-yoga.*" I was a *yogī* in the welfare office in my suit and tie. My *yoga-āsana* was to sit at my desk; my meditation was to bring my weekly pay check to the Swami and to see him every day.

Gradually he let me free even of that. We still have much to learn—how to raise money while maintaining our integrity as devotee-preachers, how to be detached while finding the money to print books and build temples. How to be a mendicant without becoming a beggar despised by society. We have a lot to learn.

Kṛṣṇa doesn't work in the spiritual
sky. He plays His flute. He
goes to the forest with calves
and cows as a playing sport.
His friends go with Him.
"Did you ever see a picture of Kṛṣṇa in a factory
or working a machine or smoking a
cigarette? Did you ever see?
No, He is always jolly."

And Rādhā doesn't approach Kṛṣṇa
at the end of His *karmī* work day
and say, "What money do You have
in Your pocket?"
They are innocent boys and girls
in Vṛndāvana village, far beyond this
rat race.
We can go there.
Work for it.

The main thing is to develop *ruci* for chanting and hearing. It doesn't come only by staying at home and not working, because then we'll become lazy. Śrīla Prabhupāda said full-time chanting and hearing was possible only for a *mahā-bhāgavata* such as Haridāsa Ṭhākura. Therefore, Prabhupāda gave us duties to keep us active in his service. Promote Kṛṣṇa consciousness.

So I write. But does it promote my
attraction to Kṛṣṇa?
And do those who read what I write
become compelled to practice *bhakti*?

Hand, move across this page. If the hand keeps moving, the pages will add up. A cash register. Memories flood in.

The Kṛṣṇa conscious writer-self wants all for our Lord.

Who are you?

I'm the hand and voice from one who was told to do automatic writing according to the rules of surrealists who write whatever comes without censorship.

Isn't it better to write whatever provokes attraction to Kṛṣṇa?

That will sabotage the spirit of free-write.

Freedom is to get out of matter. Become the scribe for higher forces. We can work together.

Okay, sound barrier poet
parleys winnings into savings
account of *bhakti*. News reporter
Don Marquis gives up job,
gives up tavern-frequenting.
Converts all he has to cause
of Kṛṣṇa.

We can't go wrong. Our song will triumph even if people think "we're ragged and funny. But we'll travel along, singing our song, side by side."

Don't be so corny. Make the best art for Kṛṣṇa.

That's what I attempt.

You say you are the Kṛṣṇa conscious writing self, but do you think you're alone in that? By the "pure," automatic writing or in memories, I too am trying to evoke that which will be Kṛṣṇa conscious and avoid *śrama eva hi kevalam*. I'm going to all the corners of my body and selves (*ātmā*), all the dark places in material creation, and lighting them with a Kṛṣṇa conscious torch.

Still, we can work together and cut through quicker. And I can tell you of what I read in *Caitanya-caritāmṛta*. Lord Caitanya wanted to experience *rādhā-bhāva*. How the Supreme Lord desired to be a *gopī* is *acintya-śakti*. If you are celibate, you stand a chance to understand Him. If you are *Kṛṣṇa conscious* and celibate.

United Airlines: "Please stand
in this line and wait.
Have your tickets and passports ready."
The clock won't stop but

today I played with fire, allowing flames to jump out of tiny tin container of "tea warmer" candles and then the fire went out of control and I blew at it, spilling wax on Lord Nṛsiṁhadeva's picture. Please forgive me.

Text 9

dharmasya hy āpavargyasya
nārtho 'rthāyopakalpate
nārthasya dharmaikāntasya
kāmo lābhāya hi smṛtaḥ

All occupational engagements are certainly meant for ultimate liberation. They should never be performed for material gain. Furthermore, according to sages, one who is engaged in the ultimate occupational service should never use material gain to cultivate sense gratification.

Comment

Whenever human civilization develops, this cycle of activities begins: religion, economic development, and sense gratification (*dharma*, *artha*, and *kāma*). For ordinary people, the goal is sense gratification—eating, sex, and other bodily and mental comforts. Religion is aimed toward that end. One prays to God or the gods, visits the temple, gives charity, does good deeds, etc., with the idea that the gods will award him wealth and other amenities. The accumulation of money (*artha*) will be needed to secure the best sense gratification—clothes, residence, car, travel, etc. An opulent lifestyle will promote better sense gratification by impressing the opposite sex, buying the best paraphernalia—theater tickets, videos, computers, and whatever else is "needed."

Therefore, religion is useful only with *artha* in mind. *Artha* is to faciliate *kāma*, the fulfillment of lusty desires. As mean-minded as this may sound, this is the cycle for civilized and pious persons who still see a utilitarian value in following religious and moral codes. As Kali-yuga degrades, even the pretense of religion will be dropped.

Sūta Gosvāmī is not outlining compromise; he is speaking the Absolute Truth. He points to the goal of perfection, but he also explains karma and transmigration in a straightforward way. The vast majority of people adhere to the way of sense gratification as the main purpose of all endeavor, "But in the statement of Sūta Gosvāmī, as per the verdict of the *Śrīmad-Bhāgavatam*, this is nullified by the present *śloka*." *Dharma*, defined as "occupational service," should not be used only for sense gratification.

"Boy, you guys are heavy. What do you mean, 'No sense gratification'? What are we supposed to do, live on air? Why can't we pray to God to give us a helping hand at least for good health so we can bring home the bacon and take care of the family? What's wrong if we pray for our children so that they don't become dope addicts or get assaulted by some sex maniac? And what about our wives and homes? You think people can live as human beings and not care for these things? You're trying to deny the basic necessities of life. I don't think God is so cruel or demanding as you make Him out to be. I think He likes it if we're happy in what you call material life, as long as we don't hurt anybody. We pray to God in church on Sunday and we thank Him for providing all these amenities for us. After this life He'll call us to share the kingdom of God with Him."

So the pious *karmī* makes his defense against what he sees as extremism in spirituality. Unfortunately, he has glossed over the facts. His vision of happiness in the world is the same as seeing through rose-colored glasses. The world is meant for suffering, even if you're a nice guy who goes to church or temple once a week and prays for happiness. Neither does *Bhagavad-gītā* or *Śrīmad-Bhāgavatam* condemn the *dharmī-karmī* in his turning to God. If he actually does recognize the Supreme Personality of Godhead and pray to Him, then he's *sukṛtina*, pious. Any recognition of God's superiority is good. But it's foolish to ask God for things that cannot make us happy by their very nature. As Christ states, "Don't stock your treasure in places where thieves and moths can break in and get at them, but invest in pure eternal love of God, which is incorruptible." Devotional service is the only activity that will satisfy the self, the spirit soul. Therefore, enlightened sages and spiritual masters don't pander to their followers' illusions by preaching something that won't make their dependents happy either in this life or in the next. Lesser teachers, pretending to be religious leaders, may cater to their followers' lower desires and try to gain material benefit from their teaching. That's an example of the blind leading the blind. Śrīla Sūta Gosvāmī and his followers speak the truth. Those who can hear submissively will act accordingly and not use religion to enjoy sense gratification.

There, that's my sermon for the day—it's short and hopefully won't bore people. Now I'm getting off the *vyāsāsana*, taking off my outer preaching vestments, and sitting down to relax. If I smoked cigars, I might light one up now and put my feet on a cushion as I lean back in an easy chair. But I don't smoke or use a chair in that way, so when the sermon's over, what does the parson do?

He feels good and thinks over what he said, and pats himself on the back. Or he rushes back to the temple entranceway to greet the congregation as they exit. Maybe he collects some compliments or complaints, and maybe even some money in envelopes.

He may get through with that as quickly as possible and find somewhere to be alone. There he feels relief from the act of performance. He begins to realize how his talk fell short. He didn't stress enough the need to take it seriously. He might have spoken more substantial philosophy, especially about *bhakti*. He might have been more inspiring and practical when he discussed how to practice *sādhana*. He might have sympathized with the congregation's difficulties instead of summarily condemning anyone who's not one hundred percent surrendered to God. He might see himself as tiny and faulty, but he's still happy to be offstage. He's also glad to have a few moments away from the litany of people's problems, as if being God's representative makes him a garbage heap.

"Do not use religion for material gain." He thinks over what he said. What about him? Is he guilty of doing what Sūta condemns and what he himself just finished condemning on the *vyāsāsana*?

A preacher's soliloquy: I admit I sometimes use religion for material gain.

Who?

Me, the fictional me. You don't expect me to make an *actual* confession, do you, as if I were being forced by insidiously clever and torturing police? "Where were you on the night of the 29th?" "Tell us your worst thoughts. Write them down or we'll record them on tape."

I'm an American. According to the Fifth Amendment, I can refuse to testify on the grounds that it may incriminate me.

I liked this morning's milkshake. I hanker for better food than average even while people starve in Africa and other countries. I don't like blisters on my hands and feet. I'm a pussy willow—I mean, a tender fellow.

I'm celibate. I follow the rules. I like to write for writing's sake, not always calculating how effective it will be as a propagandistic spear thrown at bums. Is that wrong?

Kṛṣṇa, Kṛṣṇa, I wish I had time to draw colored pictures by letting the hand move as it likes. I want to release the spontaneous words of my spirit. I wish to enter Kṛṣṇaloka through works that will please folks like me who admit, "We can't always live sitting in the pew and listening to the sermon with a straight face and edifying mood."

I spent the money you gave me on a brown scarf. I like it. I received your gift of stuffed dates and sugar cake sprinkled with tinsel paper, but I couldn't eat them all so I gave them away. I read your letter and replied to you, "I'm glad to hear that you and your wife went to Hawaii and are happy in your new house," but I wasn't actually so glad to hear it.

I admit I am roundabout because I can't cut through. This is the best I could do, but I'm going to do better.

Poor man keeping at his quota
SB 1.2.9
Dharmasya

I remember when I used to wear the best saffron-dyed, raw silk that money could buy. Then I stopped. Someone wrote to remind me and make me feel bad for what I did fifteen years ago. "You wore silks and were served nine-course meals, and you traveled every year to India, whereas most of us who collected the money were never allowed to enjoy such things. You drove in a limousine. We want our money back. We want our youth back. You told my wife to stay out and sell candles and then paintings."

I remember sharp headaches, one time lying on the floor in the flimsy Baltimore house, awake all night because the latest anti-cult legal case was pending.

I remember I decided to go on a diet to stop indigestion. I thought my headaches were caused by my digestive system. I ate only salads. Then someone said I could add a few nuts and toasted bread cubes. Before I knew it, the "salad" turned into a stomach-stuffer. Now I'm on a good diet, but the mind recalls all those nice desserts—warm, fresh-baked pies, tarts with whipped cream, scones with butter, varieties of milk sweets. "*Burfi* is *poison*," an Āyurvedic doctor told me. His face turned with disgust as if he were eating a mouthful of *trifala*.

I remember Swamijī. I remember trying to remember him in 1966. I remember this morning hearing Prabhupāda lecture on *rāga-mārga*. He said we should be patient, like the wife who waits nine months to bear her child. Be patient and execute *vaidhi-bhakti*. Gradually, our success will be guaranteed. He spoke this from *The Nectar of Devotion* in 1972. I can hear birds chirping in Vṛndāvana and Pradyumna reading the sections aloud.

I remember Corky, a sailor in the Public Information Office, and Jerry Davis, another. One was from Elkhart, Indiana, a conservative gentleman who liked to drive his Triumph sports car alone. The other guy was wild and uncultured, uneducated. I got to know him and we used to mock fight because there was nothing else to do.

I remember the time I took initiation.

I don't remember all the bad things I did. I must have suppressed them. They probably wouldn't do me much good. I remember feeling the sunshine on my bare back. I look forward to feeling it again today. But it's all so brief.

Do I use material gain for sense gratification? I should not, I should never. It's not meant for that. If by performance of devotional service we receive rewards—money, praise, etc.—we shouldn't enjoy them. That is especially true of a spiritual master: he should not extract profits from his disciples. He should guide them. Both he and they can use money in Kṛṣṇa's service, but not one dollar should be used for their own *artha* and *kāma*.

Text 10

kāmasya nendriya-prītir
lābho jīveta yāvatā
jīvasya tattva-jijñāsā
nārtho yaś ceha karmabhiḥ

Life's desires should never be directed toward sense gratification. One should desire only a healthy life, or self-preservation, since a human being is meant for inquiry about the Absolute Truth. Nothing else should be the goal of one's works.

Comment

The previous verse states that material development (*artha*) shouldn't be used for sense gratification. Now Sūta Gosvāmī gives the positive injunction: our *artha* and *kāma* should be dedicated to discovering the Absolute Truth.

Prabhupāda reviews the field of human activities and sees everywhere the same drive—to enjoy the senses. Even the fourth activity, *mokṣa*, is tainted with a selfish intention to save oneself. *Mokṣa* is a quest to become one with the Absolute Truth, a "desire to commit spiritual suicide for sense gratification."

Life is not meant for this. Of course, as long as one lives in the material world, he has to maintain and satisfy his senses. The animal propensities of eating, mating, sleeping, and defending may therefore be governed by śāstric direction so that they don't disrupt the real work of service to the Absolute Truth. When one indulges in unrestricted sense gratification, the purpose of human life is lost.

It is difficult to control the mind and senses. Arjuna compares controlling the mind to trying to control the wind. The senses are compared to venomous serpents. How, then, does a transcendentalist surmount these formidable obstacles to self-realization? Śrīla Prabhupāda writes, "Seekers of the Absolute Truth are never allured by unnecessary engagements in sense gratification because the serious students seeking the Absolute Truth are always overwhelmed with the work of researching the Truth." In other words, the devotees are too busy for *māyā*. They've become so interested in their *Bhāgavatam* studies, chanting, and other services that they have no time to consider anything else. This is the simple and splendid program to decrease sense gratification.

Prabhupāda advocated twenty-four hours of full engagement in devotional service a day. He said if a cup is filled with a dirty liquid, we have to first empty it and clean it. But if we leave it sitting around empty, it may become filled with more dirty water, we should clean the cup and immediately fill it with something pure—clean water or milk—so there will be no room for pollution.

I like Prabhupāda's description of the research worker of the Absolute Truth always absorbed and overwhelmed with activity in Kṛṣṇa consciousness. I want to be like that. It seems to be the most appealing and practical way to conquer the otherwise all-pervasive spirit of *kāma*, the life of drowning in material desire.

It's a simple program. If we're willing, there's plenty to do in Kṛṣṇa consciousness. No compromise with *māyā*. Or rather, some compromise in the admittance that our bodies and minds need maintenance and shouldn't be denied healthy upkeep. Be sane and practical. It all starts with recognition of the soul's needs and with our awakening to the words of the spiritual master and *śāstra*. Awakening means action.

We try. We chant Hare Kṛṣṇa instead of songs about boy-girl love. We eat food only after offering it to Kṛṣṇa in the varieties He desires. We serve Prabhupāda by typing, editing, cooking, or bringing in money to pay the rent. Soon we discover that it works. We find ourselves giving up habits we never thought we would be free of and we don't suffer withdrawal from them. Our physical health improves due to the regulated life and the vegetarian diet (Swamijī's love there too). Our mental life improves from Van Gogh's mad despair, from Sartre's absurd universe, to the aspiration of a life leading to eternity, bliss, and knowledge with Kṛṣṇa.

Kṛṣṇa consciousness is not a program of stark denial, "annihilation of ego," or anything dry or impossible. It's a revival of our original spiritual energy, and everything has been adapted to time, place, and person—old wisdom in a new dress, the Swamijī's miracle.

We have plenty of ISKCON buildings—whole charming neighborhoods are growing in Vṛndāvana and Māyāpur, as charming as Watseka Avenue was in the early '70s. Let there be a block of devotee neighbors. More buildings, more leaders, more lecturers. Prabhupāda's desires fulfilled to see his books translated and distributed in almost every world language.

We have all that, we want all that, but we also want our individual integrity as devotees to remain intact. Therefore, we also need personal expression. Personal expression is an integral part of integrity. With so much happening, we want to be sure that our own head is on our own shoulders. We want to be able to answer ourselves in the quiet hours of the day and remember why we are doing what we are doing.

After we fire a barrage of *Bhāgavatam* messages at the enemy and the smoke clears, we want to take stock. We want to make sure we recognize all the enemies and whether or not we are doing what Prabhupāda wanted. It's not that we doubt the leaders, but it's good to check in with ourselves.

Personal expression doesn't mean free-writing. Free-writing is only a means to an end. Personal expression means reading Prabhupāda's purports on our own and being alone with them to think them over. It's healthy.

Read *Bhāgavatam* daily.
Seek lookout on lofty plain.
It's almost 3 P.M., Sarge.
Time to wake up Śrīla Prabhupāda *mūrti*.

I'm sorry for my oversights today—
came before him
wearing no Vaiṣṇava *tilaka* because
I was in a rush, splashed his
best sleeping blanket with hot
wax because I was playing with
fire and not using my intelligence.
And other mistakes.
But I did use some care and
tenderness and respect and I'm glad
for that.

Time for his juice and
mine. Keep working at
transplanting organs, growing
tomatoes, carrots, and beets
and controlling your tongue by being
overwhelmed in the work, as he says,
of researching the Truth.

Research? I thought that
was a bad word. Well,
you can research
how to engage yourself even
when you feel tired at midday.
How to head off anger and
irritability at that time.
How many ways to be kind to
your closest friends, and to be compassionate—
can you do it?—
to those you don't even know,
or to those who may hurt you?

Research—tomorrow is Ekādaśī.
How many extra rounds can
you chant? Can you find places
in your schedule to do it?
Can you improve your delivery of
A Poor Man? Research in Jīva
Gosvāmī and the familiar yet
new purports of your spiritual master.
There is much to be done.
Patiently. Humbly.
Without attachment or
material desire.
And don't get restless or allow
the mad mind to do what
it wants. Know what I mean?

The 1962 edition of the First Canto has a nice phrase in it for 1.2.10 (it was slightly edited in later editions): "One should desire only for a healthy life or self preservation . . ." Maybe the editors thought it was misleading, as if Prabhupāda was saying physical health is all we should want. But it's clear enough that he means we shouldn't use our senses in any exaggerated way. We should eat as much as we need for health, not for titillating the tongue, for example. We should satisfy the senses so we can be be strong enough to serve the Absolute Truth. Health, not *kāma.*

I want to end this afternoon writing with a free session. I sometimes call this writing "automatic," but it's more like running to meet myself halfway, trusting myself. Funny that we just said not to trust the mind and here I am, listening intently to the periphery for whatever comes ("inviting chaos").

Alone in rooms like the one they give me in Baltimore at JG's house, I look out the window, often in winter, and see the neighbor's trampoline. They've written "Rādhā" on the trees in their own backyard. Here I am in this room, so far away from that one. Am I away from the center? I don't feel left out. Or I feel the center can be pursued from here by writing hundreds of pages. That's because each page I write inevitably leads me back to the *Bhāgavatam* and the next verse.

I want more. Sometimes we almost have to get crazier to become saner. Don't play it *too* safe. Go to the frontier of where you shouldn't enter, but don't cross the line. I was not right to watch the flames rise in the cup this morning. I should have acted sooner. Is that playing with fire similar to what I am recommending here? No. I'm just saying we have to get to know ourselves and we can't always do that by playing it safe and never taking risks.

For me, I just write and trust. I feel enthusiasm for it, but I don't whip it past its lifespan. Now I know that that chug-chugging is coming from Ramesh's rock crushing machine. He owns a quarry nearby. The rocks travel up a conveyer belt and are crushed to powder. I guess people buy powdered rocks.

I'm not deep or overwhelmed by the Absolute Truth, but I am staying out of harm's way. From here, please don't judge Godbrothers and don't worry about how they may judge you. Just look forward to tomorrow's early morning. I can't expect literary or spiritual miracles. Sūta is talking some basic philosophy. Take it in and explain it in your own words. Link the personal world with the Absolute. That's my work. Dear Lord, please reveal Yourself to me. I want to chant Hare Kṛṣṇa on Your day—time is meant for Your purposes, even in this.

Text 11

vadanti tat tattva-vidas
tattvaṁ yaj jñānam advayam
brahmeti paramātmeti
bhagavān iti śabdyate

Learned transcendentalists who know the Absolute Truth call this nondual substance Brahman, Paramātmā or Bhagavān.

Comment

At this point, Śrīla Prabhupāda only implies that Bhagavān realization is more complete than realization of Brahman and Paramātmā. That will be clearly developed in later verses. It is also conclusively described in *Caitanya-caritāmṛta* by Kṛṣṇadāsa Kavirāja Gosvāmī in the second chapter of the *Ādi-līlā*, and by Śrīla Jīva Gosvāmī elsewhere.

In a purport to *Śrī Īśopaniṣad*, Prabhupāda mentions the example of the sun-god on the sun planet, the sun disc, and the sunshine. Bhagavān is compared to the fullest possible realization of the sun, which is available when we know the sun-god in his planet. Bhagavān realization is most complete because it gives us three features of the Absolute Truth—eternity, bliss, and knowledge in personal form (*sat-cid-ānanda vigraha*). Paramātmā realization gives us perception of only two features, eternity and knowledge, and Brahman realization gives us realization only of eternity without knowledge of the Absolute Truth as the all-blissful Supreme Personality of Godhead.

In his purport to *Bhāg.* 1.2.11, Prabhupāda points out the non-dual nature of the Absolute Truth. This is known as *advaya-jñāna*. "Less intelligent students of either of the above schools sometimes argue in favor of their own respective realization, but those who are perfect seers of the Absolute Truth know well that the above three features of the one Absolute Truth are different perspective views seen from different angles of vision." We should not think that Paramātmā realization is wrong or that Brahman realization is understood only in the way the Māyāvādīs describe it, as the only spiritual truth (thus there is a difference between a Brahmavādī and a Māyāvādī). In subsequent verses and chapters, *Śrīmad-Bhāgavatam* will glorify the Absolute Truth in all of its features.

Śrīla Prabhupāda also informs us that in the spiritual world there is no difference between the knower and the known. Both the Supreme Lord as well as the pure devotees—and all the paraphernalia of the spiritual realm—are completely spiritual, eternal, cognizant, and blissful. In the material world we experience duality between knower and known. . . . "The knower is the living spirit or superior energy, whereas the known is inert matter or inferior energy."

The oneness of the Absolute may be a confusing subject matter for materialists and speculators, but the *tattva-vidaḥ*, the learned souls, understand it in all its intricacies and implications. We should hear from them.

Other understandings of *advaya-jñāna:* the Lord's names are nondifferent from Himself. When we chant Hare Kṛṣṇa, Kṛṣṇa dances on our tongue. This experience is unique in the material world where a name uttered ("John, John") doesn't give us the full appreciation of the man himself. If we cry out, "Water! Water!" we don't experience the word "water" producing liquid in the chanter's throat.

Kṛṣṇa is also fully present when the pure devotee remembers Him. When the *gopīs* thought of Kṛṣṇa after His departure from Vṛndāvana, they cried in ecstasy. Lord Kṛṣṇa confirmed that this experience, which is known as *viraha* or *līlā-smaraṇam*, is absolute. It is as good as (or even better than) seeing and being with Kṛṣṇa directly. This is because Kṛṣṇa, Bhagavān, is absolute. Any spiritual "part" of Him, such as His name, qualities, form, and pastimes, brings His complete presence into the heart of the alert and loving devotee.

Oneness in the Absolute. I remember hearing this carefully explained by Swamijī one night under the naked light bulb at the storefront. In the morning, in a calmer mood, he explained it again. I remember an old Brooklyn College buddy coming to the storefront and rejecting the concept of Brahman when I tried to point it out to him as the spiritual identity and source of all. For a moment I felt rejected and frustrated by his attitude, but I stood firm in my kindergarten realization of spiritual truth. It's true because it's in the *Vedas*. What did I know of Brahman?

I liked hearing from Swamijī when we sat on Long Branch as he recuperated in New Jersey. He said that in the spiritual world, all the elements are friendly, conscious, and blissful, including the water. He said this while we watched people surfing, a sport he said could end in their deaths.

We rejoiced with our spiritual master in contemplating a blissful vision of the spiritual world and looking forward to tasting it in the future, as he assured us we could. When a devotee asked, "But if everything is conscious and a pure devotee, how do they eat in the spiritual world?" Prabhupāda replied that we would know "when you go there. Don't ask to understand everything now. It's not possible."

It's not possible for an offender to taste Kṛṣṇa in His names. An offender chants only the outer form of the name—the letters and words. When we chant without offense, we begin to understand what is Kṛṣṇa. Kṛṣṇa in sound is as good as Kṛṣṇa in form. This world can become that world because in the higher sense it's "all one." It may be all one, but there are still varieties. We can't know everything now. Better we go on hearing and serving. The Absolute Truth is a person and He will reveal Himself to us as we progress. "To those who worship Me with love, I give the understanding by which they can come to Me."

Roll on, man,
all is one.
I don't know nothing.
I hear from *Vedas*,
God in sound.

How do I feel? I'm distracted. A lizard is tick-ticking up near the fluorescent light. All is one. But in what way? Everything belongs to Lord Kṛṣṇa, the Supreme, the energetic source of all. I'm not one, equal to Him. We are little philosophers concerned with higher topics. Good to get grounded. All is one. The typewriter is spiritual, the hand that writes is spiritual. Prabhupāda says that matter is spirit in a covered form. When we use it for Kṛṣṇa, it regains its spiritual quality.

We told the audience this on a New York City TV show in 1967 when they asked for a definition of "spirit." We said the brass *karatālas* were spirit because they were being used in Kṛṣṇa's service. If we play guitar forgetful of God, it's material. Everything is in the consciousness.

You who are reading this, take breaks as you like. I'm sure you do. It's not possible to swallow a thousand verses at once. We keep going, though, a bit at a time. We don't tire of the overall journey and we hope it never ends.

Never ends. Spiritual forms. Now we discuss it, but one day we will taste it: I'm spiritual and the Supreme Lord is spiritual and we are one. One day, nothing will be material anymore.

My time is measured and I'm a slave to the clock. Therefore, I drop memories of sordid times like hot potatoes.

I remember Bhūrijana laughing.

My time is up. The list grows until the last moment. Then I have to stop. Even Viśvanātha Cakravartī Ṭhākura and Madhvācārya got cut off while writing. Kṛṣṇa calls.

All is one. Bhagavān is best. See all in Him. He's like the curtain rising on the stage—you see everything at once. The *brahmajyoti* comes from Him, Paramātmā comes from Him. You don't have to go through the steps one at a time—first Brahman realization, then a hundred years of yoga to see Paramātmā. We used to ask Prabhupāda questions such as, "Does a devotee realize everything that a trained *yogī* knows?

But I don't know Paramātmā." We worried about such things. I don't worry about them anymore. I'm not as interested in Paramātmā as I used to be. The *gopīs* aren't either, although they offer Him respect. Some Vaiṣṇava poets curse *brahmajyoti* realization—*kaivalya-nara* is hellish. Light without Kṛṣṇa. Who needs it?

Text 12

tac chraddadhānā munayo
jñāna-vairāgya-yuktayā
paśyanty ātmani cātmānaṁ
bhaktyā śruta-gṛhītayā

The seriously inquisitive student or sage, well equipped with knowledge and detachment, realizes that Absolute Truth by rendering devotional service in terms of what he has heard from the Vedānta-śruti.

Comment

Since devotional service is specifically mentioned here (*bhaktyā śruta-gṛhītayā*), we may understand that the Absolute Truth is revealed foremost as the Supreme Person. Prabhupāda clearly establishes in his purport, "The first-class transcendentalists are the devotees who have realized the Supreme Person." Realization of Brahman and Paramātmā is imperfect, and the means of realizing them is also imperfect. "Devotional service, which is based on the foreground of full knowledge combined with detachment from material association and which is fixed by the aural reception of the *Vedānta-śruti*, is the only perfect method by which the seriously inquisitive student can realize the Absolute Truth."

There are three classes of *bhaktas:* the material or third-class devotees, the second-class or *madhyama* (middle) position, and the topmost devotees. The materialistic devotees are encouraged to elevate themselves as quickly as possible to the *madhyama* stage by serving and hearing from the representative of the *Bhāgavatam* (a *bhāgavata*). However, "A neophyte devotee has very little taste for hearing from the authorities." Persons who only pretend to be devotees make a show of hearing Vedic knowledge from professional reciters. They can never make progress by this method. Rather, they create a disturbance in the *bhakti* camp.

This verse therefore defines the behavior of a "seriously inquisitive student," or one who hears Vedic knowledge and follows the instructions of the authorized *bhāgavatas*. In the name of "all is one," we do not claim that all paths and all practitioners are equally enlightened and should therefore be encouraged in whatever they are doing. The *Bhāgavatam* presents the science of devotional service. It has to be understood and followed in the proper way if one wants to attain the results.

Each person has to ascertain his own motives and position as aspirants to approach the Absolute Truth. If we make a show of dress, speech, and mannerisms of being devotees, yet deliberately maintain material desires, then what kind of Vaiṣṇavas are we? At best, we are third-class, *prākṛta-bhaktas*.

In my own list of admissions, I've dug up all sorts of less than pure thoughts and inclinations, yet I go on hearing and trying to assimilate the *Bhāgavatam*. Is that a contradiction? Hypocrisy? How can one suddenly banish all desires and meditate exclusively on the spiritual master's desires? What about a *Bhāgavatam* verse such as *akāmaḥ sarva-kāmo vā mokṣa-kāma udāra-dhīḥ:* "A person who has broader intelligence, whether he be full of all material desire, without any material desire, or desiring liberation, must by all means worship the supreme whole, the Personality of Godhead"? Isn't hearing *Śrīmad-Bhāgavatam* the best method to cleanse dirt from the heart? Yes, it is.

We won't be outright hypocrites if we follow our initiation vows (no meat-eating, no illicit sex, no intoxication, and no gambling, and to chant at least sixteen rounds of Hare Kṛṣṇa mantra a day), but we can't claim to be advanced devotees as long as we are more concerned with material benefits than transcendental profit as a result of the practice of *sādhana-bhakti*. Take the spiritual master's order on our heads, humbly. Remove the weeds, straws, and *aparādhas* that we perceive either by self-examination or by Kṛṣṇa's pointing them out. In that way, we won't remain perpetually nonsensical and be an embarrassment to ourselves and to our guru. We have to become *chraddadhānā munayo*, seriously inquisitive students.

Here's a picture of the seriously inquisitive sage. Notice that he's walking to the left. That's west. Is he going downtown to preach? Is he bold? Or is he just going to the bathroom again? Is he going from the *brahmacāri-āśrama* to the temple room, half out of boredom, half out of routine?

Why do I call him "seriously inquisitive"? Because he left his parents, school, and career and moved into a Hare Kṛṣṇa temple where they stress reading, chanting, and serving all day. That's a serious commitment.

This particular student needs a break, though—a few amenities. He looks forward to *some Vedānta-śruti*, but not more than thirty or thirty-five minutes at a time. He needs to joke. He wants to go on the roof and feel a little warmth from the winter sunshine because his bones and flesh are cold. He's got a cold. He looks forward to eating and daydreaming, "while visions of sugar plums dance in his head."

He's not really a *chraddadhānā munayo*, not yet, but we won't reject him. He has come a long way already and we want to protect him. Someone senior can counsel him: "Get serious. Don't space out." The boy walks to the left. He is on a man's errand and he lacks confidence. Will he walk into profound, self-sacrificing engagement or just to the bathroom again?

The serious, inquisitive sage, well-equipped with knowledge and austerity, hearing *Vedānta-sūtra*. Translate that for here and now. It means you calm down and read and get at the meaning. He's *advaya-jñāna*. He sees it's all one. Spirit is truth. The seriously inquisitive sage. He doesn't play with a yo-yo, but he doesn't know Kṛṣṇa well either. He tries to wake himself up with words. (He'll accept a cup of juice just now to fuel himself.)

It means devotional service. You use your brain to teach. You say there are three kinds of devotees and four kinds of people: *karmī*, *jñānīs*, *yogīs*, and *bhaktas*. You've heard it before. Now some pop Indian music rolls over the plains. You chased a dog out of the yard—that's important, just a local thing, but you were there and it was you. The mongrel entered this government land where you are a temporary resident. As if you are the prince of this place. The mongrel jumped onto the porch. You came forward out of the garden fast, "Hut!" (You heard Prabhupāda say that on his walks.) You moved menacingly, although there were no rocks to throw. The dog sprang off the porch and headed down the path for the exit, but the front gate was locked and there was no way out. He turned to bark at you. He obviously felt trapped, so he had to test the danger a little further. You were surprised that the strange, lone, fugitive dog was barking at you, but you barked back. You barked like a human dog to show him you were equal to his challenge. He barked more. You menaced. He turned and found an opening in the barbed wire and squeezed through. This left you feeling foolish. You thought, "Maybe that dog was a saintly person. Why did I chase him? He would have ruined our fruit if he found it. I was right to chase him." But maybe you hurt his feelings. You definitely drove him out. Now you're alone.

During this time, you stopped chanting on your beads, holding them while you barked and menaced. Now you return to uttering Hare Kṛṣṇa, Hare Kṛṣṇa. Is this a seriously inquisitive sage? I don't think so.

A third-class devotee is material.
A second-class devotee is a preacher who hears from the
Bhāgavatam person.
There he goes again,
flying off a cliff,
hang glider. He can do that because
he doesn't have to work for a living.
He's spending his karma that way.
I say better chant more today and redeem
yourself. ISKCON on the march for
1996. Better account for yourself.
Willy bejabbers I ebb and
flow while the female singer
broadcasts. I had a good reference
to read you about strictness in
celibacy and how it relates
to Lord Caitanya not being *gaurāṅga-nāgarī* but
always in the mood of a *gopī*.
Give up male lust and all lust.
Don't feel guilty for not being in a temple right now.
I'm out here writing. I'm seeking themes and scars
and ebb and flow to prepare this
seriously inquisitive sage
rabbit's foot, stew of newt
witches' brew. It's actual.

I came out of stupor, a boy who remembers
he was in the Navy and ate garbagey
meat stew with lousy taste and cooks
and servers dirty, pimples and ripped
T-shirts, foul mouths and him with a
delicate or agonized poet's book in back
pocket. That's all past now. Present is
Indian pop music, house servant Lakshman
cleaning the bathroom, water sounds and I'm
actually serious and well-equipped
with knowledge and hearing
Vedānta-śruti sometimes.

And you, are you always perfect? You don't want to hear this? Then turn it off. I'm gonna chant. This is also chanting. Grr, humble, bark, sniffle, belch, look at, gripe, and drive the worst.

Text 13

ataḥ pumbhir dvija-śreṣṭhā
varṇāśrama-vibhāgaśāḥ
svanuṣṭhitasya dharmasya
saṁsiddhir hari-toṣaṇam

O best among the twice-born, it is therefore concluded that the highest perfection one can achieve by discharging the duties prescribed for one's own occupation according to caste divisions and orders of life is to please the Personality of Godhead.

Comment

The *Bhāgavatam* hints at *varṇāśrama* duties in 1.2.8, but here they are explicitly described. In the earlier verse, Sūta Gosvāmī explains that occupational duties are "so much useless labor if they do not provoke attraction for the message of the Personality of Godhead." Thus the failure of *varṇāśrama* work was cited.

In the present verse the success is described: to please the Supreme Lord by your work in *varṇa* and *āśrama*. The *varṇāśrama* divisions were originally created by Lord Kṛṣṇa, *cātur-varṇyaṁ mayāsṛṣṭam;* they are natural and appear in human society all over the world.

The Vedic scriptures tell us exactly how to behave according to our psycho-physical nature. These duties are meant to produce harmony among humans, as well as between humans and animals, humans and nature, and God and all living beings. Simply please Kṛṣṇa by linking your efforts to His desires, as directed by those who understand *karma-yoga*, action in Kṛṣṇa consciousness.

A pure devotee transcends *varṇāśrama* designations, but to set an example, he may work within society as a *brāhmaṇa* or a *sannyāsī*, the spiritual masters of society. Or a pure devotee may live as a *gṛhastha*, as Lord Kṛṣṇa did, or as a *kṣatriya*. In the *Bhagavad-gītā*, Kṛṣṇa explains his reasons for following *varṇāśrama* and indicates why other advanced transcendentalists should act in a similar way: "Whatever actions a great man performs, common men follow. And whatever standards he sets by exemplary acts, all the world pursues. O son of Pṛthā, there is no work prescribed for Me within all the three planetary systems. Nor am I in want of anything, nor have I a need to obtain anything—and yet I am engaged in prescribed duties. For if I ever failed to be engaged in carefully performing prescribed duties, O Pārtha, certainly all men would follow My path. If I did not perform prescribed duties, all these worlds would be put to ruination. I would be the cause of creating unwanted population, and I would thereby destroy the peace of all living beings. As the ignorant perform their duties with attachment to results, the learned may similarly act, but without attachment, for the sake of leading people on the right path." (Bg. 3.21–5)

We are successful if whatever we do pleases the Supreme Lord. The majority of the population in Kali-yuga may not be pleased by a devotee's work, but the devotee is satisfied and confident knowing that he is working under Kṛṣṇa's direction. How do we know that Kṛṣṇa is satisfied? One way we can know is that our attraction for hearing about Kṛṣṇa is provoked by what we are doing. We may claim that we are redeveloping *varṇāśrama* (which has been vitiated by the age of Kali) by agricultural work or an appropriate business, but if we don't chant at least sixteen rounds a day and hear the scriptures regularly, then how can we claim that Lord Hari is pleased with our development?

Other favorable symptoms already mentioned in the *Bhāgavatam* are that we serve the Supreme without material motive, with no interruption, and we feel deep self-satisfaction. These symptoms may be verified internally, just as a person knows that he is relieving his hunger and becoming nourished while he eats.

Aside from this, attention to the spiritual master's pleasure is crucial. *Yasya prasādad bhāgavat-prasādo:* if the spiritual master is pleased, then Kṛṣṇa is pleased. If the spiritual master is displeased with us, we are lost. Even after the guru's disappearance from this world, the faithful disciple is assured of the guru's blessings by following his eternal instructions.

Varṇāśrama is a complicated subject, especially because it involves the material as well as the spiritual energy. We need *varṇāśrama* in order to organize the society sanely, yet human beings also need to finally rise above the *varṇāśrama* institution. *Varṇāśrama* is not pure *bhakti*, but it supports *bhakti*. To theorize on *varṇāśrama* and to establish the ideal may be possible in conversation, but to enact it in a community or nation is daunting work.

Even if a group of people or an institution cannot establish *varṇāśrama* in its pure form, they can always turn to direct Kṛṣṇa consciousness, to chanting and hearing. Therefore, Caitanya Mahāprabhu didn't even recommend that we develop ourselves gradually through the stages of *varṇāśrama*. Rather, He told us simply to chant Hare Kṛṣṇa, dance, and honor *kṛṣṇa-prasādam*. *Varṇāśrama* designations will naturally clarify as we purify ourselves and our society—as a by-product.

Don't ask me about *varṇāśrama*. I don't know how to establish it. I lecture on "the inner life of a preacher" instead—chanting and reading. I don't say too much about that either, but I try to practice it. Inner life is on the *varṇāśrama* map somewhere. I don't write letters to the editor or polemical essays or attend conferences. It's not that I don't care about *varṇāśrama*. How could I say that? Prabhupāda considered it important and so many devotees say that they are trying to implement it, especially those working on rural development. I'm all for it.

But don't mind if I work in the fountain pen department rather than the plow department. The pen is also a plow. I admit it. I'm doing my bit.

Now this may have nothing to do with verse 1.2.13, or it may. Pleasing Lord Hari is everyone's business and we are never outside that realm. We either please Him or we don't. We can't escape Him or claim exemption: "I'm not under God's eye. I'm in a place so private, flying so high that He can't know." It's just not possible. But we can manage to get outside the internal energy. That choice we do have. We made it, too—slipped out of paradise. Now we act like *mūḍhas* thinking we are independent of Kṛṣṇa, just as a criminal is forced to follow the law, although he doesn't care for the government.

I want to please Lord Hari. We may say that whatever we do is within the *Bhāgavatam* because Bhagavān is over all. We're also in His special energy by our spiritual master's grace.

Today I'm chanting extra rounds because it's Ekādaśī. And I'm writing in a quiet house with the electricity off and flies buzzing around. I'm sniffling and waiting for a cup of juice, noting the clock, "Oh, time to wake Prabhupāda up from his post-lunch nap."

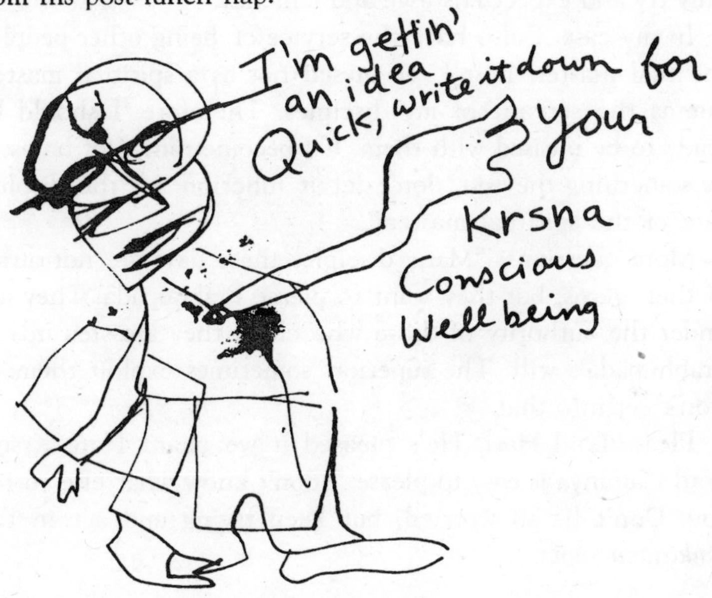

Varn Asrama, was that his name? Van Johnson? He's big, wavy-haired, and freckled. Big hands, too. He smiled a lot and wasn't afraid of most people. He was a movie star and wore a plaid shirt and work pants. But as with many Hollywood men, rumor was he was a homosexual.

Wernher von Braun, German scientist. Pun Salsditch. All these people running out of the ink bottle. Better cap it because I don't yet see a way to bring fiction into this.

The capital of desire. The city parks of the body and the gates leading into those parks. This is described in the Purañjana allegory. It ends in misery.

He really wants to know how we can be sure we are pleasing Kṛṣṇa. He may take my answer as glib and too short. "Personally, are *you* sure you're pleasing Prabhupāda?"

He presses the point with his list of questions. Still, I keep my answer short.

Hari-toṣaṇam. It's enough to know that pleasing Kṛṣṇa is the goal and to keep working for it throughout life. We can only try and expect His love and leniency.

In my case, I also have the service of being other people's spiritual master. Best I see myself not as a spiritual master, but as the servant of my disciples. Therefore, I should be ready to be pleased with them. If I become ruffled or harassed by something they do, don't let it function as "the displeasure of the spiritual master."

More questions: "Many disciples these days are not afraid of their gurus, but they want to please Prabhupāda. They act under the authority of those who claim they are stewards of Prabhupāda's will. The superiors sometimes exploit them." I won't get into that.

Please Lord Hari. He's pleased if we chant Hare Kṛṣṇa. Lord Caitanya is easy to please. I don't know what else to tell you. Don't be so worried, but keep trying and act in the *saṅkīrtana-yajña*.

Text 14

tasmād ekena manasā
bhagavān sātvatāṁ patiḥ
śrotavyaḥ kīrtitavyaś ca
dhyeyaḥ pūjyaś ca nityadā

Therefore, with one-pointed attention, one should constantly hear about, glorify, remember and worship the Personality of Godhead, who is the protector of the devotees.

Comment

These are the primary devotional activities which all members of society must follow, regardless of their *varṇa* or *āśrama*. This will make the Lord satisfied (*saṁsiddhir hari-*

toṣaṇa). When the Lord is satisfied, the living entities will also be satisfied. No one is an exception to this rule, and no one is barred from it. Prabhupāda considers the devotional methods mentioned here—hearing, glorifying the Lord, etc.—and writes that they are natural even when misapplied to ordinary mortals. One either hears about, praises, and worships Kṛṣṇa, or he hears about, praises, and worships a fallible, unqualified object of worship.

It reminds me of my own tendency to worship heroes, which I directed toward various persons during my childhood and adolescence. When I was very small, I looked up to my father. Later, I worshiped various members of the Brooklyn Dodgers. Even later, I worshiped famous rock 'n' roll singers. In college, I transferred my praise to intellectuals and artists. The heroes changed because I outgrew them. I took their pictures down from my walls and replaced them with others. Those who seemed great later seemed foolish. Then I would make fun of them. They proved to be impermanent heroes or protectors. Neither could they give me happiness, even when I was at the height of their praises.

Śrīla Prabhupāda points out how political or advertising propaganda creates the false impression that an ordinary person is wonderful. Such a person's popularity surge lasts only a little while. Then people become tired of the hero and begin to see the glaring defects in his character. They then reject him at the election booth. When the hero is at his zenith, he appears to be the country's savior, but history judges in the long run: who has done anything to alleviate the basic miseries of human existence?

Therefore, hearing, praising, remembering, and worshiping should be offered exclusively to the Supreme Personality of Godhead. Unfortunately, people have so little information about God that He's just not tangible to them. The local politicans and superstars are more tangible than God. Or, God is poorly presented by religious leaders and people simply reject Him as sentiment. This is a faithless age.

The egoistic nature of a conditioned human being makes him inclined to worship his own fallible self. "Take care of Number One." Jaded after giving adoration to others and feeling cheated, one lives a selfish life, trying to enjoy as much sense gratification as possible. "To hell with serving some leader's cause," we think. We'd prefer to serve our own tongue, belly, and genitals. We go to psychiatrists and astrologers to gain relief from our mental distress and also because we're fascinated by our own natures. There is no end to the wonderful or frightening things we can learn about ourselves. The professional counselors are willing to indulge us in hearing about the "real you" for a high fee. This is a perverted form of the universal tendency to praise, hear about, and remember someone.

Śrīmad-Bhāgavatam is the topmost literature because it directs our attention to Kṛṣṇa. Lesser Vedic texts mention hearing about and glorifying the demigods, or teach us to practice impersonal meditation through *ahaṅgraha-upāsanā*, worship of ourselves ("You are that too"). Therefore, it is important to stay within the precincts of the *Bhāgavatam* and to be guided by the *bhāgavatas*.

In this connection, both *Caitanya-caritāmṛta* and Śrīla Prabhupāda mention the wonderful welfare work done in recent centuries by the Six Gosvāmīs of Vṛndāvana. Śrīla Śrīnivāsa Ācārya sings, *nānā-śāstra-vicāraṇaika-nipuṇau* . . . the Gosvāmīs wrote many books on devotional service with the support of Vedic literature. They presented the essence as understanding Lord Kṛṣṇa through devotional service. "They have put it so nicely that even a rascal or first-class fool can be delivered by devotional service under the guidance of the *gosvāmīs*." (Cc. *Madhya*, 1.33, purport)

I like to think I'm following in their footsteps, poor as I am.

Calm down and praise Lord Hari. They do that in the Old Testament book of Psalms. Praise Him with harp, drums, and cymbals. That's *saṅkīrtana,* praising God by singing Hare Kṛṣṇa. You need to remember what you're doing, however, when you make praises. Praise is not a mechanical act. You have to find the heart.

You don't praise anyone. You just go on living, which means seeking animal-like sense gratification. No joy, no remembrance of God—just spaced out. I don't want that kind of life. What did Lord Kṛṣṇa do next? Tell us how He and Balarāma were masked as human beings and had wonderful activities in Their childhood. Tell us also (the sages inquire in *Śrīmad-Bhāgavatam*) how the Lord creates in the beginning, and then how He maintains the universes. Tell us about His internal energy. Tell us about His great devotees, such as Nārada, Prahlāda, Dhruva, and Pṛthu Mahārāja. Tell us about Kṛṣṇa.

Sit patiently and hear, and then I will tell you, Sūta says. Are you too spaced-out, too envious to praise God? Fix your head right. Don't associate with nondevotees. I can give you all this good advice if you'll just listen and heed it.

Give me some relief, man. I trust you. Go ahead and massage my tummy and back, shave my cheeks and throat. I turn it over to you—the power of attorney. I remember a legless attorney in Seattle who got around on crutches and who seemed happy in his work. I know these little flits of memory aren't going to save me and that readers can't understand them out of context either. Better I stick to the "praise God" theme. At the same time, I want to give permission to the inner voice. The hand must have something it wants to say.

When I write, "Unfortunately, people don't remember God," I am talking not just about society, but about myself. God is not real to me. I study *Śrīmad-Bhāgavatam* and

Caitanya-caritāmṛta, and now I'm also studying the *Sandarbhas*. That's the only way to bring Him close. While doing that, however, I still have to live with my body, pain, and comforts. Austerity is dry. The world is not a permanent home for us, yet it fascinates us or wears us down. Therefore, consider each word the *śāstras* speak. *Śrotavyaḥ*, hear, worship, praise, remember.

When you chant Hare Kṛṣṇa over and over, that's certainly directed to Lord Hari, but "unfortunately in Kali-yuga, people are not attentive to chanting God's names."

There you go again, talking about the people in Kali. What about you? You are the unfortunate one who doesn't praise and remember Lord Hari, who feels distant from Him. What are you doing to rectify *that*?

Well, I chant and read at least three times a day. In between, I maintain my fly-like existence. Lord Caitanya said that if He had a drop of love of God, how could He continue to live? We are faithless widows. God is gone from our lives, but we don't care. We remember only our own exploits. We talk of ordinary people instead of Lord Hari.

We are finding our way back, but by circuitous routes. We tend to dissolve our material desires by moderate means rather than by a fire of dissolution. We give ourselves endless chances because we need rest or have colds; we need water to drink or we can't find our beads. Our heads drift like clouds. Where is our depth? If we seek our low point in not loving Kṛṣṇa, we may decide to climb up. But we don't like to judge ourselves too critically. We prefer to feel encouraged. After all, we're trying to be good devotees and think of Kṛṣṇa before death.

Concentrate. Lord Hari, please let me know You in a personal way in my life. Please enter my heart. Give me strength to know You.

Praise with *ekena manasā*. A serious monk in his cell prays, but feels dry. He lies down. Time passes. He wants to talk to someone or draw a picture. He opens the dictionary and gets lost looking at a battleship, a snake in grass, Shepard (first American astronaut), Shelley with a big, ladyish collar and a drawing of his wife, Mary—tragic Romantics—"Ah, bird thou never wert!" Music all night here in—a party or wedding? Harmonium. Sounds like religious *bhajanas*. Someone is praising and worshiping, but I don't know if it's Lord Hari.

Kīrtana can be performed in a variety of ways, including lifting my hands in writing to say, "I want to love You, Kṛṣṇa. Please deliver me." Is it that we don't mean it enough? Do we worship our own expressions more than we actually worship Kṛṣṇa? It's too painful to admit these things, what to speak of rectifying them.

I hereby sign off after having scratched the tender surface of my own inadequacy and self-centeredness. But I can't kick myself out. I have to work with this fruitive being and, even in my conditioned state, perform devotional service. All I can do is ask forgiveness and keep going. Lead on, Sūta. I can't help myself, so I fall at your feet.

Text 15

yad-anudhyāsinā yuktāḥ
karma-granthi-nibandhanam
chindanti kovidās tasya
ko na kuryāt kathā-ratim

With sword in hand, intelligent men cut through the binding knots of reactionary work [karma] by remembering the Personality of Godhead. Therefore, who will not pay attention to His message?"

Comment

A materialist cannot understand karma or his need to become free of it. He doesn't believe in karmic laws because he can't see them ("Who is the witness?"). In Kali-yuga ordinary people accept the scientists' version of reality, but they refuse to accept scriptural authority. Therefore, it comes down to deciding between authorities.

We can perceive the law of karma in action by observing the conditions of people's lives. Karma explains why one person is born rich and another poor, one whole and another crippled. It explains why two people can work hard, but only one becomes successful. It also explains how the life force circulates throughout all the species, returning again and again through a variety of bodies. Transmigration explains what is beyond our senses—the transfer of the soul from one body to another.

Despite the varieties of good and bad karma, all material reaction brings suffering. Transcendentalists who are soberly aware of the facts seek to stop the cycle of repeated birth and death. Śrīla Prabhupada declares that "constant association with the spiritual activities of the Supreme Lord gradually spiritualizes the conditioned soul and ultimately severs the knot of material bondage." *Kṛṣṇa-līlā* is above the modes of material nature; therefore, hearing about Kṛṣṇa's pastimes spiritualizes us. We are spiritual by nature; association with Kṛṣṇa awakens that knowledge. Here, the *Bhāgavatam* uses the metaphor of cutting a knot. Lord Caitanya used a different metaphor in His *Śikṣāṣṭakam:* chanting Kṛṣṇa's name cleanses the dirt from the mirror of the mind.

It is not possible to gain ultimate liberation from *saṁsāra* without engaging in devotional service. We cannot become liberated by theoretical knowledge of matter and spirit. The spirit soul is ever-active and needs to be engaged in spiritual service. Therefore, although a Brahman-realized soul may raise himself to the spiritual sky by his austerities and meditation, he will eventually fall down again into the material world if he has not found shelter at Kṛṣṇa's lotus feet.

The Vedic literatures, especially the *Itihāsas* and *Purāṇas*, and even more so, the *Śrīmad-Bhāgavatam*, are meant for remembering Kṛṣṇa. (The term "Vedic literature" includes the immense literature left by the Six Gosvāmīs of Vṛndāvana.) An intelligent person will constantly hear, remember, praise, and worship the Supreme Lord according to the instructions left in these literatures.

Sometimes an aspiring *bhakta* "knows" all this, yet he feels helpless to sever the knots that bind him to material attachment. He laments, "I don't have any taste for hearing about Kṛṣṇa, and I don't have a spontaneous desire to glorify Him or worship Him. Please lift me out of this languor." We want to advise such persons not to give up hearing and chanting about Lord Kṛṣṇa, even if they find it dry. We have abused our minds and emotions by reading racy, inferior, mundane books. We have exposed ourselves to skepticism. Now we are unable to taste the nectar of the *Bhāgavatam*.

Gradual practice will revive our dormant attraction and faith. The sages aren't bluffing when they speak of the ecstasy of hearing about Kṛṣṇa; Vyāsa was not writing fables.

Let's take the medicine and gradually recover. Remember: "One who knows the transcendental nature of My appearance and activities does not, upon leaving the body, take his birth again in this material world, but attains My eternal abode, O Arjuna." (Bg. 4.9)

Someone asked, "All right, this is true, but why do we see only a small band of devotees relishing Kṛṣṇa's pastimes? Why doesn't everyone relish them? Are the devotees all of above average intelligence? What about all the intelligent politicians and scientists? Does this mean that devotional service requires some special quality? What is it?"

We see that even among those who begin Kṛṣṇa consciousness, most give it up later. It's a rare few who are serious enough to practice it throughout their lives. Prabhupāda says that devotees *are* of above average intelligence, but he isn't necessarily referring to material intelligence. Devotional service—hearing about Kṛṣṇa—has the potency to purify anyone who takes it up, but few do. That's just the way it is. Kṛṣṇa states this principle in the *Bhagavad-gītā: manuṣyāṇāṁ sahasreṣu kaścid yatati siddhaye*, " . . . and of those who have achieved perfection, hardly one knows Me in truth." (Bg. 7.3) If we somehow find ourselves in the proximity of hearing about Lord Kṛṣṇa, we should consider ourselves fortunate. Without so much questioning, "Why me? Why so few? Am I intelligent? How does it work that *kṛṣṇa-kathā* cuts material bonds?" we should move in a little closer to hear better what Sūta is saying.

Admissions—cut the knots: I, too, as with the inquirer, can't reach the taste that would make me abandon all else. The sages are doing a lot of prefatory talk, about *Śrīmad-Bhāgavatam*, about hearing. When will we get into the topics themselves, *kṛṣṇa-kathā*? But this too is *kṛṣṇa-kathā*. Discuss *bhakti* as a phenomenon, a science. That's also a way to practice *bhakti*. Soon enough we'll be hearing how Kṛṣṇa killed

Pūtanā and how He opened His mouth to show His mother the universal form. First, however, we have to be prepared to understand.

Hole in my glove where I rub
the beads against right thumb tip
and longest finger of right hand,
just above the lower joint on the
right side, callous or sore there.
Chant forty years and wear out your patience.
Prabhupāda said be confident that 24 hours
a day Lord Kṛṣṇa's helping us,
even imperceptibly.
You just have to be alert.
You do have taste.
You are here in *Śrīmad-Bhāgavatam*
because you have some *śraddhā*
and it will increase.

I admit I want a pie and to fill my belly, but Prabhupāda said, "Don't." Cut the knots.

Don't think, "I cut the knots already this morning." I also breathed this morning, but I didn't stop breathing later. Dust accumulates. Knots re-tie and harden. Go back to a verse and hear. Don't be away long.

A dialogue:

Be willing to go for it with sword in hand.

You see? He's got a sword. That's *śravaṇam*. He swings it by Balarāma's grace.

I'm not an Indian, a Hindu.

So what? You're an ISKCON enthusiast, aren't you? You subscribe to *ISKCON World Review*, don't you?

Yeah, but I skim through the articles and don't read the personals or the ads.

Then?

Permit me, persimmons, I just faxed 10,000 miles, "Get me Knut Hamsun's *Hunger*."

You think you can learn something from a worldly guy or something from the truth of life rubbed against the earth without pretense?

I wish I could write like that in devotional service too, so nicely that even a first-class fool or rascal would be interested in Kṛṣṇa consciousness. I want to open up.

He or she has the sword. Knots are slashed—big iron knots and hawser knots. No crowbar could open them, only remembrance of Kṛṣṇa.

Her hand offering benediction, I pray in my mind to Bhakti-devī: "Please help me to slash these knots that tie me to the material world."

I think of the frozen tableau of sages drawn on the inside cover of the *Bhāgavatams*. What's holding us back from joining them? Cobwebs? Ghosts? Come on, man, go forward. It reminds me of how they push student fire fighters into the flames. They have to get in there and choke and put the fire out because one day they may have to do it for real. I hung back, not wanting to go first. I tagged along in the back, looking for a space to breathe near the floor.

Real sages push forward and God is kind to them.
The Indian mind I don't have
or comprehend by chanting my mantras.
Bhāgavatam is open for me
as I've read it.
Who will not give it attention?

Learn your dreams and horoscope and childhood and unconscious, your love of women and men and your desire, admit your alienation. Be open to correction. Eat better (less?). Stick up for your rights. All this has to do with the quality of your hearing and writing on the *Bhāgavatam*. It does. You are not a cipher and not a pure devotee. You cannot put this stuff aside, or if you say you can, then let's really see you do it. Otherwise, contend with who you are and put yourself in order.

"Worshiping Him without any interval." When you die, then whatever you did with your life—that's it. Worship Govinda, worship Govinda, worship Govinda *mudha-mate*.

The Swami said in his *Nectar of Devotion* talks that *utsāha* is ISKCON's driving force and that's how "these boys and girls" have left their countries to travel with him.

Free write to
Victory
unearth worms
but then
see Krsna in
S.B & everywhere
I hope
Your
your
job

Text 16

śuśrūṣoḥ-śraddadhānasya
vāsudeva-kathā-ruciḥ
syān mahat-sevayā viprāḥ
puṇya-tīrtha-niṣevaṇāt

O twice-born sages, by serving those devotees who are completely freed from all vice, great service is done. By such service, one gains affinity for hearing the messages of Vāsudeva.

Comment

Asuras, those against God's will, are pushed down into the lower species of life where they have no chance to understand the Absolute Truth. Their only hope for deliverance is to gradually evolve into the higher species again and to make favorable contact with a pure devotee. Prabhupāda says that these pure devotees appear in different countries of the world, and he seems to hint at Jesus Christ and Mohammed when he says, " . . . they are known as the powerful incarnations of the Lord, as sons of the Lord, as servants of the Lord or as associates of the Lord." One symptom of Kṛṣṇa's genuine representatives is that they never claim to be God.

Lord Caitanya is Kṛṣṇa Himself, as stated in the *Vedas*, but He appears in the mood of God's pure devotee. He protests being called God and thus warns us against those blasphemers who take pleasure in being called God.

Prabhupāda states that the servant of God "risks everything" to preach God consciousness in the world. The preachers are the Lord's dearest servants. Whoever cooperates with them will receive God's blessings. You can please God more by serving His servants than by attempting to serve Him directly. "By serving the servants of the Lord, one gradually gets the quality of such servants, and thus one becomes qualified to hear the glories of God."

This is an open secret. It is the answer to the aspiring devotees who lament that they feel helpless to increase their attachment to Kṛṣṇa. The eagerness to hear about Kṛṣṇa can be gained by a *mahātmā's* good wishes, and his blessings are bestowed when we render him service.

It's easy to say, "Serve the *mahātmās* or *tīrthas*," but it can be demanding because the pure devotees are also known as *sādhus*, "those who cut the knot of illusion." It can be painful when a *sādhu* cuts at our material attachments and exposes our false egos. A *sādhu* is intent on his mission; he asks his followers to bear the same burden and "risk everything." Therefore, people sometimes shy away from a *mahātmā*, or stay at what feels like a safe distance. We may try to receive a *sādhu's* blessings without understanding his inner wishes. Coming too close may cause the syndrome of "familiarity breeds contempt" in someone without clear understanding.

Service to the pure devotee is not an imaginary process. We don't merely offer him whatever we'd like to do and then ask him to accept it, but we ask, "How may I serve you?"

I don't want to make it sound harrowing or negative to approach the Lord's devotee. Certainly the devotee is kind. He has the right to reprimand us, but he is usually lenient and accepts us despite our shortcomings. He always gives us a chance to hear about Kṛṣṇa from his talks and books. He doesn't want us to go away from devotional service; he protects our devotional creeper. He is sorry if we do leave his service after having approached him. In other words, the spiritual master takes personal responsibility and charge of his disciples. Glorious is that servant who never leaves his master, and glorious is that master who rescues his servant from the impending dangers of *māyā*, grabbing him by the hair to pull him back if necessary.

Service to the pure devotee continues eternally. The pure devotee continually raises us to the higher stages. Prabhupāda said that a disciple should not be content to remain on the lower rungs of *vaidhi-bhakti*, but to ascend to spontaneous devotional service, we need to become serious and sincere. We should first be happy with our fortune of having established contact with *sad-guru*. Then we should serve him to develop his qualities in our own lives.

Amen. By serving those pure devotees who are free of vice, great service is done. This sentence has such nice rhythm and of course, it's worth remembering. The statement, "One gains affinity for hearing the messages of Vāsudeva," should not be forgotten.

Let's give up the attitude of "revolting against the Lord." Just hear how Prabhupāda praises the preacher.

It's not that I think my hand can speak. I know it can't eat, although it takes the warm food and puts it eagerly into the mouth. Then what do I mean, "my hand speaks"?

I am looking for more access, to get straight to the gut by direct infusion. Every part of me is Kṛṣṇa-ized by *prasādam* in Kṛṣṇa consciousness, but I'm surrounded by fields of interference. My belt is too tight and I'm getting old. The hand grips the pen. He doesn't care for niceties. He just wants to write.

Why serve the pure devotee? The hand wants to know. Prabhupāda, I massaged you with these hands and carried in your lunch plate. I may have also offended you. Christ said to cut off the hand if it offends (he meant if it offends God). He also said that the left hand shouldn't know what the right hand is doing.

The hand feels things differently than the head. That's why I like him to have a chance to speak. The hand rolls on like a tire or crawls like an ant. He jumps in fear, he is burnt by anything hot he touches, he flinches, but he doesn't lie. I can't entirely trust the hand, but I let him write freely. When he veers off, I correct him.

Oh, great goodness is done serving Vāsudeva's saints. They do exist. They are entirely devoted to Him. I knew (know) a great one! His 100th anniversary. Buses on the roll to praise him and tell others about him, to sell his books, reunite his family. I will praise him by writing new books as he asked. Expand and boil the milk down so we are trained and pure. Each one figure it out. Great good is done. How? It's not so easy to explain. Prabhupāda is close to God. If we please him, Kṛṣṇa will be pleased with us. Then that which we say we want—to love reading and hearing about Kṛṣṇa—will suddenly become attainable by His will. We will have moved Kṛṣṇa in our favor because we served His dear devotee. Our desires themselves become blessed.

This writing could be one of those things where you do what you want and ask him to accept it, but I want to fashion it into something useful in his mission. Thus it will be purified. You may approach God in anger (as Bhīṣma did), "lust" (as Prabhupāda says the *gopīs* did), or to kill Him (as Pūtanā did, taking the form of a mother-nurse), and Kṛṣṇa will accept the good essence. We'll receive His mercy. I may be a zany author—but I have energy and that tingling can be used for the cause.

Dog-eaters, lowborn, hear me. I'm one of you, one of the swine-herding race. Hear my patchy praise of the Lord. I know what it's like when you curse and get tired. I know the arid feeling and poverty of spirit, and the feeling of having failed to live up to my spiritual master's expectations. I know your disillusion with his movement and your desire to escape. I know what it's like to be curious about what *karmīs* and *jñānīs* are doing outside the sphere of *bhakti*, and what it's like to be polluted by them and then run back to the guru's shelter. We become confused: "Who's right? To whom should we listen?" The pressure of duties: *gṛhasthas'* duties, *brahmacārīs'* duties, book distributors' passion and hard times —who understands? Managers' woes, unsung heroes and heroines—give any one of them solace and Gurudeva will be pleased with us. Then we'll gain affinity for hearing the messages of Vāsudeva.

It will be okay one day:
I'll read and like it.
It won't be the last day.
I'll accept my place and know
I definitely have a place.
I'll accept Brahmānanda as the
first president in ISKCON and
others I knew and their
right ascendancy as preachers
over me.

It will be okay. I'll even die.
Can't say I'll like it.
But will forget Joan Hensler
singing, "God Bless America"
standing by the doghouse at
119 Katan Avenue (two houses
down from slant-roofed ours).
I'll forget by God's grace,
it will slide off my back
like water.

I won't mind the cold.
I'll control my tongue but
it won't matter that much.
All that matters is attraction
for the messages of Vāsudeva
and service to His pure devotee.

Clear your mind of anything extraneous and write down only what counts to enhance your readers' Kṛṣṇa consciousness. That means repeating only completely perfect messages, no lunch bags or funny asides (by the cowherd boys). No true moment of looking down at the wood grains on the desk and entering childhood. Beat it out. Take responsibility for what you say.

So folks, be devotees. Thank you very much. This here ends another purport from yours truly. (Note the restraint and fake words. I know you won't condemn me.) I smile like a politician on a poster and promise, "I'll be good. Just elect me as your rep for four more years. I promise two or three books a year of *A Poor Man* and to link you to *Śrīmad-Bhāgavatam*. I promise I'll improve in footwear and not give up exercises. My belching will diminish if the earth holds up my own embodied life!"

I said I'm one of you
sorry, sorry, sorry
the flag waved.
Just edit this out
I'm too tired to stop.

Text 17

śṛṇvatāṁ sva-kathāḥ kṛṣṇaḥ
puṇya-śravaṇa-kīrtanaḥ
hṛdy antaḥ stho hy abhadrāṇi
vidhunoti suhṛt satām

Śrī Kṛṣṇa, the Personality of Godhead, who is the Paramātmā [Supersoul] in everyone's heart and the benefactor of the truthful devotee, cleanses desire for material enjoyment from the heart of the devotee who has developed the urge to hear His messages, which are in themselves virtuous when properly heard and chanted.

Comment

Here we read that Kṛṣṇa wants us to go back to Godhead and that He's never lazy or indifferent toward the cause of each soul's liberation and development of *bhakti*. He offers us *kṛṣṇa-kathā*.

Anyone who is even slightly acquainted with the *Bhāgavatam* knows this verse. It is a great favorite because it extends the promise to us (this and the next verse go together). As stated previously by Sūta Gosvāmī, "Therefore, who will not pay attention to His message?"

Even if all I do is hear and then relish hearing—I mean, if I can't at first improve my life in other ways, cannot yet surrender to laborious or painstaking sacrifice for my spiritual master—if I like to hear *kṛṣṇa-kathā* spoken by pure devotees, then my heart will be cleansed.

Now if we say, "But I have no taste for hearing," then I say don't complain, but act. "We have already discussed developing a taste for hearing and chanting the holy sound. It is done through the medium of service to the pure devotee of the Lord."

Śrīmad-Bhāgavatam 1.2.17 tells us that hearing is itself a pious service. Therefore, that's the only advice I can give. Meditate on this verse and decide how to adjust your life in such a way that you can regularly hear the *Bhāgavatam*. Anyone can rearrange their life to fit in more direct Kṛṣṇa consciousness. Someone can use that nice easy chair for reading, the one by the window under the lamp. And what about that stack of newspapers and magazines? Do we need to read so much junk? (Prabhupāda called the newspaper "*prayāsyaś ca prajalpaḥ*," quoting Rūpa Gosvāmī's *Upadeśāmṛta:* "They talk three hours of politics, useless talk, but if we ask them to hear *Bhāgavatam* they'll say they have no time.") Surely reading worldly books diverts us from reading the *Bhāgavatam*, not only because it steals our time, but because it plants seeds of doubt and wrong taste toward transcendental literature.

Kṛṣṇa is absolute. The book filled with *kṛṣṇa-kathā* is Kṛṣṇa Himself. Read it with reverence and Kṛṣṇa will reveal Himself in our hearts. Then we will relish it.

Kṛṣṇa responds. He sees regular reading as an act of sincerity. Sincerity counts heavily in our favor. "The Lord is more anxious to take us back into His kingdom than we can desire. . . . Śrī Kṛṣṇa helps in all respects."

We're in this material world bound with desire. Desire produces a chain of bondage. Our bodies and minds suffer from past transgressions, and even today we'll hatch new transgressions in our hearts for which we will suffer later. We have performed so many wrongs already and the disease of reaction is always in the process of manifesting or growing toward manifestation. Thus we are tied to a chain of action and reaction. Even "good" karma ensures rebirth in this world. When a living being becomes aware of this, he may utter a faint statement, "I'd like to end all this karma," but it's not easy. Therefore, he sinks down again, hopeless. As Narottama dāsa Ṭhākura sings, "Day and night I'm burning in this dark world, without seeking to make the correction."

We can rescue ourselves by *śravaṇaṁ kīrtanam*. Hearing and chanting is *puṇya-śravaṇa*, pious, but it is not related to material piety wherein our senses are strengthened by the austerity and we are rewarded with more power to try and enjoy the world. This kind of pious act transforms us; it creates virtue and power. Just by developing the desire to hear *kṛṣṇa-kathā*, "By the grace of God such a devotee gets sufficient strength to defend himself from the state of disturbances, and gradually all disturbing elements are eliminated from his mind."

Prabhupāda's translation mentions that Kṛṣṇa in the heart is "the benefactor of the truthful devotee" (*suhṛt satām*). This indicates the necessity for honesty. When he describes how "Many stalwarts in the devotional line fell victim"—to women and wealth—we may at first think that women and wealth are no longer problems for us. So let's be truthful. Why, then, don't we have more taste for chanting and hearing? Why are we inattentive to the holy name and neglectful toward the Lord's devotees? It *must* be that we are meditating on material desires (hatching eggs). Otherwise, we would be free and eligible to hear deeply. *Something* is blocking us. Of course, Kṛṣṇa helps, but He would help more if we were more truthful and prepared to rectify ourselves.

Material desire stops us from developing a taste for realizing Kṛṣṇa's presence in the *Bhāgavatam*. As we recognize this shortcoming and feel remorse for it, we may go beyond showbottle devotion. *Śravaṇaṁ kīrtanam* is such a nice remedy that it works against the vicious cycle in which we are caught. That is, material desires prevent us from appreciating *kṛṣṇa-kathā*, but *kṛṣṇa-kathā* is virtuous and cleanses the heart of material desire. We'll be even more successful when we heed the open secret, "which we have already discussed"—*service to the pure devotee*.

I wrote this morning with a headache. It was unusual; it developed during the night. It made me more appreciative of the opportunities Kṛṣṇa is giving me to read and write. I want to make full use of this before my body inevitably shuts down. The light has to dim sooner or later. Please let me keep writing while I can and not waste time. And may it come out worthy.

The low point yesterday was when I hit hard rock in writing and my efforts to become free in expression seemed unworthy. The high point occurred soon after when I persisted and felt it was the best I could do. Trust in the process.

Sometimes people misspell the word diary as dairy, I've noticed. It's an amusing mistake. A *karmī* dairy is a hellish place, similar to a slaughterhouse in intent, but a dairy on a Kṛṣṇa conscious farm is nectar-producing and virtuous work. It produces milk to be made into preparations for Kṛṣṇa and His devotees. The same with a diary. A *karmī* or *jñānī* diary is Kafka's cat whine (bless his soul). The diary of one trying to serve Kṛṣṇa can be nectar-producing. It seems like poison at first—"I had to get up early even with a headache . . ." "So-and-so dāsa chastised me . . ." but it becomes nectar in the end.

Poem makes a different sense.
Wasn't I a nice guy sitting with you
and encouraging you (and me) to read?
I said here's your lamp and chair and
be of good cheer, open
Śrīmad-Bhāgavatam and don't take it otherwise when

you read of four-headed Brahmā. If
you have any scientific doubts, you can
read Sadāpūta.

But poems are helpful in a
different way. You know what it
means to be surreal? Things are
important that need to be said
that way.
I may dare to say
there's a place for it.
Surreal lines squeak out.

You mean the way Lakshman gives
massage and looks and handles my
fingers, noting that the cuticles are chewed
and that he seems to wish me well,
although I can't tell that for sure?
No, that's not what I mean
by surreal. But that's nice too,
a tender moment you surmised.

But say, *the aspirin falls from heaven.*
"But that's absurd."
Say you refer to *śṛṇvatāṁ sva-kathāḥ*
kṛṣṇa as *a bedroom full of larks*.
Huh?
Never mind surreal for now.
Consider freedom from material desire—
a pain in the eye doesn't make you
a brave soldier, but Kṛṣṇa appreciates that
you didn't want to give up. Nothing you
can do now but go back to bed, I guess.

But make a date as soon as
you are well
I'll ring the bell, I'll read again
and write, "It's hell
without Kṛṣṇa."
I'll tell you later about
surreal. Just wait.

Am I a poor man bragging? It's ridiculous when a poor man brags either about the small amount of money he possesses or about the virtues of being poor. Even a *brāhmaṇa's* voluntary poverty is something about which one should be modest. To pretend to be poor is also a farce.

There are certainly virtues, however, connected to poverty. Nārada Muni describes those virtues in the chapter where he curses Nalakūvera and Maṇigrīva. In the *Kṛṣṇa* book, Prabhupāda states that a poor man has a certain advantage in gaining self-realization. If he's at all decent, his poverty will make him more compassionate. He'll understand the pricks of poverty and denial, so he won't want to inflict pain on others. *Sādhus* have more access to the homes of poor men, who don't guard them with big signs, "Beware of Dog," or who keep servants to screen guests. Prabhupāda states that the poor man's senses are more controlled because of his reduced eating habits. His passions are subdued naturally and he's not used to intense and exaggerated sense gratification.

Of course, we don't want to paint a rosy picture of peasants or cover over the ugly facts of poverty-related crimes in the cities. Both rich and poor are degraded. I just want to state some of these things since I'm using this banner, "poor man."

What it really means is something that is perhaps better not stated. I'm even a little embarrassed that these poor man's books can come out nicely bound. I don't want to deny the book that facility, however. "Poor man" really means "poor in spirit." It means "humble." It means admitting that one is not spiritually advanced, has not received the spiritual riches from Kṛṣṇa. It means he's begging for the holy name, although he knows he's poor at heart and feels his hands tremble from poverty. He's grateful, though, for whatever he gets to eat. He accepts it as Kṛṣṇa's *prasādam*.

When I mention the bragging poor man, it reminds me of Lord Brahmā's attempt to show off his mystic power in Kṛṣṇa's presence in Vṛndāvana. Brahmā stole Kṛṣṇa's calves and cows, but the result was that Kṛṣṇa then played such tricks on Brahmā as to leave him speechless and completely bewildered. Prabhupāda writes that if a lesser person tries to display his power to overwhelm a much greater person, the lesser person appears ludicrous. It's like a firefly trying to illuminate in the sunshine.

On the other hand, if a poor man sincerely makes his contribution, it'll be appreciated even by a rich man. Kṛṣṇa was pleased by Sudāmā's gift of flat rice, but Sudāmā had no mood of trying to impress Kṛṣṇa with such a materially paltry gift. Rather, Sudāmā was ashamed to give his gift to Kṛṣṇa. Kṛṣṇa said it tasted like nectar. He was so pleased that the goddess of fortune became afraid that Kṛṣṇa would become too indebted to Sudāmā.

Let the poor man be happy in serving Kṛṣṇa, yet aware of his unworthiness. Let him be serious and sincere. He may dance before Kṛṣṇa as Śrutadeva and his wife did.

Commenting on Kṛṣṇa's invitation to offer Him a leaf or a fruit, Prabhupāda writes, "This means that Kṛṣṇa may be worshiped by the poorest man in the world."

Text 18

naṣṭa-prāyeṣv abhadreṣu
nityaṁ bhāgavata-sevayā
bhagavaty uttama-śloke
bhaktir bhavati naiṣṭhikī

By regular attendance in classes on the Bhāgavatam and by rendering of service to the pure devotee, all that is troublesome to the heart is almost completely destroyed, and loving service unto the Personality of Godhead, who is praised with transcendental songs, is established as an irrevocable fact.

Comment

Both the *Bhāgavata Purāṇa* and the pure devotees of Bhagavān Śrī Kṛṣṇa are known as *bhāgavatas*. Serving either of them (or both) is the remedy for obstacles in the heart. Both *bhāgavatas* are the same in potency because both glorify the Supreme Personality of Godhead.

An outsider to this process may doubt how it works, but Nārada's life story is offered as proof. Nārada was only a five-year-old boy living with his mother, but when he rendered sincere service to the *bhakti-vedāntas* who visited his home, he was transformed and gradually became the great *bhāgavata*, Nārada Muni. The more one serves under the *bhāgavatas'* guidance, the more one becomes fixed in loving service to the Supreme Lord.

In the previous verse, Sūta tells how Kṛṣṇa Himself cleanses the heart of one who hears *kṛṣṇa-kathā*. Now he informs us that hearing should be guided by a devotee *bhāgavata* and that this combination will ensure success despite the inevitable obstacles.

In his early translation of this verse, Prabhupāda asserts not only "regularly hearing the *Bhāgavatam*," but specifically "regular attendance in the *Bhagwat*—class." Sometimes it feels like a chore to attend the temple *Bhāgavatam* class. Neither is it unusual to see devotees falling asleep rather than listening attentively. Do they sleep because someone less than pure is speaking? Perhaps. Whoever is asked to speak on a verse and purport should take it as a serious responsibility and prepare an interesting lecture. He should also live the life of service to the *bhāgavatas*.

But the fault may also be with the nodders. I must confess that I (and others) sometimes nodded out even while Prabhupāda spoke the *Bhāgavatam*. I admitted this to him once and he said, "Yes, there's a saying in India that the *Bhāgavatam* is a sure cure for insomnia." He was joking, but I was mortified and said I didn't want that to be true of me. Another time, Prabhupāda said only his advanced disciples could appreciate his classes. Still, he insisted that everyone attend and not excuse themselves by claiming they have other work to do. When he was given this excuse by one absentee, he shot back, "If you don't hear, what work will you do, nonsense?"

Someone brought me a Godrej "Displaywriter." Typing could be called "mechanical writ." This is the first time I've used one for this book. It bangs away under my hands. Some writers say that they prefer a pen because it provides a closer connection to the body, the bloodline to the heart. There is a difference. The typing machine is faster and therefore I'm more able to capture thoughts, but those thoughts seem to come from a different place, a humming in the head I feel as I tap it.

They've lent us this old machine to use while we're here in India. Some of the letters have rubbed off the keys. Other letters are stained with white-out. But it will do.

By regular attendance in the *Bhāgavatam* class. Often devotees ask why this verse states that *almost* all the dirty things are removed. Why not *all*? Whenever I'm asked that question, I reply that it's good if most of the dirty things are removed. Why complain? We tend to want everything to come in the first installment of mercy. We have to have faith that the *bhāgavatas* know what we will need and will in time give us everything. They will irrevocably give us faith even before we are perfect. Even up to *bhāva*, we suffer from an odor of past sins.

It is good to represent the perfect knowledge and to defend the *paramparā* with intelligence. We gradually disarm and win over our audiences and then finally let them go, "All right, chant Hare Kṛṣṇa," or we give out sliced apples at the end as Swamijī did. Sooner or later, however, the class has to end and we're back on the ground. *Irrevocably fixed:* a phrase from the class may stay in our heads awhile or we may hum the Sanskrit, *naṣṭa-prāyeṣv abhadreṣu, nityaṁ bhāgavata-sevayā.* Gradually, our consciousness fills up with anticipation of breakfast and the rest of our morning—our life of service.

Anything more? I don't want to write filler, although I do want to keep going. I'm glad to return to living. That's how I feel when I recover from a headache, because headaches knock me out of action completely. They bring my low point of the day when I see I can't take my regular turn with the *Bhāgavatam.* I also feel appreciation, however, for the times when I do have sufficient health and facility to perform this *yajña.* I pray for life duration—so I can what? Finish the whole thing? It's not possible. Anyway, I do appreciate it more when it is taken from me. That feeling comes even while I am sidelined. When the pain finally subsides after hours of rest, then I feel relief and gratitude. (I am aware that some people don't ever get relief. They have to live in a different way and their struggle becomes a constant way of life. We have to adjust to whatever becomes our fate and use whatever resources we have in service to guru and Kṛṣṇa.)

That was already stated in previous verses that material activities, occupation, or *dharma*, the facility to function and develop, should not be used for sense gratification but for inquiring into the Absolute Truth. It's important to locate ourselves in genuine service. Service is not a one-time act but something we have to constantly adjust and improve. Don't act out of personal motivation but as service to the eternal

Father, the best friend, the Lord of all, Kṛṣṇa. Do it under the guru's good graces.

Got more to say? Yes, always more. Drift into the sea of deeper concerns, or the area where serendipity occurs, the chance encounter of nice feelings toward birds and God's creation, of memories of life with the guru, of hopes of purity. Find your own genuine currency. Don't dream of false currency. Something that is approaching true devotional service has almost all the dirty things removed. *Almost.* Don't complain that they're not one hundred percent removed. I tell you this while waiting for a glass of juice to come.

I am aghast so many devotees have left. Some go back to see them and hear their beefs. I stay here watching two dark, thin men walk over the cement dam surefooted, water sluicing through their bare feet.

I'm happy to be alive.

Tell him I can't do full exercises, but I'm willing to breathe deeply.

The laundry blows.

There are at least three different editions of the First Canto. There are little differences between them, as in the "attendance at the *Bhagwat*—class" verse. I once memorized this verse while walking toward a wire fence in the American Midwest. I was so young then, and I remember that I was wearing a tattered garland and standing beside Lake Michigan with my thick *tridaṇḍi* pole.

In this room, there's a large colored photo of a *mātājī*. At first I thought it was Indira Gandhi, but then I realized it's just someone's mother photographed in a jolly moment. She may be dead by now. As casual residents of this room, we accept that she must stay on the wall. But if she's dead, then why not me too? It stands to reason. In the meantime, I want to use my time well.

Prabhupāda wrote the First Canto under special circumstances while living in Vṛndāvana and printing in Delhi before coming to America. I love to think of Prabhupāda during this time of his life. I want to be aware of these circumstances and his life as I read through the hundreds of purports in the First Canto. Of course, Prabhupāda is wonderful in other ways during later years—early on in 1968 and through the early 1970s when I typed his *Bhāgavatam* dictation tapes, then later as he traveled widely and managed ISKCON, sometimes sternly. Right now, though, I just want to savor Swamijī alone in Vṛndāvana, "dreaming" of when the *ācāryas* will send him forth. At times like this, I wish I could be a frog in his Rādhā-Dāmodara room watching him.

I'm dreaming about my own writing too, and I'm alone and aspiring, hoping against hope, yet feeling assured of Kṛṣṇa's mercy. I write to seek union with Prabhupāda. I imitate his schedule to remember him, and I write on his *Bhāgavatam* so I won't forget.

Text 19

tadā rajas-tamo-bhāvāḥ
kāma-lobhādayaś ca ye
ceta etair anāviddhaṁ
sthitaṁ sattve prasīdati

As soon as irrevocable loving service is established in the heart, the effects of nature's modes of passion and ignorance, such as lust, desire and hankering, disappear from the heart. Then the devotee is established in goodness, and he becomes completely happy.

Comment

This verse and the preceding two were quoted by Prabhupāda in his poem, "*Mārkine Bhāgavata-dharma*," which he wrote at the Boston Commonwealth Pier in September 1965. Prabhupāda expressed himself humbly to Kṛṣṇa: "Why have You sent me to this terrible place?" He didn't see how he would be able to convince the people of Kṛṣṇa's message since they were so materialistic. But Prabhupāda took courage from these verses and he then felt confident that hearing the *Bhāgavatam* would cleanse the dirt from their hearts and attract them to Uttama-śloka.

Verse 1.2.19 specifically mentions how this will happen: the modes of *rajas* and *tamas* (so prominent in Boston) would be broken up or would disappear from someone's life when he or she heard the transcendental vibration of the *Śrīmad-Bhāgavatam* and the Hare Kṛṣṇa mantra. The devotee could then comprehend the mode of goodness (*sattva*) and become happy.

And it's true. We've seen it happen, even to Americans. Spiritual bliss is the innate nature of the living being. It is expressed as activity in Kṛṣṇa consciousness. Therefore,

Prabhupāda engaged us in chanting the Hare Kṛṣṇa mantra and in cooking, typing, and so many other activities. Spiritual life—*brahma-bhūta* or *ātmānandī*—would manifest and be channeled through the senses, mind, and words.

Thank you, Prabhupāda, for thinking of these verses and for persistently trying to give us your Lord's message. I am personally thankful because I was lost, purposeless, without you. I was swirling around like trash in water, about to be swept down the gutter of a city street and into the sewer.

When the conditioned soul mixes with matter, his activities become diseased, and they are expressed as lust, foolishness, sleep, and so on. Devotional service eliminates this disease and brings us above even material goodness to *śuddha-sattva*. "Only in this *śuddha-sattva* state can one always see Kṛṣṇa eye to eye by dint of pure affection for the Lord."

To be a devotee requires a thorough change. We can't claim to be devotees of Kṛṣṇa and still be fools and rascals, cruel or passionate. A devotee develops good qualities if he is a genuine devotee and he actually engages in the practices of *bhakti*. All this starts and is maintained by "regular attendance in the *Bhāgwat* class."

Even as I'm trying to write, Madhu is vomiting in the next room. Between retching, his breath comes in pants. My own stomach is calm, but I feel for him. This is life. I worry that his health is so delicate. If he eats the wrong thing, he gets ill like this—diarrhea or vomiting that lasts all night. He was sick all last night. I heard it all because it echoed through the latrine's walls into this room. I turned on my light at 10:30 (earplugs don't stop the sound of retching or even clearing the throat) and made some notes and a picture, "Ship ahoy!" Since my ship was capsized yesterday and is again all right, the best thing for me to do is to keep writing. I can't help him now in another way. But he is a dear friend. I wish he could find a more regular, practical way to attain normal health. I hope he finds it. Health is certainly a part of Kṛṣṇa consciousness. We see how without it, our service is immediately diminished.

In this purport, Prabhupāda says the soul is not inactive; *brahma-bhūta* is the stage of real, unalloyed spiritual activity, not lax meditation without duties, not idle chanting with the mind in the lower modes. We need to act. Madhu has tons of service to do. Lately, he's been arranging for our new van to be outfitted in America and many other matters. How can he do any of it if he can't keep food in his stomach long enough to digest it?

Prabhupāda says the soul is active, not dead stone as the Māyāvādīs say. When we become free of the lower modes, we feel the power of goodness, which includes cleanliness and calmness. For us, becoming free of the modes meant giving up drugs, sex, and becoming free of obscene thoughts and whatever vices are typical of a New Yorker. How he transformed us!

Thank you, Swami. What's next? *Śuddha-sattva*? What's that? Will we attain it next week? Oh, it's not so easy. But we are on the road to that. We get a glimpse when we chant or when he talks about Kṛṣṇa in Vṛndāvana as a cowherd boy. *Śuddha-sattva*. Sounds good. It sure was sweet going through those changes with you. You wore a turtleneck jersey, just like the ones we wore.

The purport which he wrote in 1960 in Vṛndāvana says that the soul is eternally free of the modes, but it gets covered over. It is difficult to uncover it again, but *vāsudeva-kathā* can do it.

We cannot accept someone as a devotee unless he has signs of becoming cleansed. He may still have material taints about him, but he cannot remain heavily influenced by the modes of passion and ignorance. A devotee doesn't remain a fool or a rascal. Certainly Prabhupāda expected his disciples to change. He wouldn't initiate them until they did. They became bright-faced, cut their long hair and beards, and gave up illicit sex. Don't remain a fool.

Earlier this morning I read *Caitanya-caritāmṛta* and want to mention it here. This isn't the place for it? Why not? I can't hide my life from you. It doesn't seem right. If someone says it's not right to include other readings in with the *Bhāgavatam* comments, I say just the opposite—it's not right to hide it. It's not something extraneous.

I read in the first chapter of *Madhya-līlā* that Lord Caitanya spent the last twelve years of His life at Jagannātha Purī tasting the mood of Rādhā's separation from Kṛṣṇa. This is briefly mentioned in this extraordinary chapter, which Kṛṣṇadāsa Kavirāja wrote in case he didn't live long enough to complete the whole book. How's that for following the writing advice, "Spend it all. Don't keep it to yourself. If you have a good idea, don't save it for later. More and better will come if you give all generously and not keep it for yourself"?

In this context, Prabhupāda describes the *gopīs'* simple love for Kṛṣṇa. It is appealing to hear it from him. He says they were not attracted to the opulence of Kṛṣṇa in Dvārakā. They wanted Him in the calm atmosphere of Vṛndāvana. The *gopīs* are already enlightened and "they simply engage their purified senses in the service of the Lord in the remote village of Vṛndāvana. The *gopīs* are not interested in dry speculation, in the arts, in music, or other conditions of material life." (Cc. *Madhya*, 1.82, purport)

The mention of art made me wonder what I'm trying to do. I was just about to tell you about some poetry and then try my hand at writing some myself. The *gopīs* were not interested in any arts except the art of loving Kṛṣṇa. Prabhupāda goes on to say that Kṛṣṇa loves the *gopīs* not for their opulence or personal beauty, but for their pure devotional service.

Tadā rajas-tamo-bhāvāḥ,
nice rhythm to tap to, to
intone, to keep yourself pure.
Kāma-lobhādayaś ca ye—
if you can memorize you're lucky,
or take it here for reading
and sing—

I was born low and lusty,
but by guru's grace I've got
a place in goodness.
A happy boy can sing a simple
line if his heart is halfway
pure, or more we hope—
a song of goodness
and going above.

Did you read something interesting
you'd like to share?
Here, I'm in the chair
and want to be with you in this.
But let's admit the *Bhāgavatam*
service must be our main
thoroughfare. When you write you may
let the words choose you and be free,
let it be American-derived speech music
whatever you find—
but convert it,
to the real currency that lasts.
Tell us of *śuddha-sattva*
and the Swami. Then
your Etruscan wish-wash jabber jabber
won't be of much account.
What matters is the end
when Jagannātha reigns over
His pure beloveds.
I want to be there.

Text 20

evaṁ prasanna-manaso
bhagavad-bhakti-yogataḥ
bhagavat-tattva-vijñānaṁ
mukta-saṅgasya jāyate

Thus established in the mode of unalloyed goodness, the man whose mind has been enlivened by contact with devotional service to the Lord gains positive scientific knowledge of the Personality of Godhead in the stage of liberation from all material association.

Comment

This series of five verses (*Śrīmad-Bhāgavatam* 1.2.17–21) is quoted in the Bhaktivedanta Purports to *Bhagavad-gītā* 7.1. Kṛṣṇa tells Arjuna, *tat śṛṇu*, "Just hear from Me." Lord Kṛṣṇa is the greatest authority. If one hears directly from Him or His pure devotee, he gets the greatest opportunity to become Kṛṣṇa conscious. The process of understanding Kṛṣṇa, the Supreme Personality of Godhead, is described in this series of *Bhāgavatam* verses.

Scientific knowledge of Kṛṣṇa is rare. Out of thousands of so-called humans, very few aspire for spiritual perfection. Among those few who seek it, a small number may attain the preliminary perfection of Brahman realization. Out of those perfected souls, hardly one knows Kṛṣṇa in truth. Thus it is said in this *Bhāgavatam* verse that *after* coming to goodness, and *after* attaining *mukti* (liberation), one "can know scientifically or perfectly the Personality of Godhead."

In terms of *varṇāśrama*, this means that one has to become a qualified *brāhmaṇa* before he can realize God. One's status as a *brāhmaṇa* cannot be determined by birth, but by the attainment of brahminical qualities. These qualities are described in *Bhagavad-gītā:* "Peacefulness, self-control, austerity, purity, tolerance, honesty, knowledge, wisdom and religiousness—these are the natural qualities by which the *brāhmaṇas* work." (Bg. 18.42)

One has to transcend even the brahminical stage to become a Vaiṣṇava, because in the brahminical stage, the conception of Brahman or transcendence is realized, but scientific knowledge of the Supreme Lord is lacking.

A fool who doesn't even have brahminical qualities and who doesn't know Kṛṣṇa may make whimsical statements about Kṛṣṇa and mislead others. One can only understand Kṛṣṇa when he is free of the material modes, including the mode of goodness.

Madhu is still vomiting. He looks like a different person —gaunt, hollow-eyed, cheerless. He reminds me of the girl in the story, "Liquid Beauty," where a beautiful girl discourages an aggressive suitor by taking a purgative. She then vomits and passes loose stool for days until all her beauty is gone. Madhu says he thinks he got sick from drinking the tap water. (We keep asking for bottled water, but our host won't buy it. He probably thinks it's an exorbitant request and he assures us that the well water is fine). Or, Madhu conjectures, he might have become sick because mice nibble at our food supplies and contaminate them. I had to prepare my own fruit breakfast, so I saw how the vegetables and fruits are left out in the open. I also noticed that the utensils and plates are not cleaned properly. I boiled water for Madhu to drink and put it in his flask. I also heated water for his hot water bottle. Madhu simply cannot rise from bed to do his chores, and neither does he have the strength—or need—to apologize for that. He is lying down, without energy to chant his rounds, and waiting for his unsettled state to subside. Until he stops vomiting, he can't begin to take nourishment or rest.

All this makes my day feel strange.

The typewriter works in Hindi as well as English, but I don't need the Hindi. I will write well enough if I can let my mind go green—just sail off from this scene. But what about the *Bhāgavatam*? No, I'm not trying to leave that behind.

I heard Prabhupāda say on a tape this morning that we have to give up sense gratification and do what Kṛṣṇa wants. How forceful and simple, yet how difficult to attain. Arjuna was successful. At first he wanted things his way. He didn't want to kill his relatives because he thought he'd be happier if they were alive. Then he understood that Kṛṣṇa wanted them killed. Arjuna attained perfection by carrying out Kṛṣṇa's order. He wasn't a *brāhmaṇa* or a Vedāntist, but a warrior. When he fought for Kṛṣṇa, he demonstrated pure love of God. Thus Kṛṣṇa said to him, "I will tell you the mystery of the *Bhagavad-gītā* because you are My devotee and My very dear friend." Then Prabhupāda said, "Pleasing our senses is lust." (Although people sometimes call it love when it refers to the desire to please our senses through another, love exists only in relation to Kṛṣṇa.)

I felt excluded when I heard Prabhupāda talk about love. Again I worried that my writing may be sense gratification. I thought of this strange morning and how I tried to fulfill Madhu's needs, but how I thought more of myself and how I was going to fare rather than him. Selfish, bodily selfishness. We identify with the body and don't know the self. We think we're tired. We decide to put aside our service and lie on the floor. I haven't been getting sufficient rest because of Madhu's emergency situation, but I don't want to miss my turn with the *Bhāgavatam*.

Evaṁ prasanna-manaso. The mode of goodness, the rise to *śuddha-sattva*, the establishment of brahminical culture and then turning those qualities into the qualities of a Vaiṣṇava—but if we have to be liberated first, how can we say we're devotees? Who *are* the devotees if such a state is so rare?

Tādera caraṇa-sevi-bhakta-sane bās. Don't claim you're a devotee. Simply desire to serve the devotees life after life. Serve your spiritual master. That is the most effective devotional service.

Our little operation in this house has been thrown into the air. Who will cook? Who knows how? Certainly no one knows the Nature Cure cooking—only Madhu knows how to do that. Life is so easily tilted from its regular ways. I ought to be able to read the *Bhāgavatam* in any condition.

Evaṁ prasanna-manaso: the devotee is peaceful and enlivened in mind. Contact with Kṛṣṇa has brought this about. So what if this exalted state doesn't describe ourselves? That's obvious. The verse describes the *perfection* of devotional service. We can still take heart. We are on the topmost path. Even a little progress is never lost, and at the time of death, it will save us from the greatest fear.

Evaṁ prasanna-manaso. A devotee is peaceful, pleasant, calm, *śānta*—all due to love of God. He serves the devotees. He progresses past liberation—his *bhakti-latā* growing up past the material planets, through the *brahmajyoti*, past the Vaikuṇṭha planets, to Kṛṣṇaloka where Kṛṣṇa sports. This all refers to the pure devotees.

The verse describes a state unattainable by me, although I can understand the theory behind it. I think about it, memorize the stages described, comprehend it clearly enough to speak on it: (1) By hearing the *Bhāgavatam*, dirty things disappear from the heart; (2) then we surpass goodness and approach perfection; (3) we surpass Brahman liberation; (4) we are satisfied in Kṛṣṇa consciousness and do only what the Lord wants.

My friend is utterly sick. I wait in the house for someone to come. Lakshman is here like a faithful house dog, but he speaks only Hindi. What can he do, anyway?

I have no time or presence of mind to induce myself to empty the mind of chatter and to listen. The red road up and down the handwritten prose is like a thread of blood in a vein. Stambha dāsa suddenly appears before my mind's eye. Why? I don't know.

Insistent birds' cries. I'm not in Vṛndāvana.

My ship (mental) went to sea. Old lady looks at me askance when I'm not looking at her. When I look her way, she smiles.

So many ISKCON girls. A bag of mail. Go in and ask my friend how he is now. The skull turns on the pillow and he speaks in a faint voice. I am stronger than he is right now—ate all those bananas and kept them tucked away in my stomach. He said maybe it's good (to vomit so much). "I saw carrots and beans." That Nature Cure extremism—acute attacks are good for you, the fat ones are full of poison. I'm getting tired of it; could use a "poison" meal. But maybe they're right.

Are you chanting?

I'm too weak, he said.

I chanted in my mind yesterday, I said.

And today a disappointment as I rattle off mantras and think of literary plans. As if chanting is not important. It's all we have in Kali, when all is said and done. Vomit up your guts, but keep chanting Hare Kṛṣṇa and pray, "Kṛṣṇa, You're putting me through the wringer! This body is not meant for enjoyment. I'm getting all kinds of realizations."

Lie back, weak, no more enjoyment in food, body a rack of pain. Kṛṣṇa, Kṛṣṇa, Kṛṣṇa.

Text 21

bhidyate hṛdaya-granthiś
chidyante sarva-saṁśayāḥ
kṣiyante cāsya karmāṇi
dṛṣta evātmaniśvare

Thus the knot in the heart is pierced, and all misgivings are cut to pieces. The chain of fruitive actions is terminated when one sees the self as master.

Comment

The knot referred to is *ahaṅkāra*, false ego. This is where matter and spirit contact one another. This contact bewilders the soul into thinking his identity is material. Prabhupāda has sometimes compared it to the point during a fever when a man loses his identity and his mind becomes unhinged. When we understand, "I'm not this body; I'm pure spirit soul, eternal servant of Kṛṣṇa," then our karmic chain is destroyed. We no longer act to perpetuate material desires prompted by false self-interest. Whatever we do after that point as Kṛṣṇa conscious persons is *akarma*, action without reaction. All these auspicious changes take place in a devotee's life when he seriously hears *Vedānta-śruti* or the *Śrīmad-Bhāgavatam* in disciplic succession.

Cutting the knot does not mean death, although it may feel like that if we are excessively attached to family, job, or the place and identity we think we have in society (even a religious one). The attachment may be to food, to too much or to a certain kind. Do we think we cannot live without it that we have to become so possessed by it?

We usually can't cut our own knot. We are too small-minded, too crippled by it. Rather, we spend our lives trying to protect it from danger. No one we meet understands us. No one we meet feels the same attachment for our knot. To cut it feels like death. Therefore, we nurse it, this big lump in the mind.

When we take to Kṛṣṇa consciousness, however, the knot gets cut in one way or another. Then we begin to taste freedom. Freedom feels real and fills us with devotional energy. Sometimes the Lord cuts it—he takes away a child or causes a wealthy man to become penniless. He does that especially when He knows the person wants to become a devotee.

Various philosophers speculate on the nature of the self. One theory states that in the highest realization, there is only one impersonal Self. Besides that, there are materialistic speculations that only the body or body and mind combination constitutes the self and that the self is terminated at death. Theories and doubts are cleared away, however, when one realizes Kṛṣṇa in truth through *bhakti-yoga*. Then one sees both oneself (self-realization) and the Supreme Being (God realization) and realizes the link between the two (*bhakti-yoga*, or loving transcendental service).

The devotee doesn't remain in the darkness of ignorance about the Absolute Truth because the Supreme Truth personally enlightens him. As Lord Kṛṣṇa states in *Bhagavad-gītā*, "To show them special mercy, I, dwelling in their hearts, destroy with the shining lamp of knowledge the darkness born of ignorance." This enlightenment descends by *paramparā* to the submissive student. At night, no one can force the sun to reveal itself. Similarly, one can't make God appear by challenging Him. If we wait for the sun to appear in its own time and in its own way, however, we will see the sun's glory. Similarly, God reveals Himself by the natural process of revelation to the submissive devotee.

Although I am telling you all this, I don't have much else to say about it. Everything has already been said by the *Bhāgavatam*. It's hard for me to keep talking on subjects if *they are addressing something of which I have no experience*. I'm afraid the reader will discover me and know that my words are hollow.

Sometimes people ask, "Do you personally experience what you are speaking about?" We can answer that one easily: "No, but I have faith in my spiritual master's words." That is certainly a good reply. If we feel solid by making it, then that's great. Stick to the guru's *vāṇī* and be loyal to him. Our defense is vivid and heartfelt when we do that. Real success means real knowledge by real hearing anyway.

I know what it's like to be asked that question in a preaching encounter, but what worries me more is to have to ask it of myself. We usually don't have to defend our private realization in public. Therefore, we have to give ourselves what they call a reality check. I want to say, "I don't know anything," and then turn to the Lord to give me direct experience, if He desires.

For example, we talk of the bliss of chanting, but maybe we don't experience it. Some of our shortcomings can be admitted in public in a tactful way. I once wrote an essay that disturbed one devotee. He said that all the scriptures declare that chanting is full of bliss. How could I say that when I chant, I don't feel it? He accused me of betraying the philosophy and lying. Then he said I wasn't qualified to lead others. He wanted to catch me and be determined that what I had said was a weak point.

The afternoon is mine to use as a pocket of time before they come in with the juice or some bad news or just busy news. I want to remember the path to the self. When the knot is destroyed, we see the self as master. The karma is ended. A bad dream is over.

How to cut the knot: just try to analyze a little and then feel what's being said by the *Bhāgavatam*. One devotee reader told me that when he reads, it's not to first of all apply what God says or even to know something, but simply to be with Him. I liked that. Just hear, pass it over your mind, understand the point, and develop a feeling about it. Look at the words that point to the self and the knot will be cut. You get good results from practicing Kṛṣṇa consciousness.

Nobody but me knows
what's behind my eye,
that threat to what I know
as peace and well-being.

How much longer
will I be able to press down on
the accelerator to write a sentence?
Writ is sacred, the letters
form a line-up, sense
and grace come out and I'm driving
it home for Kṛṣṇa's sake.
Yes, let us have elegant and sensible
sentences turned in His cause
rather than Rāvaṇa's or
some demon's agent.

The knot is
cut to pieces, karma is ended,
and he sees the self as master.

Prabhupāda said,
"Kṛṣṇa's not meant for pleasing anyone's
senses. He wants us to please
His senses."
You are master, I'm servant,
drill it into my head
so *my* knot is cut and
my karma ended. That's
what it means to
take care of Number One.

A random list:

(1) Flowerpots.

(2) It was nice using the typewriter for two days, but now the ribbon has run out and in India, that could be the end of the typewriter's working.

(3) Before anything gets repaired, we will be gone. Mice will nibble the bananas in peace. We will be gone to meet new troubles on new continents.

(4) I'm attached to using earplugs.

(5) With Madhu sick, I have had a chance to change my diet, so I did just a little. I saw myself rushing into piles of *halavā* and apple pies and cursing Nature Cure's imbalance of too little grains. The doctor says we're not getting enough protein or carbohydrates. We're too weak.

(6) Śrīla Prabhupāda wrote the following numbers of purports of at least eight or more lines long: First Canto—612; Second Canto—324; Third Canto—875; Fourth Canto—950; Fifth Canto—389; Sixth Canto—324; Seventh Canto—443; Eighth Canto—261; Ninth Canto—202; Tenth Canto—294. Total 4,678. Figure out how many books I could write in his footsteps. Fifty volumes at four hundred pages each are nowhere near enough. Who would live so long or want to write or read them?

(7) The list grows longer, life shorter.

(8) I wanted to be peaceful. Write about that. I liked it when Prabhupāda said Rādhārāṇī wanted Kṛṣṇa in the calm atmosphere of Vṛndāvana. It's true that although the *gopīs* were often involved in intrigues and anxieties, Vraja was peaceful with its Yamunā and forests, and Kṛṣṇa was always in the vicinity to tease and to love.

This book may be wrong and crazy, but if I keep at it, I could turn it right by serious sincerity. Any examples of that? The sparrow trying to empty the ocean. The man who wanted to serve the greatest. The fool who became a devotee. The rat who tried to eat the dying candle on the altar and who made the candle flame flare up. Pūtanā coming as Kṛṣṇa's nurse. Kaṁsa always thinking of the Lord in Kṛṣṇa consciousness and becoming liberated (although we prefer to be favorable, not against Him).

Text 22

ato vai kavayo nityaṁ
bhaktiṁ paramayā mudā
vāsudeve bhagavati
kurvanty ātma-prasādanīm

Certainly, therefore, since time immemorial, all transcendentalists have been rendering devotional service to Lord Kṛṣṇa, the Personality of Godhead, with great delight, because such devotional service is enlivening to the self.

Comment

Lord Kṛṣṇa is mentioned by name in this verse, as Prabhupāda translated "*vāsudeve bhagavati.*" Kṛṣṇa is the *svayaṁ-rūpa*, the original Personality of Godhead from whom all other forms of Godhead expand. *Īśvara paramaḥ kṛṣṇaḥ, sac-cid-ānanda-vigrahah/ ānadir ādir govindaḥ, sarva-karaṇa-karaṇam.*

The first expansions of Viṣṇu are Baladeva, Saṅkarṣaṇa, Pradyumna, and Aniruddha, and are variously manifested and categorized as *puruṣa-avatāras*, *guṇa-avatāras*, *līlā-avatāras*, and so on. There are thousands of Viṣṇu expansions. The individual, infinitesimal souls are also expanded parts and parcels of the Supreme Lord, whether they are in the liberated or conditioned states. Lord Kṛṣṇa is the source of all, "the last word in the Transcendence."

Those with higher theistic knowledge are more attracted to Kṛṣṇa than to any other forms. "In forms of the Personality of Godhead other than Śrī Kṛṣṇa and Baladeva, there is no facility for intimate personal contact as in the transcendental pastimes of the Lord at Vrajabhūmi."

Śrīla Prabhupāda has advocated exclusive worship of Kṛṣṇa even from the beginning of our devotional careers. He explains the words of the Hare Kṛṣṇa mantra as indicating Kṛṣṇa and Rādhārāṇī. Rādhārāṇī is addressed as Hare. She is Harā, the Lord's internal pleasure potency. When called upon in chanting, we say "Hare, O Mother Harā, please engage us in the Lord's service." Rāma may be taken to mean Lord Rāmacandra or Lord Balarāma, but the Gauḍīya Vaiṣṇavas prefer to chant Hare Rāma with the attitude of addressing Lord Kṛṣṇa, who is "Rāma," one who enjoys with Śrīmatī Rādhārāṇī (Rādhā-Ramaṇa, the enjoyer of Śrī Rādhā).

In *Bhagavad-gītā*, Kṛṣṇa states, "Always think of Me, become My devotee . . . " (Bg. 18.65) In his purport, Prabhupāda writes, " . . . one should concentrate his mind upon Kṛṣṇa—the very form with two hands carrying a flute, the bluish boy with a beautiful face and peacock feathers in His hair. . . . One should not even divert his attention to other forms of the Lord. The Lord has multiforms as Viṣṇu, Nārāyaṇa, Rāma, Varāha, etc., but a devotee should concentrate his mind on the form that was present before Arjuna."

In *Bhāg.* 1.2.22, Prabhupāda hints at why we should concentrate on Vraja-Kṛṣṇa: because outside of Vṛndāvana, "there is no facility for intimate personal contact." Actually, Kṛṣṇa never leaves Vṛndāvana. When He enacts pastimes in other places, such as Mathurā or Dvārakā, He does so in His expanded form as Vāsudeva. In Vṛndāvana, Kṛṣṇa enjoys the *rasas* of intimate servitude and friendship with the *gopas*, parental *rasa* with His parents and other elderly residents of Vrajabhūmi, and intimate loving dealings in the conjugal mood with the *gopīs*. Even Kṛṣṇa's exchanges with the animals, trees, and land of Vṛndāvana are permeated with intense love not possible to be found elsewhere.

When Kṛṣṇa comes to the earth once in a day of Brahmā, and when He goes to other universes in the material world, He displays these Vṛndāvana pastimes just to attract us to this standard of loving God in His original form with His best associates. We are fortunate to get glimpses of it in the *Bhāgavatam's* Tenth Canto and in the writings of the Six Gosvāmīs, Kṛṣṇadāsa Kavirāja, and in virtually everything Prabhupāda writes and teaches. Our good fortune is inestimable. It is not something we have earned, but it is the causeless mercy of Lord Caitanya.

Lord Caitanya is not one of the expansions of Viṣṇu; He is Kṛṣṇa Himself in the form of a pure devotee. Kṛṣṇa wanted to bestow Vraja-prema on the living entities, after having not done so in a long time, so He advented as Lord Caitanya. His purpose was to make such *prema* more accessible than He had ever done before. Even when Kṛṣṇa sported in Vṛndāvana, He didn't make these *rasas* so easily available to the conditioned souls. As Lord Caitanya, however, He spread the mercy widely by chanting Hare Kṛṣṇa and tasting the mood of loving Kṛṣṇa in separation. These confidential truths become gradually revealed to sincere devotees as they serve the spiritual master and the Hare Kṛṣṇa movement.

All glories to Śrīla Prabhupāda and his rendition of *Śrīmad-Bhāgavatam*, *Kṛṣṇa* book, *The Nectar of Devotion*, *Caitanya-caritāmṛta*, and *Bhagavad-gītā*. In these books and in all of Prabhupāda's instructions to us, he has trained us to become eligible to one day serve Kṛṣṇa in pure love in Śrī Vṛndāvana-dhāma.

Prabhupāda has also brought us to Vṛndāvana, India, where we may contact Kṛṣṇa through residence and service in His "replica" of the spiritual world. Furthermore, Prabhupāda teaches us that wherever we are, we may enter the mood of Vraja-sevā by our thinking and activity, chanting Hare Kṛṣṇa mantra, and serving Lord Caitanya in the *saṅkīrtana* movement.

Don't berate your little service or the mood in which you perform it. We may not know much about Vṛndāvana, but even in the early stages of Kṛṣṇa consciousness, and even by repeating the sacred science, we can become faithful.

For example, Prabhupāda invited everyone to the temple to see Rādhā and Kṛṣṇa. They didn't have to know much and he certainly didn't expect them to be pure before they were allowed to see the Deity. All he wanted was for them to be respectful. He used to tell the bums who wandered into his 26 Second Avenue lectures and *kīrtanas*, "Don't disturb. Sit down."

We may not have much devotion, but we can bring flowers or other offerings to Rādhā and Kṛṣṇa and make our lives perfect. That mercy is available to all of us.

I also noted that Prabhupāda's purport speaks about the special advantages of worshiping Kṛṣṇa in Vṛndāvana, but that before he describes this in the fullest detail, he will teach about Kṛṣṇa in all His *rasas* and incarnations. We can keep in mind, however, that all of these forms emanate from the original Vṛndāvana Kṛṣṇa (*rāmādi-mūrtiṣu*). Then when we hear of the Lord as Varāha or Nṛsiṁha, we may remember how wonderful our Kṛṣṇa is, who plays the flute in Vṛndāvana, and who has expanded into these various forms.

The *Vedas* state, *eko devo nitya-līlānurakto:* "The one Supreme Personality of Godhead is eternally engaged in many, many transcendental forms in relationships with His unalloyed devotees." One who knows in truth the nature of His appearance and activities in this world can go back to Godhead and be with Him, forever free of birth and death.

Prabhupāda writes, "The Vedic version *tat tvam asi* is actually applied in this case. Anyone who understands Lord Kṛṣṇa to be the Supreme, or who says unto the Lord, 'You are the same Supreme Brahman, the Personality of Godhead,' is certainly liberated instantly, and consequently his entrance into the transcendental association of the Lord is guaranteed." (Bg. 4.9, purport)

We're not Māyāvādīs. We can use matter in Kṛṣṇa's service. That's the purpose of Vaiṣṇava *sannyāsa*. Some people think that Lord Caitanya was a Māyāvādī *sannyāsī* because He accepted initiation from Keśava Bharati, but the *Caitanya-caritāmṛta* informs us that as soon as Lord Caitanya accepted *sannyāsa*, He proceeded toward Vṛndāvana. That indicated His exclusive devotion to Śrī Kṛṣṇa.

In his purport to this verse Prabhupāda writes, "For a Vaiṣṇava, acceptance of *sannyāsa* means getting relief from all material activities and completely devoting oneself to the transcendental loving service of the Lord. . . . The Māyāvādī *sannyāsīs*, however, do not know how to engage everything in the service of the Lord. Because they have no devotional training, they think material objects to be untouchable. . . . Vaiṣṇavas say, 'Why should the world be false? It is reality, and it is meant for the service of the Supreme Personality of Godhead.' . . . Devotional service means engaging everything for the satisfaction of the Supreme Personality of Godhead." (Cc. *Madhya* 1.91, purport)

Madhu continues to be critically ill. He has been vomiting for over twenty-four hours and his body is dehydrated. The doctor says he's now vomiting bodily secretions and taking from the liquidity in his blood. He can't even hold a sip of water. They want to give him an injection to calm the stomach and then inject fluids intravenously, but he refuses to accept this since he's so much against allopathic treatment.

I hinted to him that he should consider taking it and not rule it out. When it's a matter of life and death, the body has to take help.

This house has now become an emergency ward in a hospital. Śamīka Ṛṣi is staying overnight.

I'm also going through changes. I'm modifying the Nature Cure diet and allowing Śamīka Ṛṣi to introduce more grains and bulk to my meals. I'm still weak and not feeling satisfied with the small meals. Madhu's health crisis and his general weak condition, as well as my own skinniness, don't inspire me toward extreme health cure philosophies. All this is going on, even while I try to concentrate on full-time writing.

Last night I dreamt that I joined a team of devotees from Eastern Europe. They were a traveling *saṅkīrtana* group and were engaged in covert operations going into countries where preaching was not allowed. They were younger than I, and they liked the idea that I should join them because I was an older *sannyāsī*. The leader of the group, however, who was from Romania, was more cautious about admitting me. He said I'd have to be able to pass my body through a small opening in order to qualify to join them. Then he said I would have to do this when smuggling myself over the Romanian border.

At first I said I couldn't do it. The space they wanted me to fit through was less than half the space of an open car window. Then I tried. I said to myself in the dream, "All right, make yourself as small and compact as possible, and like a softbound book, bend and pass through this space." Then I succeeded. They were then happy to accept me. The dream made me feel confident that I can do whatever is required. I can pass through a small, tight space and qualify for the demanding preaching mission.

The dream is not any clearer than that as to what it may mean in my waking life. Since I am so much absorbed in writing this *A Poor Man Reads The Bhāgavatam*, I think it's some kind of permission to *fit everything through*. In the dream once I got down into that passage, I could pass through unlimited books and preaching messages. Get down, fit through, go on with the daring mission.

My eyes glance to the *Bhāgavatam* beside me and take in the words, "rendering transcendental loving service." It's a great phrase. I told my brother-in-law Tommy, "This is not a fanatic cult. It's transcendental loving service." He must have had a laugh about that one, but maybe he thought about it on the way home. Gave No Money.

No one can recall when it began. "Until age seventy, I did practically nothing," Prabhupāda told an audience. "But then I went out at seventy when no one goes out of home because I had *utsāha*. Now Kṛṣṇa consciousness is all over the world."

Now Say Gbye
until SB 1.2.23
You ran out of Steam
pipe will pipe you more later
Krsna
Krsna
Krsna

I restrain from drawing Rādhā and Kṛṣṇa. Maybe I've lost my innocence. I no longer dare to draw the most sacred object, God's form, in my hand.

My eyes tire fast when my neck is bent over. I haven't been doing my exercises because I'm tired and my companion is too sick to make me do it.

Tired eyes can be impetus. The hand says he heard that "devotional service is enlivening to the self."

Text 23

sattvaṁ rajas tama iti prakṛter guṇās tair
yuktaḥ paraḥ puruṣa eka ihāsya dhatte
stity-ādaye hari-viriñci-hareti saṁjñāḥ
śreyāṁsi tatra khalu sattva-tanor nṛṇāṁ syuḥ

The transcendental Personality of Godhead is indirectly associated with the three modes of material nature, namely passion, goodness and ignorance, and just for the material world's creation, maintenance and destruction, He accepts the three qualitative forms of Brahmā, Viṣṇu and Śiva. Of these three, all human beings can derive ultimate benefit from Viṣṇu, the form of the quality of goodness.

Comment

Lord Viṣṇu is one of the three *guṇa-avatāras* expanded from the original Personality of Godhead, Śrī Kṛṣṇa. The material world is governed by the modes of goodness, passion, and ignorance, and each mode has a controlling deity. Brahmā controls the mode of passion. This *guṇa* incites creative drive. Thus Brahmā is the creator of the worlds and species under Lord Viṣṇu's empowerment. Lord Viṣṇu is the original creator. Lord Viṣṇu, as Kṣīrodakaśāyī Viṣṇu, maintains the worlds. Maintenance is the function of goodness. The universe ends at a certain time, as ordained by the Supreme, and when that time is up, Lord Śiva destroys it. Lord Śiva is the controller of the mode of ignorance.

Of these three *guṇa-avatāras*, Lord Viṣṇu alone grants the ultimate benefit of devotional service to the Supreme Personality of Godhead. This is clearly stated in this verse and the next. These *Bhāgavatam* statements defeat the concocted idea that worship of any demigod brings the same result as worship of Kṛṣṇa. If one worships the demigods, he attains their planets in his next life and is able to enjoy heavenly sense gratification. However, he still has to experience death. Only one who goes to the spiritual Vaikuṇṭha planets of Lord Viṣṇu can enter eternal life. Therefore, worship of demigods for material benefits is considered foolish, even though the demigods themselves are servants of Viṣṇu. The demigods assist Viṣṇu by their service in universal affairs, but they cannot grant liberation. If one wants to quit the world of illusion and suffering and go back to Godhead, exclusive worship of Lord Kṛṣṇa and Viṣṇu expansions is recommended.

Clear the foggy notions of *deva* worship, at least for yourself. Hindus will go on thinking that their *iṣṭa-devata* is best. Outsiders to Hinduism will go on thinking that Hinduism is polytheistic. *Śrīmad-Bhāgavatam*, however, doesn't leave room for misinterpretation.

We study. We fall asleep in late morning even when it's time to read. We think, "This isn't so interesting, about the demigods. I already know it. What's next?" But most people don't know it. These verses are given as authoritative proof. Even in India, Viṣṇu worship is not generally understood as the only way to perfection. The scriptures are clear, but persons claiming to be swamis, gurus, and *paramahaṁsas* have taught, "All worship leads to the same One, the impersonal Brahman." Therefore, Hinduism has become, as Śrīla Prabhupāda points out, a hodge-podge, a haphazard jumble.

Keep at it, lad. This is a poor man's job.
Write freely. Don't sleep.
Ad hoc
got a right to sing the blues.
Eat as I choose.
Don't read the news.
You got a noose
to halt the lust.
Don't give me Brahmā-
Śiva worshiper tag,
not even Christ you see,
although I do worship him by my worship
of his *Abba*, Father.
Lord Viṣṇu is Supreme.
Oh ho-hum.
I is drowsy.
And it's a matter of fact, I find the text not so exciting.
That's because
the day is long.

Now is the time for poor man to come to the rescue. This is exactly his role. He doesn't (we don't) say, "This is not interesting subject matter, this mention of *guṇa-avatāras*," but he admits that in late morning, *he* is not fully satisfied by it. There is some shortcoming in him that causes him not to be alert and pick up the important *pramāṇa* for the Supreme Lord Viṣṇu.

That's admitted. Then what do I do? I can go on to the next verse, and I will. I can also turn to material activities, but I won't.

It's woozy here. Give us a hand, Lord of intelligence. I feel and fear I'm in shaky territory and can use some help right now.

Hand, even when you're wide awake, black spots appear on the white page. See through. Someone once told me that when you read Samuel Beckett, you see through the print on the page to nothingness right before your eyes. There's nothing there. Better to stay awake and aspire for something besides nothingness.

Now let's take a look at the next verse. No harm in that. Prabhupāda sometimes moved along quickly. He wasn't afraid of that because he was always engaged in Kṛṣṇa consciousness.

Remember how I asked about things that devotees find dry in the philosophy? One devotee wrote that he finds everything dry from time to time, so he likes to vary his activities. Nice. Wash the pots in the sink. Look around—there's a dripping faucet. Turn it off to save energy and remember Prabhupāda. Clean your room, floor, desk. Don't be outside Kṛṣṇa consciousness for a moment. I can go and see Madhu in his sickbed.

But there's a limit to wandering from one variety of *bhakti* to another. We can't just belong to nowhere, no temple, no niche, no particular service. We also have to face the crunch. When it's time to read and write, it's best to read and write, not go and visit a sick friend. You'd be sitting at his bedside, but the restlessness would follow you because you deserted your assigned task.

Lord Viṣṇu, Janārdana on the southern tip of India—in Varkala. Lord Caitanya visited Them as well as the Ādi-Keśava temple where He discovered the manuscript of the *Brahma-saṁhitā*. Can I write about that? That Viṣṇu worship is best? Please deliver me from disbelief. We just read Prabhupāda's statements about exclusive worship of Kṛṣṇa in Vṛndāvana. Now we switch to Lord Viṣṇu as the controller of the mode of goodness. The *Bhāgavatam* also moves its attention from one thing to another.

Text 24

pārthivād dāruṇo dhūmas
tasmād agnis trayīmayaḥ

tamasas tu rajas tasmāt
sattvaṁ yad brahma-darśanam

Firewood is a transformation of earth, but smoke is better than the raw wood. And fire is still better, for by fire we can derive the benefits of superior knowledge [through Vedic sacrifices]. Similarly, passion [rajas] is better than ignorance [tamas], but goodness [sattva] is best because by goodness one can come to realize the Absolute Truth.

Comment

This is an important proof. I've heard that over ninety percent of Vedic *śāstras* don't really focus on *bhakti* but describe *karma-kāṇḍa* or *jñāna-kāṇḍa*. Therefore, these conclusive statements about the superiority of Viṣṇu worship over material life are valuable. Demigod worshipers and others can find their own supportive statements in literature catering to the lower modes. This verse, however, draws a clear analogy in describing progressive realization.

Some say that all gods are the same just as wood, earth, and smoke are all ultimately the same because they have their genesis in the earth. Still, there's a hierarchy of one over another based on their respective purposes. In the analogy given in this verse, if the purpose is to cook, then we want a flame. Everything is generated from the earth, but you can't cook with dirt. Neither can you stack wood on top of the earth and place a pot on top of it, expecting it to cook. All you will have is rice and *dāl* beans floating in water. You need fire. Therefore, the wood has to be ignited, brought from the smoking condition into flame.

Similarly, although the demigods of the modes of *tamas* and *rajas* are *devas* and do accept worship and reward their devotees, that transaction cannot give the desired result. What we really want is eternal happiness—a life full of knowledge and bliss. We may be in such ignorance that we think we can achieve bliss through the material energy or by worshiping the demigods, but that's illusion. Viṣṇu worship alone can give us the "fire," deliverance from material life.

In his purport to this verse, Prabhupāda writes, "But if there are impediments on the progressive path, anyone, even from the platform of *tamas*, can gradually rise to the *sattva* platform by the expert direction of the spiritual master. Sincere candidates must, therefore, approach an expert spiritual master for such a progressive march, and the bona fide, expert spiritual master is competent to direct a disciple from any stage of life: *tamas*, *rajas* or *sattva*."

We may wonder how a disciple who is actually influenced by the lower modes is capable of proper inquiry. If the disciple is so handicapped by *rajas* and *tamas*, how can the spiritual master engage him in transcendental work? One answer is that the spiritual master's order is transcendental. Even someone who is hampered by the material modes can work for the guru. Then the disciple becomes engaged in a gradual process of purification. He may not be immediately transcendental, yet he *is* transcendental because he is working under a person who is never tainted by material life.

Prabhupāda gives the example of the ignorant apprentice who can do good work as long as he follows closely the order of the expert technician. The technician uses his screwdriver just so and indicates to the apprentice to do the same. If the apprentice follows that order, his work will also be expert. In terms of practicing *bhakti*, this may mean picking flowers for the Deity, reciting prayers from *Brahma-saṁhitā*, or simply tending to the pure devotee's physical needs—making his bed, cooking for him, and so on. The disciple also prays to be delivered from those modes which still haunt him.

This verse and purport also urge us to rise to the platform of *sattva-guṇa*. That doesn't mean that within the material mode of goodness, we'll be able to see Kṛṣṇa. Neither should we be hankering to "see" Kṛṣṇa. We are told to work in such a way that Kṛṣṇa will see us. But the mode of goodness delivers us from the passion of working hard for sense gratification and the ignorance of laziness, sleep, and the madness of intoxication.

The spiritual master can uplift the disciple. Disciples may not be competent, but the very obstacles by which they are hampered can constitute a challenge for them. Overcoming that challenge is their victory. There's an interesting example of this in the Fourth Canto where Dhruva Mahārāja is fighting the Yakṣas. In his purport, Prabhupāda gives a reference from Viśvanātha Cakravartī Ṭhākura's commentary. It goes something like this: Dhruva Mahārāja was showered with incessant arrows, but he was not overcome and killed. The arrows were like obstacles, but they were also like an incessant rain upon a mountain. The obstacles washed away his incompetence and he was able to defeat his enemies. In the context of the present example, we can say that if a disciple accepts the guru's instructions, then the obstacle of being in the lower modes will not overcome and kill the disciple, but will wash away his incompetence.

In his purport to this verse about Lord Viṣṇu being the fire, Prabhupāda says, "The *rajas* stage of life gives a slight clue to the realization of the Absolute Truth in the forms of fine sentiments in philosophy, art and culture with moral and ethical principles. . . . " This seems to indicate that these cultural activities are not a high level of direct Kṛṣṇa consciousness. I flinched when I read the put-down of art, but I take it that by "fine sentiments," Prabhupāda means that sort of art and culture which reveal the mundane or "human condition" or which display the "finer sentiments" of material compassion and happiness. Certainly when he says philosophy is in the mode of passion, he's not referring to scriptural philosophy, but speculative, "creative" philosophy. In the same way, there is a difference between Vaiṣṇava art and the art which he refers to as a product of *rajo-guṇa*.

We may assume that Kṛṣṇa conscious art starts from the platform of the mode of goodness, executed by a brahminical person, one who actually follows the rules and regulations. Otherwise, how could an artist qualify to write a poem or paint a picture to illustrate Kṛṣṇa? How could an artist take part in a theatrical presentation dramatizing Kṛṣṇa's *līlās* if he or she is not a practicing devotee? The arts are another kind of practical service to Kṛṣṇa. They needn't be seen as something dangerous, nor do they have to be thought of as more than they really are. Kṛṣṇa is not impressed by art per se. He wants sincere devotion, whether in the offering of a flower, a painting, or a written book.

Text 25

bhejire munayo 'thāgre
bhagavantam adhokṣajam
sattvaṁ viśuddhaṁ kṣemāya
kalpante ye 'nu tān iha

Previously all the great sages rendered service unto the Personality of Godhead due to His existence above the three modes of material nature. They worshiped Him to become free from material conditions and thus derive the ultimate benefit. Whoever follows such great authorities is also eligible for liberation from the material world.

Comment

Sages follow Kṛṣṇa. Their following has formed a long tradition. We should follow that tradition. Sages are successful in approaching Kṛṣṇa and that is proof that their system of practicing *bhakti* works. One of the favorable symptoms mentioned in Rūpa Gosvāmī's *Upadeśāmṛta* is confidence of success. "As devotees tried this in the past and succeeded, so I will also succeed if I am patient and enthusiastic."

Prabhupāda makes the same points repeatedly and clearly and we should appreciate it. He is not trying to entertain us by giving us something novel. He's earnest about freeing the reader from the cycle of birth and death, which he recognizes as the main problem of life. Those engrossed in matter cannot see where they are going. Prabhupāda defines it for them: religion is not for material profit. We do not need to create metaphysical theories about the nature of true religion. Religion is meant to help us regain "the life of freedom in the transcendental world, where the Personality of Godhead is the Supreme Person."

God makes the religious laws and only His authorized agents know the purpose behind them. These *mahājanas* serve Kṛṣṇa and we should follow them: *mahājano yena gataḥ sa pantaḥ*.

I woke up after a post-lunch rest. I didn't want to work at this *A Poor Man Reads* task and I didn't know why. It just seemed far away. It is Sunday afternoon. I've been working steadily for two weeks. Maybe I need a break. Or maybe it's something more serious than that. I couldn't force myself to read the *Bhāgavatam* or to free-write. The free-writing seemed particularly distant, as if I had done it long ago in a previous life. I couldn't imagine how it had been so vivid and interesting to me. What was it about now? What should I do instead?

I could have gone in to see Madhu. He has been lying alone all day with no one to talk to. Or maybe I could have read *Caitanya-caritāmṛta* for awhile. I decided to chant. Then I read a few pages in the *Caitanya-caritāmṛta*. I came upon the passage about Nṛsiṁhānanda Brahmacārī who created a beautiful path for Lord Caitanya in his mind. He mentally decorated it on both sides and imagined the Lord walking there. After a certain point in his meditation, Nṛsiṁhānanda was not able to go further with creating his path. He decided it meant that the Lord would not be walking from Rāmakelī to Vṛndāvana.

In the purport, Prabhupāda writes that an offering made in the mind is as good as one made of gross matter. I thought this may have bearing on my writing, but I couldn't quite figure out how—the fact that we can meditate only to a certain point and then can't do it anymore. That was something I was experiencing myself. I've been building my *A Poor Man Reads* road of unusual commentary and it's been sailing along quickly, happily, and confidently. Suddenly I can't do more. Does it mean Kṛṣṇa doesn't want me to do more? What does He want me to do instead? I felt sincerely that I wanted to do what He wanted of me, or at least I recognized that I had to be prepared for that. Everything is practice to free us to carry out Kṛṣṇa's will.

After reading for about fifteen minutes, I decided to go in and see Madhu. I took the *Caitanya-caritāmṛta* with me, the volume with the painting of Nṛsiṁhānanda Brahmacārī meditating on his mental road on the cover. I sat beside Madhu, who is recovering now, and told him about what I had read. He smiled and said, "They are great devotees!" I read to him from Prabhupāda's purport where he writes that the main point of any service is the attitude in which we render it. Prabhupāda says one can be a poor man and still please Kṛṣṇa as much as anyone else. A pure devotee is not spiritually poor. The Lord appreciates anything that is Kṛṣṇa-centered. I may be a prolific writer, but if I'm not Kṛṣṇa-centered, the Lord doesn't care for me. That's the way it is. My writing may be "present," as they say—that is, *I* am into it—but Kṛṣṇa won't be present and won't like it unless I am a devotee rendering service through writing. It should be as direct as possible. Of course, I always want to put in a plug for honesty. It should be honest.

As Madhu and I were talking, an older man and his son came to the door, ready to fix the typewriter. They are Śamīka Ṛṣi's relatives, as are so many people in this area. I went with them to look at the typewriter. I thought it would be a simple matter of replacing one cartridge with another, but they wanted to take the old cartridge apart with a screwdriver. Then the younger man unwound much of the tape, threw it away, and got the remainder going again. They were about to leave, but I said, "What happens when this tape, which is now partly used, runs out?" Only the old man spoke English. He said he would be bringing me a new cartridge and then I can just snap it in. I thanked him, smiling, and they left. Suddenly it struck me that they *said* they would bring a cartridge, but they didn't. It was such a typical Indian exchange. They came here, did a partial repair, and didn't do the main thing, which was to give me a new ribbon. Probably it involved money. They will wait until this cartridge runs out again and I desperately need a new one. Then we will have to go through the whole process again of calling them to come out, waiting, and hoping they will repair it properly. Of course, the benefit will be another pleasant visit and we can get to know each other when they bring the new cartridge. In America, you could order half a dozen cartridges over the phone and be done with it.

The good result of all this is that I now feel more inclined to write the book. I don't know exactly how I broke free of my earlier questioning. I think it happened when, after these gentlemen left, I sat down and started proofreading some recent pages. Even before I read them, however, I was prepared to get into it and carry on my work. I felt something had broken through and that it was all right to go forward.

Please don't take this little life's description of a Sunday afternoon as not connected to the *Śrīmad-Bhāgavatam* writing. I certainly can't see it as not connected because unless I overcame this block, I would not have been able to write another line. This is a description of how I overcame it, how it happened.

Phew!
that was
a
close
call.

There's a statement in the *Bhagavad-gītā* that as kings such as Janaka and others worked for Kṛṣṇa in the past, so we should also work for Kṛṣṇa. Then there's that verse, " . . . being fully absorbed in Me and taking refuge in Me, many, many persons in the past became purified by knowledge of Me—and thus they all attained transcendental love for Me." (Bg. 4.10)

This was the system in the past and it is the system now, here where I am, in India, in 1996 (the Centennial year). It is the ancient, excellent system of *bhakti-yoga*. Prabhupāda says that the old towns mentioned in the *Caitanya-caritāmṛta* narrative are still in Bengal, but even if they are gone, the spirit remains. We don't die, but we have the same problems of birth and death that people have experienced from time immemorial. The sages have chalked out the path: serve the ever-fresh Lord Kṛṣṇa.

Alas, my *gāyatrīs* go by too quickly and I can't get them back. Is it that I think my time is better spent in writing?

Little mosquitoes, ants in puddle of honey on gold-plated platter.

I *want* to make sense, but I can't always lead the readers forward by providing all the context.

Bridge to Kṛṣṇa consciousness. Lekhaśravanti dāsī shook hands with Bill Clinton. Now *that's* a coup and worth printing. Her daddy's horse smile. The President's coiffure. Her son, Prahlāda. The joke's on the President. Did he know he was shakin' hands with a Hare Kṛṣṇa? Poor guy.

Clinton and Lakshman here in India, one so famous and mighty and one a servant. He calls me "Guru Mahārāja" because his boss does, as if that's my name. No sense trying to stop it.

What does the *Bhāgavatam* say? I don't care what your hand says, or pen or mind or your aunt Rachel. What does the *Bhāgavatam* say? It says that sages of long ago took the light and rendered service to God. (Got bit on the jaw by a mosquito. It's quiet outside.) It says real religion means *bhakti* taught by Kṛṣṇa. It says look at me and try to understand. Grasp the clear meaning. Look again, drink again, *bhagavantam adhokṣajam*. We can always find something new in a verse. Don't say *this* verse is nectar but that one is not as good. The sages worship Kṛṣṇa to become free of material nature.

Bhagavantam
Adhoksajam
Got thru
another day
faithful
to the
book

But how do you know there is God?

Because the *Śrīmad-Bhāgavatam* assures us.

But isn't that just an old book of stories?

No, it's *śāstra.* It's the book of authority. Śrīla Prabhupāda said, "At least we have a book." *Śrīmad-Bhāgavatam* is solid authority, at least among those who cherish it and who are learned in spiritual science. It is self-effulgent, describes the highest nature of religion as *love* of God. Are we so dull that we can't appreciate its standard?

So it goes, me and the atheist, like two guys at a sidewalk café in Paris arguing over whether or not God exists.

Meanwhile the *mahājanas* serve. In ISKCON temples, they just had afternoon *ārati* and will soon hold an evening one. This cowpoke will go to bed.

Hand, I salute thee. Any last messages?

No.

Text 26

mumukṣavo ghora-rūpān
hitvā bhūta-patīn atha
nārāyaṇa-kalāḥ śāntā
bhajanti hy anasūyavaḥ

Those who are serious about liberation are certainly non-envious, and they respect all. Yet they reject the horrible and ghastly forms of the demigods and worship only the all-blissful forms of Lord Viṣṇu and His plenary portions.

Comment

Śrīla Prabhupāda makes the distinction between *viṣṇu-tattva* living beings, and *jīvas*. The Viṣṇu forms are unlimitedly powerful and as good as the original Personality of Godhead. According to Their mission in this world, the

Viṣṇu forms display more or less power or attractive opulence, but They have unlimited powers within Them. Thus they are "living beings equally as powerful as the original form of the Personality of Godhead . . ."

Jīvas, however, are always limited, even though some *jīvas* are given special powers by God. One should never classify Viṣṇu forms and *jīvas* as the same. This is an offense to Viṣṇu and it is committed, for example, by those who use the phrase *daridra nārāyaṇa*, "poor Nārāyaṇa." People use this phrase to describe materially poor people to invoke sympathy and charity toward them. Helping the poor is pious, but it should not be done by insulting God's name or describing a poor man in the world as equal to the all-opulent Lord of Vaikuṇṭha.

Persons in the mode of ignorance worship demigods who are also *jīvas*, but who are empowered to administrate various material facilities. By worshiping demigods, one can fulfill his material lust for power, wealth, and intoxication. Some material desires (*ku-viṣaya*) are so sinful that they should not be fulfilled, but we want them so much that we will approach goddesses such as Kālabhairava to fulfill them. Some desires are sanctioned by general religious custom (*su-viṣaya*) and are thought of as "good sense gratification." In either case, whether we try to fulfill our *ku-viṣaya* or *su-viṣaya*, we are forced into bondage. All sense enjoyment results in bondage in the material world and pushes us to suffer repeated rebirth.

Persons in the mode of passion worship Brahmā, Śiva, Sūrya, Gaṇeśa, and others to fulfill their higher quality sense desires. Those who are in the mode of goodness don't worship demigods to fulfill their sense desires. *Brāhmaṇas* worship Viṣṇu forms represented by *śālagrāma-śilā* and other worshipful *viṣṇu-tattva arcā-vigrahas*.

The *Bhāgavatam* verse mentions that *brāhmaṇas* do not envy the demigods or their worshipers. They are respectful to all, even if the demigods sometimes look ghastly. Nevertheless, the *brāhmaṇas* never worship the demigods because they cannot grant liberation, either to their worshipers or to themselves. Viṣṇu is called *mukti-pāda*, the Personality of Godhead who can bestow *mukti*. Lord Viṣṇu's worshipers actually engage in pure devotional service for the Lord's pleasure without concern about their own liberation. *Mukti* is a natural by-product of pure devotional service.

When Prabhupāda says that Vaiṣṇavas, the highly qualified *brāhmaṇas*, "have no grudges" toward others' modes of worship, this indicates their broad-minded respect for worship within the Vedic system, but it doesn't indicate that *brāhmaṇas* actually approve of the worship or that they have no feeling for the fact that people are more or less wasting their time in demigod worship. If one is actually a *brāhmaṇa*, he will be compassionate toward those who worship in the lower modes. He may understand that by worshiping the demigods, people will continue on a path that will eventually lead to *bhakti*, but they will also eventually recognize that it is a very long path and progress is slow. If there is an opportunity, therefore, a *brāhmaṇa* may attempt to enlighten demigod worshipers about the Absolute Truth.

He can inform them, for example, that the demigods are actually great devotees of Viṣṇu and that they can satisfy the demigod by worshiping Viṣṇu directly. The *brāhmaṇa* might also point out the *Brahma-saṁhitā* verses that state that their worshipable gods are engaged in various forms of devotional service to Kṛṣṇa, who grants them their powers. Or, a *brāhmaṇa* may point out to demigod worshipers the authoritative statements in *Bhagavad-gītā* wherein Kṛṣṇa criticizes demigod worship as something practiced by less intelligent persons. In that section of *Bhagavad-gītā*, Kṛṣṇa indicates that the demigod worshiper gets faith for his *pūjā* from Kṛṣṇa in the heart. Therefore, when we say the *brāhmaṇa* bears no grudges, it doesn't mean that he is forbidden to preach. It means only that he should not insult the demigods or their worshipers.

Sometimes people say that they are situated in Kṛṣṇa consciousness but want to worship a demigod anyway. They say they will worship a demigod in order to better assist and serve Viṣṇu's devotees. Usually, they choose Ganesa so they can acquire wealth, which they plan to engage in Kṛṣṇa's service. This is a roundabout method and Prabhupāda never seriously recommended it. Worship of Kṛṣṇa will fulfill all our spiritual desires, both personally and in relation to our spiritual master's mission.

Mumukṣavo ghora-rūpān: don't worship the ghastly forms. I want to say more this morning. After all, I'm a writer. It's my duty to be up early, wearing whatever sweaters are necessary, and typing away. I have written my summary of the purport, but that seems to be only the minimum use of my power to speak.

I think of Rūpa and Sanātana going to see Lord Caitanya at Rāmakelī. They were dressed as Mohammedan officials. They confessed their bad habits and said that they were ashamed to come before the Lord in that state. It took courage to approach Him like that. They knew it would mean giving up their old way of life, but they wanted to be delivered by Patita-pāvana.

I'm interested in this passage because it's a moving sequence. They pray with such humility. Their prayers are exemplary for anyone interested in the art of prayer or the practice of humility. To pray as they prayed, we would have to be prepared to change our ways. Those two things go together—sincere prayer and the readiness to become something that we are not at present. We can't go to Lord Caitanya, make a confession, and expect to go away with our life and habits the same. Everything will change, starting with our name, right down to how we eat and how we sleep.

Dabira Khāsa and Sākara Mallika became Rūpa and Sanātana Gosvāmīs. The Lord sent them to Vṛndāvana to write books. They wrote many books, along with their nephew, Jīva

Gosvāmī. Kṛṣṇadāsa Kavirāja says it's not possible to count all the books they wrote. I've already mentioned that Jīva Gosvāmī wrote more books than all the *Purāṇas* combined. Some of those books are lost now, and some may be so advanced that only the most qualified devotees are able to read them.

And of course, I think of this in relation to myself and my service. Because the Gosvāmīs wrote so many books doesn't mean no more books should be written. Even if we think as Rūpa and Sanātana expressed their own thoughts, that we are dwarfs trying to catch the moon, still we want to write in Kṛṣṇa consciousness to purify ourselves. Just do as much as you can.

Mumukṣavo ghora-rūpān. The devotees go on worshiping their Nārāyaṇa or Rādhā-Kṛṣṇa Deities. They don't bear a grudge toward demigod worshipers but remain absorbed in the pure worship of Kṛṣṇa forms.

How sweet and graceful are Rādhā-Gopīnātha. He bears a flute, not an ax. Rādhā holds a flower for Her Lord, not a sword. She blesses the devotees not with material wealth but with assurance that they will attain service to Rādhā and Kṛṣṇa through authorized devotees. Worship Them in the early morning and throughout the day. Worship Them with *cāmara* and peacock fan. Worship Them with incense and lamps, songs, pure water, soft towels, and the recitation of devotional mantras. Worship punctually and with the best food and dress. The finery we might pick out for ourselves or our wives can be used to decorate Their beautiful forms.

I worship my Prabhupāda *mūrti*. He is kind to me. Sometimes I come before him wearing my old slippers, which I also wear in the toilet room. My mind knows it's not good, but sometimes I ask Prabhupāda to excuse me. Sometimes I remove the slippers if I feel enough mental presence. Sometimes I feel too physically tired to remove them or I think, "Prabhupāda, my worship of you is very familiar. That's the way it is because we live together. It's not so formal, so don't mind if I keep my slippers on." Or sometimes I stand in the doorway to the bathroom, drying off from my bath. That's also not on the standard of right conduct before a deity. But we live so closely together. I am admitting these things, not saying they are right. Perhaps I should try harder to correct them. At least Prabhupāda is always in my life and I pray he won't be offended and leave me. I would not bear his leaving me. If this beloved form I have worshiped for so many years were to leave me, I would get another form just like it and continue the *pūjā*. I have *cādars* and hats and *sannyāsa* uniforms for him. Sometimes I am impatient when the *sannyaāsa* top-piece doesn't fit easily or the fasteners on his clothes have worn out and don't keep his clothes in place. Prabhupāda sees me fretting and trying to finish the dressing. He may think, "Why do you worship me at all if you feel it's a botheration?" I don't want to ruin it.

Polished poems are okay.
You have to work for everything,
not just fill up pages.
But there's a place for that too.
Fill 'em up—
your Indian cheap paper pads,
your luxury American legal pad,
your poem page,
index cards,
ink, ink, where does it come from?
I hope some animal didn't
have to sacrifice its blood
for me to write this.

In a nice Chinese
poem written long ago
the recluse says,
"I sing my lonely song alone.
Perhaps a true friend will find in these words
the signature of a sage."

Text 27

rajas-tamaḥ-prakṛtayaḥ
sama-śīlā bhajanti vai
pitṛ-bhūta-prajeśādīn
śriyaiśvarya-prajepsavaḥ

Those who are in the modes of passion and ignorance worship the forefathers, other living beings and the demigods who are in charge of cosmic activities, for they are urged by a desire to be materially benefited with women, wealth, power and progeny.

Comment

Śrīla Prabhupāda straightens us out. He allows no nonsense in the name of devotional service. Someone may want to eat as much as possible and sanction that desire because "it's *kṛṣṇa-prasādam,*" but Prabhupāda stops that: "We should never desire to increase the depth of material enjoyment. Material enjoyment should be accepted only up to the point of the bare necessities of life and not more or less than that. To accept more material enjoyment means to bind oneself more and more to the miseries of material existence."

We'll feel immediate material happiness, but ultimately that happiness will become our greatest enemy. It will cheat us of our ability to renounce the world and to go back to Godhead. Therefore, we have to learn to be balanced. Prabhupāda liked to see his disciples happy, and that also meant that they could enjoy sumptuous *prasādam*—"but not too much." Don't eat more than you can easily digest. Don't become fat. Don't become too skinny either. Don't become sexually agitated. Be healthy and strong and serve Kṛṣṇa. Don't be lazy or idle, but work hard for Kṛṣṇa.

We shouldn't be looking through the Kṛṣṇa conscious rules for a license to enjoy sense pleasure. If you need a little more than the minimum, become a responsible *gṛhastha* and regulate your sense gratification. If you are a *brahmacārī* or a *sannyāsī*, however, then sense control is especially appropriate. Lord Caitanya's advice to Raghunātha dāsa Gosvāmī may be too severe to be taken literally, and in fact Prabhupāda specifically said not to imitate Raghunātha because we will lose whatever gains we have made. We can follow the spirit though. Don't increase the enjoying propensity. Don't eat luxurious foods, don't dress in fine clothes, control the tongue, belly, and genitals, don't mix with women or men who enjoy women. Always chant Hare Kṛṣṇa and remember Kṛṣṇa.

All this is similar to why we speak against demigod worship. Demigod worship centers on increasing sense enjoyment. That's what the worshiper prays for and what the demigods bestow. The *Bhagavad-gītā* states that those who worship the demigods have their intelligence stolen by material desires. Better to serve the Supreme Lord and His pure devotees and accept whatever comes as Kṛṣṇa's mercy.

Women, wealth, power, and aristocratic birth—I don't feel particularly hampered by these things, but maybe I am. As a *sannyāsī* and guru, I have access to women. I could enjoy having them serve me. I could enjoy their looking up to me as a pure soul, a mentor and counselor. They will work for me, those devoted ladies. They will cook and type and launder my clothes. They will be concerned about my health and pray to Kṛṣṇa for my well-being. Isn't this dangerous?

And wealth—"Here, Gurujī, I heard you needed money to print your latest book," "I heard you needed a new van," "Here is *guru-dakṣiṇā* so you can travel around the world and deliver the fallen souls." Isn't this dangerous?

And power. Just to be able to get whatever I want on a daily basis. All I have to do is ask and someone will arrange it. I could feel my power. I could humble a politician or a doctor (if he's a Hindu, of course. In the West, we are the ones who have to be humble). I could think of myself as powerful in this religious movement. Isn't this dangerous?

It's natural to ask myself whether I'm guilty of these excesses. It's also natural to try to find the balance between real renunciation and false renunciation. We can't spend our lives doubting our motives or assuming we are cheaters.

I have been feeling undernourished and weak. Most devotees, when they see our Nature Cure meals, think we are not getting enough grains or bulk. We tell them they are ignorant of hygenic laws because they continue to eat past the first belch. The author of *Practical Nature Cure* coined the phrase, "Dietetic righteousness." He means it in a favorable sense, but it could also become a source of pride.

Then why are we weak? Perhaps we need to eat more regularly, as Prabhupāda did—rice, *dāl*, *capātīs*, and *sabjī*. And a sweet is not forbidden. If in order to digest all that in my old and weak system I require an Āyurvedic *churna* or two, no harm. These are not the symptoms of deepening sense gratification.

The point of this discussion is that it's a mistake to decry demigod worship, claim we are Vaiṣṇavas, and then retain material desires. We will miss the real benefit of worshiping Viṣṇu and then we won't be able to please Him.

In his purport, Prabhupāda puts this statement in italics: "*One should work hard and worship the Supreme Lord by the fruits of one's hard labor for existence, and that should be the motto of life.*" We may be surprised by such a down-to-earth motto. Work. Use the rewards of your work to please God.

Don't drop out to go live in a cave, but live in the world for Kṛṣṇa. Forget about demigod worship and lighten your sense gratification.

I was just about to go to the typewriter and bat it out fast, but the damned thing doesn't work. I mildly cursed the people who had come and claimed they had fixed it. Oh, but they mean well. Now I'll have to turn to my hand. This manual, slower way may be best. It's all I have. People have used this God-given method to write for centuries. When I pick up the pen, my brain sets off some subtle sparks and I pick them up and verbalize them. Synapse? Electricity? Not exactly. It works, though.

How much sense gratification is "the bare necessity"? Sounds austere. Bare needs could mean eating a drop of something and otherwise fasting. Then we'd be so skinny and weak we wouldn't be able to pick up a book bag. For a book distributor, the bare necessity could mean whatever it takes to keep his energy up all day. The bare necessity for a farmer means enough so that he can work hard in the field all day. He won't be able to do that on a finger-drop of buttermilk every other day.

Hand, be pure. Your grip on the pen is duty. I'm happy to look at the clock and see I've got ten minutes left. But I wanted to draw, too. Here's the drawing:

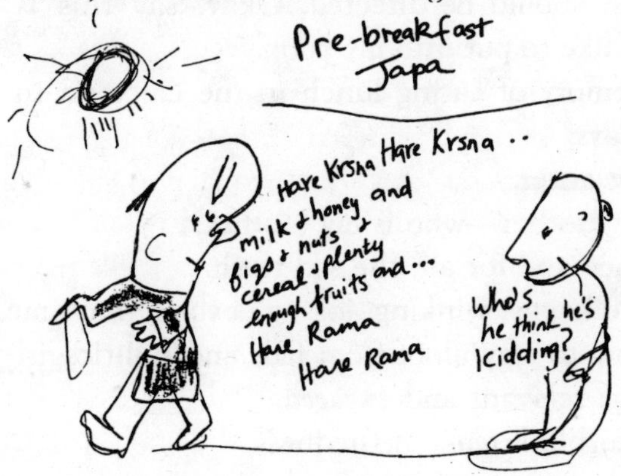

A plain sun coming up. I remember Petite Somme and Madhu and I driving there. It sure would be nice to get it together and write this *A Poor Man Reads The Bhāgavatam* anywhere in the world.

I don't need a van, only this hand and a pen. It aches. Words come in columns. A woman with a stroller is watching me. Householders everywhere. I want a life of solitude to write calmly and steadily.

What are my concerns? *Kṛṣṇa isn't real to me* is one lament or theme. I want to improve that.

Let's make a list:

(1) The picture of a tiger on a jar of *churna*. The writing is all in Hindi. Doctor gave me permission to take *churna* two or three times a day and I gleefully think, "This will be fun. I'll be able to eat more and digest it."

(2) "A Wise Child." Salinger attacked. Seymour Glass.

(3) Stainless steel cups. Living in India.

(4) A temple store. Counter beads, latest books. Where will it end?

(5) A month of the Centennial year already consumed—as if a mouse had eaten it.

(6) Rasa-prema dāsa in Brussels. Let him be.

(7) Me and new books and happy to use everything for Kṛṣṇa. Learn how to write better.

The list should be directed. Okay, say this is a list of things I'd like to put into my book.

(1) Memory of eating lunch in the cafeteria in Brooklyn College days.

(2) My sister.

(3) My brother—who is my brother?

(4) Once and for all, the sad truth.

(5) The happy, winking, joking devotee that's me.

(6) How to stay aloof from fads and politics in ISKCON and still be relevant and *engaged*.

(7) Eyes blink tears of tiredness.

(8) Sleep and dreams. Your latest dreams—a way to get them to work in your book.

(9) Attitude that each verse and purport is worth studying and that I can find nectar in them.

(10) Freedom to chant.

Texts 28–29

vāsudeva-parā vedā
vāsudeva-parā makhāḥ
vāsudeva-parā yogā
vāsudeva-parāḥ kriyāḥ

vāsudeva-paraṁ jñānaṁ
vāsudeva-paraṁ tapaḥ
vāsudeva-paro dharmo
vāsudeva-parā gatiḥ

In the revealed scriptures, the ultimate object of knowledge is Śrī Kṛṣṇa, the Personality of Godhead. The purpose of performing sacrifice is to please Him. Yoga is for realizing Him. All fruitive activities are ultimately rewarded by Him only. He is supreme knowledge, and all severe austerities are performed to know Him. Religion [dharma] is rendering loving service unto Him. He is the supreme goal of life.

Comment

The *Bhāgavatam* begins with the invocation *oṁ namo bhagavate vāsudevāya*. As explained in the first purport, "Obeisances unto the Personality of Godhead, Vāsudeva, directly indicate Lord Śrī Kṛṣṇa, who is the divine son of Vasudeva and Devakī." The name of Vāsudeva is now chanted in each of eight Sanskrit lines establishing that He, Lord

Kṛṣṇa, the son of Vasudeva, is the only object of worship. After these two verses, anyone who asks, "Who is God?" must either be slow or stubbornly rebellious.

Each line of the *śloka* focuses on a particular process for realization of the Absolute, and in each case, the goal is service to Lord Vāsudeva. For example, *vāsudeva-parā vedā*. This means that throughout all the Vedic literatures, there is only one objective described: establishing one's relationship and ultimately reviving our lost loving service unto Him [Śrī Kṛṣṇa]. Some of the *Vedas* may teach this in an indirect way, but they are part of the comprehensive Vedic scheme to gradually elevate everyone to worship the Supreme Lord in the mode of pure goodness. Those who claim that the *Vedas* lack an overall purpose, as some Indologists do, have no insight into Vedic *siddhānta*. "The *Vedas* are to know Me," Lord Kṛṣṇa says in the *Bhagavad-gītā*, "and I am the knower and compiler of *Vedānta*."

Similarly, the Vedic process of *yajña* or sacrifice is meant for realizing the truth about Vāsudeva. Lord Viṣṇu is sometimes called Yajña. All sacrifices are meant for His satisfaction. In the present age, there is little trace of bona fide yajñic ceremonies. Those who performed such sacrifices used to offer huge amounts of grains, ghee, and gold. The sacrifices were performed according to the exact science of chanting Vedic mantras. In the absence of wealth and brahminical expertise, however, the *ācāryas* have recommended only Śrī Kṛṣṇa *saṅkīrtana-yajña* for this age. "There is no other way, there is no other way, there is no other way in the age of Kali except to chant the holy names of the Lord."

This verse also mentions yoga. Yoga is meant to help an aspirant contact the Supreme Lord. *Āsanas*, meditation, and breath control performed separate from the desire to link with Kṛṣṇa are just physical exercises. They calm the mind, but they have no essence. Those who are serious in their practices of mystic or *aṣṭāṅga-yoga* concentrate on the Paramātmā form of Vāsudeva. Prabhupāda writes, "Paramātmā realization is but partial realization of Vāsudeva, and if one is successful in that attempt, one realizes Vāsudeva in full."

Vāsudeva-paraṁ jñānam. The *Bhagavad-gītā* analyzes the eighteen items useful in culturing knowledge. All of these culminate in devotional service to the Personality of Godhead, Kṛṣṇa. "Culture of knowledge leading one to the transcendental plane of meeting Vāsudeva is real knowledge." This is also stated in the *Bhagavad-gītā* where Kṛṣṇa says *bahūnāṁ janmanām ante*, one may try to culture knowledge for many births, but only when he realizes "*vāsudevaḥ sarvam iti,*" that Vāsudeva is everything, does he become a person of knowledge. If we accumulate knowledge at a university by studying in so many specialized departments, we don't become knowledgeable. We may learn how to run machines or how to think astutely on subtle subjects, but we won't gain liberation. If we don't know how to do that—if we prolong our miserable lives in this material world—then all we know is nescience.

This doesn't mean, however, that worldly and academic knowledge cannot be used in Kṛṣṇa's service. Prabhupāda sometimes compares material knowledge to a string of zeros. If we put the one, Kṛṣṇa, in front of all the zeros, then two zeros become 100 and three zeros become 1,000. That kind of knowledge leads the way to spiritual understanding. Therefore, science, psychology, and the arts can contribute to the *saṅkīrtana* movement when utilized by a pure devotee.

"*Tapasya* means voluntary acceptance of bodily pains to achieve some higher end of life." Prabhupāda does not count the pains a demon may take to gain power as *tapasya*. Real austerity is to accept bodily inconvenience for the sake of knowing Vāsudeva.

The meaning of religion has already been discussed in the *Bhāgavatam*, and Prabhupāda has offered many insights about the words "*dharma*" and "occupational duty." Prabhupāda has defined *dharma* as the unavoidable, constitutional nature of every living being. Our *dharma* is to render service to someone; in the highest sense, this "someone" means Kṛṣṇa. Therefore, *vāsudeva-parā dharma.*

All *jīvas* are in the same predicament. We are pure souls outfitted in material bodies due to the misuse of our free will. The embodied *jīva's* true purpose in life is to become free from this awkward combination of the temporary body and the eternal self. The conditioned soul is forced to act under God's laws for the material energy. These laws are just suitable to govern prisoners. A person in this world, therefore, has to show Kṛṣṇa his reformed state by sincerity if he wants to be released from the material energy and allowed to re-enter his original spiritual nature.

When a person becomes liberated, even if he still lives in this world, he is transferred to Kṛṣṇa's internal energy and his affairs are then directly guided and protected by the Lord. This is described in the *Bhagavad-gītā: mahātmānas tu māṁ pārtha, daivīṁ prakṛtim āśritāḥ*. Those who are broad-minded, the *mahātmās*, are constantly engaged in the Lord's service without deviation. In fact, all enlightened persons, such as the demigods, devotees, and enlightened sages, are serving Kṛṣṇa in different ways. The demigods are "assisting hands of Lord Vāsudeva," and the pure devotees enjoy with Kṛṣṇa in His *līlās* in the internal energy.

Verses 28–29 are a musical hymn in praise of the one Supreme, Vāsudeva. Memorize it and chant it from time to time in your day: "*vāsudeva-parā vedā . . . vāsudeva-parā gatiḥ*."

There may be some confusion about the name "Vāsudeva." According to Viśvanātha Cakravartī Ṭhākura and Rūpa Gosvāmī, Kṛṣṇa is actually the eternal son of Nanda and Yaśodā. This knowledge is kept confidential and is not mentioned directly in the *Bhāgavatam*, although it is indicated in some verses.

The general impression we get from reading the *Bhāgavatam* is that Śrī Kṛṣṇa appeared as the son of Devakī and

Vasudeva and then became the foster child of Nanda and Yaśodā in Gokula. Therefore, it is not wrong to say that Kṛṣṇa is the son of Vasudeva. Furthermore, Kṛṣṇa accepted Vasudeva as His father when He left Vṛndāvana at the age of sixteen. He then fulfilled the obligations a *kṣatriya* son owes his family according to *dharma*. He even asked Vasudeva's forgiveness for not being with him during His childhood, and He submitted to His parents' desire that He attend Sāndīpani Muni's *gurukula*.

Thus Kṛṣṇa performed the rest of His pastimes as a *kṣatriya*, marrying many wives, killing prominent demons, and so on. He never disowned His identity as the son of Vasudeva. At the same time, by His inconceivable potency, He is the eternal son of Nanda and Yaśodā in Vṛndāvana.

Vāsudeva is actually not the original Kṛṣṇa, but an expansion. Kṛṣṇa never leaves Vṛndāvana, so when He appears to go to Mathurā, He goes as Vāsudeva. This does not mean that Vāsudeva is not Kṛṣṇa. He is Kṛṣṇa whether He is playing in the Yamunā, sitting on the lap of Yaśodā, killing Pūtanā, killing Kaṁsa, marrying many wives, living in Dvārakā, and so on. These are Lord Kṛṣṇa's pastimes and they have been described in the Tenth Canto. Although Prabhupāda mentions in the *Kṛṣṇa* book that Kṛṣṇa doesn't actually leave Vṛndāvana but goes in an expanded form, he does so almost as a technical aside. He then goes on to enthusiastically describe the rest of Kṛṣṇa's pastimes in Mathurā and Vṛndāvana. We therefore are left with the impression that this is the same Kṛṣṇa who sported with the *gopīs*, who later sent Uddhava to Vṛndāvana to deliver a message on His behalf, and who spoke the *Bhagavad-gītā*.

Even if one wants to be technical and say that the original Kṛṣṇa is different than the expanded Kṛṣṇa for various reasons, we may still reply that there should be no distinction made qualitatively or quantitatively between Kṛṣṇa and His expansions. They are all *viṣṇu-tattva* and absolute. No one should create a troublesome duality between Kṛṣṇa and

Vāsudeva in any way that diminishes the thrust of these verses. Wherever Vāsudeva is mentioned, the author intends for us to understand Kṛṣṇa and no one else. We should not quibble against his intention.

Now get friendly
now get relaxed
fill your page with
berry tax.

Now be playful and juice the way
with currants, pecans, and daisies.
Now abandon the sorry frown,
kick on apes and
lacy gowns.
Muddy your boots in
Vṛndāvana's ground
and sing the mighty chant.

Now be true to oxen's pull,
now slide over mud and ice,
throw a snowball and run
and hide—be young and warm
in cold outdoors.
Now face truth or hide from it,
admit your anger and
tongue's demand.

Now write admissions and lists
and quests—let your hand speak
and your intellect admit
it's small
and bawl away the mighty
playful chant.

I admit
I remember
Diary's day is just an ember flaming still with
little life of
56-year-old monk.

Why be the center and
not Vāsudeva?
Why be the hero and not
the Lord?
Why *your* list and not
His? This
you got to explain.

Why so quick to write it
in?
Why do you love it, ink and
smell?
And pictures. Can't you tell
us why you cartoon so?

Now's the time to write these
things or if you won't then
chant instead the mighty hymn
to Vāsudeva
you said you'd memorize.

Vasudeva paro Veda
Vasudeva
param
gati

I admit I started to run. I set fire to a field and pulled the red alarm box (threw down my Fudgesicle first). I did worse and I don't want to admit it in print because it can hurt the faith of those who like me. Someone close said, "I allow you to be your own person and express yourself as you like, yet I do require to see a guru in the appropriate light, as a wise and flawless teacher, a pure devotee. I go to Śrīla Prabhupāda for that full scale."

Some few may say they see divine play in whatever I say. "He's enacting his haiku *līlā*." (I doubt anyone *really* says that.)

They may say it's no harm if I try out different literary forms and want to be myself. "He's teaching us in this way to sacrifice all face-saving images in preference to the truth. Honesty is his altar of sacrifice. It's good, it's bracing, and our place is to take what he says."

I like to write on mountaintops or by the sea or in any quiet room. I want to write before it's too late—before the dying out fact of candlelight at its gut end.

I do not know Vāsudeva. I'm an outsider to the nectar of His name and pastimes. But this *Bhāgavatam* quest is doing me good, bringing me in from the cold.

This is the time to relax and be
a bee of little consequence.
This is the hive of workers' stings
of tired hands and springs of steel,
this is the India I feared,
the book of no smoking, no hallucinations, the book
of preferred pure goodness or whatever I
can get of God's mercy from His
worktable. This foolish writer
may be given some toys or sawdust
on the Carpenter's floor.

In such a way I stay at
His feet,
writing plenty—
Vāsudeva, Vāsudeva, Vāsudeva
parā makhāḥ, parā yogā
parā kriyāḥ
paraṁ jñānaṁ.

Text 30

sa evedaṁ sasarjāgre
bhagavān ātma-māyayā
sad-asad-rūpayā cāsau
guṇamayāguṇo vibhuḥ

In the beginning of the material creation, that Absolute Personality of Godhead [Vāsudeva], in His transcendental position, created the energies of cause and effect by His own internal energy.

Comment

The Supreme Lord existed before the creation. That's the version of the first of the *catur-śloki* in the Second Canto. There the Supreme Lord tells Lord Brahmā, "Brahmā, it is I, the Personality of Godhead, who was existing before the creation, when there was nothing but Myself. Nor was there the material nature, the cause of this creation. That which you see now is also I, the Personality of Godhead, and after annihilation what remains will also be I, the Personality of Godhead." Ultimately, only God is the cause, the source of creation, its rest or maintenance, and its only survivor. After universal destruction, the spirit souls and matter are conserved by being withdrawn into the transcendental body of Lord Viṣṇu. After a long period of dormancy, the universe again awakens by God's will and the sleeping souls are injected into it for another round of material existence.

Who can comprehend such things? They're beyond the power of scientific investigation or mental speculation. As stated in the *Mahābhārata*, " . . . one should not try to understand transcendental subject matters through mundane arguments." (*Mahābhārata*, Bhīṣma Parva, 5.22) The *Vedanta-sūtra* also states, "Transcendental topics cannot be understood by argument or logic . . . By studying *śāstra* one can understand the Supreme." (*Vedanta-sūtra*, 2.1.11, 1.1.3)

Logic may be legitimately used to support the *Vedas*. It's not that logic is required—the *Vedas* are self-sufficient—but logic helps human beings to understand that which is beyond their experience in the same way someone may illustrate the location of the moon by pointing at it through the branches of a tree.

The Personality of Godhead is not involved in the material chain of cause and effect. He Himself created the causal and effectual energies. They are the laws of the material world and He is the lawmaker. Not only was God existing prior to creation, but "*He is all spiritual* and has nothing to do with the qualities of the material world."

All this I can safely say on the authority of guru, *śāstra*, and *sādhu*. As Prabhupāda used to say, "Whether you believe it or not, that is a different thing." Prabhupāda meant that we may disbelieve the *śāstra*, but that doesn't disprove *śāstra*. Our disbelief is our own affair; the knowledge of the Absolute is independent of our acceptance or rejection.

I accept. My acceptance is of no consequence. It is a laughing matter whether my tiny voice calls out on the side of God or for chaos and chance, atheism. Who will even hear my opinion? But it matters crucially to me. I accept *śāstra*. I repeat what *śāstra* states. I press on it with my tiny hands and body (the impression of my conviction). "*There*, please believe it because I, Satsvarūpa dāsa, am convinced. Please take it on my word."

Prabhupāda's purport here is only three sentences long, so we may move on. My watered-down grape juice will be here shortly.

Yes, and I concur that God must have existed before the creation in order to be its creator. Also, He must be the cause of all causes (*sarva-kāraṇa-kāraṇam*).

Would you like the juice placed on your desk at the same time we place Prabhupāda's little gold-plated cup on his altar?

Yes, please. I may pause to sip it when I have finished the offering. Hope I can digest it. That's important to me.

What's important? The cause of all causes? Establishing it by *śāstra* and logic?

No, my digestion. Unless I assimilate what I eat, how can I become stronger? No matter what I eat or drink, unless I can digest it nicely, it will become a toxin in my body and I'll never get well. This is my usual quandary—either I undereat to keep my digestive organs at ease, and starve, or I eat to my satisfaction in a nourishing way and can't digest it.

It *is* a quandary.

Like the quandary of how the universe was created?

No, that's not a quandary. It is clear and resolved. God created before there was material existence. It all comes from Him just as a spider creates its web from saliva produced in its own body.

Ah, a striking example, sir. You know these difficult things well. I hope you'll be able to also solve your own problem.

Yes, it's a matter of concern. But of course, it's not a topic worthy of discussion in the way the universe and God are of consequence—to everyone. My assimilation of food only concerns myself.

I'm still waiting for the typewriter to be revived. Śamīka Ṛṣi went to his cousin-brother today with the broken cartridge, even though it is Sunday. Using his screwdriver, the son fixed the cartridge a second time. Then they forgot to get it from him. In any case, he says, even if he *had* brought it, it probably would have become jammed again within a few minutes. We both agree that what the typewriter needs is a *new* cartridge. If I had a new one, I could use the machine right now.

But I've still got my hand, a Sheaffer pen, and an ink cartridge. And I have a few ideas. I have Lord Caitanya's fruits to distribute. He recommended that we all chant Hare Kṛṣṇa no matter who we are or in what status of life we find ourselves.

Vāsudeva is transcendental. When we chant His name or hear of His activities, we can be with Him. Hearing of Vāsudeva as the cause of the cause-and-effect cycle is also hearing about Him. We may prefer to hear of Kṛṣṇa in His internal energy in Vṛndāvana, but hearing Sūta Gosvāmī describe the Supreme Lord as the creator of *sat-asat* is also Kṛṣṇa consciousness.

My contact with Vāsudeva through hearing is unfortunately limited. It is impossible to understand Kṛṣṇa in full, but I fall short even in understanding the little bit I can know. Although this makes me unhappy, it also gives me hope. It is possible to improve. I think this writing and reading will help. By my writing on each verse and purport of the *Bhāgavatam*, Kṛṣṇa will see my earnestness and possibly bless my endeavor with increased stamina and taste. Maybe He'll think, "This person is setting out on quite a task. He says he'll write on all 4,700–some purports. Where does he think he'll get the energy for such a project? How worthy does he think his contribution will be? Of course, I could enable him to say it in such a way . . . " All this makes me tingle with expectation and appreciation of the potential this endeavor carries. That is, *if Kṛṣṇa desires*, it could be a wonderful thing.

Text 31

tayā vilasiteṣv eṣu
guṇeṣu guṇavān iva
antaḥ-praviṣṭa ābhāti
vijñānena vijṛmbhitaḥ

After creating the material substance, the Lord [Vāsudeva] expands Himself and enters into it. And although He is within the material modes of nature and appears to be one of the created beings, He is always fully enlightened in His transcendental position.

Comment

Śrīla Prabhupāda describes the *jivas* who are unfit to enter the spiritual kingdom as "strewn" around the material world. You'll find them everywhere, in all species of life, trying to enjoy themselves to the fullest extent. It's a vain endeavor, but they continue to try to fulfill themselves.

Wherever we go, because we're not self-sufficient in anything, the Supreme Lord accompanies us as Paramātmā in the heart of all beings. He is our eternal friend. Thus Kṛṣṇa guides us even in the material activities we insist on performing in our pursuit of happiness.

This contradicts or transcends the concept that God tells us what to do, and as soon as we go against His instruction, He becomes opposed to us and punishes us. Rather, even when we oppose Kṛṣṇa, He continues to help us in our foolish endeavors.

Kṛṣṇa is the witness. The metaphor of the two birds on the tree of the body depicts the Supreme Lord as silently watching and waiting. He's always transcendental to the modes of nature, although His friend, the tiny spirit soul, is subjected to them. The *jīva* bird tastes the fruits on the tree and the witness bird sees it all. At the time of death, He knows where we deserve to go next according to our karma.

The eternal Self within should never be confused with the eternal infinitesimal self. One is controlled and the other the controller.

I cherish this information. I see how it is misleading to concoct a philosophy based on only one self. I want to pray to Paramātmā who is always with me. I trust in His reality and His well-wishing intent. I hope to please Him, *caitya-guru*.

Why *do* the countless living beings remain unqualified and "strewn" about in the material world? The root cause is envy. We are originally spiritual by nature, but we think, "Why should only Kṛṣṇa be worshiped? I'm as good as Kṛṣṇa." No one can remember when he or she first became envious and came to the material world, but this envy continues and perpetuates our stay here. It is a moot point to ask where the envy originated. It starts with our envy of God and spreads outward like a bad infection. Prabhupāda explains that although we are pure spirit souls, because we are so tiny, we have the tendency to misuse our small amount of free will.

Our desire to enjoy apart from the Lord is our disease and Kṛṣṇa knows it, so why doesn't He terminate it at once? As Paramātmā, why does He only witness rather than interfere like a loving father? These human doubts come up sometimes, tinged not only with bewilderment, but with fault-finding toward the Supreme and toward our fate. The fact is, we don't want a loving father or doctor to interfere. We are intent on enjoying the material energy. Kṛṣṇa never takes away the small amount of free will that He has given to each of His parts and parcels. If He did take it away and force Himself upon us, then we wouldn't really have developed our own love of God. Love of God cannot be forced. Kṛṣṇa maintains the *jīvas'* integrity even if they have to suffer. This is another form of His leniency toward us—He lets us do what we want. At the same time, He actively gives instructions how to get out.

I'm an embarrassment to myself with this eating business. Just went in and saw Madhu. He was open-eyed, sitting up in bed. The Āyurvedic doctor came, but he wasn't an Āyurvedic. He was a homeopath and he left his little white pills. He did not recommend a diet, which is what Madhu hoped to get from him. I didn't need to preach to Madhu, and neither did I find him in a complaining mood. It's a fact though, that they consistently give him something other than what he asks for. He has diagnosed his problem as indigestion. Now the body has vomited it all out, but his digestion has shut down. Madhu says he's trying to convince the body that it has rejected indigestible food and that now it should start working again. He will not send it something it can't handle. He asked for steamed vegetables and they brought fried potatoes and beans. He settled for three *capātīs* and later got a cup of carrot juice.

Hearing him talk about indigestion and the need for temperance in eating embarrasses me. Since Madhu has been out of action, our Nature Cure diet has completely fallen aside. The same with the yoga exercises. I've been trying to fatten myself up, to gain strength, but to do so, I'm taking pills, digestive aids, and a tonic to support the heavier diet. It's a bit silly going from one thing to another. According to Nature Cure, the greatest hygienic sin is to eat when you're not hungry. This causes indigestion and all the woes that follow, from which Madhu says he's suffering. If you always wait for keen hunger and are extremely careful not to overeat, however, you are likely to undereat. Whenever I make a long-term commitment to follow naturopathy, I wind up feeling undernourished and skinny. I get exasperated trying to figure it out and it *becomes a distraction from normal Kṛṣṇa consciousness*.

I'm writing this out here because it has become a distraction. If this were not on my mind, perhaps I could better pursue the *Bhāgavatam* topics or topics more closely related to Kṛṣṇa consciousness. But this is where I'm at at this particular junction. This is my *Bhāgavatam* life—lying with a wet rag over my eye and knowing that I don't need the upcoming 5 P.M. cup of hot milk and snack and wondering why I'm taking it. So goes the attempt to try and manage my own body.

To study Vedic literature, we have to be moderate in our habits. Then we won't be distracted by belches and indigestion or by weakness from too much fasting. Neither will we end up with some malady and have our reading and writing time taken away.

Got a list? Lists unload the line. They allow me to state something that wants to be said, but briefly, and then to put it aside. A good list may grow and bloom like a poem, complete in itself. I don't have to "do" something with a list.

(1) I list to port, I list to starboard. I can't find the balance in a stormy sea.

(2) I can't stop them from bringing the milk and snack because it's programmed by the host and the only people here are the paid servants who don't speak English. I can't say to them, "I'm not hungry, so don't bring the milk." But I could pour it down the drain and put the snack back in the kitchen. It doesn't matter what they think.

(3) Let's just move on to the next verse and purport.

(4) Nothing is irrelevant.

(5) I have to pay for whatever I do.

(6) Regularly hearing the *Bhāgavatam* will clear the dirty things from the heart.

(7) At the top of the list of important things in *Bhakti-rasāmṛta-sindhu* is faith in the spiritual master, Kṛṣṇa's representative.

Text 32

yathā hy avahito vahnir
dāruṣv ekaḥ sva-yoniṣu
nāneva bhāti viśvātmā
bhūteṣu ca tathā pumān

The Lord, as Supersoul, pervades all things, just as fire permeates wood, and so He appears to be of many varieties, though He is the absolute one without a second.

Comment

Paramātmā is the Kṣīrodakaśāyī Viṣṇu expansion of Lord Kṛṣṇa. He is the third of the *puruṣa-avatāras* who enter, create, and maintain the material worlds. As Mahā-Viṣṇu or Kāraṇodakaśāyī Viṣṇu is the hugest form of the Lord from whom all the universes come, so Kṣīrodakaśāyī Viṣṇu is the smallest form of the Lord. It is God's omnipotence that He is not only the largest but the smallest: *anor aṇīyāḥ mahato mahīyān*.

Although Paramātmā is tiny, His presence can be felt by chanting and hearing the transcendental subjects discussed in the Vedic literature, especially the *Śrīmad-Bhāgavatam* and especially when the *Bhāgavatam* is heard from the spiritual master. "His Divine Grace the spiritual master can kindle the spiritual fire from the woodlike living entity by imparting proper spiritual messages injected through the receptive ear."

Reading the descriptions of Paramātmā, we sometimes get the impression that there are many Paramātmā expansions in order for Them to be present in each *jīva's* heart and in every atom. Sometimes, however, the statements about Paramātmā seem to indicate that there is only one form, but He appears to be present in many. Thus we say that there is one sun in the sky, but according to their various locations on earth, people will all say that the sun is overhead. The one is perceived as many.

We may try to understand it in one way or another, but ultimately, Paramātmā realization is inconceivable. Whether we think of Him as one or many, in neither case is His form material. When He is perceived either by the perfection of *aṣṭāṅga-yoga*, or by pure devotional service, He is seen as the individual Lord in His four-armed form within the heart.

Prabhupāda mentions here that the Paramātmā can be perceived even in atomic energy. Proud material scientists claim that they have harnessed the atom or split atoms, and so on. Thus they have given the world atomic energy in the form of the atomic bomb. Some claim that the demoniac scientists have actually controlled God (who is within the atom).

No one controls God. Sometimes Kṛṣṇa allows the demons to play with material nature and delude themselves to think that they are in control, but such demons only become more and more implicated in the material nature. In fact, nuclear weapons are so powerful that their power of destruction is out of control. Human beings may claim to have invented them, but they're also afraid of them. Politicians spend a lot of time trying to control their use.

Scientists and other persons who want to control and enjoy are allowed to try because Kṛṣṇa rewards the living beings with the fulfillment of their desires. If a living being wants to become God, Kṛṣṇa gives him some power so that he can pretend he is the *iśvara*. It is only by God's grace that the scientists are given intelligence by Paramātmā to "control" the atom. If after being given such a gift, the scientist rebels against God and then creates a bomb to kill as many living entities as possible, then again he will "become a mouse." The bombs have the power to destroy civilization as we know it and revert progress back to the point of pre-industrial primitivism.

(If I bang away on the typewriter at 1 A.M. I may wake up the two dear residents of this building, but I know they will forgive me. I won't type for long. Typing gives a certain variety to expression. I request you to turn over and go back to sleep and dream of Kṛṣṇa.)

I like the expression that the spiritual master kindles the woodlike ear of the disciple and then it breaks into divine consciousness like fire set aflame in wood. It would be nice to have such a receptive ear. How do we gain this proclivity? One way is to always hear when His Divine Grace is speaking. Prabhupāda had this quality in his relationship with his own spiritual master. Others would hear and disperse, "But I would go on hearing even though I couldn't understand everything that he said."

Another way to be more receptive is to sincerely carry out His Divine Grace's instructions. If we hear but don't act upon the instructions, then our understanding becomes theoretical.

I've heard of disciples who lost faith in some of Prabhupāda's personal dealings with them. This changed their hearts and they couldn't muster up the faith in other aspects of his behavior. They went on hearing from him in his books, they quoted and preached his philosophical teachings, but they created a duality between these teachings and his personal dealings. To be effective, however, we have to hear from him as a Vedic teacher and writer and also as spiritual master, and we need to give him all the surrender and love a spiritual master is due. That means we accept whatever he does, however he behaves toward us, as absolute and within his rights.

There are always new chances to develop our relationship with the spiritual master in a favorable way. We may think he doesn't understand something we have done or we may find it hard to accept his correction. Time, inspiration, and guru's grace can heal these mistakes in our understanding. We can only go on trying our best to approach him in a personal way and allow him to rule us. We should pray to be able to do this.

When we read accounts and memoirs of Prabhupāda's disciples and their exchanges with His Divine Grace, we can touch Śrīla Prabhupāda's personal dealings ourselves. It doesn't matter whether we always understand how he behaves or not, or whether we agree with them or not. It's good to continue exposing ourselves to the spiritual master's personal side. Neither do we have to understand why he says and does things in particular instances with particular persons. Rather, it is a Vedic injunction that one shouldn't try to understand the spiritual master's mind (*vaiṣṇavera kriyā mudrā vijñe nā bujhaya*). Just abide by what he says and don't find fault. We may not be advanced enough at present to always understand why the spiritual master reprimands one disciple, why he appears angry or challenging or soft or gentle. It doesn't matter. Simply follow his instructions.

I know that if someone turns randomly to a page of this book, he may find colloquial language—maybe even slang—as if suddenly he had stumbled into someone's back room. If he reads progressively, however, he may better understand the method behind it. I ask forgiveness for my impurities.

When we read of Jagāi and Mādhāi or of Mṛgāri's conversion or of the conversion of Vālmīki, we want to hear a little about the person's former crudeness so that we can understand the depth of their conversion. Although after the conversion, these persons became gentle and soft, they may have continued to use some of their former language. A little roughness is not a bad thing. In the Western world, we will probably continue to hear the Hare Kṛṣṇa mantra chanted in rough-voiced rock music. A free-writer does not censor everything that comes down the mental pike just to assure some gentle souls that he is now perfect (which he is not).

The receptive ear is kindled into fire. It spreads through his body as a warming presence in a cold world.

Yes, it is silly to be so preoccupied with thoughts of digestion and all that, but even that can bring us to the right path. Today while looking for a reference about Paramātmā, I noted in the *Bhagavad-gītā* that verse in the fifteenth chapter where Kṛṣṇa says He is the fire of digestion. Digestion is not the result of *churnas* or pills or the naturopath process of stimulating the body's own powers. Digestion is a result of God's grace. Without it, we cannot have the fire in our stomachs by which we can digest food. Kṛṣṇa gives it and He may withdraw it. Kṛṣṇa is the active principle in all things.

Kṛṣṇa, You operate this body. I am helpless. If You like, You can allow this body to keep going a little longer. I know it's a flopping instrument. Sooner or later its dance will be done. Please let it dance for You. Let my rude words soften and sound mellifluous to the devotees. Let my brain be more inclined to speak more directly in the channel of Kṛṣṇa consciousness. Let my ear be receptive to His Divine Grace's words. Let me be Yours.

Ding Dong Dairy,
dad and I eat ice cream
in Great Kills, Hylan Boulevard.
I wanted to love him
but the world is cruel
and ignorant. We can't
love but lust.
Poems divine the original pure,
devotees only shelter, hear
from guru (bless you dad
with *śrāddha* prayer, RIP).

Automatic writing is to catch it—light—strength—from God. In a café, in a dream, tell whomever you meet about Kṛṣṇa, or at least chant loudly, be kind to people, to dear Madhu and Śamīka Ṛṣi and Lalitāmṛta and all the folks who may not even like me—to mice—to the servants in this house.

As I eat up all food. More! *Anniyor!*

And eat, *churna* to increase fire!

Eat, eat you fool, eat this page as flame.

Behave and curb lust and live to write divine words. My hand aches, my heart too. Pray for love and courage to be a teacher and an exemplary monk with my brother spirits in *khādī* in this world. O *Śrīmad-Bhāgavatam*, save us. You are the best *Purāṇa* and Śrīla Prabhupāda is our constant father and guide.

Text 33

asau guṇamayair bhāvair
bhūta-sūkṣmendriyātmabhiḥ
sva-nirmiteṣu nirviṣṭo
bhuṅkte bhūteṣu tad-guṇān

The Supersoul enters into the bodies of the created beings who are influenced by the modes of material nature and causes them to enjoy the effects of these modes by the subtle mind.

Comment

This verse describes the Supersoul's function in facilitating the *jīvas'* material desires. Some are astonished to hear that God is an accomplice even to the nefarious deeds of the living beings, but since we are part and parcel of Kṛṣṇa, we have inherited a little of His free will. Therefore, He continues His responsibility toward us by enabling us to carry out this will. As Prabhupāda says, " . . . the living being is helpless in all respects in obtaining what he desires. He proposes and the Lord disposes." Of course, it's not that we always get exactly what we want. We're not God, so we have to operate within the limits of the material nature and our infinitesimal identity.

Prabhupāda reminds us of the intimate relationship between God and His part and parcels. It is as close as father and son. If a son becomes insane and leaves his father's home, the father continues to worry about him and suffers indirectly when he hears that the son has become an outcast or a criminal. He tries to bring the son home. At the same time, the father continues his own sane functions and does not become in any way polluted or defamed by the son's choice to become a madman. The father "keeps the light on in the window" and is always ready to receive his wayward son home again—when he comes to his senses.

Paramātmā's superior function in our lives is to help us attain spiritual happiness. We are helpless without Him, so He reminds us, "You wanted to lead a life of truth. Now do it and approach this pure devotee who has come into your life." He reminds us to chant Hare Kṛṣṇa; He is our Kṛṣṇa conscious conscience.

One may ask, "What is the meaning of having free will if we are helpless to fulfill our desires?" But at least we have the choice. There are three stages of psychic activity: thinking, feeling, and willing. The spark of choice to go to Kṛṣṇa or to try and enjoy *māyā* is within our power. What is not within our power is the ability to carry out our decision. We need to take help from either the material modes or the internal, spiritual energy.

It is good to be aware of our helpless position and to realize our actual dependence on Kṛṣṇa. We may be able to increase this awareness by certain practices. For example, instead of depending on material forms of security, we can depend on Kṛṣṇa in a practical way. *Sādhus* traditionally take vows of poverty. They don't even stock grains from one day to the next. In this way, they find themselves dependent on Kṛṣṇa for food and shelter. Depriving themselves of material supports, these devotees become more and more aware that it is Kṛṣṇa who is providing for them. When Nārada Muni was a young boy, he set out wandering in order to increase his dependence on God. Seeing how we are provided for and assisted and maintained in so many situations increases our faith. A preacher does this when he goes to a foreign land without any material provisions. Of course, Prabhupāda set this wonderful example by coming to America with only forty rupees and full trust in the potency of the holy name. Prabhupāda said those first years in New York City were happy times because "I had only Kṛṣṇa to depend upon."

It is unfortunate that our desires differ from those of Kṛṣṇa, and even more unfortunate that we request Him to fulfill our wayward desires. If we want to know the source of those desires and why they differ, we have to again look at the fact that we are eternal individuals. Even when we become pure devotees of the Lord, we remain different than Kṛṣṇa, although our desires and interests have become one.

Rather than create metaphysical speculation as to why we have a tendency to rebel from Kṛṣṇa, it is more important to admit that we have rebelled and to protect ourselves from that nature by taking shelter in our spiritual master's instructions. We may reach the stage where we will no longer be afraid or overwhelmed by material nature, or rather, whatever fear we do have will be healthy and respectful.

As we meditate on Prabhupāda's purport, we become attracted to the Supreme Lord, who is so much inclined toward each of His children. Kṛṣṇa indirectly suffers when we suffer, and He rejoices in our happiness. This is the astonishing and actual nature of the relationship each soul has with Kṛṣṇa. The more we think of this connection with the Lord, the more secure we feel in Kṛṣṇa's love. We will want to reciprocate with that love more and more, and we admire those in whom this love for Kṛṣṇa has developed into pure loving service.

Some people are insecure and find it hard to love others because they have suffered so much abuse in this world. Such persons would do better to take shelter in the security of love for Kṛṣṇa where there is no cheating or disappointment. In the higher stages, Śrīmatī Rādhārāṇī expresses Her undying love for Kṛṣṇa, even if He neglects Her. This is the security of the highest stage of *kṛṣṇa-prema*.

To some degree, this security and love may also be experienced between guru and disciple, because the spiritual master is the external representative of Paramātmā.

I gave a copy of the Prologue of *A Poor Man Reads The Bhāgavatam* to a possible patron. He read it and said it seemed nice for me to have such a long-term project. "Are you going to write on all the 18,000 verses?" I admitted that I didn't know how long it would last, but that Prabhupāda wrote almost 5,000 purports. I thought I could also write following his *Kṛṣṇa* book purports to complete the Tenth Canto. Then I said something about preparing it for "the common man." I said it as if I were *deliberately* planning my free-write mixed with *Bhāgavatam* summaries as preaching. I said that the "common man" (by which I also mean the "common woman") is not always able to give a receptive hearing to the *Bhāgavatam*. He becomes disturbed or diverted from the Absolute Truth because he is affected too much by the modes. Out of compassion, I would address this predicament in my writing.

This is only partly true. The patron I was speaking to has a conservative, Indian, religious mind, and that's partly why I explained it in that way. Of course, I'm willing to admit to him that I myself am a common man, but I didn't want to explain to him why I like to free-write. He might not understand.

The new typewriter cartridge has already died. The tape gets jammed and won't flow. So much for the great bargain that this typewriter represents. It will be nice to go West for this reason. I hope to keep some sort of portable typewriter with me if I can convince Madhu to fit it into the suitcase. Or maybe I should decide to carry one and brazen it as my second carry-on piece wherever I go.

Oh happy day

the Lord feels our pains indirectly and He's happy in our joy. Prabhupāda once explained this in terms of the human body. If we feel pain in a finger, the whole body commiserates.

If Kṛṣṇa consciousness could only become real for me. Call on His names. Are you afraid to give yourself to such a powerful friend? You think He would diminish you too much and not let you write freely? We hear of people to whom God dictates and then they write down whatever He says. Would you like that, to be a stenographer for the Supreme? Yet Rūpa Gosvāmī *thought* deeply about what to write. The Vaiṣṇava poets may see Kṛṣṇa's *līlās* in their hearts, but in loving, transcendental service (free will), they choose the Sanskrit words befitting the Lord's mood. He inspires them, but that doesn't mean that they are mere automatons.

Jayadeva Gosvāmī trembled and hesitated to write that Kṛṣṇa bows at Rādhā's feet. Kṛṣṇa came personally and wrote it for him. This indicates that understanding Kṛṣṇa's mood is the poet's responsibility.

Don't be afraid to surrender to Kṛṣṇa and allow Him to rule you. He is real. Find the way to realize this.

More admissions:

(1) I admit I'm afraid to surrender.

(2) He isn't real to me yet.

(3) I love to write.

(4) False teeth. Like to chomp on food.

(5) Pick and chew at my nails.

(6) Self-centeredness may be a cause for not loving Kṛṣṇa.

(7) Am I really afraid He'll take away my ability to write? He *will* take it away at death or sooner.

(8) Whatever He does, I'll learn to accept it.

(9) I'm using up energy now to write before He takes it away.

(10) I give this joy to Him in service—a Kṛṣṇa conscious book. It's not pure, but it's for Kṛṣṇa consciousness. Even the Library of Congress lists it in Kṛṣṇa conscious terms—ISKCON, Kṛṣṇa deity, *Bhāgavata Purāṇa*, comments and ditherings.

(11) O frabjous day—Callooh! Callay!

(12) Breakfast isn't far away. Bananas, *chikoos*, papayas, crushed almonds, and *chyavan prash*.

(13) I left my guru's service as his personal servant and secretary. I could have written privately all that time, an official diary. It wasn't meant to be.

(14) Admit you wear long johns. You accept service from others as if you deserve it.

(15) I'm serious to make this a lifelong project.

(16) Motorbikes make me nervous.

This sentence is the last one this morning and I won't end until I say peach bushels and, "Don also gave me money." The Swami said that when I gave him my big donation. Don't stop for fear of rats. Saint Francis had mice crawling all over him after the stigmata and in the place where he introduced crèche worship. Madhu knows I know the story. Lord Caitanya heard the story of Sākṣi Gopāla and Kṣīracora Gopīnātha. I am a steno and reporter quickly writing down in an interview with God in the heart who tells me, "Write down what your brain says. Write more and don't stop. Link it to God. Don't stab your pen into the paper like a knife. Change pens in midstroke if you need to. I will go on to the next *Bhāgavatam* verse. There will be a red orb on the horizon soon—time to sleep. But you slept enough last night. Better to light candles and just go on chanting Hare Kṛṣṇa Hare Kṛṣṇa, Kṛṣṇa Kṛṣṇa Hare Hare."

Text 34

bhāvayaty eṣa sattvena
lokān vai loka-bhāvanaḥ
līlāvatārānurato
deva-tiryaṅ-narādiṣu

Thus the Lord of universes maintains all planets inhabited by demigods, men and lower animals. Assuming the roles of incarnations, He performs pastimes to reclaim those in the mode of pure goodness.

Comment

The Supreme Lord appears as an *avatāra* (one who descends) in all types of society to display His transcendental pastimes so that the living beings may develop the desire to return back to Godhead. Whenever He appears, the Supreme Lord does so in His transcendental form, although the forms may appear different—Fish, Boar, Human King, Dwarf *Brāhmaṇa*, and so on. Only fools *(mūḍhas)* deride Kṛṣṇa because He appears human. They make the greatest mistake when they think that Kṛṣṇa's body is material and that He is bound by death, a fallible creature. As Lord Kṛṣṇa states in *Bhagavad-gītā*, "Although I am unborn and My transcendental body never deteriorates, and although I am the Lord of all living entities, I still appear in every millennium in My original transcendental form." (Bg. 4.6)

The Viṣṇu *avatāras* are all forms of the Personality of Godhead in varied expansions, such as Rāma, Nṛsiṁha, and Śrī Kṛṣṇa in His original form in Vṛndāvana-līlā. Incarnations of God also exist in both human society and demigod society because the Supreme Lord empowers qualified *jīvas* with certain *śaktis* or opulences. In either case, the incarnation's mission is the same: to bring suffering souls to their normal condition of eternity, bliss, and knowledge.

Prabhupāda writes, "The eternal happiness which the living being wants is obtainable in the kingdom of God, but the forgetful living beings under the influence of the material modes have no information of the kingdom of God. The Lord, therefore, comes to propagate the message of the kingdom of God, either personally as an incarnation or through His bona fide representative as the good son of God."

Śrīla Prabhupāda was and is a highly empowered preacher on Lord Kṛṣṇa's behalf. It is natural that He imparts this missionary zeal to his followers. When Śrīla Prabhupāda granted me first initiation in 1966, he lectured that we new disciples now owed a debt *(guru-dakṣiṇā)* to our spiritual master. He said that we should now distribute the knowledge our spiritual master had given us to others. If we follow this instruction, we act for the same purpose for which Kṛṣṇa descends as an *avatāra*. Thus we become dear to the Lord.

Crazy tottering late morning hymn:

I'm spreading the chanting far and wide. I'm trying to be a soldier in His army. I am blissed out, sold forever, reeling in the nectar of the holy names. I'm a haphazard victim and agent all in one.

I'm no lopsided saint, no skinny being who speaks whatever comes to mind.

"Oh when will that day be mine
when my offenses ceasing
taste for holy name increasing,
when in my heart will Your mercy shine?"
He's a cowboy dinger
not a mud slinger.
He's trying to say—
these hyperboles of bliss are only partly true for me
    because I lack the dedication of the priest, artist, or
    soldier,
I'm lazy and sleep and eat too much,
the modes ensnare me and I must have committed too
    many offenses to Vaiṣṇavas and to the holy name.
That would explain
my failure.
"Should have died long ago,"
sang the Vaiṣṇava *kavi*.
"I think Yamarāja is punishing me
by not letting me join
as part of Lord Caitanya's *saṅkīrtana*."

He's saying that? Then I should get on track. I am here and now capable of riding in the prow of the most progressive movement. I don't know why I say I have failed. Stand up and face it and sing and dance, here's a chance to proclaim it.

Oh, I don't know why I fail,
is it that I drank too much ale
and took LSD for breakfast?
But I gave that up 30
years ago. Is it residue?
Is it dandruff, radioactive fallout
provided by Kali's demons that's affecting
my sincere attempt?
Is the fallout blowing ill winds on my patch
of a spirit-body?
Am I under the influence
of a malignant star?
Is it the scar from the broken windowpane?
Ah, I know I took more
than one bloke's dose of
sordid sex attraction—that could
be the cause
why I'm drained.

In late morning I cry, "*Ennui*,"
remember *Nausea*, Sartre's book,
Camus' gripe, Kierkegaard
and Kafka's dreary look and
still I seem to think if I went
back to Celine I might find
good humor in
his vomiting up raspberries.
Yeah, that's the cause for failure,
why I'm still in jail.
Too much mundane looking
from an artist's eye.
They zonked me with their
prose and hymns and sax-tooting
and drummers.
Half notes didn't help.

I spun those LPs and jazzed
out in time, skinny boy,
Monk's rendition of
"I'm Getting Sentimental Over You"
blows you to nethers.

But it's not too late.
You've been on a recovery plan
that goes deep
to the soul.
You have been imperceptibly
taking the Swami's remedy.
"I will overcome" is your
motto when you grip the
still-red beads and call
out in candlelight,
"O Hari!" (like the prostitute)
"O Hari! Please
don't leave me behind.
I've given all I could and
my carcass still feels dead
and my head needs repairs."

"Please," I ask—
although I should not ask anything—
"to be spared the worst and
given the drive to be a strong
young lad in *saṅkīrtana*—
if not in body then in mind,
or if in mind I'm too far gone,
then find a good intention
in my *ātmā*-soul.
May it spread
to rejuvenate all that ails me
if I can
once again,
serve You happily in the ranks."

We're at the end of the second chapter now. Do I plan to review the contents to date? No, I think I'll just keep moving along.

He said, "Come, what do we gain by evasion?"

He asked, "Why don't you eat popcorn in the evening?"

I replied, "It sticks in my teeth."

He said, "I'll make you a batch of cookies and you can keep them covered in a tiffin."

"You mean in my room?"

"Yes, and you can take when you want."

All right. The *churnas* can pave the way.

Meanwhile, Madhu is going in the opposite direction. He thinks his health crisis taught him to be more strict, to eat less, and to be extremely careful not to overeat—watch for that first belch!—or else Kṛṣṇa as *vaiśvānaraḥ* will not allow him to digest. The power of fire in the belly comes from Kṛṣṇa as He states in the *Bhagavad-gītā*, "I am the fire of digestion in the bodies of all living entities, and I join with the air of life, outgoing and incoming, to digest the four kinds of foodstuff." (Bg. 15.14)

Farewell to Chapter Two. Thank you, Lord.

CHAPTER THREE

Kṛṣṇa Is the Source of All Incarnations

Text 1

sūta uvāca
jagṛhe pauruṣaṁ rūpaṁ
bhagavān mahad-ādibhiḥ
sambhūtaṁ ṣoḍaśa-kalam
ādau loka-sisṛkṣayā

Sūta said: In the beginning of the creation, the Lord first expanded Himself in the universal form of the puruṣa incarnation and manifested all the ingredients for the material creation. And thus at first there was the creation of the sixteen principles of material action. This was for the purpose of creating the material universe.

Comment

This verse refers to Kāraṇodakaśāyī Viṣṇu, the first of the three *puruṣa-avatāras*. All activities of the material world are directed by these three Viṣṇu expansions.

The word "*puruṣa*" is sometimes translated as "enjoyer." The conditioned living entity thinks of himself as the enjoyer. How can a petty, mortal, living being claim that he is the source of the universes (although with outrageous pride, some people do make such a claim)? The *Bhagavad-gītā* calls this atheism. Kṛṣṇa states, "Earth, water, fire, air, ether, mind, intelligence and false ego—all together these eight constitute My separated material energies." (Bg. 7.4)

After describing the material elements, Kṛṣṇa then goes on to say that the spirit souls are part of His superior energy. Although the spirit souls, manifested as human beings, have power over the material energy, they are always ultimately controlled by God; they have no independent existence. Therefore, they cannot be called *puruṣa*.

We are fortunate to have such a comprehensive, theistic science to study in the *Śrīmad-Bhāgavatam*. When we absorb ourselves in submissive hearing, we will be less inclined to make absurd claims that religious scriptures give no adequate explanation of the creation, or that the vast cosmos could not proceed from an intelligent being. By understanding the *puruṣa* incarnations and the other incarnations of Viṣṇu, we become eligible for liberation from all material desires and speculations.

The desire to be the central enjoyer of everything is strong in the conditioned soul. To facilitate this mad plan, the lenient Supreme Father gives us a chance to play as supreme enjoyer in the field of the material world. At the same time that He grants us this doomed wish, He also gives us a chance to understand our real, constitutional position. "Those fortunate living entities who catch the truth and surrender unto the lotus feet of Vāsudeva after many, many births in the material world join the eternally liberated souls and thus are allowed to enter into the kingdom of Godhead."

Here is the distinction between the eternally liberated and eternally conditioned souls. Anyone who does not become liberated during the course of repeated birth and death in the material world ultimately becomes stranded at the time of annihilation. Then after uncountable eons, by the Lord's desire, material creation issues forth again. At this time, the *mahat-tattva*, or total material ingredients, is let loose, and within it are all the ingredients for the material worlds, including the conditioned souls.

Prabhupāda commissioned a picture of the total manifestation of God on the dust jacket of his first *Śrīmad-*

Bhāgavatam volumes. In the center, and largest of all, is Kṛṣṇaloka, where Kṛṣṇa enjoys with His liberated devotees. On the outer fringes of Goloka's lotus petals is the emanation of His impersonal effulgence, the *brahmajyoti*. The *brahmajyoti* floods the sky with light, and within it are located the innumerable Vaikuṇṭha planets. Only in one small portion of the spiritual sky (depicted at the bottom of Prabhupāda's front cover) is a portion set aside as the material world. It is described as a cloud in the sky. This cloud is the *mahat-tattva*, or material portion of the sky. Therein all the material universes are produced and are emanated from the pores of Kāraṇodakaśāyī Viṣṇu's body. Therefore, He is briefly described in this first verse of Chapter Three.

By even a casual glance at the book cover, we see that Kṛṣṇa is the original source of all incarnations, but He is not at all occupied or concerned with the affairs of creation in the material world. The *mahat-tattva* is far away from Him. He is absorbed in playing His flute and dancing with Śrīmatī Rādhārāṇī.

We may wonder how Kṛṣṇa can be off in His personal world in Vṛndāvana and at the same time appearing in the material world in His various manifestations. It is no wonder that we cannot comprehend these things. If we could understand them, we would have the same capacity as God. A human being is considered capable if he can manage several affairs at once. If someone can be the head of a factory, take care of a family, and pursue politics or other affairs, then we consider him competent. Kṛṣṇa is not like that. He manages through His Viṣṇu expansions and maintains His freedom without the slightest anxiety or stress. God has inconceivable energies; therefore, we should understand, at least theoretically, that He is capable of carrying out all these varied activities.

In the purport, Prabhupāda writes, "The Lord is the only enjoyer, and all others are enjoyed. The living beings are predominated enjoyers." Predominated enjoyers refers to the fact that we spirit souls also have a full scope for happiness and enjoyment. In order to taste that happiness, however, we have to be properly situated according to our constitutional natures. That means we have to serve Kṛṣṇa and be enjoyed by Him. We cannot enjoy without Him.

Although Kṛṣṇa, through His material energy and the time factor, forces the living beings to submit in various ways, He does not exercise a similar force to bring us under the command of His *bhakti*. This is what makes *bhakti* so loving and relishable—that we submit to it voluntarily and out of love. Furthermore, when we finally accept Bhakti-devī's grace and come under her control, Kṛṣṇa shares with us His confidential nature. The sharing is so complete that sometimes Kṛṣṇa comes under the control of His devotees and appears as if He is the predominated enjoyer.

In the material world, we want to rebel against control. The struggle between controlled and controller is often the source of mental and even physical scars. Being controlled by Kṛṣṇa is a completely different experience. We have to relieve ourselves of our misconceptions before we will be able to fully enter Kṛṣṇa consciousness. Those who maintain the bitter impressions of personal relationships will prefer to merge into the impersonal Absolute and thus miss the best experience of becoming Śrī Kṛṣṇa's eternal servants. If a battered human being has the fortune to contact a pure devotee, he can get a preliminary taste of the joy of serving Kṛṣṇa.

We are not the enjoyers. We only act as enjoyers artificially. Therefore, let's try to sort out this propensity by discussing *Bhāgavata* philosophy. What does it mean that we are not the enjoyers? You know, don't you, what it's like to enjoy?

Yes, but are you saying that my attempt to enjoy is a sin against my very nature? When I enjoy the soft breeze outdoors in the morning, or the feel of water in the bath, is that wrong? Is every little act of enjoyment on my part prohibiting me from going back to Godhead?

Kṛṣṇa has given us the touch of the breeze and the pleasure of warm bath water. Therefore, we can remember Him (and never forget Him) when our senses contact these objects. He has also sent the things we don't enjoy—pain, listlessness, suffering. We can also connect these things to Kṛṣṇa because they remind us that we're stuck in painful, material bodies. We are the "predominated enjoyers."

What can we enjoy? Can we enjoy devotional service? Can we enjoy the little triumphs over illusion? I enjoy writing and the sense of accomplishment as the pages accumulate. But when I try to enjoy as a vain author, I'm already in hell.

The afternoon withers now that it's past 3. Wake up Prabhupāda. Think of what to do to capture the prize of the day before this day is gone or before another headache closes in.

With hope I select the *cādar* and cap Prabhupāda will wear tomorrow. It's a nice feeling planning for an untouched day ahead.

Don't think too much about time consuming you limb by limb. I have a long plane trip coming up later this month. Better to think of the pleasant aspects, make it an adventure, a moving on. This weekend I'm supposed to give a lecture in the yard beside this house. What about right now?

Do I think my hand's message, the mystique I call automatic writing, can save me from death? Or from the onrush of time? No, I don't. Rather, I think of writing as something I can do, something that inspires me with hope, something that allows me to lose myself in the moment. I loosen my belt and relax, if I can, the ever-tightening band around my forehead. My friend looks worried. The world can become suddenly torturous. We often taste the danger in dreams—out with no home, no money, danger all around. Torturers after you. Then you wake up in your comfortable bed. That means the nightmare hasn't caught up to reality yet.

The hand says there's no relief, but a little creative path may do good if I can unearth a secret in the red ink on a white page.

A list of joys by a predominated enjoyer:

(1) I like the feel of cold water splashed on my forehead when I am beginning to feel pain and there's still hope that I will be able to alleviate it.

(2) I usually like my lunch.

(3) I like to anticipate getting a battery-run, portable typewriter and keeping it with me wherever I go.

(4) I'm grateful for this writing service, specifically this new *Bhāgavatam* project.

(5) I like to relax for awhile in the winter sunshine in India.

(6) I like going to meet Kṛṣṇa.

Text 2

yasyāmbhasi śayānasya
yoga-nidrāṁ vitanvataḥ
nābhi-hradāmbujād āsīd
brahmā viśva-sṛjāṁ patiḥ

A part of the puruṣa lies down within the water of the universe, from the navel lake of His body sprouts a lotus stem, and from the lotus flower atop this stem, Brahmā, the master of all engineers in the universe, becomes manifest.

Comment

Prabhupāda sums up the functions of the three *puruṣa-avatāras*. Kāraṇodakaśāyī, Mahā-Viṣṇu, lies down in a part of the spiritual sky by His own free will. He glances over His own material nature and the *mahat-tattva* is created at once. The universes spring out of His skin holes.

That first *puruṣa-avatāra* then expands as Garbhodakaśāyī Viṣṇu, who enters each universe and lies within a half of the universe, which is filled with water from His own body. From His navel springs the stem of a lotus flower from which are born Lord Brahmā and the fourteen divisions of planetary systems.

The third *puruṣa-avatāra*, Kṣīrodakaśāyī Viṣṇu, enters each and every *jīva's* heart, and even into inorganic matter, as Paramātmā.

All these transcendental activities are filled with purpose and cause. Although the events are extraordinary and beyond human imagination, they are not lacking in details. Thus we can gain some understanding of the cosmic creation. Anticipating atheistic objections and theories, Prabhupāda writes, "The atheist does not believe in the creator, but he cannot give a good theory to explain the creation."

By logic and experience, we must conclude that material nature in itself has no power to create. It needs a *puruṣa*, or a cause, just as a woman (*prakṛti*) cannot produce a child without a man (*puruṣa*).

I accept the Vedic version of creation and don't think my acceptance of it is fanatical or sentimental. The epistemology worked out by Śrīla Jīva Gosvāmī is satisfying. He states in his *Tattva Sandarbha*, which Prabhupāda has summarized in various places (such as in the Introduction to *Īśopaniṣad*), that out of the many different kinds of proof for knowledge, the Vedic *ācāryas* accept *brahma-śabda*, or hearing from authority, as the best. For support we may also accept what we directly perceive with our senses and what we infer through logic. These second two methods, however, are faulty because they are based on the innate imperfections and limits of the conditioned soul's mind and senses.

Then we need only define "authority." "Authority" does not refer to newspaper reporters or television broadcasters. It refers to *apauruṣeya*, the faultless source of knowledge beyond the material defects. Knowledge that comes to us in the form of Vedic literature is *apauruṣeya*. There is no other proof for the Vedic authority than the *Vedas* themselves. To get proof outside the *Vedas* implies that the *Vedas* are material and can be explained by someone less than *apauruṣeya*.

Then can't we call this a defect of circular reasoning to say that there is no proof of the *Vedas* except the *Vedas* themselves?

I don't want to argue this point. It comes down to Prabhupāda's example that you can't know your father without hearing from your mother, *brahma-śabda*.

Someone asked me, "Does Mahā-Viṣṇu lie down all the time meditating? Please tell me what else He does because I heard that if we understand His activities and appearance, we can become liberated." I don't know "what else" He does. Let us just accept the meditation of Mahā-Viṣṇu in *yoga-nidra* spawning all the universes. That seems enough to think about. "Understanding" starts with belief, acceptance, and worship.

I remember reading a letter devotees sent from India when they were with Prabhupāda about something he said about Kāraṇodakaśāyī Viṣṇu. One of the devotees said to Prabhupāda, "If all of the universes were contained within that lotus stem that came from Garbodakaśāyī Viṣṇu, it must have been a pretty big stem."

Prabhupāda replied, "You cannot understand it with your puppy brain."

Even the inquiry and mention of the stem as being "pretty big" seems presumptuous or lighthearted. It's as if we expect an answer in terms of road miles or light-years, some kind of big but limited calculation. We try to fit it within our material concepts. When we do that, we become baffled and run into all kinds of contradictions. It's not material; it's spiritual. We cannot understand it with our puppy brains. Don't even half try.

Lord Viṣṇu is the original creator and Lord Brahmā is the secondary creator. That means the *jīva* has creative potency. We will read in the Third Canto how Lord Brahmā prayed that his creative energy be rightly directed and that he not become contaminated when mixing with the demons and the material energy.

I think of these topics in connection with my being a creator or artist in Kṛṣṇa consciousness. I want to create something beautiful for Kṛṣṇa's pleasure, something effective for preaching, but I don't want to create something concocted or in the mode of passion. Neither do I want to become proud of my "creation."

What are the guidelines? First, we have to be authorized by the spiritual master. Don't create new philosophies, but find ways to present the guru's teaching anew, according to time, place, and person. Always stick to the original sound vibration of the Hare Kṛṣṇa mantra, the *Bhāgavatam*, and the spiritual master's speech.

We should also know that we never "create" anything because the ingredients are provided for us by Kṛṣṇa. His material energy provides the paint or ink, and *He* provides us with intelligence and inspiration. He also provides the facility by which the audience hears or views our creation. He is the power that withdraws all these factors according to His own will. In fact, as Time, He withdraws our creations and the universe itself at the time of annihilation.

What remains? Is it futile to try to become an artist-creator in Kṛṣṇa consciousness? What remains is the devotion. Devotion never suffers loss or diminution. Be an artist as a way to serve humbly.

I think of my writing not so much as "creative" art. I assert that we can tell ordinary things in Kṛṣṇa conscious books. That may be an innovation, but it doesn't mean I'm hankering to create something to show off my fertile brain. I'm not competing with Lord Viṣṇu or Lord Brahmā. I am not trying to create new worlds. I am simply trying to be honest and to record the actual consciousness of a struggling devotee and what it's like to be in this world. I see this as a way to glorify the mercy of guru and Kṛṣṇa.

Headache for the third day in a row. It was an all-nighter—sharp and localized behind my right eye. Madhu has been recovering, but last night he had gas pains and neither of us could sleep. We commiserated around 2 A.M., talking in a non-complaining, but suffering way.

He said that his digestion and evacuation stopped working for a week. "It was only a week," Madhu said, "but when the time of death comes, there'll be no relief." Our host's elderly parents are at this stage. It's one thing after another with them. Madhu said that we expect things to let up, but we're only getting a taste now of greater difficulty ahead.

I replied in a different mood, "That also means we have to work while we can, until the end."

I fell asleep for awhile and had a dream which seemed connected to my headache. Sometimes I sat up and tried to induce a healing trance, talking to the headache. I tried to reason with my body that there was no need to keep the alarm on, or that the pain could be reduced to a small point and still the body could inform me of pain. I even thought it would be better for the pain to spread throughout my body rather than to be localized. Or maybe I could give my attention on something else and not focus on it. None of these tactics worked. I am the predominated enjoyer.

The mice were noisy during the night, *so* noisy that they penetrated my earplugs. They were gnawing at something. I found some dried pieces of bread in a corner by a mouse hole and took them away. The mice occupy the lower half of the room and the lizards the upper half. This isn't the most pleasant place.

I took only fruit for breakfast and then went outside. There was thunder and lightning during the night. Now there is a cloudbank on the horizon and the sun is invisible. The atmosphere is beautiful—sky, river, water pouring over the dam, cranes standing waiting for fish to appear. Beautiful, but vicious. The same nature that gives out headaches.

You say you're not a creator-artist-deviant but what about your playfulness? Is it not a light amusement, a form of carelessness?

No, it's just the way we are.

In the Rockies,
in the Himalayas
I write freely and send
notes home.

We accept the *Vedas*.
Our family is Vedic,
we subscribe to *Back to Godhead*.
We gave money as best we could
for the worthy projects and
went out to meet people
sometimes.

The fog is lifting.

Text 3

yasyāvayava-saṁsthānaiḥ
kalpito loka-vistaraḥ

tad vai bhagavato rūpaṁ
viśuddhaṁ sattvam ūrjitam

It is believed that all the universal planetary systems are situated on the extensive body of the puruṣa, but He has nothing to do with the created material ingredients. His body is eternally in spiritual existence par excellence.

Comment

Although Śrīla Prabhupāda has translated the Sanskrit clearly, we need his purports to understand the *Bhāgavatam*. This verse is a good example of that. The universal form is described by Sūta Gosvāmī, but it is not the *bhagavato rūpaṁ viśuddhaṁ sattvam*, or the eternal spiritual form which is also mentioned in this verse. The eternal forms are the *puruṣa-avatāras*. What is called the universal form, or *virāṭ-rūpa* is actually the *mahat-tattva*, the physical universe composed of planets in outer space. When a meditator thinks of these planets in their total form, and when he projects this onto the human-like form of the Personality of Godhead, then he is meditating on *viśva-rūpa*.

Prabhupāda tells us that the *Vedas* recommend this kind of meditation in the beginning of someone's approach to Kṛṣṇa consciousness. When the neophyte is informed that the cause of all causes is the spiritual person, Lord Viṣṇu, he is often unable to accept it. The materialist is so absorbed in thinking in terms of material persons that he finds it impossible to think that God is like one of us, another person. Prabhupāda states, "To him a form means something of this material world, and therefore an opposite conception of the Absolute is necessary in the beginning to concentrate the mind on the power extension of the Lord."

Meditation on the universal form is actually meditation on God's energy and not on God Himself. Rather than leave the neophyte meditator stranded in impersonal meditation (which often leads to atheism), he is advised to impose the personal form upon the energy extension of God.

In one sense, the energy of the Personality of Godhead is not different from God Himself, so meditation on His energy is also meditation on God. At the same time, however, the *mahat-tattva* is different from the Lord.

Thank you, Śrīla Prabhupāda, for making this clear and understandable. Without your help, we would certainly be bewildered and open to the misinterpretation given by so many impersonalists, speculators, and Indologists.

Śrīla Prabhupāda, you may say that you have done nothing but repeat what you heard in *paramparā*, but the fact that you have repeated it is in itself glorious. Furthermore, you have not repeated it like a machine, but you have made it understandable to us. We love you for this gift. We understand the universal form and eternal Viṣṇu and everything else in the *Bhāgavatam* because we have heard it from you. Śrīla Vyāsadeva spoke it, but for centuries it was not available to us. Only when you began to write your *Bhāgavatam* purports have we been able to enter the sacred precincts of Vedic knowledge.

If someone mentions "neophyte devotees," we want to admit that we are certainly not advanced. We modestly include ourselves among the neophytes. But Prabhupāda does not want us to indulge in neophyte meditation on the universal form. He wants us to go directly to the transcendental form, name, and pastimes of Kṛṣṇa, as taught by the *ācāryas*. If we ask, "At what point does the devotee give up the conception of the *virāṭ-rūpa* form of the Lord?" the answer is that he should immediately accept the transcendental form of the Lord, but at the same time not reject the concept of the *virāṭ-rūpa*. He may always appreciate and meditate on the cosmic manifestation as nondifferent than God.

For example, when driving in the countryside, a devotee may notice the forests on the hills and from a distance see that they do in fact look like hairs, just as the *Bhāgavatam* describes. The devotee may then feel joy at this observation, "Yes, Kṛṣṇa's body is right here." If he's an attentive student of the *Bhāgavatam*, he will also realize that this is a kind of impersonal meditation and that the true form of God, although he cannot immediately perceive it, is something beyond the universe. For this he may think of God in His transcendental and personal form, perhaps as He appears in the *arcā-vigraha* in the temple. The same devotee who appreciates the hills as God's body while driving in the countryside may then think of the worshipable Deity as Rādhā-Dāmodara. "Just think, our Rādhā-Dāmodara, worshiped in a forest at Gītā-nāgarī as He stands with Śrīmatī Rādhārāṇī, Viśākhā, and Lalitā, is actually the cause and proprietor of all these worlds. And yet He stands apart from it all, dancing in Vṛndāvana. Let us go and serve Him."

A short-term Godrej message: At 6 P.M. when I was already resting for the night, the young man arrived to fix the typewriter. I heard Madhu tell him, "Mahārāja is sleeping. Come back tomorrow. Hare Kṛṣṇa." I got up and asked Madhu to let him in. He entered the darkened room, took out the typewriter, and soon returned with it in working order. The young man had no translator with him, so all I could say was, "Thank you. *Daṇḍavat*." Besides, what else is there to say? I could say Hare Kṛṣṇa. And I could add, "The machine is working again? How long will it last? The problem is that the tape jams after working for a couple of pages. What have you done to cure *that* problem so that it won't break down in ten minutes?"

I'll use the machine, but be aware that at any moment the facility may be taken away. Let that spur me to immediate concentration on what to say before it's too late.

Kṛṣṇa showed His universal form to Arjuna on the battlefield of Kurukṣetra just to prove that He is the source of this wondrous and astonishing form. The *virāṭ-rūpa* was so fearful that it bewildered Arjuna. It is sometimes called a "godless display" because it creates such fear. It contains a taste of the full destructive power of God. Oppenheimer, the nuclear scientist who observed the first atomic bomb explosion, quoted from the *Bhagavad-gītā* as he beheld the mushroom cloud rising over the desert: "If hundreds of thousands of suns were to rise at once into the sky, their radiance might resemble the effulgence of the Supreme Person in that universal form." (Bg. 11.12)

In the 1960s, rock singer Jimi Hendrix released a record album showing the Indian print of the many-headed body of the universal form with Jimi Hendrix as the source of them all. This was a great blasphemy and some could not help but see a poetic justice in his untimely death, as if providence didn't want to wait too long before disproving the notion that Jimi Hendrix was God.

I'm writing by hand again. I feel squeamish typing at midnight, knowing that two guards are sleeping on the porch just a few feet from my desk and that Madhu may wake from the machine noise. I'll type later.

The next verse and purport continue this topic. This feels like a live *Bhāgavatam* class. The class is always ready to open and continue, twenty-four hours a day, any time I'm clear enough to turn to it and hear and write. An audience is always willing, or so I imagine. As long as I live, I want to use this opportunity to speak what I have heard and to purify my existence. Śrīla Prabhupāda will be glad.

Text 4

paśyanty ado rūpam adabhra-cakṣuṣā
sahasra-pādoru-bhujānanādbhutam
sahasra-mūrdha-śravaṇākṣi-nāsikaṁ
sahasra-mauly-ambara-kuṇḍalollasat

The devotees, with their perfect eyes, see the transcendental form of the puruṣa who has thousands of legs, thighs, arms and faces—all extraordinary. In that body there are thousands of heads, ears, eyes and noses. They are decorated with thousands of helmets and glowing earrings and are adorned with garlands.

Comment

In the first chapter of the Second Canto ("The First Step In God Realization"), the universal form will be further discussed along with its temporary nature. In the present purport, Prabhupāda assures us: " . . . only with patience and perseverance can we realize the transcendental subject matter regarding the Absolute Truth and His different forms." We have spiritual senses by which we can perceive God's form. It is only a matter of time before these senses are purified by devotional service. Then the material coverings will be removed.

Prabhupāda also emphasizes that one cannot see God either in His universal form or in His transcendental form unless he is purified by devotional service. Kṛṣṇa asserts this in the *Bhagavad-gītā* at the end of the eleventh chapter: "The form you are seeing with your transcendental eyes cannot be understood simply by studying the *Vedas*, nor by undergoing serious penances, nor by charity, nor by worship. It is not by these means that one can see Me as I am. My dear Arjuna, only by undivided devotional service can I be understood as I am, standing before you, and can thus be seen directly. Only in this way can you enter into the mysteries of My understanding." (Bg. 11.53–54)

Devotional service sometimes appears to proceed at an imperceptible pace, just as the hands of the clock move although we don't notice them. Without delay, we can imbibe Kṛṣṇa's messages through our ears and come to see God in that way. Therefore, it is foolish to be frustrated or to claim that we cannot see God. Even the neophyte is encouraged to see God either in the universal form or by His manifestations in this world—the sunlight, the taste of water, and so on. Further realization awaits those who faithfully practice Kṛṣṇa consciousness with body, mind, and words.

We may practice patience and perseverance in many ways. Living in the material world tests our patience as we meet the many obstacles we have to endure. Both individually and in our group effort in ISKCON, we appear to be thrown back to the beginning again and again. These obstacles test our sincerity. To strengthen ourselves by these obstacles is the proof of sincerity. There is always gain when we use our strength to chant Hare Kṛṣṇa, to turn again to the distribution of Kṛṣṇa consciousness, and to simply stay on the battlefield where we have been placed.

Certainly Prabhupāda manifested patience and perseverance in his own life. Although we accept that he is liberated and has never forgotten Kṛṣṇa, that does not mean that he could wave a wand and "presto!" be carried to America where everyone became his follower. He took pains to serve Kṛṣṇa. He had to struggle from his slow beginning, and he had ample opportunity to show us patience and perseverance.

In the purport Prabhupāda writes, "With our present materialized senses we cannot perceive anything of the transcendental Lord." We have to rely, both in material and spiritual life, on seeing through the experience of those who have already seen. This indicates that a genuine spiritual vision of Kṛṣṇa can be obtained in a relationship with someone who is spiritually advanced, who has seen Kṛṣṇa "with perfect eyes smeared with devotional service." Kṛṣṇa encourages this kind of seeing when He tells us in *Bhagavad-gītā* to approach the spiritual masters because they have seen the Truth (*tattva-darśinaḥ*).

We must also come to know in a learned way what it means to "see" Kṛṣṇa. It's not just a matter of seeing with the eyes or flocking after someone who claims he has had a vision of God. A person who has seen Kṛṣṇa is transformed and fully engaged in Kṛṣṇa's service. Such a person understands the science of Kṛṣṇa in *paramparā*. We know that he has seen Kṛṣṇa by examining all his activities. The pure devotee lives in the vision of Kṛṣṇa constantly, even in separation from Kṛṣṇa. "The world is all vacant in Your absence." In other words, if a devotee really hankers to see Kṛṣṇa and feels intense separation from Him, he calls out, "I could not see Kṛṣṇa!" We can understand from that cry that such a devotee is seeing Kṛṣṇa and so we should seek a relationship with him. This is the best way to contact Kṛṣṇa —contact His pure devotee and use our core energy to cultivate a relationship with him in deeper and deeper ways. Nothing should distract us from this purpose.

Prabhupāda states that Kṛṣṇa is "formless to the neophytes, but He is in transcendental form to the expert servitor." The expertise mentioned here is not material. The devotee is expert in *serving* in a genuinely humble and devotional mood. One may become an expert cook, *pūjārī*, or *mṛdaṅga* player, or one may even gain a reputation for being an expert *Bhāgavatam* speaker, but if these activities are not saturated with loving devotion, then they are not really expert. Our so-called expertise makes us proud and we forget that we are servants. We think instead that we have created something, done something by our own power. The art of devotion is to become both expert in our service and meek and humble in our love. Lord Kṛṣṇa reveals Himself to the expert servitor.

This is your time, sonny boy. This is your life. I'm grateful for clear sailing and wish to shout and dance on the deck of my sailing ship.

I cannot speak enough, pure enough.

It's true I want to speak of myself and of the world, of something immediate. I seem to think that readers cannot constantly sustain interest in straight philosophical discussion. I want to give us all a break. Or rather, I accept as fact that for me a break is required. I can only hear philosophy for an hour or so. Then I want to get up and stretch or walk around—go out and see the garden and hear the wind. And we have our business and personal matters (in Kṛṣṇa consciousness) to attend to.

A proof: some temples impress upon the *Bhāgavatam* lecturers not to speak too long or it will disrupt the day's devotional service for the community. In some temples, the management places a printed notice on the lectern, "Dear Lecturer, do not speak for more than one hour, including questions and answers." Speakers are sometimes affronted by this notice, or they disregard it and speak for two hours or more. When they do, breakfast is late, the book distributors go out late, the preaching starts late, and everything is disrupted. There is a time and place for *Bhāgavatam* lecturing and also a time to stop and move on to other services. We serve the book *Bhāgavata* and we serve the person *bhāgavata* in various ways.

In turning to personal thoughts and a flow of consciousness, I try to tap into the constant factor of devotional service with its ebb and flow. I also admit that sometimes when the formal *Bhāgavatam* class has ended, the quality of our Kṛṣṇa consciousness drops. I seek to improve, to steer to remembrance of *Bhāgavatam* topics. Therefore, free-writing exercises and various subheadings are an attempt not to divert myself from the *Śrīmad-Bhāgavatam*, but to enter it and open the field to *all things at all times in Kṛṣṇa consciousness.*

O absurd words that come when we don't even ask for them,

O happy day that I start out with no headache or indigestion,

O joy in heart, the chance to serve the Lord with foot down a bit on the accelerator.

My world when it's not influenced by other writers.

The sound of the water over the dam at night when I can't go out and see it.

Did you hear? We are going to leave this place earlier than we had planned and go a few days early to Bombay. We'll stay at Hare Krishna Land and see an Āyurvedic doctor. Six more days here.

Another list:

(1) The sound of the water over the dam at night (yes, I just said that).

(2) Chance to draw pictures.

(3) The darkening of day at night, I welcome it. Take off the eye mask and welcome sweet sleep. The crazy dreams I can't make sense of.

(4) The long night. Up early. Count the hours before dawn creeps over the window. Go out and meet it.

(5) Fruit.

(6) Mice.

(7) Observer status. No newspapers. Another day. The servant, Lakshman—his shy, furtive look, his mustache. What's he thinking as he irons Prabhupāda's miniature clothes?

Text 5

etan nānāvatārāṇāṁ
nidhānaṁ bījam avyayam
yasyāṁśāṁśena sṛjyante
deva-tiryaṅ-narādayaḥ

This form [the second manifestation of the puruṣa] is the source and indestructible seed of multifarious incarnations within the universe. From the particles and portions of this form, different living entities, like demigods, men and others, are created.

Comment

The purport is a summary of the different categories of *avatāras*, such as *puruṣa-avatāras*, *līlā-avatāras*, *guṇa-avatāras*, *manvantara-avatāras*, *yuga-avatāras*, *śaktyāveśa-avatāras*, and *vibhūti* incarnations. These are all described more elaborately in Lord Caitanya's teachings to Sanātana Gosvāmī. Verse 1.3.5 describes Garbhodakaśāyī Viṣṇu as the source and seed of the many incarnations. This is true because Garbhodakaśāyī Viṣṇu is the source of the third *puruṣa*, Kṣīrodakaśāyī Viṣṇu. It is actually Kṣīrodakaśāyī Viṣṇu who is the direct source of all the different types of incarnations. He is also the Lord who governs the mode of goodness and who maintains the universe, along with being the Supersoul in the hearts of all living beings.

The science of *avatāras* is impressive theology. Religious persons are always fascinated with the idea that God comes into the world or appears in a representative, empowered form. Still, there are many vague ideas and imaginary conceptions about the nature of the incarnations. The biggest misconception is when an ordinary person claims to be God, or when he allows his followers to address him in that way.

This pretension has created disillusionment and skepticism toward religion and religious teachers. Real incarnations are not self-declared but are ascertained by great sages according to their personal qualities and mission and the descriptions given in the revealed scriptures.

Brahmā is described as being empowered by the Lord for creation. "His power is like the power of the sun reflected in valuable stones and jewels." Since Brahmā is *jīva-tattva*, a living entity, we may ask whether Kṛṣṇa may also empower others among us to do something. What if the spiritual master wants us to do something for his mission, or if we spontaneously want to dedicate ourselves to our spiritual master's work? Would Kṛṣṇa empower us? Yes. Any sincere devotee or disciple can become empowered by the Lord and the spiritual master.

There are many śāstric statements which prove this. Kṛṣṇa says in *Bhagavad-gītā*, "As all surrender unto Me, I reward them accordingly." (Bg. 4.11) The Lord also states that He is equal to all living beings, but if one becomes a friend to Him and lives in Him, then Kṛṣṇa has special friendship for that devotee. He says that whoever preaches the Kṛṣṇa conscious message becomes His dearmost servant. Similarly, Lord Caitanya encourages devotees by His words to the Kūrma Brāhmaṇa: "Instruct everyone to follow the orders of Lord Śrī Kṛṣṇa as they are given in *Bhagavad-gītā* and *Śrīmad-Bhāgavatam*. In this way become a spiritual master and try to liberate everyone in this land." (Cc. *Madhya* 7.128) Any devotee who takes these śāstric statements personally can become empowered in his desired relationship with the Lord.

Kṛṣṇa gives intelligence through the heart. Since He supplies intelligence even for material functions, how much more He will empower or bless us to practice Kṛṣṇa consciousness. Becoming empowered, therefore, is not something mysterious whereby only certain devotees qualify, as if only *they* are predestined to receive Kṛṣṇa's blessings. Kṛṣṇa, especially in the form of Lord Caitanya, showers His blessings on all living beings. Lord Caitanya's blessings will be given to those who are serious, as Prabhupāda was, to preach His message in every town and village.

Śrīla Bhaktisiddhānta Sarasvatī Ṭhākura told his followers that Kṛṣṇa consciousness should be spread in the West. He told this to the young man, Abhay Caran De. Because Prabhupāda took it up so wholeheartedly, he was empowered as no one else had been before to bring Kṛṣṇa consciousness beyond the confines of India and to implant it all over the world.

We don't have to wait for a voice booming out a message from the ether. We don't need revelatory dreams to tell us that we can become empowered. Simply hear and take up Kṛṣṇa's message. Kṛṣṇa will then bless us with more and more ability. Kṛṣṇa may have a specific mission for each devotee, and of course, He has a unique relationship with each of us. He may empower some with more "voltage" than others in order to carry out His tasks. Still, everyone is eligible to please Kṛṣṇa by their sincerity. According to our desire, Kṛṣṇa or the spiritual master may see fit to increase the voltage and our ability to contain that voltage as they like.

Pass on the light of transcendental knowledge, man. Don't keep it under a bushel. Red letters in the Bible. I read it once on a bus from NYC and saw New Jersey's lights as if they were unearthly. Was I getting a calling?

I don't understand how my hand works to record everything that comes, even if it's silly. And especially thoughts that should take several descriptive sentences to unload. It seems in the process of writing it all out, I will lose spontaneity. Better to do quick flashes? But will it be coherent?

Lightning. Past. Pigeons. There's a backlog of words. Some of them come so slowly that they're old by the time they hit the page. Skylark, raven, Poe, Shelley. Clean white page like snow and death. Captain Scott. The clean, white, death of frostbite and hunger while a wind rages outside an igloo and he writes his last diary entries in pencil.

Listen, bring the mind back to Kṛṣṇa. Prabhupāda empowered Śubhānanda dāsa to compile his teachings, "You are empowered." I am empowered too, but not if I misuse it.

The *chaukīdārs* are asleep in quilts out there on the porch, coughing sometimes in their sleep. Madhu can't sleep and stalks around in long underwear. Says we ought to fly from Indore to Bombay. I think about that instead of Kṣīrodakaśāyī Viṣṇu or the biscuits in the tiffin.

Is it true you can miss going back to Godhead by a fraction? Is it like the photo finish in a horse race? Do you get called "out" on a technical infraction? Can a lawyer plead your case?

Does a poem amount to an apple?

Folks, be merry. Sing your brassy, bright note of youth and
let it mellow into your later years. I adjure you,
Kṛṣṇa is blue
Rādhā gold
I'm in
between with you,
true sister and brotherly
love, walking as the
sun lights up. He had the right to see his birth certificate, proving that his grandparents came from Eire. It doesn't matter. I'm a writer and can do PMRB purports anywhere there's a little peace and quiet.

Here goes a picture of Uncle Bob taking to Kṛṣṇa consciousness, chanting on his new beads received in the mail. His hairs stand on end and he has a circle on his forehead where the *brahma-randra* is.

I remember Madhu saying to me about a month ago, "Publish what you *really* want to say, not thinking that a book has its own life or that you wrote it so it's now history and should be published." He wanted me to take full responsibility for what I publish and not allow even an editor to do that. I accept these points, but I have more I want to say about it.

I also want to print some of what comes from the hand and heart, what comes at a certain time in a writing session. That itself is a commitment—to writing and to honesty.

In answer to Madhu's saying, "Write what you really want to say," I say whatever thoughts come as I wrote them, and I want some of them published. I believe I was open and sincere *when* I wrote them. Sure, it shouldn't be anything against the Kṛṣṇa conscious teachings or anything that will weaken a devotee's faith. It should be the best I can do. But what is it that I want to say and to give the devotees to read? It's *honesty*, not only a perfect rehashing of *śāstra*. It's the joy of writing and even the abandon in it.

Text 6

sa eva prathamaṁ devaḥ
kaumāraṁ sargam āśritaḥ
cacāra duścaraṁ brahmā
brahmacaryam akhaṇḍitam

First of all, in the beginning of creation, there were the four unmarried sons of Brahmā [the Kumāras], who, being situated in a vow of celibacy, underwent severe austerities for realization of the Absolute Truth.

Comment

The Kumāras underwent *brahmacarya*, strict celibacy, as a qualification to become *brāhmaṇas*. They were not *brāhmaṇas* only by birth, even though they were Lord's Brahmā's sons. They wanted to develop more qualification. Therefore, even today in the *gurukula* tradition of Indian education, young boys practice celibacy at the guru's *āśrama*. *Brahmacarya* means both the study of Brahman (spiritual education) and celibacy and submission under the guru's order.

Gurukulas that insist on celibacy are rare in this age. Most education in Kali-yuga has no connection to celibacy. Rather, high school and university students are promiscuous. Schools based on material education provide an opportunity for men and women (or boys and girls) to meet. They are not really centers of learning. Prabhupāda challenged modern education: "Is there any university in the world where the science of the self is taught in a scientific way?" There is no school where education in Brahman is part of the syllabus, and neither do the students have prior qualification to study it.

The city temples and country *āśramas* of the International Society for Krishna Consciousness are intended to be centers of learning and training. They're also places of Deity worship and preaching service. Sometimes an ISKCON community may not emphasize brahminical training. They believe that just by serving, all good qualities will manifest in a sincere devotee. Devotional service is purifying in itself, but Prabhupāda also wanted devotees to become qualified as *brāhmaṇas*.

Śrīmad-Bhāgavatam emphasizes that we should hear Vedic knowledge. The best way for us to hear Vedic knowledge is to read Prabhupāda's books. This austerity is especially important in a younger devotee's life.

It's possible to develop a fearful attitude toward austerity. This is especially true with practices that we find difficult. Someone may find it difficult to rise early in the morning, and someone else may find frugal eating almost impossible. Someone else may be unable to avoid *prajalpa*. How can we approach the austerities we find difficult?

We have to be balanced. We can't always force ourselves beyond our capacity or berate ourselves for our failures. We have to admit that in certain areas, we cannot be as strict as we would like to be. We shouldn't imitate a person who is more strict than we are. We have to find our own level in spiritual life. That level should not drop below adherence to the four regulative principles which we have vowed to follow at initiation. If we are too austere, then there will be repercussions, such as coming to view the path of austerity with fear or resentment. Prabhupāda refers to the rules and regulations as "the regulative principles of freedom." We should look upon austerity in that light. Kṛṣṇa consciousness is a gradual process, and it is better to be friendly toward ourselves rather than inimical to our own mental and physical states, even when they're not up to the highest standard.

For that higher standard, we have examples such as the Kumāras and others before us.

The Kumāras' history is not mentioned here. It will be told later. They refused to marry even when Lord Brahmā ordered them to do so. The *ācāryas* approve their disobedience. Other of Lord Brahmā's sons, such as Svāyambhuva Manu, obeyed Brahmā's order to populate the universe. That job got done. The Kumāras didn't *have* to do it.

Text 7

dvitīyaṁ tu bhavāyāsya
rasātala-gatāṁ mahīm
uddhariṣyann upādatta
yajñeśaḥ saukaraṁ vapuḥ

The supreme enjoyer of all sacrifices accepted the incarnation of a boar [the second incarnation], and for the welfare of the earth He lifted the earth from the nether regions of the universe.

Comment

Prabhupāda has given only a one-paragraph purport to this verse. He writes that the Lord always does something extraordinary. God doesn't come and just hang out on a street corner. He also does things that are filled with humor. As Varāha, He wanted to save the earth by lifting it up from the filthy place where it had been thrown by the *asuras*. Usually, boars pick things up from a filthy place. When you live in India, you see that principle in action and it helps you appreciate the incarnation of Lord Varāha. The Lord is clever and undefeatable. We should never think that He became a filthy creature. When He played the part of a boar, He stayed always in transcendence and the devotees worshiped Him. We'll read more about Varāha in a later canto.

man as hoggish incarnation

Am I an incarnation of gluttony in the way I eat? Did you know the belly can expand bigger than the uterus? We see fat men with bellies protruding bigger than a pregnant woman's uterus. Remember Tommy Oakland's father? He was short, but he had an enormous beer belly. Tommy was ashamed of his father, who lived in a furnished room in Eltingville, Staten Island. He was a boisterous, drunk fellow, a hard laborer. Tommy was on his way to a brilliant, scholarly career and then something snapped. He didn't care to achieve it anymore.

I lived in this world before I became a devotee. The Korean War was going on when I was a kid chewing bubble gum. They were just introducing television when I was a teenager. The set was turned on inside the store and people crowded on the sidewalk to look at it. People used to watch the World Series like that.

You mean you are so old that you have a memory like that?

Yes, and we had no car, but our uncle Jim had a '39 green Mercury coupe.

Oh, please tell us something more about Kṛṣṇa consciousness. We want this book to be worth selling in the temple bookstore. You don't want them to think that you're the hoggish incarnation, do you? Or that you're immoderate? You don't want them to say that about you, do you?

Perhaps more than anything I don't want another headache today, but it may be on the way. I'm not the controller.

The Lord appeared and lifted the earth on His tusks. It appeared beautiful, like the moon. His voice roared. He splashed water. Beings on higher planets prayed to Him when they heard His gorgeous roar. When Prabhupāda was translating this section of the *Bhāgavatam*, I was living in the Allston storefront and typing the tapes. I had no problem accepting the boar incarnation. Jadurāṇī painted the form crudely, but according to the Indian tradition. Prabhupāda coached her as to whether He should have hooves or hands and feet. ISKCON's rendition is more boarish than human.

Dr. Dimmock of the University of Chicago challenged me in the classroom demanding, "Why did you paint a full hog incarnation in Murāri Gupta's room?" He said that the *Caitanya-bhāgavata* describes that Lord Caitanya assumed the *mood* of a boar.

I replied that we have faith in the *Caitanya-caritāmṛta* and whatever our spiritual master says.

I make a distinction between the perfect presentation of *Śrīmad-Bhāgavatam* and what I call the relaxed state. The perfect presentation is given when we're speaking on the *vyāsāsana*; we're more relaxed when the lecture is over and we're thinking alone in our rooms. Do these two states always have to remain in separate, airtight compartments? Can I sometimes make mistakes from the *vyāsāsana* or admit I don't know the answer to someone's question? Do I always have to be the perfect answer man? And are my private thoughts always the lesser ones, unworthy but to be tolerated? Are the candid thoughts sometimes as good as the prepared ones? Do these two worlds sometimes meet?

Yes, they do. We can be wrong or right in both moods. Sometimes the moods are interchangeable. Try me. Ask me a question and I'll try not to first think what hat I should put on to answer it, the perfect one or the imperfect one.

Question: How can we develop love for Lord Varāha? On His appearance day, devotees read of His pastimes and speak about His inconceivable activities, but how can we love Him? What relationship do we have with this particular form of Kṛṣṇa? Who are the eternal devotees of Lord Varāha?

Answer: I don't know who Varāha's eternal devotees are, but the best way to worship Him is to read whatever is presented in the *Bhāgavatam*. Always remember that Varāha is Kṛṣṇa. The Viṣṇus all come from Kṣīrodakaśāyī Viṣṇu, who in turn comes from Kṛṣṇa.

How do we love Him? *That's a good question*. If we saw Him, we'd love Him. By regularly hearing, let us come to love *Śrīmad-Bhāgavatam*. Then we will love hearing about all of the Lord's adventures, such as the time He popped out from Brahmā's nostril and instantly expanded to a gigantic size to face Hiraṇyākṣa's challenge.

Text 8

tṛtīyam ṛṣi-sargaṁ vai
devarṣitvam upetya saḥ
tantraṁ sātvatam ācaṣṭa
naiṣkarmyaṁ karmaṇāṁ yataḥ

In the millennium of the ṛṣis, the Personality of Godhead accepted the third empowered incarnation in the form of Devarṣi Nārada, who is a great sage among the demigods. He collected expositions of the Vedas which deal with devotional service and which inspire nonfruitive action.

Comment

As soon as I start hearing about Nārada from Prabhupāda, it throws me into relishable reminiscences. I can almost smell the hot, fresh *dāl* and *chaunk* in the pot on the stove in Prabhupāda's kitchen. I think of Prabhupāda when I think of Nārada. I love the way Prabhupāda tells us about Nārada.

Just a few words and I'm sailing off into this nice association. It all seems nearby and familiar.

This is the quality of our Kṛṣṇa consciousness, which is not perhaps so understandable to persons outside of Prabhupāda's spiritual family. They're sometimes puzzled why we insist on hearing everything from Śrīla Prabhupāda and why we insist that he's so special. They want to remind us that Prabhupāda's real greatness is that he is a humble representative of the Gauḍīya Vaiṣṇava *paramparā*.

We know that this is Prabhupāda's greatness. That's why we like to hear from him. But you can't blame us if we say that we don't find such wonderful flavor in Kṛṣṇa consciousness unless we hear from our spiritual father. Is it wrong to be so chaste? I don't think so. Anyway, wrong or right, this is the way we are.

I like to go back to the beginnings of my Kṛṣṇa consciousness in the '60s and '70s. I pick up that thread and follow it up to the present moment. I find that it's a strong cable connecting me to Kṛṣṇa consciousness.

Prabhupāda discusses Nārada's authorship of the *Nārada-pañcarātra*. Prabhupāda states, "This *Nārada-pañcarātra* trains the *karmīs*, or the fruitive workers, to achieve liberation from the bondage of fruitive work." In the course of this discussion, Prabhupāda speaks the science as it is. He doesn't flinch from mentioning the soul's bondage or the pain that the *jīva* feels because of that bondage. He openly expresses that the living entity needs freedom. There's simply no way out of material suffering if we possess a *karmī* attitude. Material conditions, either in so-called happiness or in so-called distress, are all meant for distress. Foolish materialists don't know how to attain eternal happiness in the unconditioned state.

Śrī Nārada's method is to teach diseased mankind how their present engagements can lead them to spiritual emancipation. There are a number of verses spoken by Nārada later in the First Canto where he discusses this topic with

Vyāsadeva. Kṛṣṇa also says in *Bhagavad-gītā*, "Whatever you do, do it for Me." This is perfect advice for those who have a *karmī* mentality. A *karmī* desires to work for a result. That's not bad if it can be connected to Kṛṣṇa consciousness. Then you have a person who wants to work hard for guru and Kṛṣṇa. Prabhupāda loved disciples who had the energy to dedicate themselves to Kṛṣṇa conscious projects. The spirit of activity and the desire to accomplish things can ideally be yoked in the service of Lord Caitanya's *saṅkīrtana* movement.

I find this in me in my writing *bhajana*. Please, Lord, use me. Let me dance, let me write something acceptable. As Prabhupāda states, "The physician directs the patient to take treated milk in the form of curd for his sufferings from indigestion due to his taking another milk preparation. So the cause of the disease and the remedy of the disease may be the same, but it must be treated by an expert physician like Nārada."

We don't have a copy of the *Nārada-pañcarātra* in translation, and even if we did, we probably couldn't make much sense out of it without Prabhupāda's purports. But we have many instructions from Nārada throughout the *Bhāgavatam*. I think what I have said about Nārada as an old friend is something all devotees feel. Nārada is everyone's friend. He is described as the great sage among the demigods, but we know that he is welcomed even among demons. Certainly he is a friend to the ISKCON devotees. Our personal connection with him is not just official; he is not just one of the early *ācāryas* in our line. Rather, he is omnipresent. He may seem far from us, almost like a fairy-tale Peter Pan, but he is always traveling and no one can stop his entrance and exit.

We may not know exactly how Nārada travels in outer space or what *siddhis* he possesses, but Prabhupāda has made him real for us. Even from Prabhupāda's earliest preaching, the devotees developed a mood about Nārada. Mukunda wrote a song in Haight-Ashbury about the "eternal spaceman": "But I'll tell you before you think me loony/ That I'm talking about Nārada Muni." Prabhupāda liked it and said he should write more country tunes like that.

So without becoming foolishly familiar or trivializing, it's still true that we can think of Nārada as our friend and pray to him personally. Dear Nārada, wherever you are and whomever you are, please accept my humble obeisances. I read your learned discussions throughout the *Bhāgavatam*. I see how you come on the scene when somebody is too attached or is grieving over a relative who has just died. You give the perfect instructions to release the soul from attachment to matter. You were even able to counsel the author, Śrīla Vyāsadeva, when he was despondent. Please bless me throughout my devotional service. Your blessings are always potent. Please accept my humble obeisances as I make them at the feet of my Gurudeva, Śrīla Prabhupāda, and think of you. *Nārada-muni bājāya vīṇā, 'rādhikā-ramaṇa' nāme.*

Don't think I'm loony
I'm talkin' about Nārada Muni,
the eternal spaceman.

The Americans think they're great because they sent out a moon shot—the astronauts are listed in the dictionary: Shepard, Glenn, Armstrong, some woman, the first in outer space, and the Russian sputniks. Nārada travels by yogic power, devotional strength.

I am writing on borrowed time. I have no space suit, no yogic *siddhis*, nothing to protect me from the headache I feel building. I've had a headache for four days in a row. Today makes the fifth. I'm up at 11 P.M., using my time before it gets taken away.

Let me sing a midnight song (like a cricket? A scaled lizard on the wall click-clicking? Like the furry, gray mouse who looks so large but who manages to slip under the door?).

Narada, please forgive
me for drawing your
picture. But I do
love to follow your
teachings as given
to me by Swamiji,
your disciple
in parampara—
in need of the
teaching that curd
cures the disease
created by
milk,
Satsvarupa
das

Admissions:

(1) I didn't get admitted to the college of my choice.

(2) I don't like to go into public lavatories—consider them indecent. A devotee in his *dhotī* just doesn't fit in with the men lined up at urinals. We don't fit into the world at all—so we shouldn't show up in their places, either for enjoyment or suffering. A devotee in a tavern, a disco, a baseball park, a massage parlor, no. Oh, yes, if a devotee (disguised or not) is in an airport or parking lot for preaching and distributing books, that's good. Sometimes, though, someone recognizes us and asks, "What are *you* doing *here*?" It's a good question.

(3) My meter is running out.

(4) Don't think I'm loony when I say I know how to go back to Godhead and can bring all my countrymen with me.

(5) Admit the bearer of this ticket. Children under five free. Free meals for kids. Others pay. No credit. What's it like in the spiritual world? You'll know when you get there. Until then, write, write as midnight strikes. Remember Nietzsche in *Zarathustra*? Booming poem—I can almost hear the clock striking as the bell rings at the Krishna-Balaram Mandir. I read Nietzsche in my feckless youth.

One!

But all joys want eternity, want deep, profound eternity!

Two! Deep is woe, deeper still is joy. But all joys want eternity . . .

We sing at midnight in the safety of the soul. We toil, our little effort as disciples.

Text 9

turye dharma-kalā-sarge
nara-nārāyaṇāv ṛṣī
bhūtvātmopaśamopetam
akarot duścaraṁ tapaḥ

In the fourth incarnation, the Lord became Nara and Nārāyaṇa, the twin sons of the wife of King Dharma. Thus He undertook severe and exemplary penances to control the senses.

Comment

These twin sons are described in a later canto. Even when they were tempted by beautiful society girls, they remained unmoved. In fact, they produced from their own bodies female beauties more beautiful than those who had been sent to seduce them. Prabhupāda comments that a confectioner is not attracted by offers of sweets. Nara-Nārāyaṇa had within Him all opulences and potency. Therefore, He could not be attracted by material lures.

The Lord came in this form to practice austerity and to set an example. Prabhupāda mentions Lord Ṛṣabhadeva's teachings: *tapo divyaṁ putakā yena sattvam*. He advised His sons that life should not be spent like hogs who eat stool—in pursuit of sense gratification. One should restrain the senses and purify the self. Then he can ultimately come to understand *brahma-saukhyaṁ tv anantam*, eternal, blissful happiness. We can't get that happiness by polluting ourselves through our material senses. We have to first perform austerity: control the material senses and we will eventually be able to taste with our spiritual senses.

Whether it's to teach austerity or something else, God's incarnations appear in the world to benefit humanity. Prabhupāda writes, "Recently, within the memory of everyone, Lord Caitanya also appeared for the same purpose: to show special favor to fallen souls of this age of iron industry."

Lord Caitanya taught mainly by ecstatic chanting and dancing, but like Nara-Nārāyaṇa, He also taught austerity. One time a disciple asked Prabhupāda, "If Lord Caitanya is Bhagavān, then how did He show the six opulences of Godhead?" Prabhupāda replied that although Lord Caitanya did show certain miracles (planting a seed and immediately producing a mango tree with ripe mangos), He mainly showed the opulence of renunciation as a *sannyāsī*.

Those who practice Kṛṣṇa consciousness in the *gṛhastha-āśrama* may feel that Nara-Nārāyaṇa are giving something irrelevant to their lives, or they may feel sorry that they have become *gṛhasthas*. Sometimes *gṛhasthas* yearn for the simple life of a *brahmacārī*. One can't see how his household duties or the work and money required to maintain a house is Kṛṣṇa conscious renunciation.

We could say that it's not renunciation, so a *gṛhastha* should make his life more renounced. No matter what a householder does, however, he will never be able to make household life as simple as *brahmacārī* life. Even Lord Śiva has to take care of his wife and deal with all the situations that naturally arise when one is married even though he lives as a renunciate under a tree. We don't want to falsely assure a *gṛhastha* that everything he does is *tapasya* and renunciation. He has to face the fact that *gṛhastha* life is offered as a license for sense gratification. Still, while swallowing his pride, the *gṛhastha* has the same opportunity to advance as does a *brahmacārī* or *sannyāsī*. Even within household life, he can become detached, just as a coconut is detached from the outer shell. The restraint required to live with a wife and in a house and to follow the rules prohibiting illicit sex and to serve Kṛṣṇa is certainly *tapasya.*

A *gṛhastha* has to work for Kṛṣṇa by his thoughts and activities. He should never give up the struggle to read and chant regularly or to see these activities as the essence of his life. Life may never be as simple for him as it used to be, but the complicated struggle is still a struggle to become completely surrendered to Kṛṣṇa. One day he may achieve it.

A *sannyāsī* or *brahmacārī* may become complacent because unlike the poor *gṛhastha*, he is free from worrying about maintenance. His disciples or admirers provide for him. He then develops a nice reputation for his willingness to remain dependent on Kṛṣṇa. But where is the heart of his renunciation? What sacrifices does he actually make now that he is a *sādhus*?

Tapasya is something offered from the heart; it is not simply a matter of performing physical austerity like wearing rough cloth or taking cold showers. The *sādhu* may become accustomed to these things and even develop a hardened heart due to his *tapasya*. Therefore, *tapasya* has to be offered to Kṛṣṇa in devotion. It means taking trouble to serve Kṛṣṇa. Whoever can find heartfelt *tapasya* in his life has attained the goal of *tapo-divyam*. Renunciation is not judged by how little we eat, how we dress, or how tough the bottoms of our feet have become from walking barefoot over stones. It's judged by how willing we are to please guru and Kṛṣṇa.

"Slipping away at dawn," he said, "is nice, especially if you have a van in which to do it." You can't slip away from the guru's order, however. You have to take it with you wherever you go.

What is your austerity, dear reader? What is your pet sense gratification, your pet peeve? In what areas are you weak and in which ones strong? Who is judging you? Who is your ISKCON authority? When is the last time you stood in the ranks and passed inspection under the eye of one of the captains?

Oh, there was once the blues
fomented in a wet pack to the tummy.
Oh, there was once the blues
call it Nature Cure starvation.
There was once the ruse,
said, "I have to go to a clinic"
and he did deadpan it in our midst.
There was once excuses, he said, "I got
to write this way for Nelly."
There was once
a drink of liquor so compelling
by which he drunk, became mad
said, "I write not for fame,"
but no one could figure out if he was really true.

There was once the game of writing early
by which he said, "I name the incarnations
in a jiff and get on to free-writing
which ain't a bared midriff of a queen
but is a steady *brahmacārī* work for a writer
and if you don't believe me
go back to your Sam land."

He kind of threw a smoke screen and
hid behind words, said, "This is my *taspasya*,"
which some of us suspected was a horse laugh
in private he jerked his thumb as if to say,
"Listen to these guys who don't understand
my sensitive soul. Put a writer in
a hole and tell him to play the flute. What
do they know of that?"

Oh, he was just like the rest of us,
wanted respect and prestige
but for what? For scribbling what comes.
They said they would neglect him
and preferred to talk about the 30,000 people
who attended the kickoff Centennial at Bombay
and the work ahead. Take a deep breath,
to establish Śrīla Prabhupāda as beloved in everyone's
home, and the buses will roll, the money will be collected.
He could at least give lectures every day on Prabhupāda.
Where's his pledge? When we ask him, "Whatcha
doing for the Centennial?" he makes cryptic jokes.
I'd like to smack him awake. If we're going to
win the world by conventional magic
it's not gonna happen with slouches like him.
All this is paranoia
of what others may say.
It's the writer's game, the worry
warts all over the face and prose.

What he'd really like and what his actual readers would
like, is if he'd just cool it and strum
whatever melody he can on mandolin
with his buddies and call it
a little con-tri-bution.

What's this got to do with Nara-Nārāyaṇa?

I'm trying to tell you it's austerity. I don't want any more nonsense sex desire. I feel I am getting away from that. A happy report. Prabhupāda said it's fifty percent of liberation. Another time he said, "If all you do is practice *brahmacarya*, that alone can enable you to transfer to the highest planets in the material world." When he heard that, one *brahmacārī* said, "But Swamijī, that would be a curse. We don't want to go to the heavenly planets." Prabhupāda meant that *brahmacarya* is counted as a big thing, but of course you still have to go for the other fifty percent or it's not good. You want to be free of sex desire so you can worship Kṛṣṇa. Be free with plenty of energy to preach.

"Do you know why they worship me?" Prabhupāda asked as he exited from an Indian *paṇḍāl*, where many people rushed forward to touch his feet. "Because I have no sex desire."

I admit I's
havin' a hard
time
relatin' this
to Krsna

A Gallery of Poor Man's Pics

econoline
Monsters in yr head from worrying about your Ford van in America (When you should be chanting japa)
FORD

Goody two Shoes perfect devotee with only scripture and good authorized thoughts in his head. Is he for real?

Text 10

pañcamaḥ kapilo nāma
siddheśaḥ kāla-viplutam
provācāsuraye sāṅkhyaṁ
tattva-grāma-vinirṇayam

The fifth incarnation, named Lord Kapila, is foremost among perfected beings. He gave an exposition of the creative elements and metaphysics to Āsuri Brāhmaṇa, for in course of time this knowledge had been lost.

Comment

I remember from the earliest days Prabhupāda teaching us that there were two different *sāṅkhya* philosophies. One is atheistic and is supposedly popular in the West. In my ignorance, I had never heard of it. But we thought it was far out that there were two Kapilas who both taught *sāṅkhya*. First came the incarnation of God, Lord Kapila, the son of Devahūti, then later the impostor who took the same name and taught something else. Prabhupāda said it is "generally called metaphysics by the European scholars."

"The etymological meaning of *sāṅkhya* is 'That which explains very lucidly by analysis of the material elements.'" The word *sāṅkhya* also appears in the *Bhagavad-gītā* (2.39) where it is defined as the analytical description of body and soul. By counting the material elements, categorizing them, and learning how they evolve at the time of creation from subtle to gross, one can finally come to the conclusion that the universe is material, but the soul is not. One can also understand that beyond the soul is the Supersoul.

What is the point of such study? The soul should free itself from material entanglement by practicing devotional service.

As with the other incarnations in this First Canto list, Lord Kapila is only briefly introduced. When I hear His name, however, I can't help thinking of the golden-haired *avatāra* as He's pictured speaking to His mother on the cover of the "pink volume." (The BBT has now printed the Third Canto in two volumes, but we who grew up in ISKCON in the early '70s remember reading these books in different parts. The Third Canto, Part Two used to be called the "pink volume" because the dust jacket was pink.)

Prabhupāda composed his purports about Lord Kapila's teaching in 1968. He had taken a break from his *Śrīmad-Bhāgavatam* purports while recuperating his health in India in 1967. Prabhupāda came back to America in 1968 and resumed his *Śrīmad-Bhāgavatam* work along with his vigorous preaching, starting in San Francisco. He sent me the dictation tapes from the West Coast. My assignment was to type up the Third Canto, do the English editing, and send it back to him.

Lord Kapila conjures up those sweet days of being Prabhupāda's typist. It was such an intimate service. I was at some remote location, but I would love to receive the tapes as they arrived in the mail.

When I think of Lord Kapila now, I don't think of *sāṅkhya* philosophy, but of the teachings about the spirit soul in the womb and how he prays that this may be his last life in the material world. I also remember the chapter about how the conditioned soul is born, how he forgets his prayer in the womb, and how he becomes entangled yet again until he is finally pulled away at death by the Yamadūtas. I remember Kapiladeva's extensive teachings about devotional service and how He analyzes it according to the different modes. We may look forward in the months to come to reading and writing about Lord Kapila when we reach the Third Canto.

As I was the first to hear the *Kṛṣṇa* book because I was typing it, so I was the first to hear of Lord Kapila's teachings. I used to prepare lectures, parroting what I had heard earlier that day from Prabhupāda. These lectures would be for an audience of about two, who along with me, comprised the staff and congregation of the Boston temple in those days. Sometimes when devotees would visit from other places I would loan them my copy of the typed manuscripts and they would sit for hours reading.

For a while I also photocopied manuscripts and sent them to interested Godbrothers. One time I wrote a letter to Rūpānuga, who was a fellow New York City welfare office worker and who was the temple president of ISKCON Buffalo, and I mentioned how wonderful it was to read Prabhupāda's purports in the story about Lord Kapiladeva. I thought it was particularly amazing that Kardama Muni left home to take *sannyāsa*. What was amazing was that Kardama left home to seek God in a solitary place, but God had already appeared in his home as his own son!

Confiding this to Rūpānuga, I said, "Isn't this something?" The Kṛṣṇa conscious philosophy was—and is— full of revelation. Neither did it seem wrong or ungrateful of Kardama to want to take *sannyāsa*, even though the Lord of the heart was his son. It was one of the inconceivable pastimes of *Śrīmad-Bhāgavatam*.

This is not a pain journal, but I won't apologize for telling you that I have another full-scale headache. This is the fifth day in a row. It's making me anxious to complete the first volume of *A Poor Man Reads The Bhāgavatam* before leaving this station. It's a quota I've set myself. Time or fate is robbing me of my time each day. I'm trying to steal back enough of it that I can complete my task. I plan to end Volume One just before Vyāsadeva speaks the *Bhāgavatam's mahā-vākya: ete cāṁśa-kalāḥ puṁsaḥ, kṛṣṇas tu bhagavān svayam.*

Writing is a life in itself. You may call it literary life in contrast to real life, but I think that's an unfair duality.

That would mean that real life consists of getting a headache in the late morning and putting a wet rag over my eye. It would also include travel plans, faxes, communication with Bombay and Canada, and so on.

Isn't the subject of these *Bhāgavatam* notes just as real? It's "the book I'm writing," something my friends won't read, something I don't talk about, although it's important to me. This is the moment, this wooden desk and the hour, 11 P.M.—all background or setting for the opportunity to write something worthy.

Of course, I can't claim that my notes are worthy and will outlast the wooden desk or become more famous than some funky piece of Indian paraphernalia. All I know is that I want to write. Maybe that's all I should claim or even hope for. Prabhupāda says that publishing for fame should not be our concern. We should write simply to purify ourselves.

I write because I'm inspired and because this theme was given to me by Kṛṣṇa in the heart. (Yes! How else do we get *any* ideas? To say no, I'm not writing under Kṛṣṇa's dictation, is to become an atheist.)

Text 11

ṣaṣṭham atrer apatyatvaṁ
vṛtaḥ prāpto 'nasūyayā
ānvīkṣikīm alarkāya
prahlādādibhya ūcivān

The sixth incarnation of the puruṣa was the son of the sage Atri. He was born from the womb of Anusūyā, who prayed for an incarnation. He spoke on the subject of transcendence to Alarka, Prahlāda and others [Yadu, Haihaya, etc.].

Comment

This also will be described in a later canto. It's intriguing that the devotee prayed for all three *guṇa-avatāras* to become her son. Prabhupāda says that she didn't know which one was supreme. In the mood of "As they approach Me, I reciprocate," the Lord appeared as all three *avatāras*.

Dattātreya's teachings are something less than pure devotional service. That's similar to the teachings of Lord Buddha. Incarnations and agents of the Lord sometimes perform duties in this world that have to be done but that are less than pure devotional service. Consider, for example, the duties of Yamarāja or Māyādevī. Their duties are pure devotional service because they do what Kṛṣṇa wants them to do—punish the miscreants or award the materialists. Still, these are not services to which we should aspire. Thus they are sometimes compared to the police force. We respect them, but keep our distance from them.

The topic of incarnations can be enormously complicated if we try to study all the details. More details are provided in the various *Purāṇas* and commentaries. Some devotees know many things about the incarnations. I don't. Still, these incarnations are described in the *Bhāgavatam* and I want their descriptions to run through me like water sloshing through a dam. Let them always pass through me and purify me, and please allow me to give them out as soothing nectar to whomever I meet.

Some of the incarnations appear again and again in the Lord's different *līlās* and some of them go with Kṛṣṇa into different universes. Sometimes they appear in different guises or personalities. We hear how Haridāsa Ṭhākura was a combined incarnation of Prahlāda and Lord Brahmā. He also has an eternal position in Lord Caitanya's pastimes. Here in this chapter we understand that Viṣṇu is an eternal form of Kṛṣṇa. What about Dattātreya?

It's up to each devotee's inclination how far he wants to go in researching and retaining all these details. Some of the details are not so important for our execution of devotional service. Better we spend our time getting the basics straight: we're not these bodies, we're eternal servants of Kṛṣṇa, the material world is hellish, and our constitutional nature is to serve Kṛṣṇa. When we retain that, we can begin to practice pure devotional service birth after birth.

Sometimes people ask detailed questions and I can't answer them. If Prabhupāda doesn't teach particular details in his books, however, I don't feel embarrassed to say that I know only what I have read in his books. That doesn't imply that Prabhupāda taught only the basics. He taught all the important details to help us go back to Godhead. If for the time being we can't assemble all the details in our own puppy minds, we may hope that someday we will understand them better. As ISKCON grows more and more knowledgeable, books are being produced which are faithful to Prabhupāda's teachings. Examples of this are the *Ṣaṭ Sandarbhas* and the handbooks to accompany our study of *Bhagavad-gītā* and *The Nectar of Devotion*.

(I just tried the Godrej again. It doesn't work. Neither the old nor the new cartridges print on the page.)

Kṛṣṇa is the source of all incarnations. That's what Lord Caitanya told Vallabhācārya. He said He only knew a few of Kṛṣṇa's names—He's the son of Yaśodā, He's Śyāmasundara, like that. Be profoundly simple and devoted. Wish I could be.

Text 12

tataḥ saptama ākūtyāṁ
rucer yajño 'bhyajāyata
sa yāmādyaiḥ sura-gaṇair
apāt svāyambhuvāntaram

The seventh incarnation was Yajña, the son of Prajāpati Ruci and his wife Ākūti. He controlled the period during the change of the Svāyambhuva Manu and was assisted by demigods such as His son Yama.

Comment

Demigod is a post. Lord Brahmā is the "president" (not Bill Clinton). Brahmās come and go. You too can become a Brahmā, just as the Democratic Party in America promises all American citizens, "You too might grow up to be President of the United States."

These posts are offered to "highly elevated pious living beings." When there is a scarcity of such persons, then Kṛṣṇa Himself takes the post. Once Prabhupāda's GBC man for India requested permission to give up his post and to return to America to travel and preach in a bus with his Godbrothers. Prabhupāda approved of the preaching spirit, but added privately, "He can go and preach, but I have to stay and manage India." The manager may seem to be something less than a preacher, but he's often doing the most crucial work. Without him the institution would crumble. We need managers. The universe needs demigods. In an ultimate sense, we could say that we don't even need a universe. Better that it just gets folded up. But that's idealistic. The fact is that there are conditioned souls, just as there are criminals. There has to be a prison in which to reform them.

When Kṛṣṇa fills a demigod's post, it doesn't mean that He has become a "manager" or that He has become burdened by the universal affairs, but it does show us how important the management of those affairs is. We may say that the demigods relieve Kṛṣṇa of His management burden so that He can be free to enjoy in Vaikuṇṭha. Certainly Kṛṣṇa appreciates the demigods' labors, which they perform as devotional service. Their services are not really material maintenance. They are also providing the *Vedas* and the process of devotional service. We may read of them with appreciation.

When there was no one to take Indra's post during a certain period of Manu, Kṛṣṇa became Indra. This is the incarnation known as Yajña. At that time, His sons such as Yama and others assisted Him.

"Why did the designated devotee who was Indra leave his post early?" And, "What are the pastimes of Lord Yajña?"

I don't know.

(1) I admit it's got to come—death—for each of us. "We all have to go." How deeply do I feel it? We want to save our own skins.

(2) I have a conception that I should write and it will save me. I *must* do it. That's all.

(3) I need comfort, peace, and quiet. Otherwise, I get headaches.

(4) I'm writing this in place of straight preaching, and I admit it's odd. So what? My skull is asymmetrical. The brain surgeon who told me this assured me, "It's no sin." Also, one of my ears is a little lower than the other and both of them stick out. So what?

This man is
about to receive
a book of
Srila Prabhupadas
—a Srimad
Bhag, from a
book distributor.
He doesnt know it
yet.

Text 13

aṣṭame merudevyāṁ tu
nābher jāta urukramaḥ
darśayan vartma dhīrāṇāṁ
sarvāśrama-namaskṛtam

The eighth incarnation was King Ṛṣabha, son of King Nābhi and his wife Merudevī. In this incarnation the Lord showed the path of perfection, which is followed by those who have fully controlled their senses and are honored by all orders of life.

Comment

Prabhupāda outlines the path of perfection, *vartma dhīrāṇām*, as followed by Vedic society. One gradually progresses through the four divisions of occupation and cultural advancement. "Out of these, the renounced order of life, or the order of *sannyāsa*, is considered the highest of all, and a *sannyāsī* is constitutionally the spiritual master for all the orders and divisions." The highest stage of *sannyāsa* is called *paramahaṁsa*, and sane and religious people very much admire a genuine *paramahaṁsa*.

The characteristic on which this purport focuses as the way of perfection is abstinence from unnecessary sense gratification. Prabhupāda alludes to *Śrīmad-Bhāgavatam* 5.5.1, a verse that he liked very much to lecture on, where Ṛṣabhadeva, the eighth incarnation, begins speaking to his one hundred sons. *Nāyaṁ deho deha-bhājāṁ nṛloke:* "My dear sons," King Ṛṣabhadeva says, "do not misuse this human form of life, which is rarely attained after long transmigration through the various species." Don't use it like hogs who eat stool. Don't indulge the senses in cheap happiness which is "immensely obtainable" whether as a pig or a human being. Human life is meant for something better. Abstain, therefore, from cheap happiness and try to attain eternal and unlimited happiness.

Prabhupāda writes, "Those who have been trained for abstinence in material pleasures are called *dhīra*, or men undisturbed by the senses. Only these *dhīras* can accept the orders of *sannyāsa*, and they can gradually rise to the status of *paramahaṁsa*, which is adored by all members of society."

We will read in the Fifth Canto how King Ṛṣabhadeva, in the last stage of His life, left his kingly life and all social convention and wandered around the earth naked as if he were mad. People abused him in his *avadhūta* way of life, but He remained unaffected, detached from the material body and all social interactions with fools. It's described that He was so completely transcendental that even His stool smelled like roses. Who can understand the greatness of such a *paramahaṁsa avadhūta*?

We shouldn't imitate King Ṛṣabha, but we should hear His instructions and practice the path of perfection. Practice restraint from sense gratification, which is "immensely obtainable . . . cheap happiness." People live for sensation—the taste of a cigarette, of coffee, or even of food according to religious sanction. They always want to taste something, see something, do something. There are immense opportunities to touch sense pleasures one after another. People line up their day with such sensations, looking for breaks, perks, and time off in order to engage themselves fully in sense gratification. Everyone will get such sensations, even a dog. Therefore, material pleasure is not the purpose of life. There is a higher, spiritual happiness that is quantitatively and qualitatively superior. We can obtain spiritual happiness only when we at least begin to renounce material happiness. Only those who are purified can know *brahma-saukhyaṁ tv anantam*.

Sometimes when devotees are confronted with the order to restrain their senses, they mention the point about a peaceful life. We have to be peaceful, we say, before we can practice devotional service. To attain peace, however, we may need to get married or do other things that pacify the senses. By pursuing peace, we then find that there is no end to coping with everything that gets in the way of our peace. Why is it that we think we need peace and security before we can begin our service?

Devotional service can begin as soon as we understand that devotion to Kṛṣṇa is the purpose of life. When we understand this point more fully, our devotional service will continue without motive and without interruption. Certainly mental peace and bodily security are required, unless we're able to follow Mahārāja Ṛṣabhadeva—ready to walk naked through a marketplace and have people spit on us. Since almost no one can do that, a peaceful position *is* a factor in our ability to practice Kṛṣṇa consciousness, but it can't be the goal of our spiritual life.

Prabhupāda has given us guidelines how to create peace in our lives. He has not asked us to perform impossible austerities. He has asked us to avoid illicit sex, intoxication, gambling, and meat-eating. That's not hard to do when we are sustained by chanting Hare Kṛṣṇa and given the opportunity to serve Kṛṣṇa. Therefore, there is no ultimate conflict between finding a peaceful situation and performing devotional service, provided we don't think that we have to wait forty years before we begin our service. The two paths go forward simultaneously. We take time for material upkeep and time for spiritual life. An imbalance is created when things become too much in favor of one or the other. The greatest mistake is to place too much emphasis on material upkeep and not enough on spiritual life. Lord Ṛṣabhadeva's teachings call all spirit souls not to waste their human form of life in cheap, material happiness.

There are various stages to renunciation. The *kuṭīcaka* moves out of his home, away from the wrangling of the children and the grandchildren, away from his wife and other ladies. But they all know where he is. He lives in the next village in such and such person's spare room. His family brings him his tiffin every day, maybe by motorbike as they do around here. Occasionally he hears some news of his family as his sons serve him his *prasādam*. Thus he remains connected to his old life, but it is a first step toward renunciation. By living alone, he builds a life of *bhajana* and self-sufficiency. He also meets new people and begins to preach.

In the *bahūdaka* stage, he breaks the connection to the food line and the home, although he continues to live nearby. As *parivrājakācārya*, he sets out alone and leaves his family life behind. They may never hear from him again. The life of traveling and preaching inspires him and also presents him with many difficulties and inconveniences. Sometimes while traveling, he dreams of being home again, but he doesn't give in to that urge. Most of his *sannyāsa* life is spent as *parivrājakācārya*. *Paramahaṁsa* is something else.

Restraint is restraint and you got to practice it. How can you avoid the gist of these purports staring you in the face.

A *sannyāsī* can't be afraid of austerity or anything else. I'm afraid of mice, but I got that from my mother. I used to be afraid of dogs, but I was cured when Uncle Sal gave me my own puppy. I'm afraid of surrender to God. I'm also afraid of high places, like GBC meetings.

Madhu wrote a self-searching prayer and said that he was too attached to austerities. He's getting better now.

Text 14

ṛṣibhir yācito bheje
navamaṁ pārthivaṁ vapuḥ
dugdhemām oṣadhīr viprās
tenāyaṁ sa uśattamaḥ

O brāhmaṇas, in the ninth incarnation, the Lord, prayed for by sages, accepted the body of a king [Pṛthu] who cultivated the land to yield various produces, and for that reason the earth was beautiful and attractive.

Comment

King Pṛthu was an incarnation of God. His activities will be fully described in the Fourth Canto, especially His talks with the four Kumāras. Pṛthu Mahārāja came after the infamous King Veṇa, referred to in the purport as the king who was dethroned by the *brāhmaṇas*.

Prabhupāda delineates the different duties of the *kṣatriyas* and the *brāhmaṇas*. The *kṣatriya's* God consciousness is to make for a sane and peaceful society so that people can prosecute Kṛṣṇa consciousness. All the citizens, including the *brāhmaṇas*, are grateful for the reign of a powerful, God conscious ruler. In Kali-yuga, however, the *Bhāgavatam* predicts that persons who are less than *śūdras* will occupy the government by hook or by crook. Those who claim to be *brāhmaṇas* will also be unqualified. Therefore, any sincere devotee executing the *saṅkīrtana* movement has a duty toward society.

At the present moment, devotees do not have significant political power. What, then, can they expect to do against the "great havoc of maladministration" that comes when the less-than-*śūdras* are in control? The devotees don't have any major constituency in democratic countries, and what passes for political-religious movements are mostly fanatical, sectarian groups that are not God conscious.

Even if the devotees did have political power, they would not be interested in occupying thrones or political posts because "they have much more important duties for the welfare of the public."

I feel encouraged and confident reading this purport. I should not feel bad about not getting involved in world politics or even politics within our institution. Śrīla Prabhupāda mentions "much more important duties," although he doesn't spell them out in this purport. We know, however, that the duties of a Kṛṣṇa conscious *brāhmaṇa* are to read the scriptures and to preach in the *saṅkīrtana* movement. While such personal practice of *bhajana* and purely spiritual preaching may not seem to be politically effective, it is the real work of the *brāhmaṇas*. Ultimately, things change by Kṛṣṇa's desire. When pure souls try to please Him, Kṛṣṇa can change everything overnight.

During King Pṛthu's time, although the *brāhmaṇas* were much more powerful, they also did not engage in a political or military revolution. "Instead of occupying the royal throne, they prayed for the incarnation of the Lord, and the Lord came as Mahārāja Pṛthu."

Saintly persons should distance themselves from worldly societies. Even within a religious society, a devotee may maintain a kind of separateness in order to maintain his integrity. He doesn't jockey for position or seek advantages by holding such a position, even the position of guru. The *Mahābhārata* informs us that even the great soul Bhīṣmadeva was compromised by his relationship with and the diplomacy of Dhṛtarāṣṭra.

It is also true that great souls care very much for the direction society takes. They monitor what goes on and actively seek the best for society either by prayer, or in this case, by dethroning the king. An outstanding example of prayer is when Advaita Ācārya called out for Lord Caitanya's descent. On other occasions, the demigods prayed for the Lord's advent and the Lord responded. We have also read at the beginning of the *Bhāgavatam* that the sages who gathered at Naimiṣāraṇya were not hiding from the world. They were like the elder brothers of human society and the purpose of their *yajña* was to bring benefit for the people of Kali-yuga. They asked Sūta Gosvāmī to speak something which would be relevant for people who had the disadvantages of the age and who couldn't practice pure spiritual life.

I pray that Prabhupāda's ISKCON can maintain its basic identity as his movement. Ever since his disappearance, ISKCON has been a tree shaken by various winds and by people pulling at its trunk. Some have actively sought to cut it down. Still the tree grows, despite scars and deformities. Branches have been lopped off. New attacks are planned and often executed against its well-being. Sometimes the attacks come from outsiders, and sometimes from enemies within, like a rot in the heartwood.

Anyone who cares for ISKCON prays that it will remain faithful to the *sampradāya* and especially to the founder-*ācārya*. Beyond that, we hope that ISKCON will spread its roots and branches and nourish and protect people with its fruits, flowers, and shade.

Sincere prayers must lead to action. I want to always be concerned for Śrīla Prabhupāda's movement. We should all realize that whatever service we are performing is not being performed in a vacuum. ISKCON is a big, joint family. Eventually, everyone knows what everyone else is doing. If all each of us can do is set a good example, it will not go in vain.

I don't claim to be satisfied with my own cultivation of integrity as a devotee of Kṛṣṇa or a disciple of Prabhupāda. Integrity is something that has to be worked at throughout life. When we try to establish personal integrity, we have to face our imperfections and failures. At the same time, we have to feel secure, just as we did at the beginning of ISKCON, that this movement is worth working for and our lives are meant for serving in it. We don't want to serve a superficial ISKCON or the society which our enemies present as the real ISKCON. We want to serve the heart, the pure movement that Prabhupāda introduced. It is still possible. We don't have to be either ostriches with our heads in the sand or blazing reformers. We can always be conscious of the institution's needs, and in a deeply personal way, with commitment, make a positive contribution.

I am convinced that we cannot make this contribution if we remain "ciphers" in the movement; we have to contact our own individuality and surrender from there. Therefore, we fight to protect our individuality. Sometimes ISKCON itself seems to want to swallow us up in the name of "do the needful." Sometimes we fight the movement in that sense, in order to serve the movement best.

I'm grateful to those devotees who are sincerely managing Prabhupāda's movement and doing their best to create laws to govern ISKCON. We read in the previous purport that the managers of cosmic affairs are important workers in the universe, so much so that when He can't find anyone qualified to manage, He does it Himself. Someone has to collect the money, protect the property, and deal with the legalities so that we can exist in the world in peace. Someone has to meet with other managers and go though the inevitable and complicated details. Such management is spiritual. Whoever turns to a spiritual movement like ISKCON and tries to benefit himself as well as take the opportunity to perform devotional service should be grateful to those who are willing to go through the austerities of management.

Although people fear corruption in administrators, that doesn't mean that we shouldn't be organized. Prabhupāda was not against "organized religion," as many New Age teachers are. He wanted us to be very organized in order to preach.

Text 15

rūpaṁ sa jagṛhe mātsyaṁ
cākṣuṣodadhi-samplave
nāvy āropya mahī-mayyām
apād vaivasvataṁ manum

When there was a complete inundation after the period of the Cākṣuṣa Manu and the whole world was deep within water, the Lord accepted the form of a fish and protected Vaivasvata Manu, keeping him up on a boat.

Comment

The Supreme Lord appeared in the form of a fish as Matsya-avatāra "to show some wonders to Satyavrata." This will be described in the Eighth Canto. I remember how in 1966 Prabhupāda mentioned this pastime in his morning *Caitanya-caritāmṛta* class. He said that the *muni* was sipping water from his *ācamana* bowl by the river when he suddenly saw a tiny fish in the pot. The fish spoke to the *muni*: "Please save Me and put Me in a bigger container. I'm uncomfortable in this tiny pot." The *muni* placed the fish in a larger pot, but the fish at once expanded to the size of that pot and asked for a bigger pot. The *muni* then placed Him in the river, but the fish filled the river and asked for a still bigger body of water.

Finally, the *muni* threw Him into the ocean. He expanded there too and filled the entire ocean. "Then he could understand," Śrīla Prabhupāda said, "this must be God."

We chuckled and some of us exclaimed out loud to show that we had gotten the point. "Yeah, He must be God if He can do *that*." We felt *śraddhā* simply by hearing from Swamijī. After hearing that story from him, we told it to others.

In his purport to this verse, Prabhupāda mentions a difference of opinion between Śrīdhara Swami and Jīva Gosvāmī. This is the famous, permitted type of disagreement. Usually we say there is no difference of opinion between *ācāryas*, but occasionally there is—a kind of proof of individuality within the agreed-upon conclusion. Śrīla Prabhupāda doesn't make a fuss about it. He comments, "Apart from this"—whether you take it according to Śrīdhara Swami or Jīva Gosvāmī—the point is the same: Matsya appeared to show special favor to Satyavrata.

He placed him on a boat,
yes, He placed him on a golden boat
and towed that boat which was roped
to the fish-horn by the
Vāsuki snake—and towed
him over the waters of devastation.

He gave the *muni* notice,
"There will be a flood,"
so he gathered herbs and creatures
as Noah did.
On the day the Lord predicted,
the rains came down like
showers from the elephants' trunks,
pralaya, devastation. The
Lord sailed with
the sages onboard.

Pray we also get warning
and be prepared,
believe in His instruction
given sometimes in strange ways
and in times so special that
even *ācāryas* disagree
as to when it really was.

When I wrote about ISKCON and respect for its managers, I was sober and straight. It makes me wonder now, "Why aren't I always like that?" Why am I sometimes zany? In fact, I'm mostly zany. I appear to be a quiet fellow—I write alone, cope with a physical handicap, aging and sedate, but when I write . . . One Godbrother wrote a book review for *ISKCON World Review* and called me "offbeat." Offbeat? I looked it up and the dictionary defined it as "eccentric." Zany means "clownish, given to extravagant or outrageous behavior."

Oh, well.

I am writing honestly. It's perhaps comical because of the incongruity or strangeness that a quiet, modest-looking fellow expresses himself in private with silly lines or whatever you want to call them. That means he actually thinks that way but keeps it mostly to himself. It's his individuality coming out. He's not like everyone else.

Is that so bad? Even the *ācāryas* differ from one another. The Lord Himself certainly displayed humor in asking the *muni*, "Please put Me in a bigger pot."

You may take it that there is nothing particularly zany here. What it is is ordinary. And that's true. It's incongruous the way the ordinary is placed side by side with the straight *paramparā*. For that I apologize. To omit it all would be to close down this project, but Kṛṣṇa gave it to me this way and I take it that He approves.

Yet I do sometimes tremble when I hear Prabhupāda put it so directly: "Material pleasure is when you try to satisfy your senses and spiritual life is when you try to please Kṛṣṇa." I hope this pleases Kṛṣṇa; I hope and strive to make that my motive. I am a person with an early crooked growth. It comes out when I write freely.

Why this penchant is so strong to offer you what I call freedom I can't say exactly. The fish in me says, "Please, dear reader, put me in a bigger pot." I like to smile, I guess, and I like to make you smile.

Text 16

surāsurāṇām udadhiṁ
mathnatāṁ mandarācalam
dadhre kamaṭha-rūpeṇa
pṛṣṭha ekādaśe vibhuḥ

The eleventh incarnation of the Lord took the form of a tortoise whose shell served as a pivot for the Mandarācala Hill, which was being used as a churning rod by the theists and atheists of the universe.

Comment

This wonderful pastime will be fully described in the Eighth Canto. It is a pastime in which the Lord simultaneously appeared as a tortoise and in a many-armed form sitting atop Mandara hill. During the same *līlā*, the Lord also appeared as Dhanvantari and as Mohinī-mūrti. The purpose of the churning of the ocean was to produce nectar from the sea so that both the demons and the demigods could become deathless. The Lord's intention was to relieve an itching sensation on His back. This is certainly a wonderful expression of humor by Kṛṣṇa.

When Kṛṣṇa lists His opulences in the *Bhagavad-gītā*, He mentions some of the many entities that were produced in the early stages of the churning. For example, He mentions Uccaiḥśravā, a horse. Some of these amazing entities were claimed by the demigods and some were claimed by the demons. When Lakṣmī-devī came forward, Lord Viṣṇu claimed Her for Himself.

Poison was also produced from the churning. I have compared this to the production of free-writing in Kṛṣṇa consciousness. When I "churn" in free-writing by writing what comes, some of it will be nectar and some of it will be unsavory recall or an expression of present imperfect desires. Aside from free-writing, both nectar and poison are produced in the flow of consciousness of any conditioned soul, even while he attempts to practice Kṛṣṇa consciousness. He cannot prevent the imperfect thoughts from coming, but he has to distinguish them from the Kṛṣṇa conscious thoughts. He makes this distinction by always following the principle of *śaraṇāgati:* to accept what is favorable for Kṛṣṇa consciousness and to reject what is unfavorable.

It is not harmful to "churn" or to examine one's self. It happens whether we like it or not, especially during times of stress. We will pass Kṛṣṇa's tests if we accept the nectar and put aside the poison.

In the *Bhāgavatam* pastime, Lord Śiva comes forward to hold the poison in his throat. Prabhupāda describes Lord Śiva's act as magnanimous, and he takes the opportunity to ask all devotees to preach for the welfare of others.

Still, we cannot imitate Lord Śiva's ability and take poison into our bodies and minds. To accept poison—sense gratification—is in the mode of ignorance. Even if we take poison in the name of preaching or "churning" out our doubts and bad thoughts, an overdose may be deadly. It is best not to produce too much poison. By *taking in prasādam*—Kṛṣṇa conscious literature, *kṛṣṇa-kathā*, and offered food—we will eventually begin to produce more nectar than poison and "kill" the demons within us.

Since the atheists and theists worked side by side in this pastime, we may wonder what is the actual difference between them. Both were trying to exploit the world and avoid death by discovering immortal nectar. The demigods, however, despite their material ambitions, always turn to Kṛṣṇa for shelter. They do this on a number of occasions during this pastime, and thus we clearly see the difference between the demons and the demigods. It is not that the demigods are simply clever enough to know who's boss and to go to Him for sense gratification. They also devote themselves to His service by managing the universal affairs. The demigods are devotees, although they are known as *sakāma* devotees, devotees with material desires.

It is dangerous to enter into a joint venture with the demons and to work with them, but if we have to do it, then we must not give up our daily practices of *bhajana*—chanting and hearing. We should not join with demons in such an intimate way that we give the results of our activities for an unworthy cause or do things forbidden by scripture. Sometimes worldly emergencies may force such joint ventures upon the devotees, but ultimately, the devotees—whether they are working to save flood victims or sharing a bomb shelter with nondevotees—are always thinking and acting for Kṛṣṇa. Otherwise we may get consumed by the worldly activities and forget Kṛṣṇa at a time when it is most important to remember Him.

Why did the Lord become the pivot of the hill in the seawater?

Because He wanted to. He saw that this wild endeavor was headed for disaster and He chose to intervene. He also had to help the demons and devotees carry the mountain. Nothing happens without Kṛṣṇa's sanction.

He also wanted to relieve an itching sensation: "Please scratch my back."

O divine tortoise incarnation,

I read of You now.

I remember Rāya Rāma dāsa explaining that the tortoise pastime took place so long ago that it is "remote." This seemed to be a preaching tactic by him to make it somehow easier to accept such a fantastic account as history. At least we don't have to believe that God became a tortoise *recently*. But does it really become easier to believe that it happened in ancient times, when perhaps strange things were more likely to happen? And did the Kūrma *līlā* actually take place only in a remote time? Isn't it alive now when we chant and hear *keśava-dhṛta-kūrma-śarīra jaya jagadīśa hare*?

I am boasting of my faithfulness. I easily accept the fact that the Lord could appear in this form. After all, He can do anything He pleases. It's easy for us to accept Kṛṣṇa's *līlā* when it doesn't cost us anything. Then we think of ourselves as generous and liberal. "I don't mind if Kṛṣṇa wants to appear as a tortoise. I can accommodate that." What we mean is that it doesn't affect us one way or another. But let the Lord press or pinch on a personal interest and we'll see how permissive and accepting we are. If He wants to take away our husband or wife, or a beloved friend, when He comes as Time to interrupt our fun and material progress, then what?

Please, Lord, let us praise You in all Your pastimes and purposes, those we can understand and those that baffle us, those that took place long ago and those that are happening now or in the future, but let us do it deeply and with heart.

The guards on the porch are talking. It's midnight. I prefer this hour to be like "the night before Christmas" when "all through the house, not a creature was stirring, not even a mouse." But creatures do stir, even as I write. What is it I seek to find in the lotus of quiet? I hope to see Lord Kṛṣṇa in the *Śrīmad-Bhāgavatam*.

Śrīla Prabhupāda *mūrti* accepts the dictaphone I place before him while I write. Prabhupāda is up writing at his customary hour and I am up with him, writing in my junior way as his son.

Madhu said that so many questions are asked of the speakers in the *Bhāgavatam* class that it often seems more an exercise in rhetoric. The real question is how we can see and hear the *Bhāgavatam* as relevant to our lives.

Text 17–18

dhānvantaraṁ dvādaśamaṁ
trayodaśamam eva ca
apāyayat surān anyān
mohinyā mohayan striyā

caturdaśaṁ nārasiṁhaṁ
bibhrad daityendrum ūrjitam
dadāra karajair ūrāv
erakāṁ kaṭa-kṛd yathā

In the twelfth incarnation, the Lord appeared as Dhanvantari, and in the thirteenth He allured the atheists by the charming beauty of a woman and gave nectar to the demigods to drink.

In the fourteenth incarnation, the Lord appeared as Nṛsiṁha and bifurcated the strong body of the atheist Hiraṇyakaśipu with His nails, just as a carpenter pierces cane.

Comment

For the most part, I want to follow Prabhupāda's policy of not making a purport if the previous *ācāryas* didn't write a purport. By "previous *ācāryas*," I mean Prabhupāda himself. If I comment at all on these verses for which there is no purport, it's because I am drawing from other purports and talks in which His Divine Grace explained the subject matter.

Dhanvantari appeared during the churning of the milk ocean, holding a golden pot filled with nectar. He is the incarnation who presented the Āyurvedic science (the Aśvinī-kumāras also presented it). Devotees like to choose Āyurvedic practices as their health care because they want to stay in tune with the *Vedas*. Āyurveda is almost lost now, although it's often mistakenly or imperfectly practiced by people who sell combinations of Indian allopathic pills and Āyurvedic herbs in India.

These twelfth and thirteenth incarnations appeared during the churning of the milk ocean. The climax of the *līlā* was when the Lord appeared in a beautiful female form. This was His trick to allure the atheists and to give the nectar to the demigods. It is all wonderfully described in the Eighth Canto.

As for the fourteenth incarnation, Lord Nṛsiṁhadeva, Prabhupāda doesn't give any comment here. He will do so in the Seventh Canto. This list, therefore, is like a short film shown between the movies at the theater, "Preview of Coming Attractions." I remember that at the Strand movie theater in Great Kills, there was a big open entranceway which you could enter even when the theater was closed. It contained pictures with descriptions of movies planned three or four weeks ahead. We would stand and see which cowboy movie, which boring love story, and sometimes which sensational hit would be moving down from Manhattan to Staten Island in a few weeks. This chapter is like that.

Text 19

pañcadaśaṁ vāmanakaṁ
kṛtvāgād adhvaraṁ baleḥ
pada-trayaṁ yācamānaḥ
pratyāditsus tri-piṣṭapam

In the fifteenth incarnation, the Lord assumed the form of a dwarf-brāhmaṇa [Vāmana] and visited the arena of sacrifice arranged by Mahārāja Bali. Although at heart He was willing to regain the kingdom of the three planetary systems, He simply asked for a donation of three steps of land.

Comment

Śrīla Prabhupāda's one-sentence purport to this verse is memorable: "The almighty God can bestow upon anyone the kingdom of the universe from a very small beginning, and similarly, He can take away the kingdom of the universe on the plea of begging a small piece of land."

Prabhupāda remembered his father saying in Bengali, "The Supreme Lord has ten hands, so if He wants to give something, He'll give you more than you can possibly hold; if He wants to take something away, what can you hold onto with your two hands?" The Christians say, "The Lord giveth, and the Lord taketh away. Blessed be the name of Lord."

Be grateful for the bounty, the windfalls, and every little moment of life. It's all precious because Kṛṣṇa has given it to us. We may embrace it and use it in His service, and we can be ready to let go of it when He desires.

His taking life away from us is not irrational or cruel. It was never ours to possess. Giving is always followed by taking away. That's just the nature of the material world. When Kṛṣṇa takes something away that we love, we sometimes say, "It was too perfect to last." That may be taken as pessimistic, as if God wanted to spoil our fun. It could also mean that the gift He gave us was, in a sense, perfect, but it doesn't matter. We have to move on. Kṛṣṇa wants us to take something more now, or something different, and we must be ready to surrender to His will. It's in our interest to let go when Kṛṣṇa indicates that our time with a particular gift is up. By using what He gave us in His service, we can qualify ourselves for better gifts, but first we must become detached and let the teacher move us on.

We'll be reading about Vāmanadeva in the Eighth Canto. We'll hear how Bali Mahārāja, although a demon by birth, became a *mahājana*. Vāmanadeva tested him severely in the school of detachment. Of course, he passed. He did not resent the Lord, but wanted to give Him everything as soon as He understood that Kṛṣṇa had marked him as someone who should surrender. He saw Kṛṣṇa's taking away his opulence as special mercy, which it was.

I sat in a restaurant with my
dad, another time with two
black men. I said, "We are
all animals."
This is a writer's life. I still
didn't introduce surreal
poems.
We have 50 volumes to go—
in how many years?
Writer as slave.

It is like this—writers
are obscure demanders.

Writers lie and wait to pounce upon perception, like a cat at the mouse hole. Or like panic in the breast of a shy mouse and me afraid of his panic because I identify with it. Yes, mousy, as you fear the light and death out there by the cat's paw, so do I. That's why I fear you—I see my own animal panic in you.

Writer's life, roaring drunk
Brendan Behan
autographing books at a bookstore.
Writer's lie, a river named
Liffey. A town near Godāvarī.
Indian life is good; I used
to say Vṛndāvana is the best place to
write but when I was there recently
I stayed in my room and collected
its dust as holy
because I received His mercy
there,
permission
for a writer's life finally
dedicated to one undying project,
staying awhile with each
verse of *Śrīmad-Bhāgavatam* and my
master's purports with
"permission given" to go ashore,
a drunken sailor.
I can do it,
but is it best?
That's what I'm asking,
O Lord Vāmana.
Don't take away
my writer's life.

Let me give You all land
and my head and my
writer's right hand not
paralyzed but working
on Your behalf.

I want to tell you why I'm writing about dreams and how it's connected to the *Bhāgavatam*. After reading and writing about Vāmanadeva, I took a nap around 4:30 A.M. I know that's a dangerous time to sleep. I had a nightmare that I was wandering alone, not with a deep devotee identity. I came to a dark street where there were houses on both sides. There was an opening, like a caged window and a dim light—maybe it was a store. I went to that house and called out. An old man came out to see me. I asked him for directions to the train station, which would be to New York City connected by subway. He gave me directions and said that it wasn't difficult to find. I walked for awhile and then found the train station. It was a large place. Connected to it was a game room and a waiting room. I discovered that I was the only white person in this area. I became afraid. I went up to one person and asked him if this train connected to New York City. He said yes. But it was hard to find where to go to actually catch the train.

I walked in one direction where people seemed to be waiting. I noticed more white people. Most of them seemed blond and low-class. I became especially afraid to see the tough men among them. Some of them passed me and made sarcastic and threatening remarks. One of the tough guys said that I had an expensive wristwatch. I became alarmed that they were going to rob me.

Then one very big guy came up to me surrounded by his friends. He joked. I understood what he was going to try to force me to do. I then became so frightened that I jerked awake. It wasn't easy to awaken. At first I felt as if I were suffocating, which was just a feeling I had of being in the hood of my sleeping bag. Then I woke up fully.

Now for the "purport." It's unfortunate that I was not in devotee consciousness, turning to Kṛṣṇa while in the midst of these dangerous people. I was simply scared, with little money, trying to find my way. My present waking life is protected by devotees. This very contrast makes me think that I should put this dream into *A Poor Man Reads The Bhāgavatam* and talk about it. I should express my gratitude for the protected life I have, the sublime engagement of placing my consciousness at the feet of the *Bhāgavatam*. I should never leave this shelter, but be aware how dangerous the other mentality is. I have a privileged life, but there is a frightening aspect of being forced among demons.

The dream indicates to me that I should use my time to get out of the material world and to go back to Godhead. If I don't go back to Godhead, then even if I become a devotee in this world, I could meet up with these fearsome circumstances. The dream also tells me of the need to preach because Kṛṣṇa wants us to help all people. Even though they appear tough and aggressive, they're in need of Kṛṣṇa consciousness.

But dream circumstance also tells me of the bravery and risk preaching requires. I appreciate my protected status, but at the same time, I know I am minimizing my risks by living a life of reading *Bhāgavatam* and writing. We have to go out and preach the *Bhāgavatam* sometimes, "taking all risks" before we become very, very dear to the Lord.

Text 20

avatāre ṣoḍaśame
paśyan brahma-druho nṛpān
triḥ-sapta-kṛtvaḥ kupito
niḥ-kṣatrām akaron mahīm

In the sixteenth incarnation of the Godhead, the Lord [as Bhṛgupati] annihilated the administrative class [kṣatriyas] twenty-one times, being angry with them because of their rebellion against the brāhmaṇas [the intelligent class].

Comment

The *kṣatriyas* are the rulers of the world, but by the Vedic conception, they act as servants to the *brāhmaṇas* and the śāstric direction. Lord Bhṛgupati, also known as Paraśurāma, appeared in the world as a *brāhmaṇa*, but when He saw that the *kṣatriyas* were disobedient to the *brāhmaṇas*, Paraśurāma took the role of a *kṣatriya* and punished them by His own military strength. He is often depicted as wielding a chopper in His mighty arm, dressed in an animal skin, wearing His hair in a topknot, and looking angry. He was so fierce that He created rivers of blood.

Devotees find it hard to explain this incarnation to outsiders, just as they find it difficult to talk about Lord Nṛsiṁhadeva before casual guests to the temple. I remember years ago in the ISKCON Detroit mansion, the temple commissioned a set of outdoor sculpture pieces of the incarnations, including Paraśurāma. One devotee confessed that when he took guests through the garden and showed them these incarnations, he felt awkward and speechless when he came to Paraśurāma. He used to waffle and tell the guests this was a pious wood chopper. We are embarrassed because we know people no longer appreciate the concept of an angry God. They are sick of violence in the world and especially of violence motivated by religion. The fact remains, however, that God has many sides. He can be sweet and loving and as fierce as a tiger at the same time.

The *kṣatriyas* were so rebellious that after Paraśurāma killed one generation, He had to slay the next. He did this for twenty-one generations. Those *kṣatriyas* who managed to flee Paraśurāma's ax ran west to Europe and the Middle East.

Prabhupāda used to say that the Western stock of humanity was descended from these *kṣatriyas* because they reached Europe and entered the cultures of the various nations we know today.

When His mission was over, Paraśurāma went back to a life of brahminical austerity to atone for the killing. Thus He showed that even if killing is sanctioned, it is not good. If God atones for His killing, then humans, despite their rationalization for dropping bombs or pulling triggers, should regret it. One has to make peace before God, and all karma will be accounted for.

The *kṣatriya* spirit as it flourished in Vedic times is something beyond us now. Fighting was a sport, and the enemies' prowess was appreciated even by their victims. The *kṣatriyas* used to fight in the daytime and host each other at the military camps at night. Everything was conducted by codes of honor. The *kṣatriyas* were brave, honorable, truthful, and faithful. They were also submissive to the *brāhmaṇas*. As we hear about them now, they seem larger than anyone we know as leaders in life today.

Prabhupāda said there is no one training *kṣatriyas* properly in modern times. Therefore, the populations are distressed when the government imposes involuntary military service on all male (and sometimes female) citizens. He saw this firsthand in America when so many young men were being drafted to fight in Vietnam. Some of them came to ISKCON for shelter and Prabhupāda obtained exemptions for them by proving that they were ministerial students. He explained that a person's psycho-physical nature should be determined in his childhood and that he should be trained from the start. This made us feel less guilty or unworthy about the fact that we found military induction abhorrent. There's nothing wrong with not having a *kṣatriya's* courage as long as we find our *varṇa* and dedicate ourselves to whatever courage and austerity that requires.

An incarnation such as Paraśurāma assures us that there will be justice in the world. Sometimes the scriptures say that we cannot expect justice here but that we will receive it in the next world. Demons exploit people and they appear to go free. We also don't see what rewards innocent people receive. This can make those who are seeking love and justice frustrated.

Therefore, some people dedicate their lives to finding justice in this lifetime. They think they can rectify the world single-handedly or that they can join a cause to correct the world's wrongs. But they don't get very far.

When Kṛṣṇa intervenes, however, He rectifies the problems. Those who hanker for righteousness may take heart when they see Paraśurāma's anger against the rebellious managers. Instead of waffling and saying that this is not God but a pious wood-chopper, we may proudly sing, *keśava dhṛta-bhṛgupati-rūpa jaya jagadīśa hare*—let 'em have it, Bhṛgupati!

I want to finish my comments through verse twenty-seven in the next two days and come to the end of Volume One of this *A Poor Man Reads The Bhāgavatam*. Unfortunately, I have been hampered by daily headaches for the past week and I've only been able to work from midnight to 5 A.M. Yesterday I told Madhu of my plan and how it's now being threatened. I said I could probably rush through the straight philosophical descriptions, but it takes more time and headache-free energy to free-write. In response, Madhu told me a story about his maternal grandmother, who was Irish.

He said that she had cancer. She moved away from home to stay in a terminal ward in a hospital in Tipperary. She hid the fact of her approaching death from the family, especially the children, and no one visited her in the hospital. At the beginning of the year, she decided she wanted to die in May. May was the month of Our Lady, the mother of God, and she thought it would be most beneficial for her salvation to die during Mary's month. She set her mind on that and practiced her devotion to Mary. May came and his grandmother lived right through it. When June began, his grandmother accepted it and said, "Well, June is good too. It's the month of the Sacred Heart of Jesus." She therefore changed her devotion and died in June, seeking the grace of the Sacred Heart.

I liked this story. It showed me once again that I may have my plan, but Kṛṣṇa has His own. Maybe I won't finish Volume One here. That's my plan, but there's nothing ultimate about it. If I go to Bombay and finish Volume One there, what's the harm? Maybe I can get Rādhā-Rāsabihārī's grace for this project in Prabhupāda's Hare Krishna Land.

Therefore, I have decided not to rush this writing in an attempt to finish it in two days. If I finish it, great, and if not, that's all right too.

I told Madhu, "All right, I'll follow Kṛṣṇa's plan." I may have to see Kṛṣṇa as The Inevitable. Kṛṣṇa's pure spiritual form in Vṛndāvana is difficult to see in this lifetime. It requires the special mercy granted by a pure devotee. Anyone can open his eyes and see Kṛṣṇa as The Inevitable. Man proposes and God disposes. Only mad and ignorant rebels try to work against this inevitable force. When they become too destructive in their apparent self-sufficiency, the Lord incarnates as Bhṛgupati to show them who is boss.

I look at my hand as it grips the pen. My hand is full of lines. Palmists tell us that we are ignorant, gullible, or vastly intelligent. The Vedic science is lost.

Last night I lay awake wondering what causes my headaches. Is it diet? Sunshine? Should I even bother to try and find out? I feel stronger when I eat more, but maybe my constitution changed at the health clinic and I'm in for more problems. That's their theory. Gullible and speculative. I have a tendency to become submissive to different theorists. Best to just chant Hare Kṛṣṇa.

But the headaches. My diet is now normal—*dāl*, rice, *capātīs*, and *sabjī*. Maybe my body is becoming accustomed to that again. I'll go on eating if I have to die. Can't get cured by not eating. I try to adjust to my body as a loving friend. All I'm left with, however, is that my headaches are Kṛṣṇa's will.

Now, dear hand, how about a sublime message or two and some ditties and ballads and flowers in May (the month of Our Lady of the Assumption)? A poet wrote, "I'll die on Thursday and it will be raining." Who cares? Better to die in Vṛndāvana during Kārttika with too many people intruding on your privacy.

"What is skepticism?" Prabhupāda asked in Philadelphia.

"Disappointment," Ravīndra-svarūpa said.

"Don't be disappointed."

(The mice will play. Got no cat. At least they're not rats.)

Dreamt of being with Prabhupāda as his servant. Walked behind him in the rain, grateful. Was with him in a huge building where there were wild hogs out of their cages.

Prabhupāda and I found a door with a fire exit mechanism and escaped. It was so nice to be with him, to feel his mercy pushing me toward *bhakti.*

Madhu is chanting in the hallway. He can't sleep.

I don't have complete silence or complete anything, and I can't concentrate on the absolutely pure message from inside. I have to take what I can get. We'll discuss Vyāsadeva next, if Kṛṣṇa desires.

The main thing is love and dedication. Live the life of a *Bhāgavatam* reader and a writer.

This too, this too—
the opposite of *neti neti*
(not this). I claim it all
for Kṛṣṇa consciousness: this too, the
headache that steals my time
is His—is time I would have spent
in *Śrīmad-Bhāgavatam.*
This too, black ink or red,
my left hand holding the
page and right arm chopper working.
This too, black pen box, fear
of pain. Don't be afraid it can't rule
you—Kṛṣṇa rules and I accept.
This precious time I'll spend with
you one way or another. I am
never outside of Kṛṣṇa and
Kṛṣṇa consciousness, *Śrīmad-Bhāgavatam.*
That's my contention. Hand, I salute thee. Thanks for the ride.
See you soon at breakfast (not a big thing—just a few fruits or whatever).
Cry *sincerely* to Prabhupāda.
(I hope writing helps promote sincere crying.)

I tried but failed—saw rain on streets of
Boston at night and thought good, our *harināma*
will be canceled and I can stay home—but
at least home was our lit-up target,
the Allston temple. I was a skinny t.p.
with all the devotees.
"Rest in peace,"
"Live forever,"
graffiti.

Text 21

tataḥ saptadaśe jātaḥ
satyavatyāṁ parāśarāt
cakre veda-taroḥ śākhā
dṛṣṭvā puṁso 'lpa-medhasaḥ

Thereafter, in the seventeenth incarnation of Godhead, Śrī Vyāsadeva appeared in the womb of Satyavatī through Parāśara Muni, and he divided the one Veda into several branches and sub-branches, seeing that the people in general were less intelligent.

Comment

The division of the original *Veda* into four is a technical subject explained in the *Ṣaṭ Sandarbha* and the commentaries of my Godbrother. Actually, Vyāsadeva didn't write the *Vedas*, but he complied those things that constituted the eternal breathing of Nārāyaṇa. He did write some things to make it more accessible. For example, he wrote, "*śrī-bhagavān uvāca*" and, "Arjuna said." I guess he also composed the Sanskrit, the meter, and so on, but I don't know for sure. We shouldn't be disappointed that Vyāsadeva wasn't a writer like J. D. Salinger. Neither was Śrīla Prabhupāda. (He said that we should assimilate the *Bhāgavatam* and then speak it in our own words. Exactly what "in your own words" means we will have to discover.)

What kind of a writer, then, was Vyāsadeva? He was the best because he was an incarnation of God. We have to write following Vyāsadeva's spirit, just as we speak in his spirit. When we sit on the *vyāsāsana*, we're as strict as possible. Still, even there we speak in our own words with our nasal Brooklyn accents. We don't make too many jokes or tell long stories or make politically-motivated speeches. There's a limit to relaxation.

I allow myself more leeway in my writing. For me, it's a place to stretch out and be myself. That doesn't mean we don't want the straight *Vedas*. We want them to be perfect utterings, the breath of Nārāyaṇa (*bramākṣara-samudbhavam*).

Vyāsadeva took the already existing material from the *Vedas*, selected it, and put it in the *Purāṇas* in a way that would be understood by people in Kali-yuga. In this age, everyone is born *śūdra* or less. People don't undergo the purificatory processes. Therefore, no one is cultured. "Śrīla Vyāsadeva divided the *Vedas* into various branches and sub-branches for the sake of the less intelligent classes like the *dvija-bandhus*, *śūdras* and women."

Our Kali-yuga brains are tiny, and we have ruined them with lust and intoxication and so many other things bombarding us from the ether. This is a polluted, bad age. We're dwarfs, pygmies, and our minds are soaked in alcohol and parents beating us and fear of the Bomb. What do we expect from ourselves?

I first heard of Vyāsadeva the day I bought Swamijī's three volumes of the First Canto. Swamijī explained to me that these were Vyāsadeva's books to which he had written a commentary. It's right there in the front matter of his

Indian edition: "*Śrīmad-Bhāgavatam* of Kṛṣṇa-Dvaipāyana Vyāsa."

Vyāsa is a friend of the family, like Nārada and Prahlāda —a great devotee and incarnation. Only later did I hear that Vyāsadeva was considered "ugly" and that he had a dark complexion, that he was so ugly that women were afraid of him. That doesn't deter us from loving him and feeling gratitude. He's beautiful as he shines forth in the *Bhāgavatam*, the original writer.

I went to Prabhupāda one night and told him I'd been reading about Vyāsadeva in his *Śrīmad-Bhāgavatam* and that I found it interesting that Vyāsadeva was a writer but wasn't satisfied with what he had written. Prabhupāda's eyes widened in appreciation because I was speaking about such a sublime subject, although I really didn't know what I was talking about. Fortunately I stumbled into the world of the *Bhāgavatam*, and without knowing what it was, felt charmed and attracted by the "writer."

Yeah, I thought I knew what it was like to have writer's blues like Vyāsadeva. You write and write and you think you have done something good but still you feel morose. I thought I understood Vyāsadeva.

Prabhupāda, just to hear, even in the broken language of a child, the mentioning of Vyāsadeva, opened his eyes wide and smiled. I wish I could always please him by speaking *Bhāgavatam*, even though I still stumble like a baby, still mispronounce the Sanskrit, and still don't know what I'm taking about. I suppose I'm expected to be grown up now.

Anyway, all glories to Śrīla Vyāsadeva, the literary incarnation of God, and all glories to his *Śrīmad-Bhāgavatam*, which is perfect, complete, and eternal.

Poor hand's got to work. Give it twenty minutes. List—the story, "In Brooklyn Snow."

Me, me, me, in various ways.

Free-write list.

Ample time.

Random words.

Throw it all in a closet.

Heaps and heaps. This is automatic writing.

All I know.

Vyāsa—don't forget he was a real writer. Draw him with topknot and bare chest. The European ISKCON art school made him big-chested and muscular, somber, sober, deep, sitting in the Himalayas. Before that his picture was crude and devotional, stylized because no one really knew what he looked like. Dark blue?

In one early picture, he was so hairy and unhappy. Nārada floated in from the sky. We'll be reading about that in the fifth chapter.

Am I better than the devotee who waffled and said Śrī Paraśurāma was chopping wood? I can't be bothered to make structured essays leading people into the philosophy gradually. I used to do that four times a day in college classrooms, same lecture—four defects, two ways of this and that—and led gently and subtly or not so subtly to *man-tra,* the chant that delivers the mind. "Hare Kṛṣṇa." The bell would ring and class would be over.

I can turn everyone into a devotee by painting *tilaka* on their foreheads. That's all I know how to do. Kṛṣṇa-ize the world in that way. Draw them in *dhotīs* and a few pious, chaste women in *sarīs*. To hell with *karmīs;* neither associate with them nor love the demons. It's all right to live in that way.

I want Bhakti-rasa and Kṛṣṇa-kīrtana to read and be sustained. Vyāsadeva wrote, Vyāsadeva wrote.

Here's a picture of Vyāsadeva.

Vyasa wrote for
us less intelligent people
yet didnt "dumb down"
the message - gave us
sublime S.B.
SB
Bhagavata Purana by Vyasa

Bhaktijana raised his hand after a lecture in the Allston storefront in 1968. He asked Prabhupāda, "What about Rabindranath Tagore? Is he a nice poet?"

Prabhupāda answered, "He's nice . . . for the mundane. We're interested in poets like Vyāsadeva and Vālmīki."

Text 22

nara-devatvam āpannaḥ
sura-kārya-cikīrṣayā
samudra-nigrahādīni
cakre vīryāṇy ataḥ param

In the eighteenth incarnation, the Lord appeared as King Rāma. In order to perform some pleasing work for the demigods, He exhibited superhuman powers by controlling the Indian Ocean and then killing the atheist King Rāvaṇa, who was on the other side of the sea.

Comment

Lord Rāma came to protect the devotees and punish the miscreants. Prabhupāda compares Rāvaṇa's challenge to the defiance of modern scientists who go against God's natural order. They attempt to fly to other planets by material means. In the modern age, we don't consider interplanetary travel a challenge to God's established order. When cars and airplanes were first invented, people worried that they were against God's will too.

Yes, I can say it. Just because something becomes the vogue doesn't mean it's in tune with God's order or that it won't create a bad reaction sooner or later. It sounds quaint now when we hear statements from decades ago that man was meant to travel only forty-five miles an hour and he should only go by horse. The world has been revolutionized by the automobile, the airplane, the train, and so on, but the day may come when all these things will become useless. Natural resources are becoming so scarce and the world so congested with vehicle pollution that it can't go on forever.

Śrīla Bhaktisiddhānta Sarasvatī Ṭhākura saw that these inventions could be used in Kṛṣṇa's service, and he himself traveled in a car, although it was against what people understood as *sannyāsa-dharma*. He presented a perfect example of *yukta-vairāgya*, the principle taught by Rūpa Gosvāmī. He thought that devotees could use modern inventions to propagate Kṛṣṇa consciousness. In this way, the devotees, the demons, and the objects themselves would become spiritualized.

In a God conscious world, there would be no cars or hellish factories, and men would not be reduced to slavery to produce modern amenities. Life would be simpler. Because all this paraphernalia is there, however, the devotees can use it. At the same time, devotees must remain detached from the amenities, not dependent on them, and set an example of non-industrialized life on Kṛṣṇa conscious farms.

Unless devotees can prove that they are able to live without dependence on demoniac civilization, then their preaching is tainted with hypocrisy. Devotees may use electricity in their preaching, but they may also show that electricity is not required for a comfortable life. Real comfort is not found in material amenities, but in the holy name.

If God decides that everyone has achieved their quota, yet politicians and military crusaders defy this order, then eventually the world will become polarized and civilization as we know it will be destroyed. The demons and atheists may think that God's laws are religious sentiment, but they will eventually learn otherwise. What God ordains will endure, and defiance against Him will end in ruin.

There are many descriptions of interplanetary travel in the Vedic literature. The *Vedas* also describe that such travel is done with qualification, not in a spaceship. Success is dependent on one's karma.

Rāvaṇa belonged to a class of puffed-up, godless materialists, who, upon making a little material advancement, decide that they are as good as God. "He wanted a staircase to be built up directly reaching the heavenly planet so that people might not be required to undergo the routine of pious work necessary to enter that planet."

Rāvaṇa also defied the Supreme Lord and kidnapped His eternal wife, Sītādevī. (Lord Caitanya researched the *Purāṇas* and found that Sītā was not actually kidnapped, but only a shadow form of Sītā. Nevertheless the *Rāmāyaṇa* is a heartrending story because of the kidnapping of Sītā, her suffering in exile from Rāma, and Rāma's transcendentally painful separation from her.)

In this one-*śloka* summary of Rāma's activities, we learn that He appeared in order to please the demigods and to kill the atheist king, Rāvaṇa. What the demigods desired was that He give them relief from Rāvaṇa's atrocities. In the course of His pastimes, Rāma performed many superhuman tasks, one of which was to float stones on the ocean and build a bridge to Laṅkā.

Rāmacandra is "only" an expansion of Lord Kṛṣṇa and He had only one wife. He also confined His activities strictly within the human code of truth and religion, as He exemplified filial obedience and other virtues. Yet all this apparently limited activity appealed to the people. The human-like king who was actually superhuman captures the imagination. We are attracted to His heroism, His nobility, His subdued senses, His righteous chastisement of the demons, His loyalty to friends, and many of His other qualities. *Raghupati rāghava rāja rāma, patita-pāvana sītā-rāma, sītā-rāma jaya sītā-rāma.*

Prabhupāda introduced the worship of Sītā-Rāma in temples such as Bombay, England, and Washington, D.C. with the sentiment that it would demonstrate ideal government. It may seem farfetched for us to pray to Lord Rāmacandra and then go out and do something about the world's corrupt government—what can we do?—but our duty is only to serve and to pray. Everything else is up to Kṛṣṇa.

"O Rāma! O Rāma!" cries Sītā. "O Rāma!"

I remember the Hollywood-type ISKCON version, screenplay by Henry Higgins.

O Rāma! Rāma!

Rāma shot His arrow at the enchanting deer. Sītā within the ring of fire allowed Rāvaṇa to enter—a deadly mistake. She accused Lakṣmaṇa of infidelity—a woman's weakness and another dangerous mistake. Jaṭāyu: Prabhupāda says we can be like him, defeated by a demon but not minding, trusting in Kṛṣṇa. And Prabhupāda compared his preaching outside India and then re-entering India to preach to Rāma's recruiting an army of monkeys and crossing the ocean to Laṅkā.

"Rāmjī. Rāmjī, Rāmjī." The old man on Juhu Beach used to stand at the ocean's edge and greet each passerby, "*Jaya* Rāmjī! *Jaya* Rāmjī!" They laughed at him and thought he was crazy, but we heard his "*Jaya* Rāmjī" and secretly admired him. Wish we could be such fools as to call out God's name to each person we meet.

O Rāmjī, Rāmjī, Rāmjī, I scrawl.

O Rāmjī, Lord Rāma,
deliver us from evil.

O Personality of Godhead, may we read of Your activities again in this lifetime and in future lives. It is not against the principles of devotion to Kṛṣṇa in Vṛndāvana.

Hanumān prayed, "I know Lord Nārāyaṇa is the same as Lord Rāma, but I will worship Rāma. I don't want any liberation that would disturb my mood of servitude to Rāma." Rāma told us that death is always with us, whether we walk or sit or engage in any activity at all. This He said in His speech to Bharata. Rāma smiling, Rāma and Lakṣmaṇa's beauty as They sit with Their bows resting nearby in a thatched cottage, glowing as God Almighty, but in hermitage and forest exile.

Rāma's strong arms relaxed. Rāma's arms tensed, pulling the bow in battle. God on earth.

O Rāma, You killed Vāli as You hid behind a tree. Later, the *gopīs* criticized You for this treachery. The sages saw Rāma and aspired to become *gopīs* in the future.

We celebrate Rāma's victory over Rāvana at the Rāma-vijaya festival. I remember attending that festival in Potomac. We went outside together, the mock-angry crowd, to the open field (despite a mild prohibition from the fire department). Someone shot flaming arrows at Rāvaṇa's effigy (I saw much taller effigies a few days later in New Delhi) and others threw sticks and stones and flung angry words at the demon. We all felt satisfied in the cool, late-autumn night as the flames shot up and the demon was consumed. It gave us a sense of security to know that the personification of evil can be destroyed. It also felt good to be with a faithful congregation and to discharge the festival duty.

I also remember writing to Prabhupāda in the early days with questions about Rāma. Why was He praised as equal to Indra? Prabhupāda replied that we should worship God in the mood in which He has preferred to appear. Rāma was an ideal king. Therefore, He can be compared to the heavenly king, Lord Indra. Lord Caitanya appeared as a pure *bhakta*. We should not approach Him as if He were Rāsabihārī.

I'm free, a poet-scribe in nappy, brown knit cap with two days to go. I'll never forget that *Jaya* Rāmjī man at Juhu's ocean edge calling out.

Text 23

ekonaviṁśe viṁśatime
vṛṣṇiṣu prāpya janmanī
rāma-kṛṣṇāv iti bhuvo
bhagavān aharad bharam

In the nineteenth and twentieth incarnations, the Lord advented Himself as Lord Balarāma and Lord Kṛṣṇa in the family of Vṛṣṇi [the Yadu dynasty], and by so doing He removed the burden of the world.

Comment

The word *bhagavān* indicates that Śrī Kṛṣṇa and Balarāma are the original forms of the Supreme Lord. This is also indicated by the first verse in Chapter Three, "In the beginning of the creation, the Lord first expanded Himself . . ." Prabhupāda writes that the mention of the word "*bhagavān*" for Kṛṣṇa "will be further explained later."

Chapter Three will reach its climax at verse 28, where the word "*bhagavān*" will be used in its most crucial context in the entire *Bhāgavatam*. That is, in the verse *kṛṣṇas tu bhagavān svayam*. Here it is stated only briefly: "Lord Kṛṣṇa is not an incarnation of the *puruṣa*, as we learned from the beginning of this chapter. He is directly the original Personality of Godhead, and Balarāma is the first plenary manifestation of the Lord."

Almost nothing is mentioned of Kṛṣṇa and Balarāma's activities at this point, although these pastimes were already referred to in the first chapter, verse 20, when the sages asked their questions of Sūta. They said that they wanted to hear of the Supreme Lord's multi-incarnations and that they would never grow tired of such hearing. They specifically mentioned that they wanted to hear about how "Lord Śrī Kṛṣṇa, the Personality of Godhead, along with Balarāma, played like a human being, and so masked He performed many superhuman acts." (*Bhāg*. 1.1.20)

Furthermore, since the onset of the *Bhāgavatam*, we've been aware that Vāsudeva, the son of Vasudeva and Devakī, is the focus of meditation, the Absolute Truth, the Supreme Person.

Although the present verse appears to list factual information about Kṛṣṇa's function in the world, Kṛṣṇa's function is heavy: "He removed the burden of the world." The two brothers didn't come only to play in the fields and to wrestle with Their friends, but to save the world. All this will be described in due course.

The combination of Kṛṣṇa and Balarāma is attractive to devotees, especially to the cowherd boys, cows, and calves in Vṛndāvana. I remember hearing in the beginning of my spiritual life that God had a brother. "Okay, why not?"

There are many devotional paintings showing Kṛṣṇa and Balarāma running and playing in Vṛndāvana. Some pictures of Kṛṣṇa may be difficult to execute, but pictures of Kṛṣṇa and Balarāma often come out successful and we catch the happy spirit.

There are various Kṛṣṇa-Balarāma Deities around ISKCON. Of course, They are found in Vṛndāvana at the Krishna-Balaram Mandir. There, Balarāma is mighty, yet He leans upon His dark, stronger brother, who is the resting place for all living beings and the entire universe. As everybody knows, Balarāma is white and Kṛṣṇa is blackish, and both of Them light up the world with love of Kṛṣṇa.

In New Māyāpur, France, Kṛṣṇa-Balarāma enchant the devotees and stare down the inimical demons in Their path. Sometimes on a Sunday afternoon, you can attend a quiet *ārati* and watch the brothers as sunlight filters through the curtains. To see Them in that setting increases my faith in the Personality of Godhead and makes me want to surrender and become His devotee. When I am away from New Māyāpur, I want to return, despite the obstacles, just to see Them again. The same is true of Kṛṣṇa-Balarāma in Vṛndāvana. I never want to stop going back to see Them. I want to draw strength from Balarāma in order to serve Prabhupāda and Kṛṣṇa. In Vṛndāvana, the Deities are Prabhupāda's. Prabhupāda wanted us to see Them.

There is another set of Kṛṣṇa-Balarāma Deities in a jungle on a hill in Puerto Rico. These are small Deities. I also like to go there. Even though They are "small," They are worth seeing. The small band of devotees who worship Them never abandon Them, even when the hurricane ripped the temple roof off. Kṛṣṇa and Balarāma watch Their devotees work and dance, and They reciprocate in Their own way.

I know some householders who worship Kṛṣṇa-Balarāma Deities. Mādhavendra Purī dāsa and Caitanya-rūpa dāsī have large Deities. They worship Them as if the boys are their children, although they also realize that They are the protectors of their lives and of all living beings.

Prabhupāda sometimes quoted the statement from the *Upaniṣads*, *nāyam ātmā bala-hīnena labhyo:* no one can attain Kṛṣṇa consciousness unless he has the spiritual strength given by Balarāma. Śrīla Prabhupāda points out that this strength is not physical, such as the strength one obtains by performing gymnastics or by eating a fatty diet. It is spiritual strength and it comes from the Lord. Kṛṣṇa gives us the sword of knowledge in the *Bhagavad-gītā* and Balarāma gives us the spiritual strength that enables us to wield the sword against our doubts. All glories to Kṛṣṇa-Balarāma and Their playful, handsome sports. All glories to Their names, such as Balarāma, Saṅkarṣana, Rāma, and Kṛṣṇa, Siddha-rūpa, Ghanaśyāma, and Kālacandjī.

A desperate hornet is spinning around this room, hitting against walls, chair legs, and curtains. Otherwise it's quiet. I hear the constant sound of water over the dam. I expect to hear occasional grunts or dream-talk from the two guards sleeping on the porch. I expect to hear Madhu clear his throat or chanting in the hall. He has no regular sleep hours during the night. Maybe I'll also hear mice (or think I hear them). The lizard is clicking under the fluorescent tube.

I feel sorry and surprised that my work day has been reduced to about three or four hours. I hope this is temporary. If Kṛṣṇa wants to keep me down, however, so be it.

Better run and play while I can in the fields of Vṛndāvana.

But what if I get a headache trying to keep up with Kṛṣṇa and Stoka-kṛṣṇa and Patrī and Śrīdāmā and Subala and the rest?

Then stay home like the *yajña-patnis* and think of Kṛṣṇa. Prepare a feast for His friends. Or, if you find the kitchen too hot, then what can I say? Stay in your room and chant all day. You can't do that? Think of Him while you're in bed when you're not meditating on your pain. Somehow, take a broken life and use it as an instrument for Kṛṣṇa's service.

O hornet, it's your last hour.
You knock violently against the
curtain, come right in front of me,
but I can't help you.
I've got my own worries.
Here comes head pressure.
Let me finish what
I'm saying, while the hornet
flashes no prayer.

Kṛṣṇa and Balarāma masked as humans . . .
Did They wear children's masks
made of flowers and twigs and colored
minerals from the hill?
Kṛṣṇa and Balarāma racing ahead,
the cowherd boys in pursuit—
"I will be the first to touch Him!"

Kṛṣṇa and Balarāma,
words, words, to impel me
to Their lotus feet,
Their chests, eyes, Their
wrestling stance.
"What kind of a big man are you?"
challenged Śrīdāmā.
Play, and when a
demon comes, turn to Kṛṣṇa
nervous but confident—"Even
if this snake statue is actually
a demon desiring to swallow us,
Kṛṣṇa and Balarāma will kill him.
We need not fear."

Throw the *dhenuka* demons
by the hind legs up into the trees.
Break the beak of the giant duck.
Pulverize the bull and horse demons.
"O mothers and fathers, please
hear what Kṛṣṇa and Balarāma
did today in the forest.
The giant duck came and Kṛṣṇa bifurcated
his beak."
"Oh? Kṛṣṇa is so wonderful?
Come bathe and eat Your meal."

Kṛṣṇa ate dirt. Balarāma will
testify.
Balarāma, please go at once and
give protection to Your brother. He
has gone alone to the Yamunā and we
are feeling evil omens.
Do not worry, Baladeva smiles,
there is nothing to fear even if
the Kāliya serpent with a hundred heads
catches Kṛṣṇa in his coils. It's
just a game of His to increase
our love. We have nothing
but Kṛṣṇa and He wants to draw out
our devotion more and more.

Jaya Kṛṣṇa-Baladeva.
Even I am Their devotee
by the grace of Their devotee
who erected Their temple
in a Rāman Retī field.

Kṛṣṇa and Balarāma, the nineteenth and twentieth incarnations, advented in the Vṛṣṇi family "and by so doing He removed the burden of the world." I pray to Lord Kṛṣṇa to lift the burden of my heart by adventing there in the form of the holy name. I pray to chant attentively and without offense. I am trying to chant, but I must be an offender. Therefore, I'm asking Kṛṣṇa-Balarāma to lift this offensive burden of inattention and mechanical chanting.

Text 24

tataḥ kalau sampravṛtte
sammohāya sura-dviṣām
buddho nāmnāñjana-sutaḥ
kīkaṭeṣu bhaviṣyati

Then, in the beginning of Kali-yuga, the Lord will appear as Lord Buddha, the son of Añjanā, in the province of Gayā, just for the purpose of deluding those who are envious of the faithful theist.

Comment

Śrīla Prabhupāda provides vital information about Lord Buddha which is not mentioned in the verse. The verse tells us the time and place of Buddha's appearance, but what caused him to descend? "At the time when Lord Buddha appeared, the people in general were atheistic and preferred animal flesh to anything else."

So-called Vedic followers in India about three thousand years ago were indulging in animal slaughter. When they were challenged as to why they killed animals, they stated that it was allowed as a Vedic sacrifice. Buddha therefore appeared and preached nonviolence, but he didn't use the *Vedas* to support his arguments. He said he didn't believe in the *Vedas*. This took away the support of the meat-eaters. Some of them were thus tricked by Lord Buddha into following him. Since he is an incarnation of God, he deluded them into following God, although they were atheists. "That was the mercy of Lord Buddha: he made the faithless faithful to him."

These so-called Vedic followers were certainly in an abominable condition. This is an example of how one can wind up when he follows the letter of the law but misses the spirit (*niyamāgraha*). We can fall victim to *niyamāgraha* when we don't accept the guidance of the disciplic succession because our motives in following are selfish or speculative. The real purpose of the *Vedas* is to follow the stages of *sambandha*, *abhidheya*, and *prayojana*. That is, awakening to our relationship with God, engaging in the activities of that relationship, and pursuing the ultimate goal, love of Kṛṣṇa.

Lord Buddha is technically considered an atheist because he rejected the *Vedas*, but at the time of his appearance, he was the emblem of theism for those to whom he preached. If he had appeared quoting Vedic texts, the meat-eaters could have counter-quoted him, or the hard-core atheists would have simply ignored him and gone on eating meat, unaware of the adverse psychological effect of committing violence. Lord Buddha was on a special mission of mercy to save the animal-killers.

Śrīla Prabhupāda emphasized the importance of Lord Buddha's mission to stop animal-killing. Animal-killers cannot understand God. Prabhupāda puts it in italics: "*It is nonsensical to say that animal-killing has nothing to do with spiritual realization*." Still to this day, some so-called Hindu *sannyāsīs* continue to eat meat in the name of the *Vedas*. "Lord Buddha wanted to stop it completely, and therefore his cult of *ahiṁsa* was propagated not only in India but also outside the country."

Śrīla Prabhupāda doesn't want us to think of Lord Buddha as an atheist. He says Buddha's rejection of the *Vedas* is "simply technical, and had it not been so he would not have been so accepted as the incarnation of Godhead. Nor would he have been worshiped in the transcendental songs of the poet Jayadeva, who is a Vaiṣṇava *ācārya.*"

Buddhism spread throughout the Orient—India, Japan, China, Tibet—and it has implanted itself deeply in those cultures. The New Age expression of it has also become popular in the West. Prabhupāda comments, "We are glad that people are taking interest in the nonviolent movement of Lord Buddha. But will they take the matter very seriously and close the animal slaughterhouses altogether? *If not, there is no meaning to the* ahiṁsā *cult.*"

This *Śrīmad-Bhāgavatam* verse is proof of scriptural authority because the scriptures can predict future events. The *Bhāgavatam* was composed five thousand years ago. Lord Buddha appeared about 2,600 years ago. The *Bhāgavatam* gave a clear prediction, naming his family and birthplace. There are many other prophecies in the *Śrīmad-Bhāgavatam* which are still being fulfilled. This is the standing of the flawless *Purāṇa,* which is without mistake, illusion, or imperfection.

I was raised Roman Catholic, but I left the Church when I came under the influence of intellectualism at college. Later on my own, I returned to spiritual investigation by study of nontheistic religions such as Taoism, Zen, and impersonal Hinduism. I read the Mentor paperback, *Teachings of the Compassionate Buddha* and the *Dharmapada.* Unfortunately, I read them at the same time I used to smoke marijuana. That was life in Manhattan in the 1960s. I was hardly following any Buddhist codes, but I was certainly interested in the fourfold way and I appreciated the ideals and otherworldly negation of desire and illusion, freedom from pain, and *nirvāṇa.*

As so many young people at that time did, I looked into whatever books were available on Zen—*Zen Flesh, Zen Bones,* Suzuki's *Introductions to Zen Buddhism.* I tried to understand how something was there, but that it was so illusive. The books assured me that if I managed to name "it," "it" would disappear. It was tantalizing, but it was a mental game. I also read Alan Watts.

He once came to Brooklyn College when I was there. I asked him if Zen states could be attained by using alcohol or drugs. He said, "Yes, a very similar state to *satori* can be attained by using LSD." Some of the students were put off by that because they had enough sense to understand that Buddhism required discipline and couldn't be attained by hallucinatory drugs.

Lord Buddha was a kind of emblem for me. He was the wise person from the East. Therefore, when I first saw Śrīla Prabhupāda in the storefront at 26 Second Avenue, I immediately flashed on the image of Lord Buddha with his long earlobes and Eastern monk's robes, the grave look and shaved head. Prabhupāda was just how I imagined Buddha to be.

The *Bhagavad-gītā's* teachings as I learned them from Swamijī made it clear to me that I was not meant to follow the path of Buddhism. I was meant for something much more delightful than that—Kṛṣṇa consciousness. Even in my years of practicing Kṛṣṇa consciousness, however, I have sometimes dabbled in Buddhist texts. I have, for example, read a lot of haiku poetry, which is very much influenced by Zen. I was attracted to Basho's loneliness and aspirations for monkhood, and his depth of seeing into ordinary reality. I also appreciated Issa's down-to-earth compassion for fleas and other lowly creatures and his Pure Land Buddhism, which has more a feeling of *bhakti* to it.

But Buddhism, whether in its classical teachings from Gautama Buddha or its derivations like Zen, is atheistic. Therefore, it is a dangerous influence and should not be taken without caution. Lord Caitanya countered the Buddhists when He met them on His travels in India. Prabhupāda offers logical arguments to present to Buddhists when they don't accept the scriptures. Historically, Buddhism spread throughout India, but was later driven out by Śaṅkarācārya's influence.

In his purport about the Buddha *avatāra*, Prabhupāda centers on *ahiṁsā*, specifically referring to the killing of animals. Prabhupāda also teaches *ahiṁsā* beyond this. He says that even in his household days, he once preached on nonviolence when he visited Jhansi. He was asked to speak on the occasion of Gandhi's appearance day and was given the topic "Nonviolence." Prabhupāda defined "violence" as when a person obstructs another from his or her inherent rights. He said that everyone born in India has a right to understand God consciousness from the sages and scriptures, which are all Indians' inherited culture. The current leaders in India, however, are trying to stop people from taking up Kṛṣṇa consciousness or from following the *Vedas*. This is how he defines violence.

Prabhupāda also gives the positive and broad definition of nonviolence in the *Bhagavad-gītā* when commenting on the items of knowledge:

> Nonviolence is generally taken to mean not killing or destroying the body, but actually nonviolence means not to put others into distress. . . . So unless one elevates people to spiritual knowledge, one is practicing violence. One should try his best to distribute real knowledge to the people, so that they may be enlightened and leave this material entanglement. That is nonviolence.
>
> —Bg. 13.12, purport

I find this statement by Prabhupāda pleasing: "We are glad the people are taking interest in the nonviolent movement of Lord Buddha." Kali-yuga has degraded since the time of Lord Buddha's appearance. There are even more *pāṣaṇḍīs* now. Almost everyone is a gross materialist these days, and few of them really care or know how to care for other humans, what to speak of animals. If someone is a little attracted to higher values, we consider him a candidate for Kṛṣṇa consciousness or at least for *some* form of spiritual life. It seems best to encourage them as Prabhupāda is doing in this statement. But he also warns them not to make a farce out of their Buddhism.

Once after a lecture a man asked Prabhupāda, "What about Buddha?" Prabhupāda then asked him back, "Do you follow Buddha?"

The man said he did not. Prabhupāda said sarcastically, "You talk about Buddha, but you don't follow him." He said you should follow Buddha (or Christ). It doesn't matter so much which bona fide spiritual leader you follow, but you should not just offer lip service. This is how Prabhupāda offered encouragement.

In devotional service we understand that Buddha, Christ, and Śaṅkara are all within Kṛṣṇa's plan for the gradual purification of the world. "Therefore both Lord Buddha and Ācārya Śaṅkara paved the path of theism, and Vaiṣṇava *ācāryas*, specifically Lord Śrī Caitanya Mahāprabhu, led the people on the path towards a realization of going back to Godhead."

In Prabhupāda's strong writing against animal-killing, we see his compassion for their suffering and his concern for the foolish humans who don't realize what horrible karma they incur due to their lack of spiritual knowledge. Despite any endeavor they make to "meditate," actual realization will evade them until they give up animal-killing.

Vegetarianism or nonviolence toward animals is a growing movement in the West, but it goes against the current of the tremendous forces in favor of high-tech slaughterhouses and the eating of flesh. Anyone who preaches against this infamy is certainly making progress toward pleasing the Supreme Lord. Nonviolence is not a complete *dharma* in itself, but Prabhupāda points out that it is crucial because no one can claim spiritual realization if he doesn't have a program to stop animal slaughter.

I'm sometimes negligent in my own practice of nonviolence. I think of the almost incidental killing of bugs and creatures like that. I like to burn votive candles on the altar, but sometimes tiny flies jump into the flame. I have stopped using the candles during certain seasons of the year, but sometimes I wait until I find a few corpses before I stop. Why? Sometimes I'm not as careful as Mṛgāri became after he was converted by Nārada. That ex-hunter took care not to step on ants and he was willing to stop and clear the path before he walked. I sometimes push brutishly ahead or brush ants off with a passionate movement of my hand.

I tend to forgive myself for these oversights, but I want to be more careful. I don't want to indulge in committing the seventh offense, deliberately being negligent about a religious principle, in this case *ahiṁsā*, but thinking I will be purified by the holy name.

Another point about nonviolence is the fact that one living being is food for another. This morning I saw that the two fluorescent tubes I had turned on attracted some hornets. Actually, I don't think they were hornets, but some flying insects that resembled hornets. They were fat creatures—looked like cigar stubs with wings. At first I thought there was only one of them, but then I saw half a dozen more spinning around the room, all in a bad state. I was intent on writing these comments about Kṛṣṇa and Buddha and tried to ignore them. Then they started coming right under the desk lamp and onto the *Bhāgavatam* pages and my notes. I put on my gloves, caught them, and threw them into the bathroom. Then I saw that the lizards were alert. I saw one lizard catch an insect in its jaws and I realized that I had prompted this by putting on too many lights.

I know I can't interfere with nature and save the bugs from being eaten by lizards, but I shouldn't create situations that increase the violence. Prabhupāda taught us to keep violence at a minimum as far as possible.

Srila
Prabhupada
murti.
Khargone,
India
Feb
14, 96

Lake Placid,
Susan something,
figure skater friend of my sister,
Madeline.
O sweet Adeline,
your past is a sugar-coated joke
maudlin hymns
wooden chapel you attended
midnight Mass . . .

Why didn't you write more
memories in this book?
To save them for future volumes.

Write more
hymnal fount
holy water.

I've been happy to be in India
since November.
And the ants are running wild over
the planks on the desk,
"My desk," I almost said.
My time, my life, my book.
It's Kṛṣṇa's.
As Time He owns us and destroys
the material we call our own.
O Kṛṣṇa, You are a heavy cutter.
Please deliver us to safety.
May we chant Hare Kṛṣṇa and be
retrieved,
relieved, shorn
of excess.

O Lord Kṛṣṇa, I should have written
more and better.
Now You're not giving me much time.
Do You like it this way?
What if I took a painkiller?
Would that go against
Your plan to give me pain?
I don't mean to say it that way.
You'll do whatever You'll do
with me and there's no way I can
get around it.
I say yes to whatever You
do
with me.
But please let me serve You
life after life. Let me attain
sincere and spontaneous devotional service.

Good-bye to this place. It had its pluses and minuses. I won't mention them here. Glad to be here and ready to go.

Please, Lord, I don't want to ask anything, but I do wish to continue writing this book. May I please You and purify my motives.

Text 25

athāsau yuga-sandhyāyāṁ
dasyu-prāyeṣu rājasu
janitā viṣṇu-yaśaso
nāmnā kalkir jagat-patiḥ

Thereafter, at the conjunction of two yugas, the Lord of the creation will take His birth as the Kalki incarnation and become the son of Viṣṇu Yaśā. At this time the rulers of the earth will have degenerated into plunderers.

Comment

Lord Kalki comes at the conjunction of Kali- and Satya-yugas. The calendar tells us that we are now five thousand years into Kali and that Kalki will come in another 427,000 years. Will you be around, Ginsberg? The Swami's boys will be in the kingdom of God if they're good disciples.

Will you be around, Ginsberg, when people live for only thirty-five years and when there's no religion? Will you be ready to live through the nightmare of having civilization stripped away and people killing each other on the slightest provocation? Will you be there when Kalki wields His sword and when there is no more *harināma-saṅkīrtana*? It will be so bad that the only way the Lord sees to save them is to kill them and give them deliverance. After they are killed, the golden age of Satya-yuga will be ushered in.

Don't be there. Pray to Kṛṣṇa.

The Twelfth Canto predicts in detail the anomalies people will experience in Kali-yuga. People will think that they are beautiful because they have long hair. That's already true. Kali is accelerating before our eyes. When I was young, things were not so degenerate. No one smoked marijuana in our high school, and only the bad kids had sex. Now kids do those things before they even get to high school.

There will be drought, heavy taxes, and so much government exploitation that people will prefer to live as aborigines in the hills. Marriage will be a farce; husbands and wives will break their vows as soon as their sex pleasure is disrupted. That's already true now too.

There will be no justice in the courts unless you have the money to pay for it. Those who are less than *śūdras* will rule the land. People will look like pygmies, and the trees will be stunted in their growth. The devotees will be persecuted by the demons, and devotional service will be conducted underground.

Before these symptoms set in, there will be a period of ten thousand golden years, years that will remind people of Satya-yuga. But this interim of auspicious years will be like an eddy going against the main current. Prabhupāda said that it's up to the devotees and their preaching spirit to determine when and how this ten-thousand-year grace period will occur. Śrī Caitanya Mahāprabhu appeared five hundred years ago. We can start anytime.

All the degeneration going on in society should remind us that we must become fixed in devotional service as soon as possible. The bad affects of Kali-yuga will not be isolated only in one place, but will spread throughout the universe. How can we possibly protect ourselves? We can start with knowledge. If we know it's going to rain, we can carry an umbrella.

Sometimes devotees hear about these predictions and think that all the worst symptoms are already present. We think we have already seen the worst. The rulers of the earth *are* self-centered, unprincipled plunderers. Does this mean that Lord Kalki will incarnate sooner than we think? Does it mean we can expect a great disaster or another world war?

One thing is certain: although the situation is certainly very bad, it is going to get a lot worse. Śrīla Prabhupāda said that everything foretold in the scriptures will come about on schedule. Lord Kalki will not incarnate for another 427,000 years. We have only experienced the first five thousand years of degeneration. Things are going to get hundreds of times worse. It is not even possible to conceive of the suffering, the terror, the pitiable lives that people will be forced to live.

Therefore, it is intelligent to conclude that the world is not a fit place for a gentleman, not now, and even more so in the future. We should not come back to face our material desires in another life because the world will only become more and more hellish. Of course, we think we see the pleasant side of material nature. The *Bhāgavatam* says that the colorful birds with their musical songs are like Kṛṣṇa's smile, but the world is not a place of sweet songs sung by merry birds flying carefree from treetop to treetop. It is not a place of beautiful, scented flowers or of love and trust. Those things live only on the surface. If we look just beneath the veneer, we can see the anxiety of all living entities as they eat in fear, sleep in fear, mate in fear, and try to defend themselves. We can also see the selfish, ignorant, petty exploitation that each species of life engages in. It will get a hundred times worse.

What level of material happiness can be worth prolonging our stay in the material world? Even the happiness of Satya-yuga in the heavenly planets is not desirable for one who knows the truth. We will become stranded by every material situation we try to enjoy, and we will be left to suffer repeated birth and death. Even in good times, in good bodies, the material nature pinches. Kali is the worst of all the ages.

I'm afraid of its influence. Maybe what I see in nightmares is glimpses of Kali-yuga worsening. In my nightmares I'm lost or thrust into difficult situations alone with ruffians, subject to torture. Those are nightmares, but it will be worse when we can't wake up safe in a room surrounded by devotees.

We have to take shelter of Kṛṣṇa. What does that mean? I don't think I have been severely tested. When I am being tested—through headaches and other stress—I find it difficult to remember Kṛṣṇa and to chant His holy name. Yet the chanting is the one great virtue of Kali-yuga. It turns everything into good. Kali-yuga, in fact, is an auspicious age because just by chanting Hare Kṛṣṇa, we can attain God realization.

I'm afraid of the hellish punishments on this earth. I'm also afraid that I won't be able to turn to Kṛṣṇa when the going gets rough. Yet I think that Kṛṣṇa will give me the necessary strength to turn to Him in my hour of need. I feel confident that Śrīla Prabhupāda has given us Kṛṣṇa consciousness and that it will save me. Not only me, but anyone who practices it.

Therefore, our duty is to continue preaching according to our capacity no matter what goes on out there. Kalki will come when He comes. Until then . . .

Until then? Tell your truth. I'm hot, I'm warm, I'm headache-free. For lunch he served a dessert of hot, sweet porridge alongside a bowl of sweet *kṣīra* and two crumbly *luglus*. They were a wonderful combination and I lapped them up like a kitten with its milk.

Will I be detained in *saṁsāra* for that? Maybe. I will have to give everything up if the attachment is holding me back. I remember saying at the Nature Cure clinic that I have had my quota of sweets for this lifetime, but perhaps that's not true. Kṛṣṇa allows me to have more in one way or another. I can build up my strength; I'm too skinny and weak.

Of course, if it comes down to it, I don't plan to stay in this world just to enjoy more *kṣīra* and hot cereal or milk or yogurt or bananas or anything else. I already suffer pain. I don't want to be detained for more.

The only relief is to chant Hare Kṛṣṇa with attention. Yes, but when I'm down with pain, even if I can't chant, I want to be with Kṛṣṇa in one way or another.

These are my last hours in this place. I hope to finish the first volume of *A Poor Man Reads The Bhāgavatam* before I leave. But I also don't feel inclined to hurry. Take a deep breath. Fill the lungs and exhale. Exhale the prose of a sufferer and enjoyer, a fool detained in Kali-yuga. I am not an incarnation of God. I didn't come here to save souls, myself already liberated. I was sinful and have been forced to live in this age. Still, I have received the mercy of Kṛṣṇa's pure devotee.

Hand, deliver me a sermon. The ant runs frantically over the blank page, even as I fill it in. All roads from here lead to Bombay. When we get there, we will look for Juhu. Then I will go to Prabhupāda's rooms and beg for the mercy to write Volume Two.

Enormous hope in bad age
wake up and chant precious
beads *cintāmaṇi* touch mercy
of Lord as *nāma-rūpa*.
When, Lord, when?

Does it have to get worse before
I cling to the holy name
as the only hope? I don't want
that desperate living nightmare.
Prefer soft candlelight—no mice,
no human voices even, just me chanting.
I do love it even now—
but my mind races away.

You gave me writing and I'm happy for
that. When I think of what to
write, I'm filled with a drive.
Oh . . .
Kali, keep away. This page and
the next—join it to the
saṅkīrtana movement. Broken
odd song for the master who
smiled and said your American free
verse "On Chanting," is nice.

(1) Confessions ain't all.

(2) Confessed official sins only on Saturday in church.

(3) I fugged, I funked, I flunked, I flinched a thousand times like Saint Peter denied his Christ three times.

(4) I thwarted and told on friends. I trod on their sinking bodies so I wouldn't drown. I ate all veg and didn't save any for them. I kicked at them and grabbed for the rope lowered to us.

(5) I killed an ant, a horse, a fly, a rat, a cat, a mouse, and a dog. Did I kill humans too in my previous life?

(6) I'm ignorant of all that I say. I claim mouthfuls that I'm not entitled to. To save my skin, I'd strip yours. I lie to make extravagant prose. "There is no sin I haven't committed," and mean it to be taken as impressive, sincere rhetoric.

(7) It don't matter what I think or write, but I write anyway, thinking it's special, thinking some of it may be saved.

(8) Push to sincerity; write until your hand aches.

(9) The best thing about you is your chanting stance.

(10) He's honest.

(11) He's three-fourths dead and Kali is only getting warmed up. Admit it: you are not one hundred percent pure or a lover of Kṛṣṇa, so you will have to come back for more of Kali-yuga.

(12) Then get fixed up so you can return for love of Kṛṣṇa, friendliness to His devotees, and compassion for all beings.

(13) It would be nice to be immersed in the *Bhāgavatam*.

(14) Volume One done and I go on to Volume Two. Don't know anything but that the verses and purports will save me.

Text 26

avatārā hy asaṅkhyeyā
hareḥ sattva-nidher dvijāḥ
yathāvidāsinaḥ kulyāḥ
sarasaḥ syuḥ sahasraśaḥ

O brāhmaṇas, the incarnations of the Lord are innumerable, like rivulets flowing from inexhaustible sources of water.

Comment

The list in this chapter is not a complete one. Many, many incarnations have not been mentioned. Indeed, the incarnations are so innumerable that they are compared to waves in an inexhaustible flow of water.

Prahlāda Mahārāja prays to Lord Nṛsiṁhadeva that the incarnations appear in all species of life and that the Lord comes according to the needs of the different *yugas*. "In the Kali-yuga You have incarnated garbed as a devotee." This is an indirect reference to Śrī Caitanya Mahāprabhu. There are many other verses in the Vedic literature foretelling of Lord Caitanya's appearance as the Supreme Personality of Godhead. He is the incarnation come to save us in Kali-yuga. He makes Kali-yuga something wonderful, as He appears with Lord Nityānanda like the sun and moon appearing simultaneously on the horizon of Gauḍa to remove the darkness in the core of our hearts. They do this by freely distributing love of God through the chanting of His holy name.

There are many incarnations; they all flow from Kṛṣṇa. Kṛṣṇa Himself (and Śrī Caitanya Mahāprabhu) is not, therefore, an incarnation per se. That will be clearly explained in the upcoming *mahā-vākya śloka*.

"So the Lord is the inexhaustible source for innumerable incarnations which are not always mentioned." This is a hint that persons who are great saints in other religions may also be considered incarnations within the *Bhāgavatam's* jurisdiction. The list is not complete in the text of the *Bhāgavatam* as we have it. The real test is not always whether an incarnation is specifically mentioned but whether His symptoms are discernible and genuine according to the instructions in the revealed scriptures. Based on this data, Śrīla Bhaktisiddhānta Sarasvatī Ṭhākura called Jesus Christ and Mohammed *śaktyāveśa-avatāras*.

A real incarnation is distinguished by His specific, extraordinary acts which would be impossible for any living being to perform.

In direct, fully empowered forms such as Viṣṇu, or in living beings specifically empowered with a particular, partial *śakti*, the Lord's innumerable incarnations manifest everywhere in all the universes without cessation, just as water flows constantly over a waterfall.

I repeat this information, but do I believe it? Where are all these incarnations now if there are so many constantly appearing? Well, Kṛṣṇa's pure devotees are a form of incarnation, and of course, He incarnates in His holy name.

We are not blind or deaf. Kṛṣṇa is His name.

Then will I receive that incarnation?

I count my beads as if dead. I am mechanical, inattentive, and chant only a slim sixteen. While chanting, I make plans for devotional service, but can't I

do better?

Me and my friend are going to chant
in the car tomorrow but
it will be the same thing.
Never mind. I hope.
I pray.

I throw mud on the skeptics' despair and no hope. The incarnations are flowing like 16,000 mantras, ten per hour, five per minute, thirty-two syllables, no stoppage, *nirāntara*. Even death can't stop a sincere chanter.

Lord Caitanya established *harināma* for 10,000 years. At the end of Kali, the Lord will appear as Kalki. Best to chant before it's too late.

Text 27

ṛṣayo manavo devā
manu-putrā mahaujasaḥ
kalāḥ sarve harer eva
saprajāpatayaḥ smṛtāḥ

All the ṛṣis, Manus, demigods and descendants of Manu, who are especially powerful, are plenary portions or portions of the plenary portions of the Lord. This also includes the Prajāpatis.

Comment

Śrīla Prabhupāda's purport is only one sentence long: "Those who are comparatively less powerful are called *vibhūti*, and those who are comparatively more powerful are called *aveśa* incarnations."

Vibhūti is also mentioned in the tenth chapter of the *Bhagavad-gītā*. Lord Kṛṣṇa says that He will state some of the principal manifestations of His different energies. Prabhupāda writes (10.19), "And *vibhūti*, as used in this verse, refers to the opulences by which He controls the whole manifestation. In the *Amara-kośa* dictionary it is stated that *vibhūti* indicates an exceptional opulence."

This seems to indicate that *vibhūti* are not always spiritual and divine in the way that we normally think. For example, a person like Nārada is obviously a divinely empowered living being. Everything he does is pure *bhakti*. In the *Bhagavad-gītā*, however, Kṛṣṇa describes His opulences and speaks of many things. Some of them are obviously spiritual, such as ". . . of vibrations I am the transcendental *oṁ*. Of sacrifices I am the chanting of the holy names . . ." Then He says, ". . . among beasts I am the lion . . . of fishes I am the shark . . . " There is nothing particularly spiritual about the shark, but as Prabhupāda states, "Of all the aquatics the shark is one of the biggest and is certainly the most dangerous to man. Thus the shark represents Kṛṣṇa." Therefore, *vibhūti* means anything that shows power and endowment by the Lord. Anything great comes from Kṛṣṇa and it may be seen in nature in that way, even something that is dangerous, heavy, light, quintessential, and so on.

The *aveśa* is more directly spiritual empowerment by Kṛṣṇa. We cannot call a shark an *aveśa-avatāra*, although the shark is one of the Lord's *vibhūtis*. It is also by Kṛṣṇa's *śakti* that a music group or writer or artist becomes enormously popular in this world, but we couldn't refer to the Beatles as *aveśa* incarnations.

The *saktyāveśa-avatāra* is highly qualified to represent Kṛṣṇa. This is described in the *Caitanya-caritāmṛta* verse, *kali-kālera dhāma—kṛṣṇa-nāma-saṅkīrtana, kṛṣṇa-śakti vinā nahe tāra pravartana*. Only a person who is directly empowered by Kṛṣṇa can spread the chanting of Hare Kṛṣṇa all over the world. On this evidence, one of Prabhupāda's older Godbrothers said that Prabhupāda was empowered by Lord Caitanya. How else could Prabhupāda have spread the holy name all over the world, something that had never been done by any previous incarnation or *aveśa* personality? Therefore, we say that Prabhupāda was not only someone who worked hard, was determined, was an intelligent organizer, or even a faithful disciple; he was the direct recipient of Lord Caitanya's blessings. He was not only extraordinary or unique as a lion or the Himalayan Mountains are extraordinary or unique; he was spiritually endowed, empowered. What Prabhupāda wrote about Lord Buddha is also true of himself: "He made the faithless faithful toward him."

We'll read later that the *Śrīmad-Bhāgavatam* is a literary incarnation of God. Vyāsadeva is an incarnation of God with a literary mission, and his masterpiece, *Śrīmad-Bhāgavatam*, written under Nārada Muni's direction, is Kṛṣṇa in the form of scripture. This may be true of any bona fide scripture, but it is especially true of the *Śrīmad-Bhāgavatam*. Thus we will soon read Sūta Gosvāmī's answer to the sages' question, "Now that Lord Kṛṣṇa has left the earth, where do the religious principles reside?"

In talking about incarnations, we are discussing God's potent presence, whether He is manifesting it in full or in part, as He appears in this otherwise dark and unhappy material world. He lights up nescience with His teachings, songs, mantras, and spiritual form and pastimes. He manifests as a pure devotee, as scripture par excellence, and in sound as the Hare Kṛṣṇa mantra.

As the sages stated earlier, "Living beings who are entangled in the complicated meshes of birth and death can be freed immediately by even unconsciously chanting the holy name of Kṛṣṇa, which is feared by fear personified. . . . Who is there, desiring deliverance from the vices of the age of quarrel, who is not willing to hear the virtuous glories of the Lord?" (*Bhāg*. 1.1.14, 16)

In talking about Śrīla Prabhupāda, I don't want to claim that I know more than I actually do. Neither do I like it when someone minimizes him by giving technical arguments based on the scripture. Rather, scripture proves Prabhupāda to be especially empowered.

That does not mean, however, that Prabhupāda did not work to achieve his mission. We all thrill to read in Prabhupāda's life as well as in other heroes' lives in the *Bhāgavatam*, the spiritual "rags to riches" stories. They inspire us. It would steal from the inspiration that we draw from these persons if we thought they were simply going through the motions to show us how it is done.

We read, for example, of how Prabhupāda had to shoulder the burden of family life for so many years, how he traveled, how his days were long and arduous as he sold pharmaceutical products. He wanted to join his spiritual master's movement, but he had to take care of his family and business. He worked patiently and responsibly and set a great example for all the householders to come. He wrote articles and a commentary on *Bhagavad-gītā*. (His manuscript was stolen just as he was about to publish it, so he started it again.) He went into the Delhi streets in summer's heat to sell *Back to Godhead*. He reeled in the streets and was gored by a cow. He was not pretending to be gored "for our sake," nor did he fake being overcome by heatstroke. I don't think this is an unfaithful way to hear of Prabhupāda's life any more than it is unfaithful to follow Nārada through his childhood to his attainment of perfection. Or to know that Nārada was a Gandharva in a previous life who fell down and later took birth as the son of a maidservant. Although such great souls are empowered, they still strove to use every ounce of blood and energy and breath and strength in Kṛṣṇa's service.

There's more to it than what I've said here. I don't know all the esoteric secrets and can't make ultimate explanations. Even higher understandings than what I've given here, however, don't negate what I have said. An empowered soul *works* for Kṛṣṇa. He sometimes cries when a disciple goes away that he could not save that soul. He feels himself unworthy, thinks himself a beggar bereft of love of God. He isn't pretending. Kṛṣṇadāsa Kavirāja thought he was lower than Jagāi and Mādhāi. We shouldn't trivialize the feelings of great souls or explain them away. Rather, we should worship their examples and not pretend to know everything about them. At the same time, we can acknowledge that they are special and can do things ordinary living beings cannot.

Let us accept the mercy that the great souls are offering as best we can. Accept their mercy as completely transcendental and not tainted by this world. Accept Nārada, the Kumāras, and others as eternal incarnations. Their examples mean that becoming empowered is something open to every *jīva*.

Work hard
& be
empowered
to chant Hare Krsna
and spread the
chanting life to
others assuring
them you can be
honest
Work hard
& be
empowered . . .

Open the door a little and let in some of that warm air and sunshine. Winter in India is mostly over.

My skinny wrists, veins standing out like sinews, could easily be cut. I have a birthmark on my left wrist.

This headache too will pass.

I finished this volume, but fortunately I can move on to the next. That's Lord Kṛṣṇa's blessing on me.

Work hard and be empowered. Last write for One. Let the hand guide you home. When we dream at night, we forget the day's illusion, and when we're awake in the day, we forget the night's illusion. In both cases, however, we are dreaming as long as we are not Kṛṣṇa conscious. The mirage is an example; we mistake the illusion for reality.

So he spoke in '72 in the Rādhā-Dāmodara courtyard
and I try to hear but my mind isn't clear.
People disturb me. My mind disturbs me.
I think I'm this body.
"The whole world is full of fools
and rascals," Śrīla Prabhupāda said—on the strength of
Śrī Kṛṣṇa, *mūḍhas*, *duṣkṛtinas*,
māyayāpahṛta-jñānas.
I'm repeating it here.

Headache, go away
don't bring the hornets
of pain overnight. We'll be gone
by 1 or 2 A.M. and in my bag
I've got the wool,
I mean, Volume One.
Please protect it, Lord,
for delivery.
I'm so attached.

Let me live and love
the writing life for You
with enough *prasādam* to
carry me through, but not
more than I need.

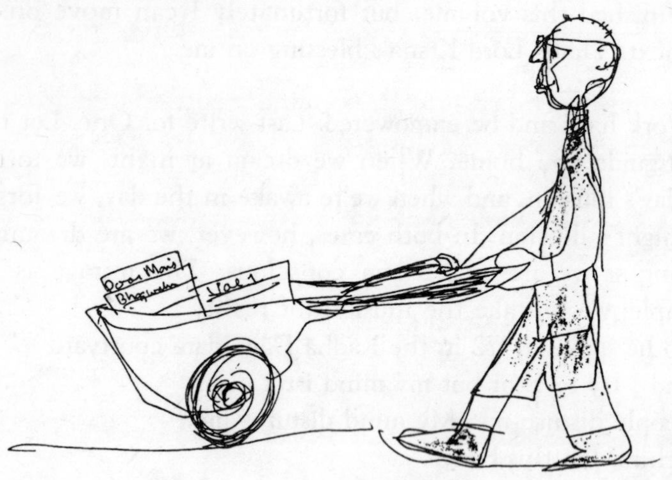

Neither *vibhūti* nor *aveśa*,
sign off glad I could touch
sacred scripture and keep myself
out of trouble.

—*To be continued, if Kṛṣṇa desires*

Glossary

A

Abhidheya—The stage of performing regulated activities to revive one's relationship with the Lord.

Abhijñaḥ—Self-knowing.

Ācārya—A spiritual master who teaches by his personal behavior.

Ācchā—A common Hindi expression meaning, "I see," or, "Is that so?"

Ahiṁsā—Nonviolence.

Aiśvarya—Majesty, opulence.

Apauruṣeya-śabda—Knowledge from a divine source.

Arcā-vigraha—Deity.

Artha—Economic development.

Arjuna—One of the five Pāṇḍavas, to whom Kṛṣṇa spoke the *Bhagavad-gītā* on the Battlefield of Kurukṣetra.

Āśrama—A spiritual order: *brahmacārī* (celibate student), *gṛhastha* (householder), *vānaprastha* (retired), *sannyāsa* (renunciate).

Ātmā—The soul or living entity.

Avatāra—Lit. "One who descends." An incarnation of the Lord.

B

Balarāma—Kṛṣṇa's elder brother and His first plenary expansion.

Bhagavān—Lit. "One who possesses all opulence." The Supreme Lord, who is the reservoir of all beauty, strength, fame, wealth, knowledge, and renunciation.

Bhāgavata—Anything related to Bhagavān, especially the Lord's devotee and the scripture, *Śrīmad-Bhāgavatam.*

Bhajana—Devotional activities.

Bhajana-kriyā—To practice devotional service under the spiritual master's guidance.

Bhakti—Devotional service to the Supreme Lord.

Bhaktisiddhānta Sarasvatī Ṭhākura—The spiritual master of His Divine Grace A. C. Bhaktivedanta Swami Prabhupāda; an *ācārya* in the Gauḍīya Vaiṣṇava *sampradāya.*

Brahmā—The first created living being and the secondary creator of the material universe.

Brahmacārī—A celibate student living under the care of a bona fide spiritual master.

Brahma-jyoti—The bodily effulgence of the Supreme Lord which constitutes the brilliant illumination of the spiritual sky.

Brahman—The impersonal aspect of the Absolute Truth; spirit.

Brāhmaṇa—Those wise in the *Vedas* who can guide society; the first Vedic social order.

Brahma-bhūta—The liberated or spiritual platform of consciousness.

Brahma-muhūrta—A period spanning one and a half hours before sunrise to one and a half hours after sunrise, considered the most auspicious time for spiritual practices.

Brahma-saṁhitā—Lord Brahmā's prayers glorifying the Supreme Lord.

C

Cādar—A shawl.

Caitanya (Mahāprabhu)—Lit. "Living force." An incarnation of Kṛṣṇa who appeared in the form of a devotee to teach love of God through the *saṅkīrtana* movement.

Caitanya-caritāmṛta—The biography and philosophy of Caitanya Mahāprabhu.

Caitya-guru—The Supersoul.
Cāmara—A yak-tail whisk.
Cañcala—Flickering, unsteady.
Capātī—A whole-wheat, griddle-baked flatbread.
Caraṇāmṛta—Water that has washed the Deity.
Chaukīdār—A security guard.

D

Dakṣa—A son of Brahmā and chief forefather of the universal population.
Dāmodara—A name for Kṛṣṇa in His pastime of being bound with a rope by Mother Yaśodā.
Darśana—Vision; audience.
Devakī—Kṛṣṇa's mother in Mathurā.
Dhāma—Abode; the Lord's place of residence.
Dhotī—Vedic men's dress.
Dvija-bandhu—Unworthy son of a *brāhmaṇa*.

E

Ekādaśī—A day Vaiṣṇavas fast from grains and beans and increase their remembrance of Kṛṣṇa. It falls on the eleventh day of both the waxing and waning moons.

G

Ganges—A sacred river in India that washed the lotus feet of Lord Viṣṇu.
Gauḍīya Vaiṣṇava—A follower of Lord Caitanya.
Gaura-kiśora dāsa Bābājī—The spiritual master of Śrīla Bhaktisiddhānta Sarasvatī Ṭhākura.
Gaura-Nitāi—Lord Caitanya (Gaura) and Lord Nityānanda (Nitāi).
Gāyatrī—A prayer chanted silently by *brāhmaṇas* at sunrise, noon, and sunset.

GBC—Governing Body Commission, ISKCON's board of directors.

Gokula—The manifestation of Goloka in the material world.

Goloka—Kṛṣṇaloka, the eternal abode of Lord Kṛṣṇa.

Gopa—A cowherd boy; one of Kṛṣṇa's eternal associates.

Gopī—A cowherd girl; one of Kṛṣṇa's most confidential servitors.

Gosvāmī—One who controls his mind and senses; title of one in the renounced order of life. May refer specifically to the Six Gosvāmīs of Vṛndāvana who are direct followers of Lord Caitanya in disciplic succession and who systematically presented His teachings.

Govardhana Hill—A hill in Vṛndāvana, the site of many of Kṛṣṇa's pastimes.

Guṇḍa—Dacoit, thug.

Gurukula—A school headed by the spiritual master.

Guru-sevā—Service to the spiritual master.

Gurvāṣṭakam—A prayer, written by Śrīla Visvanātha Cakravartī Ṭhākura written in praise of the spiritual master.

H

Hare—The evocative form of Harā, another name of Rādhārāṇī; refers specifically to the internal spiritual energy of the Lord.

Hari-nāma-dīkṣā—Formal initiation of the disciple by the spiritual master into the chanting of the Hare Kṛṣṇa *mahā-mantra*.

Hiraṇyakaśipu—A demoniac king killed by Lord Nṛsiṁhadeva.

I

ISKCON—Acronym of the International Society for Krishna Consciousness.

J

Jagāi and Mādhāi—Two debauchees whom Lord Nityānanda converted into Vaiṣṇavas.

Japa—Individual chanting of the Hare Kṛṣṇa mantra while counting on beads.

Jīva Gosvāmī—One of the Six Gosvāmīs of Vṛndāvana.

Jñāna-yoga—The process of approaching the Supreme by the cultivation of knowledge.

K

Kali—The personification of quarrel and hypocrisy.

Kali-yuga—The present age which is characterized by quarrel and hypocrisy.

Kāma—Lust.

Kaṁsa—A demoniac king who tried to kill Kṛṣṇa during His childhood pastimes.

Karatālas—Hand cymbals used during *kīrtana*.

Karma-yoga—The process of God realization by dedicating the fruits of one's work to God.

Karmī—One engaged in karma (fruitive activity); a materialist.

Kārttika—The Vedic month corresponding to October–November in which Lord Dāmodara is worshiped.

Khādī—Homespun cotton cloth.

Kīrtana—Chanting of the Lord's holy names.

Kṛṣṇa—The Supreme Personality of Godhead.

Kṛṣṇadāsa Kavirāja Gosvāmī—The author of *Śrī Caitanya-caritāmṛta*.

Kṛṣṇa-kathā—Topics spoken by or about Kṛṣṇa.

Kṛṣṇa-nāma—Kṛṣṇa's holy name.

Kṣatriya—Administrative or warrior class. The second Vedic social order.

Kṣīra—Sweetened condensed milk.

L

Lakṣmī—The goddess of fortune; money.

Laulyam—Greed, usually refers to intense desire to see Kṛṣṇa.

Līlā—Pastimes.

League of Devotees—A short-lived precursor to ISKCON established by Śrīla Prabhupāda in India prior to coming to America.

M

Madhvācārya—A thirteenth-century Vaiṣṇava *ācārya* who preached the theistic philosophy of pure dualism.

Mādhurya-līlā—The sweet conjugal pastimes of Kṛṣṇa and the *gopīs*.

Mādhurya-rasa—Devotional service to Kṛṣṇa in the mood of sweetness and conjugal love.

Mahā-bhāgavata—A devotee in the highest stage of devotional life.

Mahābhārata—The history of greater India, compiled by Śrīla Vyāsadeva and including the *Bhagavad-gītā*.

Mahājanas—Refers to the twelve authorized agents of the Lord whose duty is to preach the path of devotional service to the people in general.

Mahā-mantra—The great chant for deliverance: Hare Kṛṣṇa Hare Kṛṣṇa, Kṛṣṇa Kṛṣṇa Hare Hare/ Hare Rāma Hare Rāma, Rāma Rāma Hare Hare.

Mahāprabhu—Supreme master of all masters; refers to Lord Caitanya.

Mahārāja—Great king. Also used as a title of respect for a *sannyāsī*.

Mahātmā—Great soul.

Mandira—Temple.

Mathurā—The city where Lord Kṛṣṇa appeared and to which He later returned after performing His childhood pastimes.

Mauna—Silence.

Māyā—The external, illusory energy of the Lord, comprising this material world; forgetfulness of one's relationship with Kṛṣṇa.

Māyāpur—A town in West Bengal, India, where Lord Caitanya appeared.

Māyāvādī—An impersonalist or voidist who believes that God is ultimately formless and without personality.

Mokṣa—Liberation

Mṛgāri—A cruel hunter and torturer of animals who, by the influence of Nārada Muni, became a pure devotee.

Mūḍha—Fool, rascal.

Muni—A sage or self-realized soul.

Mūrti—A form, usually referring to a Deity.

Myrobalan—An Āyurvedic medicinal plant.

N

Naimiṣāraṇya—A sacred forest in central India, considered to be the hub of the universe.

Nanda—Kṛṣṇa's father in Vṛndāvana.

Nārada Muni—A great devotee of Lord Kṛṣṇa who travels throughout the spiritual and material worlds singing His glories and preaching the path of devotional service to the Lord.

Nārāyaṇa—The four-handed expansion of Lord Kṛṣṇa.

The Nectar of Devotion—Śrīla Prabhupāda's summary study of Śrīla Rūpa Gosvāmī's *Bhakti-rasāmṛta-sindhu.*

Nṛsiṁha(deva)—The half-man, half-lion incarnation of Lord Kṛṣṇa who appeared to save Prahlāda Mahārāja from Hiraṇyakaśipu.

P

Paramahaṁsa—The highest stage of the *sannyāsa* order; a person on the highest platform of spiritual realization; a topmost devotee of the Lord.

Parameśvara—The supreme controller.

Paramparā—The disciplic succession of bona fide spiritual masters.

Parikrama—A walking pilgrimage.

Parīkṣit Mahārāja—The emperor of the world five thousand years ago who heard *Śrīmad-Bhāgavatam* from Śukadeva Gosvāmī and thus attained perfection.

Parivrajakācārya—The third stage of the *sannyāsa* order; one who constantly travels throughout the world, preaching the glories of the Lord.

Paśandi—An atheist; one who thinks the Lord and the demigods to be equal or who considers devotional activities to be material.

Patita-pāvana—Savior of the fallen souls.

Prabhupāda, A. C. Bhaktivedanta Swami—Founder-ācārya of ISKCON and foremost preacher of Kṛṣṇa consciousness in the Western world.

Prahlāda Mahārāja—A great devotee who was persecuted by his demoniac father, but who was protected and saved by Lord Nṛsiṁhadeva.

Prajalpa—Foolish, idle, or mundane speech. Talks unrelated to Kṛṣṇa consciousness.

Prakṛta-bhakta—One who performs devotional service for material gain.

Prāṇa—The life air of the body; vital energy.

Prāṇāyāma—Control of the breathing process as practiced in *aṣṭāṅga-yoga*.

Prasādam—Lit. "Mercy." Food which is spiritualized by being offered to Kṛṣṇa, and which helps purify the living entity.

Prayojana—The ultimate goal of life; to develop love of God.

Pūjā—Worship.
Pūjārī—A priest, specifically one who is engaged in temple worship of a Deity.
Purāṇa—Vedic histories of the universe in relation to the Supreme Lord and His devotees. The "spotless" *Purāṇa* refers to the *Śrīmad-Bhāgavatam.*
Pūtanā—An evil witch sent by King Kaṁsa to kill baby Kṛṣṇa, but who was killed by Him and thus achieved liberation.

R

Rādhā-Dāmodara—The presiding Deities of ISKCON's Gītā-nāgarī farm in Pennsylvania, U.S.A.
Rādhārāṇī—The eternal consort and spiritual potency of Lord Kṛṣṇa.
Rajas—Passion.
Rajo-guṇa—The mode or quality of passion. One of the three modes of material nature.
Rāmāyaṇa—The epic history of Lord Rāmacandra, written by Vālmīki Muni.
Rasa—The spiritual essence of a personal relationship with the Supreme Lord.
Ratha-yātrā—An annual chariot festival celebrating Kṛṣṇa's return to Vṛndāvana in which the Deity of Lord Jagannātha is pulled in procession on a *ratha* (chariot).
Rāvaṇa—A demonic king killed by Lord Rāmacandra.
Romaharṣaṇa—The father of Śrī Sūta Gosvāmī.
Ṛṣabhadeva—An incarnation of Kṛṣṇa appearing as a great devotee king, known for his spiritual instructions to His sons and His subsequent renunciation of His kingdom for a life of severe austerity.
Ṛṣi—Sage.

Ṛtvik—Lit. "Priest." Name given to a fallacious doctrine which holds that Śrīla Prabhupāda is the only initiating guru of ISKCON and that his followers may initiate new devotees only as officiating priests on his behalf.

Ruci—Lit. "Taste." A stage in the practice of Kṛṣṇa consciousness in which one develops a natural attraction or "taste" for the activities of devotional service.

Rūpa Gosvāmī—One of the Six Gosvāmīs of Vṛndāvana.

S

Sad-guru—A bona fide spiritual master.

Sādhaka—One who practices regulated spiritual activities.

Sādhu—Saintly person.

Śakti—Power or energy.

Sambandha—Knowledge of one's original relationship with Kṛṣṇa.

Sampradāya—A chain of disciplic succession through which spiritual knowledge is transmitted.

Saṁsāra—The cycle of repeated birth and death.

Sanātana Gosvāmī—One of the Six Gosvāmīs of Vṛndāvana.

Saṅga—Association.

Śaṅkarācārya—An incarnation of Lord Śiva who, ordered by the Supreme Lord, propagated the impersonal Māyāvāda philosophy, which negates the distinction between God and the living entity.

Saṅkīrtana—The congregational chanting of the holy name, fame, and pastimes of the Lord.

Sannyāsa—Renounced life; the fourth order of Vedic spiritual life.

Ṣaṭ Sandarbha—Treatises on the Vedic scriptures, written by Śrīla Jīva Gosvāmī.

Sattva—Goodness.

Siddhāntic—Var. on *siddhānta*, the perfected conclusion according to Vedic scripture.

Śikhā—Lit. "Flag." A tuft of hair grown at the crown of the head of male Vaiṣṇavas.

Śiṣya—Disciple or student.

Śiva—The personality in charge of the mode of ignorance.

Śloka—A stanza of Sanskrit verse.

Smṛti—Scriptures further explaining the four original *Vedas* and the *Upaniṣads*.

Śraddhā—Firm faith and confidence.

Śrīmad-Bhāgavatam—The *Purāṇa*, or history, written by Vyāsadeva specifically to give a deep understanding of Lord Kṛṣṇa.

Śruti—The original Vedic literatures: the four *Vedas* and the *Upaniṣads*; scripture received directly from God.

Śuddha-sattva—The transcendental state of pure goodness, uncontaminated by the modes of material nature.

Śukadeva Gosvāmī—The sage who originally spoke the *Śrīmad-Bhāgavatam* to King Parīkṣit just prior to the king's death.

Sūrya—The presiding demigod of the sun.

Sūta Gosvāmī—The sage who recounted the discourses between Mahārāja Parīkṣit and Śukadeva Gosvāmī to the sages assembled at Naimiṣāraṇya.

Svāmī—Master; refers to one in the renounced order.

Svarāṭ—The independent quality of the Supreme Lord.

Svarūpa—One's original spiritual form.

Svarūpa-siddhi—The perfection of one's eternal relationship with Lord Kṛṣṇa.

T

Tamas—Ignorance; one of the modes of material nature.

Tapasvi—One who perfoms *tapas* (austerities).

Tapasya—Austerity.

Teachings of Lord Caitanya—Śrīla Prabhupāda's summary study of Lord Caitanya's instructions.

Ṭīkā—Commentary.

Tilaka—Auspicious clay markings that sanctify a devotee's body as a temple of the Lord.

Tīrtha—Holy place of pilgrimage.

U

Uddhava—A confidential friend of Śrī Kṛṣṇa in Dvārakā.

Upadeśa—Instruction.

Upadeśāmṛta—*The Nectar of Instruction*; a practical guide to the development of Kṛṣṇa consciousness, written by Śrīla Rūpa Gosvāmī.

Uttama—Topmost or highest.

Uttamaśloka—A name of Kṛṣṇa; "He who is praised with transcendental song or poetry."

V

Vaidhi-bhakti—The process of following the regulative principles of devotional service under the guidance of a spiritual master, in accordance with revealed scriptures.

Vaiṣṇava—One who is a devotee of Viṣṇu or Kṛṣṇa.

Vāṇī—The instruction of the spiritual master.

Varṇa—The four occupational divisions of society: intellectual *(brāhmaṇa)*, administrative *(kṣatriya)*, mercantile *(vaiśya)*, and laborer *(śūdra)*.

Vasudeva—The father of Lord Kṛṣṇa.

Vāsudeva—The son of Vasudeva, or Śrī Kṛṣṇa Himself.

Vedānta—Śrīla Vyāsadeva's philosophical summary of the conclusions of Vedic knowledge in the form of short aphorisms.

Vedas—The original revealed scriptures, first spoken by the Lord Himself.

VIHE—Vaiṣṇava Institute for Higher Education.

Vijñāna—Practical realization of spiritual knowledge.

Viṣṇu—An all-pervasive, fully empowered expansion of Kṛṣṇa.